BEFORE LEWIS AND CLARK
VOLUME I

BEFORE LEWIS AND CLARK

DOCUMENTS ILLUSTRATING THE HISTORY OF THE MISSOURI 1785-1804

Edited

with an introductory narrative

by

A. P. NASATIR

VOLUME I

Introduction to the Bison Book Edition by
James P. Ronda

University of Nebraska Press
Lincoln and London

Introduction to the Bison Book Edition © 1990 by
the University of Nebraska Press
All rights reserved
Manufactured in the United States of America

First Bison Book printing: 1990
Most recent printing indicated by the last digit below:
10   9   8   7   6   5   4   3   2   1

Volume I: ISBN 0-8032-8361-X (paper)
ISBN 0-8032-3320-5 (cloth)
Set of Volumes I and II: ISBN 0-8032-3322-1

Library of Congress Cataloging-in-Publication Data
Before Lewis and Clark: documents illustrating the history of the Missouri, 1785–
1804 / edited, with an introductory narrative, by A. P. Nasatir.
p.   cm.
Reprint, with a new introd. Originally published: St. Louis: St. Louis Historical
Documents Foundation, 1952.
"Bison book edition."
Includes bibliographical references.
ISBN 0-8032-3322-1 (set).—ISBN 0-8032-3320-5 (v. 1).—ISBN 0-8032-8361-X
(v. 1: pbk.).—ISBN 0-8032-3321-3 (v. 2).—ISBN 0-8032-8362-8 (v. 2: pbk.)
1. Missouri River Valley—History—Sources. 2. Fur trade—Missouri River Valley—History—Sources. I. Nasatir, Abraham Phineas, 1904–   .
F598.B44   1990
978—dc20
89-25080   CIP

Originally published as the first of two volumes by the
St. Louis Historical Documents Foundation in 1952.
This Bison Book edition omits five foldout maps that
appeared on unnumbered pages.

To my Wife

IDA HIRSCH NASATIR

Introduction to the Bison Book Edition
By James P. Ronda

In the summer of 1673, the French explorers Jacques Marquette and Louis Jolliet engaged in an epic voyage of discovery down the Mississippi. Toward the end of June the adventurers came to the confluence of the Mississippi and Missouri rivers. Amazed by the great volume of water flowing from the mouth of the Missouri, Marquette pondered the river's ultimate source. "Pekitanoui," he wrote, "is a river of Considerable size, coming from the Northwest, from a great Distance." The French, like other Europeans, had long sought a water route across the continent. Marquette seized upon his "Pekitanoui" as that path to the Pacific. "I hope by its means," he declared, "to discover the vermillion or California sea."[1] For Marquette and his successors, the Missouri became a river of dreams and destiny. It might lead missionaries to souls yet unevangelized. It might yield commercial riches in pelts and minerals. And, of course, the river might prove yet another means to extend the reach of French power in North America.

Something more than a century later, Thomas Jefferson echoed Marquette's prophetic words. In his *Notes on the State of Virginia* (1787), Jefferson described the Missouri as "the principal river," one filled with both commercial promise and geographic mystery. Less than ten years later, writing instructions for André Michaux's abortive transcontinental venture, Jefferson clearly pointed to the Missouri as the young republic's highway to empire. "As a channel of communication between these states and the Pacific ocean, the Missouri, so far as it extends, presents itself under circumstances of unquestioned preference." By the time Jefferson wrote detailed instructions for the Lewis and Clark expedition, his commitment to the Missouri as America's sovereign river was complete.[2]

The years between Marquette and Jefferson saw the Missouri capture the imagination of many a trader, bureaucrat, and entrepreneur. First Frenchmen and then Spaniards traveled the river in search of profit and national domain. And in their journeys they met native people—Osage, Omaha, Ponca, Sioux, Arikara, and Mandan—all of whom found the bearded strangers both fascinating and more than a bit dangerous. Nowhere are the Missouri and its diverse peoples more fully chronicled than in Abraham P. Nasatir's magnificent documentary history, *Before Lewis and Clark*. With remarkable dedication, Nasatir spent years combing through both American and European archives tracking down those records that might illuminate the river's murky history. The reward for that quest came in 1952 when the St. Louis Historical Documents Foundation published *Before Lewis and Clark*. What the prospective reader found on the shelf that year were two stout volumes holding some 230 documents. Most of the documents had never before been published and none had been so conveniently offered to both the interested lay reader and the professional historian. But Nasatir did more than simply present accurate transcripts of little-known documents. He also provided detailed annotations, carefully putting each bit of evidence in proper context. Nasatir must have realized early in his studies that the documents called for more than annotation. He answered that requirement with an extensive introductory essay. Here he launched a pioneer effort aimed at sorting out the twisting currents of Missouri River history. Although later scholars have added a detail here and a correction there, Nasatir's essay remains required reading for all those who seek to know the wide Missouri.[3]

Both the introductory essay and the historical records reveal a story with as many twists and turns as the river itself. Because the cast and the script for the Missouri drama are so large and often unfamiliar, it is useful here to clarify the major themes in *Before Lewis and Clark*. Geographic discovery, scientific curiosity, personal power, national rivalries, and cultural conflicts are all present, and each needs its moment on the river. The documents in Volume I cover the decade between 1785 and 1795. Those ten years saw a dramatic expansion in Spanish exploring activity up the Missouri. Before the mid-1780s Spanish officials in New Orleans and St. Louis saw little reason to probe the Louisiana country and the lands that bordered the Missouri. New Mexico and Texas—the Provincias Internas—seemed far more important than any distant Missouri lands. But events at the edges of Spain's American empire forced a shift in that policy of benign neglect. Rivals for American domain, especially the Russians, British, and Americans, began to peck away at Spanish territories. Russian expansion south from present-day Sitka and the explosive confrontation with Great Britain at Nootka Sound compelled Spain to move to protect its Pacific coast borders. At the same time, fur traders from the Hudson's Bay Company and the North West Company planted themselves firmly on the northern plains and along the Missouri and upper Mississippi. Those traders, and their Indian partners, posed a genuine threat to Spanish influence. Added to this already complex imperial tangle was the growing presence of aggressive merchants and settlers from the new American republic. These challenges, coupled with the geographic misconception that the Missouri arced directly into New Mexico, sparked a remarkable burst of Spanish exploring activity up the muddy river.

Surrounded by dangerous rivals, Spanish officials moved to shore up Missouri defenses. Just how little men like Governor-General Esteban Rodríguez Miró knew about the river and its peoples is revealed in a 1785 report sent to the Commandant of the Provinicas Internas, Antonio Rengel. That report and those drafted by St. Louis officer Manuel Pérez (pp. 119–27, this volume) showed the weakness of the Spanish position in the face of British and American encroachment. As was so often the case in the Spanish colonial empire, knowledge did not necessarily lead to action. Whereas Miró and Pérez could only plead for action against what seemed a rising tide of interlopers, it fell to private traders to meet the threat. Men like Juan Munier, who made important trade contacts with the Poncas on the Niobrara River, and Jacques D'Église, Spain's first trader at the Mandan villages in present-day North Dakota, offered the first response to trouble on the Missouri. Of those venturesome river traders, none proved more important in the earlier years than D'Église. *Before Lewis and Clark* holds many documents revealing D'Église's journeys up the Missouri and his often troubled dealings with Indians. Whatever his financial fortunes, D'Église made it plain that private traders could also be agents of empire.

Perhaps the most important development chronicled in the first volume of *Before Lewis and Clark* was the founding of the Company of Explorers of the Upper Missouri. Commonly known as the Missouri Company, the firm proved to be the principal weapon in Spain's fight for commerce and sovereignty on the river. Private trading companies that blended corporate profit and national objectives had long been a part of the exploration of the American West. The Hudson's Bay Company, the North West Company, and the Russian-American company suggest ways that imperial powers sought to use grizzled trappers as diplomats in buckskin. In the fall of 1793 Jacques Clamorgan and a group of St. Louis merchants founded the Missouri Company. Most of those merchants saw the company as a means to gain a trade monopoly along the lower reaches of the river. Clamorgan had other ideas. By the spring of 1794 the company was ready to engage in an ambitious program of exploration and enterprise.

The dimensions of the Missouri Company's scheme can be judged by looking at Clamorgan's instructions to Jean Baptiste Truteau, leader of the company's first upriver venture. Truteau was directed to build a substantial trading post at the Mandan villages. That post was to represent not only the investment of the company but Spain's sovereign claim to the region. But Clamorgan and his associates had more in mind that a Missouri-based trade empire east of the Rockies. Like Peter Pond, Alexander

Henry, and eventually Thomas Jefferson, Clamorgan dreamed of a Pacific domain. At the end of the eighteenth century most geographers and cartographers imagined a West filled with narrow mountain ranges easily portaged. There were surely rivers that interconnected, allowing an almost continuous water passage from Atlantic to Pacific. Truteau was ordered to get what news he could of such waterways in preparation for company journeys west of the Great Divide. And like the instructions Jefferson drafted for Lewis and Clark, Clamorgan's directions (pp. 243–53, below) sent Truteau after a wide variety of scientific and ethnological data. Here was the explorer as scientist, merchant, and agent of empire. Truteau's journal and his "Remarks on the Manners of the Indians Living High up the Missouri," both printed in this volume, reveal much about the complex river world. Truteau was no trained observer but he did note everything from the location of important Indian villages and patterns of native leadership to plant and animal life. Science, in the form of Enlightenment natural history, was on the river long before Lewis and Clark.

Truteau's expedition never reached the Mandan villages, but his success in gathering important information spurred the Missouri Company to launch a second venture. In the spring of 1795 Clamorgan selected an obscure trader named Lecuyer to lead a large party up the Missouri. That expedition was to stop at the Mandans and then press on over the Rockies and plant a permanent post "on the shores of the Sea of the West" (p. 337). The bold venture fell apart when Lecuyer's men ran afoul of the Poncas. Undaunted by this failure, Clamorgan hurriedly prepared a third river party.

The first volume of *Before Lewis and Clark* closes with documents relating to the journeys of James Mackay. Born in Scotland, Mackay came to North America in the mid-1770s. From 1776 to 1793 he followed the Canadian fur trade. These were important years in that fur business and Mackay seens to have played some part in the North West Company's efforts to find routes to the Pacific. For reasons that are now obscure, Mackay left Canada for Spanish Illinois. There he took Spanish citizenship and in 1795 became chief field agent for the Missouri Company. Like Clamorgan, Mackay sought Pacific waters. With men such as these directing efforts on the Missouri, Spain seemed destined to dominate the Northwest as fully as the Southwest.

NOTES

1. Reuben G. Thwaites, ed., *The Jesuit Relations and Allied Documents*, 73 vols. (Cleveland, 1898–1901), 59:141.
2. Thomas Jefferson, *Notes on the State of Virginia*, ed. William Peden (Chapel Hill: University of North Carolina Press, 1955), 8–9; Donald Jackson, ed., *Letters of the*

Lewis and Clark Expedition with Related Documents 1783–1854, rev. ed., 2 vols. (Urbana: University of Illinois Press, 1978), 2:670.

3. For some examples see Frank Norall, *Bourgmont, Explorer of the Missouri, 1698–1725* (Lincoln: University of Nebraska Press, 1988); W. Raymond Wood, "Nicholas de Finiels: Mapping the Mississippi and Missouri Rivers, 1797–1798," *Missouri Historical Review* 81 (July 1987): 387–402; W. Raymond Wood and Thomas D. Thiessen, eds., *Early Fur Trade on the Northern Plains* (Norman: University of Oklahoma Press, 1985).

PREFACE

The vast territory of the Trans-Mississippi West has intrigued me ever since I began to study history as an undergraduate in the University of California many years ago. My attention was attracted by the fact that very little was known or had been printed about the Upper Mississippi, the Missouri, and the Arkansas valleys before the Louisiana Purchase drew the interest of the American people. Thomas Jefferson, indeed, had been concerned about that region for many years before 1803, but until the publication of the results of the explorations of Lewis and Clark, Pike, Dunbar, Freeman and Hunter, and others the area remained unknown.

My researches in the archives of Spain and elsewhere, however, have resulted in the unfolding of a long story of attempts to discover a route to the Pacific, of expansion to Santa Fe. Lewis and Clark were but the ones who fulfilled the dreams of the French and Spanish fur traders and explorers who had spread out over the vast Trans-Mississippi area and had reached the mountains and perhaps even traveled beyond them before the turn of the eighteenth century. The entire documentary record of the Missouri from 1673 to 1804 would require a good many volumes for its presentation. In the present work I have chosen to give in detail the story of the Missouri during the last decade and a half before Lewis and Clark.

My principle of selection has been the importance of the document to the continuous story of exploration of the river. It must be kept in mind that exploration in the colonial decades meant Indian trade, for the advance of the Missouri was only by means of Indian trade. Consequently, I have included much more than mere geographical or topographical reports: the Indian policy of the Spanish government, the activity of the merchants involved in the Missouri trade, the international complications caused by the "invasion" by English traders of territory beyond the Mississippi which Spain claimed as its exclusive property, and the attempts of Spain to enforce its hold on the northeastern frontier of New Spain are essential parts of the whole story of the Missouri in these years.

To make this story complete for the period chosen I have included all documents of importance for the years 1790-1804 whether they have been previously published or not. Previously printed documents, with a few exceptions, have been collated with originals or copies in my possession; all printed translations have been carefully gone over and in some instances corrected. Documents have, almost invariably, been given in full rather than in extract. The bulk of the documents are now translated and published for the first time. In translating I have always believed in rendering word for word in so far as it was possible to do so: I have wanted the writers to tell their own story in their own words. Many of the writers were not literary or highly educated persons; they wrote as ordinary persons do in letters, forgetting certain principles of grammar, punctuation, and, sometimes, intelligibility. I have not attempted to improve upon their writing. Some routine details in correspondence I have standardized: for example, the many styles of address at the beginning and close of letters I have simplified from "My Lord," "Your Highness," "Your Lordship," and so forth to "Your Excellency." I have used the latter style in all instances of a subordinate addressing a superior; in the reverse case I have used the simple pronoun "you."

The documents are allowed to tell their own story. I have not attempted to edit them fully (such procedure would double the size of these volumes); I have generally limited myself to notes indicating the source of the documents and to cross-references. In case of documents republished here for sake of continuity of story I have not included the full editorial notes but I have of course indicated where they may be found. I have not included a bibliography but I have given full citation for documents either printed here or quoted from. In the documents I have kept the original spellings of place, tribal, and personal names; in the titles supplied for the documents, however, I have used the correct form for such names.

To introduce these documents effectively I have written a short history (the first such account, I believe) of the Missouri River from its discovery in 1673 until the expedition of Lewis and Clark. In the first and least known portion dealing with the river in its French days I have wished to be rather full and have included considerable excerpts from original documents. Section II, covering the Spanish period up to about 1790 I have sketched in rather lightly, for little actual progress was made in exploration of the river during those years. The last division contains the story of a very active period of exploration and of the Anglo-Spanish rivalry there at the close of the century. This introductory history, which I have annotated fully, therefore, gives a sustained account of the river from 1673 to 1804, whereas the remainder of the present volumes is devoted to the documentary detail of the story for the last fifteen years before the time of the Americans.

Five maps have been chosen to illustrate this narrative and documents; of these the Soulard and the Finiel are published for the first time.

In such a work as this it is a pleasure to acknowledge help which I have received from many persons. My first encouragement to prepare it came from Mr. Charles E. Peterson, then the energetic and magnetic president of the St. Louis Historical Documents Foundation. The editorial board of the Foundation (Mr. Peterson, and Professors John Francis Bannon, S. J., and John Francis McDermott) helped me in the selection of documents. Dr. Bannon has carefully gone over my introduction and aided me materially with it. Professor McDermott has never failed me whenever I have called upon his vast storehouse of information relating to St. Louis. My colleague Dr. Leslie P. Brown, Professor of Romance Languages at San Diego College, has been of inestimable help to me. His intimate knowledge of grammar and of French and Spanish philology has been given unstintedly to me. It is due to him that I have been saved the pitfalls of the translator who has not always seen the peculiarities of expression of persons writing in Spanish but whose native language was French, and vice versa. Dr. Brown has aided me with many difficult passages. What errors remain, of course, are mine and mine only. My materials have been assembled from so many archival repositories that space will not permit the mention of the many, many kindnesses I have received from their staffs, but I am deeply appreciative of all the time and knowledge they have spent in my behalf. I do wish to add, however, a special word of appreciation for the staff of the Missouri Historical Society who have never failed to furnish me with materials for which I have asked. In the painstaking work of proofreading I have had the excellent assistance of my nephew, Robert Hirsch, to whom I am much indebted. The magnificent index I owe to Miss Ruth Fleming of San Francisco.

Finally, my wife, to whom this work is dedicated, has directly and indirectly contributed to it. She has foregone many pleasures and luxuries and given up her vacations that our time and resources could be concentrated on this project. In short, she is responsible for seeing it completed.

San Diego, California   A.P.N.
April 19, 1952

CONTENTS
VOLUME ONE

[Volume I is indexed at the end of Volume II]

INTRODUCTION

THE EXPLORATION OF
THE MISSOURI
1673-1804

PART I

UNDER THE FRENCH RÉGIME

1.

THE IMPORTANCE OF THE MISSOURI AREA

St. Louis, Missouri, today a great city in the heart of the continent, was from its beginning strategically located for the control of commerce and trade in a vast territory. Pierre Laclède wisely placed his settlement near the confluence of two great rivers: the Mississippi, which extends from its source near the northern boundary of the United States to the Gulf of Mexico, bisecting the nation, and the Missouri, which rises close to the continental divide and turbulently flows from the northwest, crosses the plains, and finally merges with the greater river. Around St. Louis in every direction stretches the rich and fertile Mississippi Valley, now one of the leading agricultural and industrial areas of the world. Early explorations of this important region by Spanish, French, and English adventurers, soldiers, fur traders, and missionaries form one of the most fascinating and least known chapters of our country's history.

It might at first seem strange that the Mississippi Valley was not explored shortly after the great feats of Coronado and de Soto. But those expeditions into the southern half of the present United States uncovered neither the elements of romantic appeal nor the material inducements which Mexico and Peru had held. Consider the difference. Where in the Mississippi Valley were gold and silver? Where did one find native populations and cultures comparable to the Aztec or Inca, or even to the Pueblo Indian? What inducements could the Osages, Sioux, and Kiowa

1

hold forth? Not even to spread the faith would the Spanish push beyond the troublesome Apaches and Comanches. What other incentives could have aroused them? Indeed, only her claim to exclusive ownership and a desire to surround her empire with an iron wall in order to keep out people of other nations finally moved Spain to take an active interest in the vast mid-continental region.

In the early part of the seventeenth century, France, England, and the Netherlands—strongly impelled by rivalry, nationalism, desire for economic profit, mercantilism, and honor—simultaneously challenged the exclusive Spanish monopoly, all planting permanent colonies in North America. The French, led by intrepid pioneers, explorers, fur traders, and missionaries, occupied the St. Lawrence basin, pushed their frontier to the Great Lakes, spread their empire between the English on the Atlantic coastal plains and the Spaniards in the southwest, and began exploring and exploiting the vast Mississippi-Missouri Valley. It was, for France at least, fruitless effort. Complicated competition and pressure later caught her between the aggressive and buoyant Anglo-American frontiersmen who crossed the Alleghenies and the Spaniards with whom those Americans competed, fought, and whom they ultimately defeated.

For a time, however, the clever, profit-seeking, paternalistically-supported Frenchmen monopolized the trade of the trans-Mississippi West. Here the French earnestly sought an "exclusively owned" route through the continent to the Sea of California and the lucrative trade of the Orient. This urge alone accounts for the rapid advance of the French, who dipped their canoes in every leading river highway in the west from Canada to the Gulf of Mexico. Furthermore, the French were covetously eyeing the rich Spanish Empire, especially New Mexico, a prize which they sought to win chiefly by trading with and making alliances among the Indian tribes. But time was running out, and in their reaching westward, the mountain barrier stopped them.

To oppose these fast-moving French, the Spanish, too late, embarked upon a policy of defensive expansion. They explored the great plains and attempted to counter the French through trade and friendship with the Indians. Nevertheless, defeat stalked the Spaniards. This is the story of the seventeenth century.

In the eighteenth century European politics combined with imperial ambitions to oust the French from the "heart of America." The French area was divided at the Mississippi between Spain and England. Spain now occupied the western portion of the valley and attempted to strengthen it purely as a bulwark for her far more rich and important Mexican colonies. Several urgent motives combined in the latter part of the century to lead the Spaniards to seek geographical enlightenment concerning

2

the great encircling and protective northeastern frontier of colonial New Spain (now the southwest of the present United States). Though opportunities for private gain played their part, perhaps the most urgent need was to check British encroachment on Spanish territory. For such defense Louisiana was strategically located. It served as a protecting barrier against British threats to the mineral wealth of New Mexico, a chief source of metal income to the Spanish crown. In order to prevent incursions into this region from the west, as well as to check Russian aggression from the north, Spain occupied California almost at the precise time that she took over Louisiana. British activity on the northwest coast of North America and British penetration of the "unknown west" in present-day Canada, taken together with the virtual monopoly which British merchants held of the trade with the Indians of the Upper Mississippi-Missouri regions, injected fear into the hearts of the Spanish officials that such activity might result in the British conquest of the rich kingdom of New Mexico from the north. (Witness, for example, the activities of Carver, Pond, Ducharme, the Northwest Company's agents, Todd, La Rocque, MacKenzie, and others, as well as the Nootka Sound Controversy and the events leading thereto.)

Spain had still other motives for extensive explorations. She desired to open up the country in the watershed of the Missouri River to the enlightenment of the world, to acquaint unknown tribes of Indians with the Spanish government and customs, and to develop commerce with them for the purposes of self-defense and private profit. All these desires combined to produce a series of expeditions by the Spaniards which led them from the Niobrara River to the forks of the Missouri. This work of expansion was carried to its logical conclusion when Lewis and Clark reached the Pacific Ocean, and the traders of St. Louis reached Santa Fé.

First, however, we must trace the progress of discovery along the Missouri River during the French régime. Credit for discovering the Missouri must be given to Louis Jolliet and Father Jacques Marquette who, accompanied by "five men who were quite determined to do anything and to suffer anything for such a glorious expedition," towards the end of June, 1673, passed the mouth of the Missouri River, which they called "la rivière Pekitanoüi." They were astounded by this water's rapidity, for undoubtedly they saw the river of the "oumissouries" rushing eastward at full flood-tide. Father Marquette remarked that "Several villages of the savages are located along this river, and I hope by means of it to make the discovery of the Vermillion Sea or California."[1] Nine years later

---

[1] R. G. Thwaites, [ed.], *Jesuit Relations and Allied Documents* (72 volumes, Cleveland, 1900), LIX, 141. For the circumstances of the Jolliet-Marquette expedition see the scholarly *The Jolliet-Marquette Expedition, 1673*, by Francis Borgia Steck (second ed., Glendale, 1928); Ernest Gagnon, *Sieur Jolliet* (Quebec, 1902); Baron Marc

3

Robert Cavelier, Sieur de La Salle, passed the mouth of the Missouri and set down an accurate description. After La Salle's assassination, Joutel, in making his way from Texas to the Illinois Country, passed the Missouri River on the first day of September, 1687.[2]

The great fame of La Salle's expedition, according to Baron Marc de Villiers du Terrage, gave rise to many legends among the *coureurs de bois*

---

de Villiers du Terrage, *La Découverte du Missouri* (Paris, 1925) ; L. P. Kellogg, *The French Régime in Wisconsin and the Northwest* (Madison, 1925). For original sources see, Pierre Margry [ed.], *Découvertes et Établissements des Français dans l'Ouest et dans le Sud d'Amérique Septentrionale 1614-1754* (6 volumes, Paris, 1876-1886) ; J. G. Shea, *Discovery and Exploration of the Mississippi Valley* (New York, 1852) ; L. P. Kellogg, *Early Narratives of the Northwest* (New York, 1917). For a discussion of Marquette's and other maps see R. N. Hamilton, "The Early Cartography of the Missouri Valley," in *American Historical Review*, XXXIX (1934), 645-662, and the following articles by Jean Delanglez: "Discovery of the Mississippi: Primary Sources," *Mid-America*. XXVII (January, 1945). 219-231; "Discovery of the Mississippi River: Secondary Sources," *Mid-America*, XXVIII (January, 1946), 3-20; and "The Jolliet Lost Map of the Mississippi," *Mid-America*, XXVIII, (April, 1946), 67-144. In 1948 Delanglez gathered together his various studies on Jolliet and printed them in his *Life and Voyages of Louis Jolliet, 1645-1700* (The Institute of Jesuit History, Chicago, 1948). The Jolliet-Marquette exploration was the culmination of French exploration and occupation and trade to the headwaters of the rivers flowing into the Great Lakes. Jesuits had urged exploration of the unknown territory since the early days. (Thwaites, *Jesuit Relations*, volumes XVIII, LI, LIX, etc.). The memory of Coronado and the lure of Quivira were known to the French, and the desire for the opening up of a route to the South Sea. Marquette was actually fired with the idea of winning new territory for the cross. Some few scholars have accepted the fact that Radisson and Groseilliers had visited the Missouri and even saw and spoke with some Osages (Houck, *History of Missouri*, I, 151 ff., based upon Father Allouez; see also Thwaites, *Jesuit Relations*, LIV, 225; XLIV, 237).

[2]La Salle arrived at the mouth of the Missouri, February 14, 1682. He catalogued some of the native tribes of the interior—e.g., the Pana nation, 200 leagues to the west —and estimated the course of the "grand rivière des Emisourites" as navigable for more than 400 leagues. Garraghan suggests that this meant as far as the Platte (G. J. Garraghan, *Chapters in Frontier History* [Milwaukee, 1934], 55). Margry, *op. cit.*, I, II, and III, contain documents on La Salle, the originals or copies which he made are in Bibliothèque Nationale, Paris, Manuscrits Français, Nouvelles Acquisitions, volumes 9288, 9289, 9290, 9291 (hereinafter cited, B.N., n.a.). Father Zenobius Membré's narrative of the La Salle expedition is in J. G. Shea, *Discovery and Exploration of Mississippi Valley* (New York, 1852). *Joutel's Journal of La Salle's last voyage, 1684-1687* was edited by H. R. Stiles (Albany, 1906) ; and also edited by I. J. Cox in *Trailmakers* series (3 volumes, New York, 1902) and in *American Explorer* series (2 volumes, New York, 1922). For Joutel see also Shea, *op. cit.;* Margry, *op. cit.*, III, and B.N., n.a., 9289 folios 1-149. See Delanglez' discussion of maps in *Mid-America*, and by same author, *Some La Salle Journeys* (Chicago, 1938). Douay accompanied La Salle; his narrative is printed in Shea, *op. cit.*, (second edition, Albany, 1903), 201-233. See also Hennepin's *New Discovery* (ed. by R. G. Thwaites, Chicago, 1903) and Father Christian Leclerq's, *First Establishment of the Faith in New France* (ed. by J. G. Shea, Paris, 1882). Tonti's narrative is printed in Kellogg, *Early Narratives*, and in B. F. French, *Historical Collections of Louisiana* (New York, 1846), vol. I. Tonty, writing to Renaudot, spoke of a map and told of the Missouri coming from the west "about 300 leagues from a lake which I believe to be the lake of the Apaches," B. N., n. a., vol. 7485, folios 119-120, and printed in Werner and Pease, *French Foundations* (Springfield, 1934), 276-282, from Archives Nationales, Colonies, (hereinafter cited A. N. Col.) C[13] C3, folios 142-143. See also E. R. Murphy, *Henri de Tonty* (Washington, 1941).

4

concerning the Missouri, echoes of which stories Mathieu Sagan,[3] Baron La Hontan, and Bossu published in their narrative volumes. La Hontan's narrative has been discredited by Houck and others, though Houck at least accepts as true the evidence that La Hontan visited the Missouri. The scholarly Villiers du Terrage accepts not even this, relegating the narrative to the category of "legends" in no uncertain terms:

The expedition which La Hontan is supposed to have made in company with the Outagamis (Foxes) on the Missouri in the month of March, 1689, never took place; and the astounding rapidity of his trip to the river of the Osages is not the least improbable thing [phase] of the matter. Everything that the author tells of the fort[s] of the Missouri, of the Wabash and of the country of the Illinois superabundantly proves that he did not know those regions.[4]

La Salle, in 1683, wrote of two Frenchmen who had lived among the Missouri tribes. According to another record, in May-June 1693, two other French traders, accompanied by some Kaskaskia Indians, visited the Missouri and Osage Indians, hoping to set up trade with them and to establish peace between their tribes and the tribes residing in the vicinity of the Kaskaskia.[5] The last mention of the Missouri in the course of the seventeenth century was that of Father St. Cosme, who visited the Missouri region in 1698 and reported that a large number of savages lived upon that river.[6]

---

[3]Archives du Service Hydrographique de la Marine (hereinafter cited A. S. H.) volume 67[2], numbers [liasses] 2 and 3. Number 1 is La Salle. See also Margry, op. cit., VI, and in B. N., n. a., vol. 9287. N. Bossu, Nouveaux Voyages aux Indes Occidentales (Paris, 1768), I, 167-169. B. N., n. a., vol. 9287 contains voyages of La Hontan, letters xii à xviii, 1687-1689, pp. 89-202, and "Relation de Mathieu Sagean, ancien campagnon de Cavalier de La Salle" in Relations des Voyages aux Sources du Mississippi, à la Californie . . . par Danycan. Also others. See A. P. Nasatir, French Activities in California: An Archival Calendar Guide (Stanford University, 1945), 373-374. Most of these are notes and are printed in Margry, op. cit., V and VI.

[4]Lahontan, Louis Armand de Lom d'Arce, Baron de, New Voyage to North America, (ed. by R. G. Thwaites, Chicago, 1905); Villiers du Terrage, Découverte du Missouri, 28; Houck, History of Missouri, I, 239. Le Maire in 1714 wrote that, "In this country we regard what the Baron de La Hontan wrote of this western district of Louisiana as an account written to please rather than to inform the reader. It must be expected that this region will have to be more settled by the French if we are going to be able to explore regions yet unknown to us." (A. N. Col. C[13] C, II, 109-138, extract printed in Margry, op. cit., VI, 185, and translated in Missouri Historical Review, XXXIX (1946), 388, is folios 114 vo-115).

[5]Louis Houck, History of Missouri (3 volumes, Chicago, 1908), I, 240, says May, 1694, but Father Gravier's letter recounting this information is dated February 15, 1694 (R. G. Thwaites [ed.], Jesuit Relations and Allied Documents, LXIV, 159 ff., especially, 161, 169 ff.). La Salle says that in 1680 or 1681 two French coureurs-de-bois were captured on the Mississippi by Missouri Indians and were taken off to their village, (Margry, op. cit., II, 203, 325-326; cited by Garraghan, Chapters in Frontier History, 56-57).

[6]Letter of Jean Frs. Buisson de St. Cosme to the Bishop of Quebec, dated in the Arkansas Country, January 2, 1699, Archives Nationales Series K, Volume 1374, dossier 20, number 81; A. S. H., vol. 115[x] no. 14; Kellogg, Early Narratives, 342-361; J. G. Shea, Early Voyages Up and Down the Mississippi (Albany, 1861), 64-69. On page 342 of Kellogg, op. cit., is Franquelin's map.

On July 13, 1700, Le Sueur, searching for mines and returning up the Mississippi, reached the Missouri. He described the Missouri and spoke of tin and lead mines; he commented curiously that Missouri means "canoe," so named for the Indians who are called the "peoples of the canoes." Moreover, he told of warfare being waged against the Panis established all along the river of the Missouri and added that no one had as yet discovered the source of the river.[7]

On July 10, 1700, Father Marest of the Kaskaskia mission wrote to Iberville (then at L'Île Dauphin) recounting all the geographical information he had been able to gather. He declared that the Missouri was as long and as large as the Mississippi and was well peopled with Indian nations; he spoke of the Kansas and Panis as living in the Missouri valley, stating that they carried on commerce with the Spanish; he had seen Spanish horses. He also mentioned the Oto and Iowa tribes, the latter allied with the Sioux, but confessed that neither he nor any other Frenchman had ever been among these tribes of the Missouri. He stated that his information was derived from the savages who do not know "the upper country and could not tell exactly the distance of or from each village; therefore, I will say nothing to you about it, I wishing to tell you only the truth; as for the Pekitanoüi [Missouri] I may tell you that it is the country of the beaver."[8]

Meanwhile religious endeavors resulted in the founding of missions near the Missouri and the planning of still others. The center of activities among the Indians of the Missouri was to be the Tamarois mission (Cahokia) founded in March, 1699. Jesuit Father Limoges, arriving at Cahokia, March 9, 1700, made known to Father St. Cosme his desire to plant the cross farther among the tribes of the Missouri, especially the Osages. Two years later, Father Bergier, successor to Father St. Cosme, wrote of his desire to establish missions among the Kansas and Panimaha tribes on the Missouri river, the Osages being too numerous and the Missouri Indians reduced to nothing; he sought from Quebec and Paris permissions for mission activity.[9]

A highly interesting but short-lived episode was the planting of a mission establishment where St. Louis now stands. The site had previously been seen by Jolliet and Marquette, July 4, 1673; by Henri de Tonti, on December 7, 1698;[10] and on December 8, Fathers Montigny, Davion, and

[7]On Le Sueur see: *Jesuit Relations,* LXVI; Margry, *op. cit.,* V, 416-420; Shea, *Early Voyages; Wisconsin Historical Collections,* XVI, 177 ff.; Villiers du Terrage, *op. cit.,* 31-32. Pénicaut's narrative is printed in *Minnesota Historical Collections,* vol. III; Margry, *op. cit.,* VI, 69 ff; and is in A. S. H. 115ˣ no. 9. Delisle's map based on the *mémoires* of Le Sueur is in A. S. H., Portefeuille 138 *bis,* division 3, number 2.
[8]A. S. H. vol. 115ˣ *liasse* number 15; quoted in Villers du Terrage, *op. cit.*
[9]Garraghan, *Chapters in Frontier History,* 60-61.
[10]Kellogg, *Early Narratives,* 346; J. H. Schlarman, *From Quebec to New Orleans,* (Belleville, 1929), 139-140.

St. Cosme celebrated mass there.[11] The mission was established late in 1700, when the Kaskaskia Indians moved from the Illinois river to the mouth of the Des Pères river (within the corporate limits of present St. Louis.) A mission was maintained here for better than two years; though the settlement was abandoned its location, nevertheless, gives some evidence of the "pull" of the Missouri.[12]

With the opening of the eighteenth century the history of the exploration of the Missouri may be said to begin. The chief motives of the French were to anticipate the Spaniards who were pushing—or at least writing about pushing—northeast towards the Missouri and to blaze a trail to the famed mines of New Mexico. Commerce and friendship with the Indians were only means to those ends. To these motives should be added (but not from the direction of Missouri) the interest in discovering a route to the western sea.

In 1700 an as yet unidentified writer who had had long talks with Iberville and access to his Journals reported that nothing was new in Louisiana and that the land west of the Mississippi, at least beyond three or four leagues inland, was entirely unknown. He suggested that in order to derive benefit from the vast cost of the past twenty years' exploitation it would be necessary to send *coureurs de bois* to the strait which separated California from the mainland and to have qualified personnel make maps of the area.[13]

Undoubtedly many *coureurs de bois* did penetrate to great distances, their activities no doubt retarded by the *méfiance* of the Plains Indians. However, since, as Villiers du Terrage maintains, the objective was the mines of New Mexico, these intrepid, unrecorded adventurers probably made their sallies up the branches of the Missouri, as for example, the Osage, Kansas, and the Platte rivers, rather than ascending further on the Missouri itself. Further strengthening this opinion is the fact that no mention of contact with the Sioux is found in documents from this area, since in the main the Sioux and Upper Missouri river country belonged to the Canadian spheres of interest.

---

[11]St. Cosme's letter is printed in Kellogg, *Early Narratives*, 342-361, esp. 346-355.
[12]This is based on Gilbert J. Garraghan's essay "The First Settlement on the Site of St. Louis," which first appeared in *Mid-America* and is more conveniently found in his *Chapters in Frontier History*, 73-84. See also, by the same author, "New Light on Old Cahokia," in *Illinois Catholic Historical Review*, XI (1928), 99-139; and "Earliest Settlements of the Illinois Country," in *Catholic Historical Review*, XV, (1930), 351-362. Letters of Father Marest are in *Jesuit Relations*, LXVI. See also Sister Mary Borgias Palm, *Jesuit Missions in the Illinois Country 1673-1763*, (Cleveland, 1934). See the map published in Schlarman, *op. cit.*, 151. The existence of this Indian village was established by Lawrence J. Kenny, *St. Louis Catholic Historical Review*, I (1919), 151-156.
[13]Margry, *op. cit.*, VI, 177, extract from a letter dated Rochefort, November 15, 1700. This is most likely Michel Begnis' letter of November 13, 1700, to Villermont which is in B. N., Mss. Français, vol. 22808, folio 204, and in extract in *Ibid.*, n. a., vol. 9287.

Iberville, desiring to open up commercial relations with New Mexico and thinking also of reaching California and exploring on the sea,[14] wrote in 1700 that he would undertake the exploration that everyone wished to be made in the west by way of the Marne or Arkansas Rivers. Two years later Iberville in his *mémoire,* dated June 20, 1702, listed a number of Indian nations who dwelt on the Missouri, giving the number of their families and including the Missouris, Kansas, Otos, Iowas, Panimahas, and Panis.[15] On February 15, 1703,[16] he recounted that twenty Canadians left Tamarois (Cahokia) to discover New Mexico, trade there, and see whether the mines of which the savages told them really existed. In his plan for relocation of the Indian tribes Iberville proposed establishing western trading posts on the Arkansas, Ohio, and Missouri rivers around which settlers would be encouraged to settle.[17] On September 6, 1704, Bienville reported that the Canadians were traveling on the Mississippi and the Missouri in small bands of seven or eight.[18]

In the following year a Frenchman named Laurain arrived at Biloxi and gave Bienville a confused account of his travels, of the Indians in-

---

[14]Margry, *op cit.,* VI, 178. This is *Mémoire des choses que le Sr. Iberville demande par le Mississippi, 1701.* It is in A.S.H. 67² no. 4.

[15]Iberville's *Mémoire Sur le Pays du Mississippi,* dated June 20, 1702, is in Archives Colonies F³24, folios 38-45. (Surrey's *Calendar* states that Iberville's Journal, December 15, 1701—April 27, 1702, is this document and is printed in Margry, *op. cit.,* IV, 503 ff.) The names given above are quoted in Villiers du Terrage, *op. cit.,* 35, but the full list includes:

> Sioux—4000 families
> Maha—1200
> Toctata—Iowas—les Aymons—300
> Kansas—1500
> Missouris—1500
> Arkansas—Aesetones—Tongenge—200
> Manton—100
> Panas near Arkansas—2000
> Illinois of Great Village—Otamoroas—800
> Les Messigamea, Chepanchie, Medehiaquoins—200
> Les Quiapou et Mascouten—450

Iberville stated that several of those nations could be moved to the Arkansas. The purpose of removal was the war with the Spaniards and their allied Indians, and the control of trade.

[16]Margry, *op. cit.,* VI, 180. Margry copied this inaccurately—see B. N., n. a., 9295, folios 254-255.

[17]*Ibid.,* IV, 593 ff. Inefficiency in government and the War of the Spanish Succession prevented any carrying out of this comprehensive scheme of Iberville. Father Bergier at Tamaroa stated that in March, 1702, seventeen Frenchmen left that village to ascend the Missouri about 200 leagues and there build a fort between the Pawnee and the Iowa. They were attacked *en route* but probably returned in safety (Garraghan, *Chapters in Frontier History,* 62).

[18]A. N. Col. C13A, vol. I, pages 449-465. The short extract printed in Margry, *op cit.,* VI, 180, is badly garbled. On August 6, 1702, Remonville wrote that the Missouri was larger than the Mississippi and that fourteen very populous tribes lived on the Missouri. Margry, *op. cit.,* VI, 179. This is in B. N., Mss. Fr., vol. 9097, folios 127-128 *vo.* The first part of this extract from the original letter is printed in Margry, *op. cit.,* VI, 89-90.

habiting the Missouri, and of the Spanish establishments on the frontier of New Mexico.[19]

In 1706 or 1707 Derbanne with a small party of men ascended the Missouri nearly four hundred leagues and credited himself with being the first Frenchman to penetrate so far into the interior. Derbanne claimed he had discovered horses either stolen or purchased from the Spaniards by the Indians, a fact suggesting Spanish penetration. He asserted that New Mexico was not far from the Missouri but that the Spaniards, who perhaps wished to deceive the Frenchmen, reported there was no silver in New Mexico.[20]

On April 10, 1706, Bienville reported that two Canadians had told him they had spent two years going from village to village on the Missouri, they had been near the Spanish mines, and had been arrested in an Indian village which the Spaniards had just left. The Spaniards had come to trade for buffalo hides, with which to make harness for their mules. The Canadians claimed that the Spaniards had been at war with three or four large Indian nations. They assured Bienville that the Missouri country was beautiful, and from three mines they brought samples of copper and of an unknown metal.[21] Two years later, on February 25, 1708, Dartaguiette was assured by a Canadian, Boudon, who proposed to furnish the western posts with lead at six *sols* per pound, that there were many tin mines and that the Missouri river was as yet not well known.[22]

On October 16, 1708, Nicolas de la Salle wrote that it was very important to explore the Missouri. He had questioned some slaves of the Indian nations of Missouri, had learned that iron of the same color and quality as *piastres* had been discovered, and that Spaniards frequented the region with mules. Some Canadian *voyageurs* had ascended the Missouri three hundred or four hundred leagues without being able to discover its source. With the aid of 40,000 *livres* in merchandise, munitions, and food, an expedition of one hundred men could be undertaken, the voyage probably to take from twelve to [15] months. He suggested that an engineer accompany the proposed expedition in order to map the river.[23] The idea of exploring the Missouri was further urged in 1709.[24]

Nicolas de la Salle wrote again on June 20, 1710, that Ensign Darac

---

[19]Margry, *op. cit.*, VI, 181, and Villiers du Terrage, *op. cit.*, 35-36. This is taken from *Journal Historique de l'Établissements des Français en Louisiane*, compiled by Beaurain (Paris and New Orleans, 1831).

[20]Garraghan, *Chapters in Frontier History*, 62-63. For Spanish reaction to French activities and of their explorations northeast of Santa Fé, see A. B. Thomas, *After Coronado* (Norman, 1935).

[21]A. N., Col. C13A vol. I, folio 502-513. Folios 503-504 only are printed in Margry, *op. cit.*, VI, 181-182.

[22]A. N., Col. C13A, vol. II, folio 25, quoted in Villiers du Terrage, *op. cit.*, 37.

[23]Incomplete letter in A. N., Col. C13A, vol. II, folios 221-223. A slightly different account of this letter is the original in *Ibid.*, vol. II, folios 229-233; printed in Margry,

and two soldiers had been sent by Bienville to ascend the Missouri, ostensibly to make presents to the Indians friendly to the French, but actually to trade in peltries and for slaves to sell in the Islands; La Salle urged the minister at Paris not to pay their salaries.[23]

Diron Dartaguiette twice mentioned the Missouri in 1710. On one occasion he stated that it was necessary to make discoveries on the Missouri which, according to those who had been there, even the Spanish, cut between Old and New Mexico. From such accounts it was learned that the Missouri flowed directly to New Mexico, and was called the Rivière Blanche.[26] On May 12 Dartaguiette forwarded a map based on information derived from *coureurs de bois* and savages who had visited there.[27] At that time relations between the French and the Missouris must have been good, for in 1712 these Indians went to the aid of Dubuisson, when he was besieged in Detroit by the Fox Indians.[28]

Governor Cadillac wrote on October 26, 1713, that a man named Saint-Michel had told him that the Spanish mining area was traversed by the Missouri.[29] Depending, perhaps, on this information, Le Maire tells

op. cit., VI, 182-183. A good part of this is quoted in Villiers du Terrage, *op. cit.*, 37-38 where some added comments on the "iron" are given.
   [24]*Mémoire* of Sr. Mandeville, 1709, printed in Margry, *op cit.*, VI, 184. The original is in A. N., Col. C13A, vol. II, folios 471-480 and an extract in *Ibid.*, F³24, folio 55. It is dated April 27, 1709.
   See an extract which is different in A. N. Col. C13A; vol. II, folios 481-490, especially folio 487.
   [25]A. N., Col. C13A, vol. II, folios 519-527. La Salle and Bienville did not get along well. Bienville sent Ensign Darac to Illinois. See Bienville to Minister, February 20, 1710, as listed in Surrey. *Calendar,* I, 157. I have not seen this letter. On October 27, 1711 (A. N. Col., C13A, vol. II, folio 585) Bienville said that Darac was a gentleman, brave, wise, and a strong friend of the Indians and had served in the troops of Canada for a long time.
   [26]February 12 and June 20. The first is listed as being in A. N., Col. C13A, vol. II, folio 536 (Villiers du Terrage cites folio 236—extract printed in Margry, *op. cit.*, V, 371,) and the latter is in A. N. Col. C13A, vol. II, folios 541-546. Quoted in Villiers du Terrage, *op. cit.*, 39.
   [27]Dartaguiette to Minister, Bayonne, May 12, 1712. *Mémoire* on the present situation of the colony of Louisiana. "I shall have the honor of taking to *Monseigneur* a map that I had made of what is known to us of this [Missouri] river, according to the reports of the *coureurs-de-bois* and the savages who have been there. This map explains more and better than I would be able to say here". Archives du Ministère des Affaires Étrangères, Correspondance Politique, États-Unis (hereinafter cited A. E. Corr. Pol.) Supplément, vol. VI, folios 4-8; also A. N., Col. C13A, vol. II, folios (pages) 803-809.
   [28]Report of Dubuisson to Vaudreuil, Detroit, June 15, 1712. This is a long letter in A. N., Col. C11A. vol. XXXIII, folios 161 ff., printed in *Wisconsin Historical Collections*, XVI, 267-287, esp. 272; also in *Michigan Pioneer and Historical Collections,* XXXIII, 537-562. See also P. F. X. de Charlevoix, *History and General Description of New France,* translated by J. G. Shea (6 vols., New York, 1900), V, 258 (the story of the siege is told beginning on page 257) ; and L. P. Kellogg, "Fox Indians during the French Régime," in *Wisconsin Historical Society Proceedings, 1907*, 142-188, and by the same author, *The French Régime in Wisconsin and the Northwest*, 268-289, esp. 280-282.
   [29]A. N., Col. C13A, vol. III, pages 31-32, quoted in Villers du Terrage, *op. cit.,* 39-40. This is from a long report of Cadillac to the Minister discussing conditions in

us in his *mémoire*, dated January 15, 1714, that the Missouri had been ascended more than four hundred leagues without a Spanish habitation being found, and that not until reaching a point more than five hundred leagues from the mouth of the Missouri did one begin to hear news of Spaniards from the Indians, who were at war with them.[80]

On December 27, 1714, the King ordered five posts established, of which Natchez would be the *magasin*, where the *voyageurs* of the Missouri could send their pelts.[81]

In the French archives are a number of other *mémoires*, some dated, others undated, all thought to have been written in the second decade of the eighteenth century, all bearing on the Missouri and activities along its banks. Let us examine some of them.

One such document states that the Missouri "divides into several branches which water a vast extent of magnificent countryside, as rich it is said, in mines as it is abundant in all kinds of animals. There are a number of nations, populous enough, established on its banks who are quite warlike. One could draw many beaver and other furs from that section."[82]

De Ganne's *mémoire*, though dated October 20, 1721, refers to activities much earlier than that time. According to this report several Missouri and Osage Indians, coming to trade among the Illinois, had given the information that by the Missouri, lakes, and other rivers, one could reach the Western Sea. The Pawnee and Wichita who lived in Missouri territory had relations with the Spaniards, from whom they procured horses.[83]

Another *mémoire* declared that quite possibly it would become necessary to establish a post on the Missouri, either to protect French traders or in order to "come closer to the Spaniards, or because of some mines which are more precious than those of lead."[84]

Louisiana and opens volume three of the C13A series. Saint-Michel understood from the Spaniards that the mines were on the Missouri. Saint-Michel left for [from?] the Illinois and the Missouri. He said that the mountains where the Spanish mines existed were crossed by the Missouri at 400 to 500 leagues. Perhaps these accounts were exaggerated but suffice it to say that they were based on official reports of the explorations of the Missouri by the French. See also for the Spanish side of the story, Thomas, *After Coronado*.

[80]Margry, *op. cit.*, VI, 185. This is from a long *mémoire* of Le Maire written from Pensacola. A. N. Col., C13C II, folios 109-138. The paragraph quoted is in A. S. H. 115ˣ no. 22. Only a short extract of this *mémoire* is printed in Margry, *op. cit.*, VI, 184-186. The fourteen excerpts printed in Margry, volume VI, are in the main translated in *Missouri Historical Review*, XXXIX (April, 1945), 384-388.

[81]A. N. Marine BI vol. IX, folios 273-293. Made by Council of Marine held in the Louvre, August 29, 1716; A. N. Col. C13A Vol. IV, p.p. 211-231.

[82]A. N., Col. C13C vol. I, folios 366-369; extract given is on folio 368 *verso*.

[83]Printed in Werner and Pease, *French Foundations*, 303-395.

[84]A. N., Col. C13C vol. I. folios 117-132. This is undated but under the Company, after 1717.

11

Hubert's *mémoire* told of mines only a short distance up the Missouri, and he included another *mémoire* about the Missouri which stated that thirty-five leagues up the river was the Osage, fourteen leagues farther the Rivière à la Barque, five leagues farther the Rivière à la Mine de Plomb, seven more leagues the Rivière au Portchicore, and eleven leagues farther the village of the Missouri. From this Missouri village to the Kansas river it was thirty *(sic)* leagues, and at one hundred twenty leagues up the Kansas that river forked to the west-northwest, where was a variety of mines. It was only a short distance from the branches of the Upper Kansas to the Arkansas and the country of the Paducas (Comanches) who traded with the Spaniards. One hundred forty-seven leagues from the Kansas was the Rivière des Panis, which at thirty-five leagues forked into three branches; along this river were various Panis villages. On the right were the Maha river (sixty leagues by land) and the Iowa. Further up was the Platte river and near it on the left another river nearly as large as the Missouri; above this point lived the Aricaras, who spoke the same language as the Panis.[35]

In another *mémoire* entitled *La Louisiane—Sur L'État de cette colonie, des production et les avantages qu'on en peut retiré[r]*, the author stated that he could not "speak of the Missouri nor other uninhabited country."[36] All of these references show the ever-increasing interest in the Missouri River country.

2.

THE EXPLORATIONS OF BOURGMONT AND OTHERS

The first definite and detailed exploration of the Missouri is the voyage of Étienne Veniard de Bourgmont. Bourgmont was a *coureur de bois* in Canada, a man fired by the spirit of adventure, who replaced Tonti in January, 1706, as commandant of Fort Detroit. At the siege of that post by the Foxes in 1712, he first became acquainted with the Missouri Indians when they arrived to aid the French. He accompanied the Indians to the Missouri on their return and became the idol of the tribes which he visited in 1714.[37] He deserted from Detroit and joined others living a fascinatingly adventurous life, married an Indian woman, and went to live among the Missouri Indians about whom he wrote. One of his writings, *Route Qu'il fau tenir pour monter la rivière du Missouri*, gives a diary of

---

[35]A. E. Mémoires et Documents, séries, Amérique, vol. I, folios 216-221, and *mémoire* on Missouri in folios 221-224.

[36]A. N., Col. C13C vol. I, folios 375-385. This was probably written a little later, for it speaks of the French living in harmony with the Spaniards established at Los Adaes—seven leagues from Natchitoches.

[37]Bourgmont was later pardoned and reinstated in the service by Cadillac.

his activities in 1714.[38] He had sojourned among the Osages, but he says very little or nothing about them in this document. How far he went up the Missouri at this time is uncertain, but Le Page du Pratz, who knew him well, claimed that he ascended the river a distance of eight hundred leagues. We know that Vermale's map, drawn in 1717, indicates the course of the Osage river.

Bourgmont's description of Louisiana, however, written probably in 1717, does include some information about the Osages. The Osage river, he said, ran to within forty leagues of the Cadodachos, a "nation sauvage à peu près de mêmes espèces." The Osages, as well as the Missouris, were allies and friends of the French. All their commerce, he intimated, was in fur; they could offer the best furs of the Missouri region. These folk were not numerous, but their blood was good, and they were the most alert of the Indian nations. After describing the Missouri River as far as the Arikara and Caricara villages, six hundred leagues up the river, Bourgmont noted that by way of the Missouri commerce could be carried on with the Spaniards, who were not far distant from the branches of this river, according to the reports of the savages who trafficked with them.[39]

Just when Bourgmont departed from his Missouri friends is not known, but on September 25, 1718, Bienville requested from the king the award of the cross of St. Louis for him. We know that he took part in the capture of Pensacola in May, 1719. On September 13, 1719, the Council in France spoke of Bourgmont's services in the Missouri district and resolved to send him back there. However, Bourgmont went to France. About this time, Bienville wrote to the directors of the Company asking them for permission to found a post on the Missouri.[40]

Bourgment's information was of great value to Louisiana, for the French were by now learning that it was impossible to reach New Mexico easily by the Red or the Arkansas Rivers. Between 1716 and 1719 several *mémoires* on the Missouri river were sent to Paris, seeking to win attention for the Missouri valley. Hubert proposed to reconnoitre the Missouri;[41] Le Maire gave space in his *mémoires* to the Missouri.[42] Another *mémoire* stated that it was certain that several private *voyageurs* had found some mines in the Missouri country, of which they did not speak for fear that the Company would take possession of them.[43] Still another

[38]Archives du Service Hydrographique de la Marine, volume 67², number 18, and printed in Villers du Terrage, *Découverte du Missouri*, 46 ff. See also *mémoire* (1716) in A. N. Col. C13A, vol. XLIII, folios 187 to end of vol.
[39]A. N. Col. C13A, vol. I, folios 253-255.
[40]A N. Col. C13A, vol. V, folios 337-339.
[41]June 21, 1718, in A. N. Col. C13A, vol. V, folio 134.
[42]B. N., Mss. Fr., vol. 12105. Le Maire's map gives the Missouri, Kansas, Osage rivers. A. S. H., Bibliothèque, vol. 4040C, no. 46.
[43]A. E., Mémoires et Documents, Amérique, vol. I, folios 193-197.

mémoire stated that up to the time of writing the French had not discovered any gold or silver mines but that there should be mines as rich as those of New Mexico, since the mountains of New Mexico projected themselves into Upper Louisiana. "It is known that the Spaniards trade with the savages of Missouri and that the latter give them gold under the name of copper."[44]

Again, in 1716, a *mémoire* urged that France take measures to keep in her possession all her territories west of the Mississippi and to prevent the Spanish from seizing these countries. The Spaniards, said the *mémoire,* had already moved eastward in the lower part of the Mississippi valley and had occupied Los Adaes to oppose the French at Natchitoches. The writer feared the possible loss of all the country between the Mississippi, the Red River, and the sea coast, up to the Spanish territories of New Mexico; there was also a large territory between the Mississippi, the Red River, New Mexico, and the Missouri, where the Spaniards could very well take possession. Indeed, they had already tried to settle along the Missouri, and would have succeeded had not the savages prevented them. Safety required taking possession of all the land up to Spanish-occupied New Mexico, an operation which involved expansion from Natchitoches, with Jesuit missionaries, and the establishment of a post at the mouth of the Arkansas. The Missouri, he emphasized, was a very important river for the French—it passed through lands inhabited by numerous populous nations ready for rich trading enterprise, and its source must be quite near some other river which would flow down to the western sea. To keep this prize from the Spaniards, France must maintain and even enlarge the post which *Monsieur* de Bourgmont had established on the Missouri (the writer suggested forty soldiers) and establish Jesuit missions as far as the river's source on all the spots where the Spanish could penetrate this great river. The Jesuits would win the savage nations to French interests and trade, thus preventing the Spanish from taking possession of the Missouri and of all the rivers which are tributary to it on the southern side.[45]

On June 21, 1718, the Council in Paris recorded receipt of a *mémoire* by Hubert, begging the Council to appoint him to direct the establishment of the Missouri, and to search for and exploit mines on that river, since he was a man of prudence, experienced in handling the Indians.[46] Council discussion of the *mémoire* brought out that mines like those of New Spain could probably be found up the Missouri, since the Spanish mines were in mountains thought to be the Missouri's source—but the Indians in the region were hostile. It would be necessary to establish a fortified post

[44] *Mémoire* of Sr. Le Bartz, in *Ibid.,* vol. I, folios 156-175.
[45] A. N. Col. C13A, vol. XLIII, folios 189 *verso*—191 *verso*. This *mémoire begins* on folio 187. The document, dated 1716, is either incomplete or the end is missing.
[46] A. N. Col. C13A, vol. V, folio 121.

under command of an officer and thirty soldiers and staffed with workmen well chosen, also twelve Canadian traders who could aid in discovering the mines, with twelve rowers to man the pirogues, four miners with implements, an engineer, two surgeons, and one *aumonier* or chaplain. This detachment should be established on the upper Missouri to help protect commerce with the Spaniards, who, it was assured, traversed the river en route to their mines. Since the Spaniards in that area were far from their bases, the French could easily maintain themselves with the aid of the Indians who held the Spaniards in horror but would in return for presents, be friendly to the French. The Indians might aid the French in reaching the mines of New Mexico and even in driving out the Spaniards. Even if the French did not evict the Spaniards they would get much silver in exchange for merchandise. Such possessions were always advantageous for the future; and the Spaniards had no special title to the land, for it was just as far from there to New Mexico as it was to Natchitoches, "which we have just established."[47]

The Council continued the discussion. M. de la Motte's discoveries had been superficial and hasty, for he feared attack and did not have enough men to make a defense. Such a plan as described above would be adequate defense for passage through the nations. Moreover, exploration of the rivers would lead to the Western Sea and trade with China and Japan. Those who had ascended the Missouri asserted it was the real source of the Mississippi, which should rightfully be called the Missouri; these were not the opinions of a single *voyageur,* but of several who had been questioned separately. The chief practical difficulty seems to have been the dispatch of a company of more than seventy persons, nine hundred leagues up a rapid river, with provisions, munitions, and goods, an expedition which would require at least twelve pirogues, and for which the payment of the soldiers, at the ordinary rate, would cost twenty-thousand francs annually, an extraordinary expense, (which would be expended in France on goods selected and suitable for trade).[48]

Other comments on the importance of controlling this region appear in the record. Gallut, former treasurer of the viceroy of Mexico, had written from Natchitoches in 1715-16 concerning Spanish activities in Texas and French activities in the area beyond Natchitoches. He asserted that the French could also trade there, that in fact merchandise could come from Canada for the Illinois, and that the French had already passed the Missouri river and the mountains, beyond which they had always hoped to find the South Sea, and even had passed the chain of mountains con-

---

[47] A. N. Marine BI, vol. XXX, folios 58-68 *verso,* and also in C13A, Col. vol. V, folios 127-138.

[48] A. N. Marine BI, volume XXX, folios 64 *verso—*69 *verso,* including itemized account of expenses. Same also in C13A, Col. vol. V, folios 127-138.

taining the mines of St. Barbe. This territory was neither French nor Spanish and should be delimited.[49] Charles Legac, ex-director of the Company of Indies, arrived in the colony August 25, 1718, and supplied information until March 5, 1721. He spoke chiefly of Lower Louisiana, but mentioned Missouri and Osage Indians, reporting that it was from the Osages that Du Tisné purchased horses.[50]

Bienville believed it would not be advisable to put more than twelve soldiers in the little stockade fort which Bourgmont had built on the Missouri. These could maintain the French alliance with the Indians and assist the *voyageurs* who traded in that area among the Indians. He wrote: "Any other establishment appears to me to be visionary for the present." He recommended direct trade through the lower part of the colony with the Spaniards as "surer and sounder than the fantastical idea that some have attempted to give the Company of opening up a large commerce with New Mexico by the Missouri river. It is true that one of the branches runs toward the west, but the most navigable goes to the Northwest, flowing in the general direction of the Mississippi, and is nearly three hundred leagues distant from New Mexico, as one can see by the fragments of the journal,[51] which I sent to France, of the Spanish caravan that was defeated in 1721."[52]

Boisbriant, commandant of the Illinois country, intended to ascend the Missouri in 1720, but he lacked munitions and merchandise. He had promised the nations which had come to see him that he would send both merchandise and men. All the nations had made peace with the Panis-Maha nation, but would not consent to do the same with the Padoucas (Comanches). The Otos and Kansas, at war with the Padoucas, had carried off two hundred and fifty Padouca slaves and had also found Spaniards among the Padoucas. This information was reported to Boisbriant by four Frenchmen to whom he had given permission to seek horses among the Panis-Ouasas. In reality this was the Villasur massacre by the Pawnees, aided by the French, of which the circumstances have only recently been brought to light.

It seems that the Spaniards had information of the French advances into the west. As early as 1703, as we have already seen, twenty Canadians

[49]Relation du voyage des Canadiens au Mexique [joined to letter of Gallut, La Rochelle, August 1, 1716], A. N. Col. C13A vol. XXXVI, folios 415-416 *verso;* Minutes of Council of Marine on Gallut's account dated La Rochelle, August 1, 1716. A. N. Marine BI, vol. IX, folios 333-336. See also minutes of Council of Marine, March 30, 1716, *Ibid.,* BI vol. VIII, folios 273 *verso-274.*

[50]A. E. Mémoires et Documents, Amérique, Vol. I., folios 81-129.

[51]Published by Villiers du Terrage in "Le Massacre de l'Expédition Espagnole du Missouri," *Journal de la Société des Américanistes de Paris,* n. s., XIII, 230-255. translated by Thomas in *Nebraska History,* cited in note 53. See Thomas, *After Coronado,* for full documentation.

[52]A. N. Colonies, C13C vol. I, folios 398-401 and published in *Mississippi Provincial Archives, French Period,* III, 512-539. See note 61 for full citation of this work.

had left Illinois seeking a route to New Mexico in order to investigate trade and mines thought to be there. In 1706, Ulibarri encountered evidence of French commerce and trade, and heard of a white man and woman who had been killed. Besides further advances up the Missouri and its branches and the founding of Natchitoches by St. Denis, who had extended French activities to the Rio Grande, the French had, as we shall see, established posts among the Cadodachos, had ascended the Red and Arkansas rivers, even proposing, as did La Harpe, a post among the Touacaras, from which to trade with New Mexico. Du Tisné, as we shall later recount, had gone via the Osages to the Arkansas, had made an alliance with the Pawnee nations, and had traded in Spanish horses. Valverde's expedition, north from Santa Fé in 1719, had learned of a French-Pawnee alliance menacing the Apaches. Villasur's expedition was, therefore, intended to rid the Spaniards of this growing threat. Leaving Santa Fé in the early summer of 1720, Villasur proceeded to the northeast where his expedition was cut to pieces by the French and their Pawnee allies.[53]

Boisbriant, in a letter of October 5, 1720, recounted the French dilemma with respect to the Indians of the Missouri. If the French made peace with the Padoucas, they would irritate all the other tribes, enemies of the Padoucas but friends of the French. On the other hand, if they allowed their friends the Missouris, Osages, Kansas, Otos, and Pani-Mahas, to continue carrying off slaves and horses from the Padoucas, they would be forced to renounce all hope of reaching New Mexico through the country overrun by the Padoucas (or Comanches as they were later called.) Moreover, when the French would not buy Padouca slaves from their Indian allies, the slaves were sold to the Foxes, enemies of the French. In this complicated situation, it was evident that the French needed peace among all the Indian tribes, if they were to ascend the Missouri in safety. Hence, the commandant advised that the slaves be purchased from the Missouris and that Bourgmont (at that time still in France) be sent immediately to build a post and force the tribes to make peace. Bourgmont should also seek to make peace with the Spaniards that both nations might direct their respective Indian allies to peace. The fallacy in the argument was the failure to take into full account the number and nomadic nature of the Comanches.

---

[53]Villiers du Terrage, "Le Massacre de l'Expédition Espagnole du Missouri," *Journal de la Société des Américanistes de Paris,* Nouvelle Séries, XIII, 230-255. (A. N. Colonies C13C vol. IV, folios 232-237.). A. E. Sheldon, "Battle at the Forks of the Loup and the Platte," *Nebraska History,* VI (1923), no. 1, 13-19; also *Ibid.,* VII, (1924), 83-87. W. E. Dunn, "Spanish Reaction Against the French Advance towards New Mexico, 1717-1727," *Mississippi Valley Historical Review,* II (1915) 348-362; A. B. Thomas, "Massacre of the Villasur Expedition," *Nebraska History,* VII (1924), 68-81. A. B. Thomas in his *After Coronado* (Norman, 1935) has collected all of the available new information. See also Le Page du Pratz, *Histoire de la Louisiane* (3 volumes, Paris, 1758), II, 246 ff.

In response, the Company in Paris, noting what information they had and what Bourgmont now gave them, ordered Bourgmont's appointment as commandant of the Missouri and Arkansas river territory, authorizing him to stop all unlicensed *voyageurs*.[54] We will see more of Bourgmont's activities later.

Meanwhile, Charles Claude du Tisné was endeavoring to visit the Osages, Paniouassas, and Padoucas by means of the Missouri river and later he was to try by overland routes. Du Tisné, the son of a well-to-do Parisian family, was a witty, audacious Canadian gallant, a gentleman, and one of the first officers who had come to Louisiana with Bienville. Volunteering for American service against his family's wishes, he had first gone to Quebec, where he was sent out among the Indians by a Quebec merchant. He was quick to learn the language and manners of the Indians. In 1714 he went to Mobile and was frequently employed by Bienville in making alliances and negotiating with the Indians. He was left in command of Natchitoches when St. Denis went westward in his attempt to open commerce with the Spaniards.[55]

Du Tisné, at the order of Governor Bienville, sought to visit the Paniouassas by way of the Missouri River. He could not, however, reach his destination, because the Missouri Indians forced him to remain with them, a circumstance which obliged him to return to the Illinois and offer himself to Commandant Boisbriant in order to go by land. With the commandant's permission, Du Tisné in the spring of 1719 set out from Kaskaskia, intending to visit the Missouris, Osages, Panis, and Padoucas. Ascending the Missouri to the Osage, and up that river eighty leagues to the Osage villages, Du Tisné became the first official visitor to arrive among them, though, doubtless, independent or individual traders had frequented the district for many years. He found an Osage village on a height of one and one-half leagues northwest of the river, a village of a "hundred *cabanes* and two hundred warriors." Du Tisné traded with these folk, obtaining some horses, which the Osages had stolen from the Panis, and some skins. He described the Osages as well-built savages, having several chiefs of the various bands, though these leaders seemed to wield little power; he added that the Osages were sly, treacherous, and given to breaking their word.

The Osages received him well and listened to his harangue, but balked when he told them of his design to go on to the Panis, who were their enemies. Despite their opposition, Du Tisné pushed on, but agreed to

[54]Villiers du Terrage, *Découverte du Missouri*, 71-76 *passim*.

[55]Du Tisné was twice in temporary command of Fort de Chartres, once after De Boisbriant in 1724 and again after the death of Des Liette in 1729. He died in 1730 from a gunshot wound inflicted by a Fox Indian. See Le Page du Pratz, *Histoire de la Louisiane*, II, 297-305. Bossu, who met his son in 1757, gives some incidents of Du Tisné's life. *Travels*, I, 202.

leave most of his guns behind. Within four days he had covered forty leagues distance to the southwest and arrived at a Panis village in Oklahoma. The Osages, still determined to prevent friendly relations between the French and the Panis, had sent runners ahead to the Panis warning them that the French were coming to trap and enslave them. When he reached the Panis, Du Tisné very nearly lost his life before he could convince them that the French were their friends, not their enemies. Du Tisné's boldness and audacity saved his life. He secured an alliance with the Panis and opened up trade, exchanging his three guns, some powder, hammers, and knives for two horses, and a mule marked with a Spanish brand.

Du Tisné asked the Panis for permission to pass to the Padoucas, their mortal enemies. This request was flatly refused, and he had to content himself with what information the Panis were willing to give him concerning the folk beyond. They told him that although the Spaniards had visited their villages, nevertheless, the Padoucas barred the Spaniards' way. Du Tisné later suggested to Bienville that the French might be able to unite the Panis and Padoucas, thereby securing entrance to Spanish territory, but first the French would be obliged to return Padouca slaves and be prepared to grant presents. He also reported that cruel war existed between the Panis and Padoucas, who even ate each other. On September 27, Du Tisné planted the royal white flag in the Panis villages, and returned alone to Illinois, since the Osages refused him guides.[56]

The Osages and Missouris frequently raided the Panis-Noirs, and other neighboring tribes to take horses and slaves, which the Illinois French traders were so eager to obtain that they supplied arms to the Osages and their neighbors. The French government disapproved of this traffic and ordered it stopped,[57] but without success. Pani slaves became so common that the French adopted the names of *Pani* and *slave* as synonymous. Most affected by these slave raids were the Panis-Noirs in Oklahoma, the Pani-Maha in Nebraska, and perhaps also the Arikaras. The Mentos on the Canadian river were probably not affected at this early date, for Du Tisné speaks of their visiting the Osages and of his giving them slaves to sell for him at Natchitoches; but La Harpe speaks of a Mento war against some Panis. Later, as more traders supplied the Osage and other Siouan tribes with guns, their raids increased, and even the Mentos suffered. The

[56]Documents in Margry, *Découvertes et Établissements,* VI, 309-315, from La Harpe's "Journal" which in its complete form is in B. N., mss. Fr. 8989, folios 20-22; badly translated in Anna Lewis, *Along the Arkansas* (Dallas, 1932), 55-59, and also in *Kansas Historical Collections,* IX, 252-254. Du Tisné's letter to Bienville, November 22, 1719, is in B. F. French, *Historical Collections* (new series, New York, 1869), 151-152.
[57]Order, dated Paris, October 25, 1720, A. N. Col. B42 *bis,* p. 390, printed in Margry, *op. cit.,* VI, 316.

John Law colony in eastern Arkansas[58] offered a good market for the slaves; according to La Harpe, the colonists first attempted to open up the slave trade directly with the Mentos, but the jealous Osages stopped this. In fact, says La Harpe, in 1721, when Richard [Pichart] and five Frenchmen were sent to obtain horses from the Mentos they were plundered on the Arkansas by a war party of Osages. Despite this, the French party succeeded in reaching and wintering among the Mentos, returning down the Arkansas in the spring of 1722. As these Osage raids increased, the Panis-Noirs, Wichitas, and others moved north into Kansas, and the Tawakanis, Iscanis, Tonkawas, and Kichais retired southward, where they in turn began to raid Spanish Texas to get horses to replace those captured from them by the Osages.[59]

The expeditions of Du Tisné and the Spanish defeat in 1720 awakened the French to the necessity of a military occupation of the Missouri. To accomplish this, Bourgmont, whom we left in Paris, was appointed commandant of the Missouri, and his departure set for January 17, 1722. He was instructed to found an establishment on the Missouri, make an alliance with the Padoucas, and then return to France with some Indian chiefs. All these things, as we shall see, Bourgmont accomplished.

Bourgmont left Paris in June, 1722, but found upon his arrival in New Orleans that nothing in preparation for his journey north had been done. He departed in February, 1723, encountering en route many difficulties and delays. On August 20, 1723, Bienville wrote Boisbriant that he would order Bourgmont to the Upper Missouri, "if you judge it à propos"; Bourgmont could be given twenty soldiers to establish a small post and some presents for the Indians. Boisbriant did not look unfavorably upon the project, though he doubted that a lasting peace could be made with the Padoucas; he suspected the nations of the Missouri of being always in confusion and of embroiling themselves in disputes so that they might receive presents from the French as the price of reconciliation.

Bourgmont's party reached the Missouri village on November 9, 1723, where he erected Fort Orléans[60] on the north bank of the Misouri in Carroll County, Missouri, thus fulfilling the first part of his commission. By this time ice in the river forced him to delay his trip to the Padoucas. Reporting his delay to the Council of Louisiana in January, 1724, Bourgmont

[58]Documents on John Law are in Archives du Ministère des Colonies, Series G¹ volume 465, Louisiane, dossiers rélatifs aux concessions.

[59]H. E. Bolton, *Athanase De Mézières and the Louisiana-Texas Frontier* (Cleveland, 1914), I, 160. Brindamoor was a French leader of the French outlaws who supplied guns to the Indians in exchange for horses, mules, and slaves. Margry, *op. cit.*, VI, 363.

[60]On Fort Orléans see: Villiers du Terrage, *La Découverte du Missouri*, see esp. pp. 88, 94; Garraghan, "Fort Orleans on the Missouri," *Missouri Historical Review*, XXXV (1941), 373-384; Villiers du Terrage, "A Hitherto Unpublished Map of Fort Orleans on the Missouri," *Mid-America*, XII (1930), see map on p. 263; Garraghan, "Some Newly Discovered Missouri Maps," *Missouri Historical Society Collections*, V (1928), 256-264, see esp. pp. 262-264, and also in his *Chapters in Frontier History*, 91-93.

wrote also that he had learned that the Otos and Iowas had made an alliance with the Sioux and Foxes, both enemies of the French. When the Otos and Iowas made gestures of friendliness, he refused at first to receive them; when he did, they promised to break the offending alliance. Bourgmont feared that an alliance of Otos, Iowa, Mahas, Panimahas, and Sioux might render the Missouri valley and even Fort de Chartres untenable by the French; but he felt that with presents he could secure an alliance with those tribes, who had seen but one Frenchman in five years. He desired them to join him on his visit to the Padoucas.

By June, 1724, Bourgmont was ready to visit the Kansas and the Padoucas. He formed two separate forces, one under Saint-Ange, who departed by canoe on June 25, the other commanded by himself. The two parties were to meet at the Kansas, those Indians having agreed to accompany Bourgmont to the Padoucas. Saint-Ange did not rejoin Bourgmont until July 16. Bourgmont had left Fort Orléans by land, July 3, with a party of eight Frenchmen, one hundred Missouris, and sixty-four Osages. When a fever broke out among his men, the Osages abandoned them fearing to contract the illness. Bourgmont, himself ill, was forced to return to Fort Orléans, sending an advance party with Gaillard in charge to take presents to the Padoucas. The Padoucas welcomed the party on August 25. Bourgmont again set out from Fort Orléans on September 20, reaching the Kansas on October 2, presiding over long speeches of friendship among the Missouris, Otos, Kansas, Iowas, and the Panimahas in the Padoucas camp.

The party left the Kansas village on October 8, 1724, and were welcomed by the Padoucas on October 18. The next day he harangued the tribesmen: the French were friends and allies of the Missouris, Osages, Kansas, Otos, and Panimahas, and desired an alliance with the Padoucas also. He presented a French flag and other gifts to the chief, who promised peace and trade and agreed not to make war on those Indians allied with the French. On October 22, Bourgmont left the Padoucas, reaching Fort Orléans on November 5.

Three weeks later a general council of Indians authorized several chiefs to accompany Bourgmont to France. He left a short time later with one Oto, four Osages, four Missouris, a Missouri girl, four Illinois and Chicagou, and a Metchegamia chief.[61] For economy, however, the council at New Orleans sent only the young Missouri princess, one Oto, one Osage, one Missouri chief, one Illinois, one Chicagou, and the ambassador of the Metchegamias. The party arrived in Paris on September 20, 1725, were

[61]Minutes of the Council, January 10, 1725, in A. N., Colonies C13A, Vol. VIII, folios 122-182, and vol. XXII, folios 238-375, giving the minutes from May 31, 1724, to February 3, 1725, printed in: D. Rowland and A. G. Sanders, *Mississippi Provincial Archives, French Domination,* (Jackson, 1932), III, 416-487, see esp. pp. 476-478. See also Le Page du Pratz, *Histoire de la Louisiane,* I, 324-327; III, 141-221, and Dumont, *op. cit.*

given a grand reception by the Duke and Duchess de Bourbon and the Directors of the Company of the Indies, and were presented to the King. They were fitted out in Paris and performed their war dances at the opera. The Missouri princess was baptized in Notre-Dame.[62]

At Fort Orléans the Seminary missionary, Father Jean Baptiste Mercier, worked for fourteen months, frequently visiting the Osage Indians.[63] He wrote that he needed missionaries for work among the Missouris and Osages, who had in fact asked for them;[64] but in 1732, after the abandonment of Fort Orléans,[65] the good father wrote that the mission to the Missouris was not to be thought of, now that there was no longer a commandant on that river, for the missionaries would be too much exposed to Indian attacks. In spite of presents and alliances, the astute French had by that time learned not to be too certain of the Missouris and Osages.

---

[62]Villiers du Terrage, "Le Massacre de l'Expédition Espagnole," *loc. cit.*, 242-244; Dumont, *Mémoires;* Bossu, *Nouveau Voyages; Nebraska History,* VI, (1923), No. I, 33-38. The documents relating to Bourgmont's expedition are in Margry, *op. cit.,* VI, 385 ff.; the document on pages 388-389 is similar to that in A. N. Colonies, B43, folios 90-91. Bourgmont's instructions are in Colonies B43, folios 91-93, and printed in Margry, *op. cit.,* VI, 389-391. The document printed in *Ibid.,* VI, 391-392 is in A. N. Colonies C13C, vol. IV, folio 129; that on pages 392-396 is in A. N. Colonies C13C, vol. IV, folios 105-106; that printed on pages 396-397 is in A. N. Colonies C13C, vol. IV, folios 107-108; 109-110; see also 111-117. Bourgmont's journal (pages 398-449) is in A. N. Colonies, C13C, vol. IV, folios 130-160 *verso* (copy in B. N., n. a. 9287, folios, 166-186; original is in A. S. H., 115ˣ no. 26) and is partly translated by Henri Folmer, "De Bourgmont's Expedition to the Padoucas in 1724." *Colorado Magazine,* XIV (1937), 123-128; see also article by the same writer in *Missouri Historical Review,* XXXVI (1942), 279-298. The document printed in Margry, *op. cit.,* VI, 449-452, is in A. N. Colonies, C13C. vol. IV, folios 159-160. Bourgmont's return is noted in a letter of February 27, 1725, in A. N. Colonies, C13A, vol. IX, folio 68. The best account of Bourgmont is Villiers du Terrage, *La Découverte du Missouri.* His map is reproduced in Gilbert J. Garraghan, *Chapters in Frontier History* (Milwaukee, 1934) 90-91. For the visit of the Osages and other Indians to Paris in 1725 see *Nebraska History,* VI (1923), no. 1, 33-38; Dumont, *op. cit.,* II, 74-78; Bossu, *op. cit.,* I, 161-162. Mrs. Caroline Foreman has discussed this matter in her *Indians Abroad* (Norman 1943); and also in *Missouri Historical Collections,* V (1928), 110-112. Affidavit that Belisle ordered stealing of horses from Kansas Indians, Fort Orléans, January 1, 1724, A. N. Colonies, C13A, vol. VIII, folio 219. Letter of Bourgmont, Fort Orléans, January 7, 1724, concerning installation of post in *Ibid.,* Vol. VIII, folios 210-218 *verso.* Henri Folmer has an excellent summary in *Missouri Historical Review,* XXXVI (1942), 279-298.

[63]An extract of the letters of the Conseil de la Louisiane for May 20, 1725 (A. N. Colonies, C13A. vol. IX, folios 147-150, extract on folios 147 *verso*-148) speaks of Deslittes going to Illinois and of Father Mercier, "aumosnière du poste des Missouris," and declares "we beg you *Messieurs* to pay attention as we have already remarked to you that in all the posts where there are neither inhabitants nor consequently any fees, it is morally impossible for a priest to be able to live there and maintain himself on 600# for all things." Quoted in Garraghan, *Chapters in Frontier History,* 67. État. des Prêtres Missionaries 20 Xbre 1724: "At Fort Orléans is Mercier and he is not furnished by the Company" (A. N. Colonies D2D10). On May 19, 1722, a commission was issued to Sr. François Mariette to be chaplain and missionary at the Missouri post (A. N. Colonies B, vol. XLIII, folio 116).

[64] A *mémoire*, perhaps erroneously dated 1716, in A. N. Colonies, C13A, vol. XLIII, folios 187 to end of volume, speaks of the need of Jesuits on the Missouri.

[65]The Company of the Indies wrote to Perrier and La Chaise from Paris on October 27, 1727, regarding the Illinois country and the expenses incurred and sustained by the Company. Regarding the missionaries and the Missouri post we read: "The post

22

Troubles with the Indians were frequent. In 1722, Chassin reported that early that year, or late in 1721, some French *voyageurs* arrived at the Illinois, having wintered among the Octoctatas and Kansas in the Missouri, and brought some species of minerals which had been taken from the Spaniards. Less agreeable news, however, came soon after; one of the *voyageurs* had witnessed the pillage of some Frenchmen who had been with him at the Osages. Fear was expressed for the fate of another French *voyageur*.[66] By this time the French traders were well entrenched with the Missouri Indians, and indeed, in 1725, following Bourgmont's peace with the Padoucas, it was suggested that the Missouri Indians might be used together with the Illinois and forces from Canada to fall upon the Foxes.[67] On July 22, 1727, the Minister replied to Governor Perrier's letter of May 2, which had relayed the report of Desliettes, Commandant of Illinois, that the Foxes had killed a lieutenant and seven Frenchmen who were on the way to the Missouri.[68]

---

of the Missouri, in which the Company has been kind enough graciously to reserve a garrison of eight men, is absolutely useless, its [the Company's] intention is that you should send a positive order to abandon it, leaving there only the Missionary if he believes that he can make some progress in the preaching of the gospel among the savages. You will recommend at the same time to the officer who commands this post to have his garrison carry back to Illinois all the effects of the Company which are worthy of transportation." An inventory was to be made by Desliettes and Chassin of the goods that arrived at the Illinois from the post of the Missouri, and they were to state what would be appropriate to send to New Orleans. They were ordered to complete this as soon as possible. Perrier and La Chaise replied on March 30, 1728, replying to the Company's letter article by article. "As for the Missouri, it will be relieved and the post of Ouabache which perhaps is not yet begun will be reduced as you wish to ten men." The Company's letter is in A. N. Colonies, C13A, vol. XI, folios 66-108, extracts on folios 91 *verso*-92 *verso*. The reply is in *Ibid.* In this regard, see Garraghan, *Chapters in Frontier History*, 66-70 *passim;* and J. H. Schlarman, *From Quebec to New Orleans* (Belleville, 1929), 289-290. Villiers du Terrage states that Fort Orléans was re-established in 1736 and during the 1740's (*Découverte du Missouri*, 124). For location of Fort Orléans see *Ibid.*, and January, 1930, issue of *Mid-America*, p. 263; and Garraghan, *op. cit.* Garraghan has summarized Villiers du Terrage in his article on Fort Orléans in *Missouri Historical Review*, XXXV (1941), 373-384.

[66]Extract of a letter of Chassin, Illinois, July 1, 1722, A. N. Colonies, C13A, vol. VI, folios 297-300 *verso*, printed in Rowland and Sanders, *Mississippi Provincial Archives, French Domination*, II, 298-300. Father Charlevoix discussed the possibilities of routes to the Vermillion Sea and on April 1, 1723, suggested two routes, viz: (1) ascending the Missouri whose sources most certainly must not be very far from the sea; (2) or less hopefully, to establish a mission among the Sioux, who carry on trade with the Iowas who are near the Missouri and know all the upper reaches. The missionaries would learn within a short time the necessary information. Charlevoix thought that as the crow flies there were some 700 leagues from the Sioux to the Ocean. Bourgmont knew as much of the Upper Missouri as the Iowas did. It was this second proposition, less costly, that was adopted by the King on May 11, 1723. See N. M. Crouse, *In Quest of the Western Ocean* (New York, 1928); "Delisle's Conjectures of the Existence of a Sea." Pierre F. X. de Charlevoix, *Journal of a Voyage to North America* (ed. by L. P. Kellogg, 2 volumes, Chicago, 1924); and Charlevoix, *Letters to the Duchess of Lesdiguieres*, (1763; French edition, Paris, 1744).

[67]A. N. Colonies, C13A, vol. IX, folios 59 *verso*-61, 67 *verso*.
[68]A. N. Colonies B50, folios 543-544.

Despite all difficulties it appeared that furs could and should be brought from the Upper Mississippi valley to New Orleans, and that this procedure was better for the Company than sending the furs to Canada, as had been previously done. In 1728 the Company made a contract with several Canadians trading in the Upper Mississippi. Again it granted the exclusive trade of the Missouri and Ouabache rivers for five years beginning January 1, 1729, to Outlas and Marain on condition that they ship all their furs to the Company at New Orleans at stated prices. Despite the high prices to be paid for peltries "inferior to those coming from Canada," and the long period of time for which the grant was made, nevertheless, the Company approved this exclusive trade, confirming the contract on December 4, 1728.[69]

Perrier wrote to Maurepas from New Orleans on April 1, 1729, that he had relieved Fort Orléans, an establishment which had caused considerable expense to the Company without giving it any advantages. In fact, "all" the Frenchmen who had been killed had been on their way to the Missouri where it was easy for the Foxes to surprise them.[70] Perrier had earlier been given instructions by the Company to reduce or abandon the post.[71] An undated *mémoire,* probably referring to 1729, stated that, since trade with the Spanish was not secure because of Spanish defenses and decrees, it was imperative that the French form alliances with all the Indians between New Orleans and Illinois and distribute soldiers among the posts. The *mémoire* suggested twenty-five men each for Natchitoches and Arkansas and two companies, one hundred men, for Illinois. It was further suggested that some Canadian families be sent to Arkansas to trade with Osages and Spaniards. Without more men the lead mines could not be worked in safety. "It is very possible that it will become necessary to establish a post on the Missouri either for supporting our traders or for us to approach the Spaniards or, according to report, of some mines more precious than those of lead."[72]

Murders committed by the Indians caused Bienville to write that he intended to send soldiers to the Illinois in order to protect *voyageurs,* convoys, and traders. In fact, in the winter of 1732-1733 the nations of the Missouri killed eleven French *voyageurs.*[73]

---

[69]MM. Perrier and De la Chaise to the Company of the Indies, November 1, 1728, A. N. Colonies, C13A, vol. XI, folios 129 *verso*-131, and 154-155 *verso.* The conditions of the contract are detailed here.

[70]Perrier to Maurepas, New Orleans, April 1, 1729. A. N. Colonies, C13A, vol. XII, folios 15-17.

[71]*Mémoire* to serve as instructions to Perrier, Paris, September 30, 1726. A. N. Colonies C13BI, p. 18; *Ibid.,* Colonies B43, p. 678, printed in Margry, *op. cit.,* VI, 452.

[72]A. N. Colonies, C13C, vol. I, folios 117-132.

[73]Bienville, Louisiana, July 25, 1733. A. N. Colonies, C13A, vol. XVI, folios 267-269 *verso.* This violence might have been due to a lack of trading goods as was the case in 1724. Margry, *op. cit.,* VI, 427, and quoted in N. M. M. Surrey, *Commerce of Louisiana* (New York, 1916).

On April 22, 1734, Bienville wrote:

The news that I have had the honor of sending to Your Excellency concerning the letters I have received about the murder of the eleven voyageurs *of which the Osages have been accused has only been partly confirmed. It is true that they killed a slave and a* Bohème [tramp], engagé *with the hunters, whom they mistook for a savage. The others, who were away when the blow was struck, were frightened when they returned to the* cabanage *where the murder had been committed, and not daring to trust any nation, they decided to go to the Illinois by land, where they arrived after two months' march. Thus the officer who commanded at Arkansas, not seeing them return, judged that they had been killed and advised me of it.*

The Osages, according to the advice which they have had from the Missouris, that Monsieur Dartaguiette had resolved to send the nations against them to avenge this death, have charged the traders who were at the Missouris to make excuses to him in their behalf, and of assuring him that they had no thought of killing Frenchmen, and that they would submit to all satisfaction required of them. Not content with that, they have been to the Arkansas to bear their excuses to the officer who commands there, and covered this death of a slave in such a way that I do not believe that it suits the state of our affairs to push this matter any further. We do not need to seek new wars. We know that one has just been started in the district of Canada, in which truly the affairs of the Illinois will have a large part.

. . . . .

I learn by the same occasion that a Frenchman who has lived for several years with the Pani-mahas, who are established on the Missouri, having gone with these savages to the Ricaras who inhabit the upper part of this same river and who had not yet seen any Frenchman, found in that district many silver mines which appeared to him to be very rich. One of them he believes virgin. He adds that two voyageurs *from the Illinois propose to return there with the former to verify this report. Moreover, one can go there in a canoe. It will be easy for them to bring the minerals which I shall have the honor of sending to you as proof.*[74]

[74]A. N. Colonies, C13A, vol. XVIII, folios 142-152. The third paragraph is poorly printed in Margry, *op. cit.*, VI, 455. That there were priests in Missouri—see Salmon and Bienville to *Monseigneur*, New Orleans, April 15, 1734. A. N. Colonies, C13A, vol. XVIII, folios 98-103. For the sending of Dartaguiette see C. W. Alvord, *The Illinois Country, 1673-1818* (Chicago, 1922), 174-179. St. Ange and Du Tisné, both sons of former commandants of Illinois, were sent to stir up the tribes of the Missouri valley against the Foxes. They accomplished nothing. A second attempt in 1735 also accomplished little. At that time Louis St. Ange was commanding a post on the Missouri, probably built by two men who had received a grant of the monopoly of the trade on the Missouri and the Ohio rivers. St. Ange was summoned from this fort in 1736 to aid in reinforcing post Vincennes. *Ibid.*, 180.

Writing again on July 27, 1734, Bienville further clarified the situation. He repeated that instead of the Osages killing eleven Frenchmen, they had killed only one, a man named Petujean, a *bohème*. However, the Osages, hearing that Dartaguiette was going to send the nations friendly to France against them to avenge the murder, hastened, as Bienville had stated in his last report, to make excuses. Dartaguiette decided not to pursue the matter any further, being content to forbid commerce with the Osages to all the Frenchmen "who are in the Missouri, under penalty of corporal punishment," a course which the superior authorities opposed, asking him to continue to render accounts.[75]

On May 21, 1735, the minister wrote to Salmon, the *ordonnateur*, that Bienville had informed him that the *armement* which had been ordered prepared for the nations of the Missouris to go against the Foxes had not been assembled. That was a shame, said the minister, but, since the trouble with the Chickasaws was soon to end, Dartaguiette could march the nations of his district against the Foxes.[76] However, Bienville reported differently. He was informed by letters from the Illinois dated June 15 that the nations established on the banks of the Missouri had joined together to go against the Foxes. In fact, led by De Morieres, a cadet from the garrison of Illinois, and twenty Canadian *voyageurs,* five to six hundred of these Indians had left in May, 1735.[77] Indeed, Bienville notified the Count de Beauharnois that, because of Indians murdering Frenchmen, especially Le Norman, he had been forced to prohibit trade with the Sioux, Panis, Padoucas, and others.[78]

Thus the Osages early showed their mettle and the technique which they were to perfect in later days. When pinched and hurt, or in imminent danger of revenge, punishment, or starvation, they always cringed before the superior power and profusely shed crocodile tears until their immediate objective was attained—then they could relapse into their barbarous and cowardly habits of double-crossing and lying.

It appears, however, that the entire matter was not closed, or else that other murders were committed by the Osages for we find the Minister replying from Versailles on September 16, 1737, to Bienville's letters of June 17 and 21, and saying that "if the Osages bring to Bussonière the

[75]A. N. Colonies, C13A., vol. XVIII, folios 225-226—extract on Osages. This was approved (marginal notation).
[76]A. N. Colonies, B64, folios 504 *verso*-505. For a discussion of the second Fox war see Kellogg, *French Régime in Wisconsin*, 316-340. Documents are in *Wisconsin Historical Collections,* XVII.
[77]Bienville to Minister, New Orleans, August 20, 1735. A. N. Colonies, C13A, vol. XX, folios 152-159. Salmon writing to the Minister, New Orleans, August 28, 1735, said that he was informed that four savage villages established in the Missouri, about 400 men, left to go against the Foxes at the instigation of Pondret, an Illinois *voyageur* who joined with them 12 other Frenchmen of which number was Sieur de Morieres. A. N. Colonies, C13A, vol. XX, folio 253.
[78]Minister to Bienville and Salmon, Versailles, October 4, 1735, A. N. Colonies, B63 folios 608-609.

authors of the deed perpetrated by that nation upon the Frenchmen of the Arkansas river, this will be an indication that the nations will have disapproved of this act of treachery, and that will terminate the matter." However, he ordered the commandants to refrain from doing anything that would cause war among the Indians, but admonished them to take care that "the authority does not suffer."[79]

Bienville next took up the matter in his letter of April 26, 1738:

With regard to the coup *struck by the Osages upon our hunters of the Arkansas river: the nation is not yet prepared to give satisfaction for it. Regarding this subject, I have only learned that a party having come* en calumet *to the Arkansas, they were very badly received there; that it was a question of pillaging them, but that, having assured the Arkansas that the nation had no part in this murder, which had been committed by some* coureurs *who had been thrown out of their village, they returned without any evil [having been done to them] but at the same time not at all content with the welcome that had been given them.*[80]

Such attacks were not stopped. On June 20, 1740, Jean Baptiste Benoist (Benoît), Sieur de St. Claire, the commanding officer at the Illinois, learned that a Missouri Indian had killed a Frenchman named La Grillade, who had been among the savage villages for eight or nine years. Since the killing, the Missouris had not dared come to Illinois to obtain their needed goods. On July 15 an Illinois arrived at the post of the commandant and informed him that the previous winter the Osages had killed some Frenchmen of the Arkansas district and had even brought the head of one of their victims to their village and that in addition they had pillaged a Frenchman who had come from the Missouri district, "whom some wished to kill, but were prevented." Further reports stated that, forty days previously, a party of ten Missouris had gone to make an attack on the Arkansas and would strike the French whenever an opportunity could be found.[81]

3.

NEGOTIATIONS WITH THE INDIANS

Meanwhile, the French, much to the chagrin of the Spaniards, had achieved two of their original objectives. Forts had been established, peace made with the Indians, and now, beginning in 1739, French traders

---

[79]A. N. Colonies, B65, folios 529-531.
[80]A. N. Colonies. C13A, vol. XXIII, folios 48-51 *verso.*
[81]Benoît de St. Claire to Salmon, July 28, 1740, copy in A. N. Colonies, C13A, vol. XXVI, folios 190-191; Flancour to Salmon, Illinois, July 29, 1740, *Ibid.* folios 192 *et verso.* Three Frenchmen were killed, including La Grillade. The Missouris also organized a war party against the nations, allies of the French, to the south. They were allied with the Otos, Iowas, and Kickapoos.

actually reached New Mexico. Several of these expeditions involved the Osages.

Bourgmont's early achievements in erecting Fort Orléans and securing permission for Frenchmen to pass through the Comanche country to the Spaniards had, meanwhile, suffered setbacks. Fort Orléans had been either destroyed or abandoned; the Fox wars further checked the westward advancement of French traders. Although a new fort, Cavagnolle, was built near present Kansas City, for the same purposes as those of Fort Orléans, and although traders continued in the valley bartering with the Osages, Kansas, and other tribes, yet not until 1739 do we find definite information that the French had broken through the Comanche barrier and reached the Spanish emporium at Santa Fé.

Curiously enough, this trip was made by way of the Missouri, which was thought to have a northwesterly direction. In 1734, a Frenchman, who had resided for several years among the Pani-Maha, had visited the Arikaras and claimed to have found silver mines. When he descended the river, telling his story, two *voyageurs* from the Illinois proposed to return with him in order to verify his reports.[82] Whether this was done or not we do not know, but in 1739 Pierre and Paul Mallet, with a party of eight or nine, taking a different route, reached the Platte River on June 2, ascended it, and, after making their way through the Comanche country, reached Taos and Santa Fé. Mallet's journal records that they left the Pani-Maha villages on the Loup fork in Nebraska on May 29, 1739, and arrived in Santa Fé July 22. After having been detained in Santa Fé for months, on May 1, 1740, seven of the party (one man, Moreau, having married in New Mexico), left to make the return trip, four descending the Canadian and Arkansas rivers, and the others going northeast to the Illinois.[83]

The Mallet party had succeeded in getting through the Comanche barrier to New Mexico and had returned safely with evidence that New Mexican residents would welcome commerce. The brothers' success, after so many official French expeditions had failed, seemed a marvel. Governor Bienville seized upon their knowledge of the country, and in 1741 he sent Fabry de la Bruyère, guided by four members of the Mallet party, including the brothers themselves, bearing a letter to the governor of New Mexico. Fabry was instructed to ascend the Arkansas, observing the geography, astronomy, botany, and other natural features of the

---

[82]Bienville to Minister of Marine, April 22, 1734, in A. N. Colonies, C13A, vol. XVIII, folios 142-152; printed with two lines omitted in Margry, *op. cit.*, VI, 455.
[83]A. N. Colonies, F³, vol. XXIV, folio 387; also folios 377-379 *verso,* 381-382, 383-386, 387-391; and Colonies C13C vol. IV, folios 228-231—printed in Margry, *op. cit.*, VI, 455-462. See also *Ibid.*, VI, 462-465. This is translated in part by Henri Folmer in "The Mallet Expedition of 1739 through Nebraska, Kansas and Colorado to Santa Fé," *Colorado Magazine*, XVI (September, 1939), no. 5.

country. If he encountered unknown nations of Indians, he was to propose peace and alliance with the French.

He shall inform himself concerning these nations, whether they are at peace or at war with the Spanish nation, and as we have learned that the Osages, Panis, and Padoucas were making incursions in New Mexico, attacking and pillaging caravans, he shall assemble the chiefs of these nations allied to us, and exhort them to cease their incursions against the Spaniards, representing to them that the crowns of France and Spain are allied.

To this end he was to give the chiefs presents. In their letter to the governor of New Mexico, Bienville and Salmon said that they were sending Fabry with a detachment of fifteen men to discover the western sea and unknown lands in the west and begged the Spanish official to lend aid to them.[84]

Leaving New Orleans in September, 1741, the Fabry party immediately ran into difficulties. With low water in the Canadian river, they took from December 7 to January 15, 1742, to reach a point no more than forty-two leagues above its mouth. Here, on January 24, Fabry was visited by a party of thirty-five Osages, on their way to war against the Mentos or the Panis. The Osage chief asked Fabry to cross the river to their camp, informed him of the arrival of the Chevalier de Villiers among the Missouris, said that they had six French traders in their villages, that good feeling had been re-established between themselves and the French, and assured him that the Osages no longer wanted to make trouble. The next day Fabry gave them some gunpowder, bullets, knives, and similar wares; the Osages were not contented, wanting guns, but, given nothing else, they departed before noon, promising that if they made an attack they would return in six or seven days and would bring some slaves. They did return on February 3, seventeen of them, with seven horses, a mule, and two scalps; they said that the remainder of the party had separated from them

[84]Bienville and Salmon to *Monseigneur,* New Orleans, April 30, 1741, in A. N. Colonies, F³, vol. XXIV, folios 377-379, printed in Margry, *op. cit.,* VI, 466-468, and translated in Folmer, *loc.* cit. Instructions to Fabry de Bruyére, New Orleans, June 1, 1741, A. N. Colonies F³ vol. XXIV, folios 242-243 and printed in Margry, *op. cit.,* VI, 468-471; Bienville and Salmon to Governor of Santa Fé, New Orleans, June 1, 1741, in A. N. Colonies, F³ vol. XXIV, folio 243, and printed in Margry, *op. cit.,* VI, 471-472; Fabry's journal is in A. N. Colonies, F³ vol. XXIV, folios 392-406 *verso,* and printed in Margry, *op. cit.,* VI, 472-492. Salmon to Minister, New Orleans, September 24, 1741, A. N. Colonies, C13A, vol. XXVI, folios 156-157, stated that in his and Bienville's letter of April 30, they gave reasons for sending the expedition to New Mexico. However, he, Salmon, was opposed to it until he received orders from the Minister, but Bienville said if the Canadians returned it was important to form a commerce. Fabry offered to go and Salmon did not oppose. Fabry left at the end of last August and Bienville gave him six soldiers and a sergeant. They accompanied the convoy of Illinois as far as the Arkansas river which river they were going to ascend. The cost was 17554£ 19s. paid by the treasury. They gave Fabry a letter to the Governor of Santa Fé.

on their way to the Mentos and that they had not seen them since. After they had departed, Fabry, fearing them, fortified his camp, but he did not wish them to know it. When they returned he told them he had strengthened his camp as a precaution against a possible attack by the Panis-Noirs, who had been raiding those districts. The Osages believed Fabry's story but were somewhat disquieted about his trip, fearing he was out to make an alliance with the Panis and Padoucas and would give them guns. Fabry reassured the Osages, saying he was going to see the Frenchmen in the west, who were old brothers. The Osages informed him that the river above that point had little water. Taking counsel with his Canadians and concluding that, if no rain or snow fell, it would be useless to ascend in canoes, Fabry decided to try to purchase horses from the Osages, which they had previously offered to sell him. Fabry had at first refused the offer, contrary to the advice of his associates. Now, when he actually wanted the horses, the Osages determinedly refused to give them up, saying they needed the beasts to get to their villages.

The Canadians then proposed to follow the trail that the Osages had previously taken. Fabry unsuccessfully attempted to dissuade the men, finally ordering them to be silent. He then wrote to the French traders of the Missouri to procure horses; he offered to pay for the horses and to pay two hundred francs to any two traders who would come with the savages bringing horses. He handed the letter to the Osage chief, who said the trip could be made in seven days. Fabry waited in vain until the end of the month and then decided to push on, but shallow water slowed his progress seriously.

Meanwhile the Canadians proposed to Fabry that they go in search of the Mentos to obtain horses from them; accordingly, Fabry dispatched the elder Mallet and three companions. In two attempts they failed to find the Mentos. The Mallets proposed to go northward and obtain horses from the Panis-Noirs, but Fabry scouted the idea. The Canadians then offered to guide him to Santa Fé in less than twenty-two days. After much discussion, many proposals and counter-proposals, Fabry left the Mallet party and most of his own men in camp on the Canadian river and went down to the Arkansas to obtain horses from the French settlements. He instructed his men to wait for him four months, until August 1; the *voyageurs* agreed to wait three months. If by that time he had not appeared, they would be free to continue the trip; but the troops were to return to New Orleans.

Fabry left on April 4, encountered more low water, and did not reach the Arkansas until the twenty-sixth. He procured only five horses but went to look for the Caddos, from whom he procured more horses. By the time he returned to the Canadian river, he found that the Mallets and their men had taken most of the goods and set out for Santa Fé afoot. The

Mallets blamed Fabry for all their difficulties, saying that he had refused to trade for the Osages' horses on the terms the latter had suggested; that Fabry had refused to let them hunt horses at the Panis villages; that birch bark canoes which could ascend the river might have been made, but Fabry refused; and that during Fabry's absence the river had been navigable for forty days. Fabry now gave up hope of completing his expedition, sent part of his men down the river, and with the rest mounted on horses started across country to the Red River. He saw the Tavakavas and Kitsais villages and, travelling *via* the route of the Caddos and Yatassé, arrived at Natchitoches.

Meanwhile, activities and discoveries on the Upper Missouri were taking place from another quarter. These were connected with the search for the western sea which had agitated romantic Frenchmen and others for many years. Fact and fiction, mixed with motives of gain and fame, urged on the Latins. The officials in New France endeavored to eliminate some of the friction through the work of Father Charlevoix, whom they had sent for the purpose of gathering at first hand the necessary data for such an undertaking. The good father questioned every trader who had returned to Quebec from activities in the west. Father Charveloix's report sums up the real knowledge then known of the "far west." He suggested several possible routes to the Western Sea. He also suggested the establishing of missions among the Sioux. France chose to follow Charveloix's proposition of placing missionaries among the Sioux and of not undertaking further search for the Western Sea until more accurate knowledge could be obtained. We do not have need here to trace in detail the various efforts of the French to push westward towards the Western Sea in the north. Suffice it to say that Jesuits mixed with traders and ofttimes combined the functions of trader and missionary. The search for the Western Sea again became an issue of importance with the early activities of Pierre Gaultier de Varennes, Sieur de La Vérendrye.

Pierre La Vérendrye was born at Three Rivers, Canada, in 1685, son of the then governor of that post. He became a cadet at the age of twelve and served against the British in Newfoundland and in New England. He then went to France where he served during the remainder of the War of the Spanish Succession. At Malplaquet he was wounded and was rewarded with a lieutenancy for his distinguished services. Unable to avail himself of the offered lieutenancy, he returned to Canada where the Marquis de Vaudreuil awarded him an ensignship in one of the colonial regiments. Such peaceful activities did not appeal to the restless Pierre, and in 1726 he was appointed commandant of the trading post of Nipigon, to the north of Lake Superior. He plunged into the development of the fur trade with his accustomed zeal and energy but never lost sight of the great object of his ambition—the discovery of the Western Sea. Undoubtedly information given him by the Indians aided him in his desire. Determined to carry out this objective, La Vérendrye went to Quebec. There he discussed his projects with Governor Beauharnois, who supported him in his plans to discover a route from Winnipeg to the Pacific—one further north than the Sioux habitat. The question was how to finance his projected expedition. La Vérendrye offered to lead an expedition to the Western Sea if the King would pay and equip one hundred men. Despite the efforts of Beauharnois the government of France would not commit itself to any definite amount of money. Determined to go ahead La Vérendrye succeeded in obtaining a monopoly of the fur trade of the country he proposed to explore. In Montreal he won the backing of several leading merchants, who, though not particularly concerned about his projects of discovery, were interested in his monopoly of the fur trade of the area.

Apparently the French policy was to establish gradual French influence through establishment of posts in the territory. Moreover, they desired to placate the Sioux. La Vérendrye attempted to accomplish these purposes as well to make his discovery of a route to the Western Sea. Accordingly, in 1731 he again turned westward. He left the heart of New France accompanied by three of his sons, Jean Baptiste, Pierre, and François, his nephew La Jeremaye, who had already seen service in the west, and a party of *voyageurs* and soldiers. Thus in effect La Vérendrye had to found trading posts on the lakes to the north of Lake Superior in order to collect furs enough to provide funds for his great enterprise. First, he established a post at Rainy Lake. On the western shore of Lake of the Woods he established Fort St. Charles in 1732. In 1734 he established Fort Maurepas on Lake Winnipeg.

La Vérendrye was forced again to descend to Montreal, and again he failed in his efforts to get the King to finance his project. Undaunted he returned to his field of the fur trade. The many hardships which he was forced to endure we cannot begin to recount here. Suffice it to say that more trips had to be made to Montreal. His nephew, La Jeremaye, who had rendered invaluable service to him, died. However, La Vérendrye's youngest son, Louis, who had been studying cartography, joined his father, and so did a young missionary, Father Aulneau. The latter was interested in the Mandan Indians, who lived on the shores of a great river on which, the explorers hoped, they would not be very far from California.

Returning from one of his several trips to Montreal, La Vérendrye and his party reached Fort St. Charles in June, 1738, determined to go to the Mandans. He built Fort La Reine on the Assiniboine, near the modern Portage La Prairie, and proceeded in a southwesterly direction to the Mandan villages on the Missouri, which received him in a very friendly

32

manner. When he asked about the Indians lower down on the Missouri, the Mandans informed him of five forts their own tribes held, of the Pananas, and Pananis (Pawnees). La Vérendrye thought he had found the river flowing to the South Sea. Leaving two men among the Mandans to learn the language, La Vérendrye returned to Canada. He sent his journal to Beauharnois, who sent excerpts from it to France.

News of La Vérendrye's activities was mildly welcomed in France. The ministry acknowledged from Versailles on May 2, 1740, Beauharnois' dispatch of extracts from La Vérendrye's journal, and was pleased to hear of his "making progress in the discovery, and that he is on the verge of making more." The way the Mandans had received La Vérendrye gave hope that they would provide him with help in making the discovery, especially "if the report which had been made to him by the son of one of the chiefs concerning the Pananas and the Pananis is sincere, but one must not rely too much on details of this type." The minister further declared that ". . . the decision which Sr. de la Vérendrye has taken—to leave two Frenchmen among the Mantanes in order to learn the language of this nation—may . . . put him in a position if these two Frenchmen might succeed, of pushing the courses further and with more facility; and when once he will have reached the Pananis and will have been able to reconnoiter 'the river' which he has mentioned in his relation and [of] which he has been told that the water was salty, it is to be believed that he could obtain more certain notes concerning his object. I shall wait until you inform me of what you have learned, but please recommend to him again by the first occasion that you will be attentive not to give too much hope concerning the success of his enterprise and will render matters just as they were so that one might finally be able to judge knowingly."[85]

Business and other setbacks prevented La Vérendrye from immediately following up his southwest trip. However, he sent his son Pierre to the Mandans to obtain guides for an expedition to the sea. La Vérendrye did not take part in the final explorations, but his sons, Louis and François, started off in April, 1742, for the Mandan villages. With guides they proceeded in a west southwesterly direction to reach the Horse Indians. They visited Indians who spoke Spanish. They went as far as the mountains, where Indian conditions and the return of their guides forced them to abandon their plan and turn back. On their return trip they found a man among the Arikara who spoke Spanish; he told them that the route to the Spanish settlements was three weeks on horseback and danger-

[85]A. N. Colonies, B70 folio 345. Several references to the early search for the western sea have already been made. For a full discussion of this subject see Nellis Crouse, *In Quest of the Western Ocean*, chapter VII especially. A number of documents there cited, especially those of Father Bobé, Delisle, etc., are calendared in Nasatir, *French Activities in California: An Archival Calendar-Guide*. See also La Hontan, *op. cit.*; Daniel Coxe, *Carolana*, in French, *Historical Collection of Louisiana;* Charlevoix, *op. cit.*, Moncach-Apé, etc.

ous owing to the Snake Indians through whose territory it passed. The Indians further told the La Vérendryes that at three days' journey from the Arikaras, they would find a Frenchman who had lived in that locality for several years. The party was too tired to visit the Frenchman, but wrote him a letter urging him to visit them. They waited in vain for the visit, then left the Arikaras in April, returned to the Mandans, and from there to Fort La Reine, arriving in July.[86]

We have further details, though scattered and spotty, of activities on the Missouri from below. The Indians continued at times to create problems for the French in Illinois, though we are told that the Indians were not actually numerous, that the Missouri tribes possessed hardly five hundred men and the Osages even fewer.[87] Following the killing of La Grillade in 1740 (which has previously been mentioned) Benoît and Flancour admitted that they did not know what was going on in the Missouri with regard to the *voyageurs* among the tribes of that area. They hoped to send there to get information.[88] Much of the Indian trouble was the result of abuses in the trade by *coureurs de bois* and other lawless elements. In 1741, Benoît informed Bienville that the Missouri Indians had brought him complaints against most of the traders, who were cheating them and making violence upon them. In reply Bienville ordered Benoît to send a detachment, an officer and six soldiers, from his garrison at the Illinois to reside among the Missouri in order to restrain the traders there. "Without that the traders would not fail to cause us some affairs with these Indians." Bienville also ordered Benoît not to grant licenses to traders for the Missouri, "except to men well known, wise, and under the condition that they will take the necessary things for the subsistence of this small garrison."[89] The Minister, in replying to Bienville's letters of September 29 and 30, said: "Since you have judged that it is best, in order to stop the fraud and violences of which the Missouri savages complained on the part of the French traders with whom they were in trade, to establish a garrison among them, you have done well to send it there. But on the other hand it is necessary that in the choice of the men who compose it you give the

---

[86]This is based on Nellis M. Crouse, *In Quest of the Western Ocean* (New York, 1928), chapter VIII. Documents and letters are in *Journals and Letters of . . . De La Vérendrye and His Sons* (ed. by L. J. Burpee, Toronto, 1927). Many of the letters dealing with geographical exploration mentioning California are calendared in Nasatir, *French Activities in California: An Archival Calendar-Guide.* Concerning La Vérendrye see also: "Journal du Voyage faite par le Chevalier de La Vérendrye," in A. S. H. 5[11], no. 18, printed with a few errors in Margry, *op. cit.*, VI, 598-611, translated in *South Dakota Collections*, VII, 349-358; *South Dakota Historical Collections*, VII 195-260; and *Mississippi Valley Historical Review*, III (1916), 143-160; 368-399.

[87]*Mémoire* on Louisiana, 1746. A. N. Colonies, C13A, vol. XXX, folios 258-259.

[88]Copy of a letter written by Flancour to Salmon, Illinois, July 29, 1740, A. N. Colonies, C13A, vol. XXVI, folios 192-192 *verso.*

[89]Bienville to Minister, Louisiana, September 30, 1741, A. N. Colonies, C13A, vol. XXVI, folios 97-99, whole letter is folios 97-106.

utmost consideration so that there might not result any inconvenience from it. It is wise to permit only known persons to go to trade at this post as well as in the others which are established in the colony. And this is why His Majesty can only rely on you."[90]

De Bertet was sent to the Illinois to take command in 1742[91] and succeeded in devising a solution to the problem. His plan was evolved in 1744, when it was agreed to farm out the Missouri trade to an individual or group of individuals . . .

It has been represented to us that for several years the savage nations established on the Missouri, dream only of having a French fort established in their territory to protect them from the vexations of many voyageurs from Canada who would have been able in the future to cause disturbances and dissension among them, which it would have been quite difficult for us to appease and in addition to that the disorder which these voyageurs were causing daily, competing with one another by giving away their goods at very low prices, and even selling them at a loss, which would bring about the voyageurs' ruin, and also prevent commerce from increasing with the nations because of the ease which they had of satisfying their needs, which has made them up to the present time indifferent to the opportunities for the abundant hunting in the whole extent of this river. Add to this also the liberty enjoyed up to now by many vagabonds from this government and that of Canada who would frequently cause quarrels which could have had further consequences and cause the loss of many Frenchmen. This happened only two years ago to a man named Sans Peur, who was killed by the Panimahas, and to the ones named Petit Jean and Dupre, who were killed by the little Otos since that time. Therefore, in order to prevent such abuses from happening again which up to now have found their way among these nations, and in order that the trade of this country and that of Canada may not suffer from them, we have, with the consent of the King, granted to Mr. Deruisseau, Seigneur en partie de l'isle Perrot, in Canada, whose ability and integrity are known to us, the exclusive trade of the entire Missouri River and of all its tributary streams, subject to the conditions hereinafter enumerated for the duration of five years, commencing the first of January, 1745, and ending only on the 20th of May, 1750, we reserving the right to alter, add or withdraw the conditions of this agreement, depending upon the circumstances of the time in the future, and consequently to make such decisions as we will deem advisable for the good of this trade and of the colony. We give to him and to his associate full power to make use of it immediately in order to finish the con-

---

[90]Minister to Bienville, Versailles, January 19, 1742, A. N. Colonies B74, folios 622-623 *verso.*

[91]Bienville to Minister, July 30, 1742, A. N. Colonies, C13A, vol. XXVII folios 81-84 *verso.*

struction of the fort and to take there all the goods fit for trade with all the nations of the Missouri, and we instruct them to maintain concord and peace among them, to prevent injurious practices which they might suffer from their men or from traders to whom they have granted special permissions, and in case of disputes and agitations among the savages, they are expected to appease them at their own expense. They shall expressly forbid anyone to organize trade, or hunt along the entire river; those who violate the rule shall suffer confiscation of their belongings and goods, which will go to the fermiers, and a more severe penalty, unless they have express permission from the fermiers; they will then be free to travel and carry on transactions with whomever they please, bearing themselves all responsibilities; thus they will keep this trade for the number of years mentioned above, during which time they will be required to discover at their own cost all mines and minerals within the range of their business, reporting their discoveries to the commander of the post, and to penetrate from that place at the end of the Missouri even as far as Santa Fé itself, in order to discover the exact location of the route, and in order to be able later to establish trade easily with the Spaniards, and also to increase on that river the trade of beavers, martens, peckans, and other fine furs for the use of Canada, (which will probably find infinitely more advantages in such discoveries even more than this colony), all mentioned fine furs obtained from this trade being reserved for Canada, and for her trade, particularly the beaver, in order that the Company of Indies may not suffer, reserving only for the commerce of this Colony the hides of deer, roe-bucks, cows and others customary for commerce.

ARTICLE I

That he accepts the obligation of building and furnishing the fort which he began at the Kansas on the Missouri River, at the place designated by Mr. Legantois, following the plans which Mr. Bertet, commander of Illinois, has communicated on the eighteenth of December, 1743, i.e. "a fort of eighty feet on each side, surrounded by good posts, made of the best wood found in the place where the fort is located, with two bastions on the front side, and on the back side, according to the plan which has been made, twice as many stakes, and storied bastions.

There shall be in the said fort a house for the officer designated as commander; it shall be thirty feet long and twenty feet wide, with rooms distributed according to the plan, already made, with wooden separation walls, and upper and lower floors. It shall be built of posts covered with bark, with a kitchen contiguous to the building, built as a shed, covered also with bark, with a chimney as on the boussilage . . . Also a guard house, twenty feet in length, according to the plan already made, built of posts

36

covered with mud [boussilage] *the whole structure covered with bark, and a chimney in said building made with mud* [boussilage] *with a high and low floor of split stakes, the upper being well coated with mud on its upper side. A square powder room, ten feet on each side, from post to post, covered with a high and a low floor of split stakes. Also a house to lodge the* fermiers *of the post, the size of which shall be determined at their convenience. Also another house for their men, the size of which will suit them."*

ARTICLE II

The said Deruisseau and his associate will be required to pay the commander of the post, for each year of the lease, a contribution of one hundred pistoles, in furs, priced according to their sale at the Illinois, beginning from the first year of their lease, at the first of January, 1745.

ARTICLE III

Moreover, they will be required to carry his [other] supplies and belongings from the Illinois by the Kans, evaluated from twelve to fifteen hundred Kgs. for each year of said lease, as a compensation for his food, which his fermiers *will not be required to provide, as had been previously decided, their only obligation being to furnish his table with venison available in each particular season.*

ARTICLE IV

These fermiers *will be required also to feed the garrison of the post at their own expense, depending upon the circumstances, with the food available, i.e., one half of a barrel of corn each month per man, and one half pound of venison each day, or if such meat be lacking, bear oil or fat mixed in the right proportions.*

ARTICLE V

These fermiers *shall also have the duty of providing the soldiers of the garrison with transportation for their dry goods and their clothing.*

ARTICLE VI

As for the presents to the savages, the fermiers *will be required to give them presents whenever among these nations agitation arises, which the commander of the post considers necessary to appease in order to maintain calm and concord among them, being careful however, to only give presents for essential reasons, for fear of abuses.*

37

Article VII

When the savages shall come to see the Commander the fermiers *will be required to give them presents only once for each first visit of the different nations, and in the case that they come later bringing the Commander a message pertaining to the interests of the colony, the Commander will give them some small presents in powder or vermillion, at the expense of the King, with moderation, however, and only on important occasions.*

Article VIII

When a conference with the nations shall be considered the fermiers *will have to provide the Commander with an interpreter understanding the Kans language; they may choose the interpreter from among their own men, but shall allow the Commander to choose and make use of the man in which he has most faith.*

Article IX

They will be required to make reports to the Commanding officer in the post on the discoveries which they or others make pertaining to minerals, and also other discoveries taking place within the range of their activities during their years of exploitation.

Article X

The traders shall also be required to return, at the expiration of their leave, and in good condition, not only all the buildings mentioned above, but also all the little forts which they might build in the different villages of those nations for the safety and facility of their trade.

Article XI

They will not be permitted to give or to sell to these nations any drinks such as wine, brandy or other intoxicating liquors, directly, or with their men as intermediaries, or through traders carrying their permission, under any circumstances: he who disobeys will be subject to corporal punishment.

Article XII

These fermiers *may appeal to the Commander of the Post if they are in need of soldiers from the garrison, whether it be to maintain peace among the French and safety in the posts, or to pursue fugitives . . . in the latter case they will have to pay the soldiers, in addition to the ordinary food ration, 10 francs a day per man, in local money.*

Article XIII

No traveler will be allowed to hunt in the whole Missouri region except to the Tanerie; offenders are subject to confiscation of their belongings and goods which they might have for the benefit of said fermiers *and to punishment, unless they have permission from the* fermiers.

Article XIV

They will also appeal to the Commander of the post in case of dissension among the French or among the savage nations on the entire Missouri territory, or in case of dissolute behavior of their men towards the women, and bad talks which the travelers might give the savages.

Article XV

The Commander of the Post will do justice to them with regard to their men who do not live up to the conditions of their engagements.

Article XVI

They shall be maintained in all the territory covered by their trade by the Commander of the Post, to whom they may appeal in case of usurptation of their right by travelers who might go beyond the conditions fixed with them by the fermiers; *the* fermiers *in this case shall support the costs of the troops granted to them for the purpose, since the King must not have anything to do with it.*

Article XVII

They will be permitted to take to Canada the furs enumerated hereafter, i.e., beavers, martens, peckans, *and other furs which will not be a threat to its commerce, and to bring back to this country the product of the sale, in goods fit for trade on this Missouri River. Said* fermiers *will be required to bring down to New Orleans all the other hides such as deer, roe-buck, cow, all of those, in short, which would be profitable to commerce in this province.*

Article XVIII

These tenants shall receive, if possible, from the warehouses of the King at the Illinois, by paying, some goods which they might need; the price will be fixed each year by the commissaire ordonnateur *of the colony.*

Article XIX

And if the garrison is to move, the fermiers *will be required to pay for the trip from the Kans to the Illinois, and from the Illinois to the*

Kans, their only obligation, however, being to feed the soldiers of that garrison on the supplies found at the place, and on the same basis as their own men.

ARTICLE XX

Finally, the fermiers will retain their exclusive trade for the whole duration of their lease, beginning today, without anyone having power to hinder them on the entire territory covered by their trade on the Missouri and tributary rivers.

We hereby instruct Mr. Bertet, major commanding for the King at the Illinois, and also the officer commanding this Missouri post, to see to the execution of the present agreement made and in duplicate at New Orleans this eighth of August, one thousand seven hundred and forty-four.

Signed: Vaudreuil.[92]

The plan was an old one—in return for an exclusive control of the trade the grantee would undertake to support French power as well as to extend exploration to the southwest. The Canadian, *Sieur* Deruisseau, having been granted the monopoly, was obliged to build a fort, quarters for officers, barracks, a powder house, and a storehouse. He further agreed that he would pay the officer of the post, transport the effects of the garrison from the Illinois, and support them at his own expense. He was to bear part of the expenses of keeping the savages on good terms and furnish a part of the presents. It was expressly provided that no intoxicating liquor was to be sold to the savages. Vaudreuil's orders were to separate the trade of the Illinois and Missouri rivers from that of Canada.[93]

On December 6, 1744, Vaudreuil wrote the Minister concerning the necessity which he and Bertet, Commander of the Illinois, felt of having traders among all the Indian nations, and of measures, previously proposed in his letter of August 30, designed to further the fur trade and to prevent the frequent desertions and the frauds committed by brigades from Canada and Illinois. Among the steps taken was the grant to Deruisseau, whose agreement and contract Vaudreuil enclosed with his letter. To help Louisiana, Vaudreuil asked the Minister to order Beauharnois better to regulate and pay for licenses from Canada to the Mississippi valley.[94] The Minister

[92]A. N. Colonies, C13A, vol. XXVIII, folios 224-232.

[93]Beauhornois to Minister, Quebec, October 21, 1744, in A. N. Colonies, C11A, vol. LXXXI, folios 186-188 and especially the ministerial note. On April 28, 1745, the President of the Council wrote to Beauharnois that Vaudreuil had established small posts on the Missouri in order to stop the disorders caused by the *coureurs-de-bois* from Illinois (A. N. Colonies B, vol. 81, folios 282 *et verso*). The Minister approved the action (A. N. Colonies, B81, folio 282, extract in *Wisconsin Historical Collections*, XVIII, 5, and see page 41, 43-44, appendix VI, in *Report* of the Canadian Archives for 1905).

[94]A. N. Colonies C13A, vol. XXVIII, folios 245-247. Entire letter is folios 245-250 *verso*.

approved the grant of the exclusive trade privilege to Deruisseau upon the conditions stated: "That you complete the fort which has been begun, feed the soldiers of its garrison, and provide for the greater part of the presents to be made to the savages. And there only remains to be desired that this arrangement may stop the disorders and the abuses which have prompted you to take it without occasioning on the other hand justified complaints from those who have been accustomed to making the trade."[95]

For reasons, some of which have been suggested here, Louisiana and Canada were divided in their jurisdictions. In a document entitled *"Mémoire* on the limits which should be given to the government of Louisiana and that of Canada," some of Vaudreuil's suggestions were incorporated. On the River of the Peorias the boundary should be at "le Rocher." In his letter of August 30, 1744, Vaudreuil suggested the transfer to this location of the Post of Kans, which was expensive due to the presence of all the nations of the Missouris. This new post would be a check on *voyageurs* from Canada. Beauharnois was to be prohibited from granting licenses to *voyageurs* from Canada to trade south of his jurisdiction or in the Missouri.[96] There was a small settlement on the Missouri river, about ninety leagues from its mouth, which contained perhaps a score of *habitants* who owned about one-half that number of slaves. The people were chiefly engaged in hunting and trading, but did raise some corn.[97]

Deruisseau's fort on the Missouri became a fact, so Vaudreuil reported on March 15, 1747, that Bertet had written him. The governor of Louisiana reported to the Minister that the activities of Deruisseau happily had largely contributed to checking the disorders and abuses which had caused him to be granted the exclusive trade. Moreover, that grant to Deruisseau had not occasioned any complaints from those who had customarily engaged in trade on the Missouri; these were mostly vagabonds and *coureurs-de-bois,* who often caused desertions.[98]

It is not possible to ascertain with certainty whether or not Deruisseau's fort was Fort Cavagnolle. However, we know that the post on the Missouri was commanded by the Chevalier de Villiers, who had been a cadet in Canada, and had become an ensign on October 15, 1736, and

---

[95]Minister to Vaudreuil, Versailles, April 25, 1746. A. N. Colonies B83, folios 310-311 *verso.*

[96]November 9, 1745. A. N. Colonies, C13A, vol. XXIX, folios 85-87 *verso.* On this matter see N. Caldwell, *French in the Mississippi Valley, 1740-1750* (Urbana, 1941), 56-57. See also *Wisconsin Historical Collections,* XVII, 512-518 and Vaudreuil to *Monseigneur,* August 26, 1749, A. N. Colonies, C13A, vol. XXXIII, folios 57-58.

[97]*Mémoire* on Louisiana. A. N. Colonies, C13A, vol. XXX, folios 242-282, see especially folio 252.

[98]Vaudreuil to Minister, New Orleans, March 15, 1747, A. N. Colonies, C13A, vol. XXXI, folios 17-23; printed in Pease and Jenison, *Illinois on the Eve of the Seven Years War* (Springfield, 1940), 9.

finally a lieutenant in 1746. He was capable, and Bertet said he was an officer of good intelligence and exemplary conduct.[99]

4.

EXIT THE FRENCH

With Fort Cavagnolle established on the Missouri at the Kansas village, the Arkansas route was now rendered safe by concluding a treaty with the Jumanos and Comanches. The treaty was immediately in force, and at once new expeditions to New Mexico under all types of leaders—deserters, private traders, and official agents—were made. The Comanches, enemies of the Apaches on the south, and until then hostile to the Jumano, Pawnee, and other tribes to the east, had little contact with the French; but early in 1748 it was reported that thirty-three Frenchmen had traded with the Comanches. Several Frenchmen, including Pierre Satren and others, had traded with the Comanches *via* the Arkansas river. The French had also established regular trade with the Jumanos. Other Frenchmen likewise succeeded in reaching Santa Fé from Arkansas; some also reached the Spanish *entrepôt* by the northern route. Largely through French effort, alliances had been made between the Comanches and Jumanos, and the Comanches and Pawnees, although the Comanches were still at war with the Osages and Kansas.

Several Frenchmen reached Santa Fé *via* the Missouri, and one party in 1752 probably went there with the official sanction of the authorities in Louisiana. In August, 1752, Jean Chapuis and Luis Feuilli arrived in New Mexico. Chapuis had obtained a passport from the commandant of Michilimackinac, permitting him to return to Illinois. At Fort de Chartres he spoke to Benoît de St. Claire about opening a trade route to New Mexico; St. Claire approved and issued a license. Chapuis set out from Fort de Chartres, and was at Fort Cavagnolle on December 9, 1751. On his way, Chapuis traded with the Osages and the Kansas. Leaving the Kansas tribe in March, 1752, the party proceeded to the Pawnees and thence to the Comanches, who guided them to Santa Fé. There, the Spanish confiscated the traders' goods, imprisoned the party, and later apparently sent them to Spain.[100]

Although there is no further record of Frenchmen pushing through to Santa Fé in this period, there are many reports of contact with the

[99]List of officers and troops of Louisiana, no date [1746 ?], A. N. Colonies D²C51, folios 189-196.
[100]Herbert E. Bolton, "French Intrusions into New Mexico, 1749-1752," in H. E. Bolton and H. M. Stephens, *Pacific Ocean in History* (New York, 1917), 389-407. See also documentation in A. B. Thomas, *The Plains Indians* (Albuquerque, 1940).

Indians of the Missouri River.[101] In 1748 Governor Vaudreuil wrote that the *voyageurs* "have only too frequently" been pillaged by the Osages, "with whom, nevertheless, Louisiana has never been in open war." Such a statement leads one to believe that steady and frequent contact with that tribe had been established.[102] In further support of this assumption can be cited the remarks made by the governor a year later: Benoit de St. Claire, *ad interim* commandant of the Illinois, had reported to him that the Indians under his jurisdiction were all "quite tranquil and appear very content"—in fact, the Osages and Iowas, who were "suspected of having killed two French *coureurs-de-bois,* and of being very bad subjects," had sent several chiefs to the Illinois commandant "to exculpate themselves and beg him to ask me [Vaudreuil] for forgiveness to them." The governor continued:

As it is not best to increase the number of our enemies for slight causes, and on the other hand, if the case would seem to require it, we should not be in a position to make war, especially on the Osages, who are more than two hundred leagues from our establishment in the vicinity of the Spaniards, I wrote Sieur Benoît to profit by the good disposition of both of those tribes, assuring them that I would forget the past, but I would like very much to take them again into our friendship.[103]

In reply the minister warned Vaudreuil to increase the productivity of the Illinois Country and to pay attention to the enterprises of the British in the north, going on to say, "Since the Osages and Iowas have been cleared of the suspicion that was held against them concerning the murder of two French *coureurs-de-bois* who were killed, His Excellency has approved that you push this affair no further."[104]

In the summer of 1749, a conspiracy against the French was initiated among the Illinois Country Indians, presumably by the English, which threatened to reach the tribes on the Missouri. Not only were *parolles,* collars, and English flags sent to the Miamis and nations of the Wabash and Illinois districts; the Illinois themselves and the Cahokias agreed to the plot, and the Peorias were approached. Rumors were afloat that the

[101]A. N. Colonies, vol. XXXIII, folios 219-221 *vo.*, sent December 17, 1749. See also *Ibid.*, vol. XXXIV, folios 400-403. An interesting *Mémoire* on Louisiana by Le Bailly Mesnager, probably dated 1748 or 1749, to which no serious consideration was ever given, advocated exploration of the sources of the Mississippi and the Missouri as an area of great importance to France (Pease and Jenison, *Illinois on the Eve of the Seven Years War*, 132-148).

[102]Vaudreuil to Minister, New Orleans, November 2, 1748, A. N. Colonies, C13A, vol. XXXII, folios 113-121, printed in *Wisconsin Historical Collections*, XVII, 512-518.

[103]Vaudreuil to *Monseigneur*, New Orleans, August 26, 1749, A. N. Colonies, C13A, vol. XXXIII, folios 57-58. Printed in Pease and Jenison, *op. cit.*, 102-104.

[104]Minister to Vaudreuil, Versailles, September 26, 1750, A. N. Colonies, B91, folios, 394-394 *verso*, printed in Pease and Jenison, *op. cit.*, 232-234. This letter was in reply to several letters from August 26, 1749, to January 31, 1750.

Indians of Illinois were inducing the Missouri and Osage tribes to unite with them in attacking the French. The bait to the Indians was merchandise which they could obtain cheaply from the English.[105] In the same summer, three Frenchmen were killed by the Sioux on the Mississippi, and another Frenchman, together with his slave, was killed on the Des Moines river by the Petit Osages. Commandant St. Claire demanded the murderer from the Osage tribe, but at that time knew "not what they will decide. We are having much trouble in our territories. I know not what the result will be, but I hope to avert everything."[106]

As it turned out, satisfaction was given for the murder of this Frenchman, a man named Giguière, who had been hunting on the upper part of the Des Moines river; the Little Osages apprehended the murderer, put him to death, and sent his scalp to Commandant Benoît. Following this incident, prior to October, 1750, the Missouri nation spread a report that the Little Osages had killed not the guilty man but his brother, that the murderer, who at first disappeared, had returned to the village. When the Little Osages heard of this, they seized the real murderer and brought him bound to the commandant of the Illinois.[107] The Little Osages begged Benoît de St. Claire to send Portneuf, apparently the second in command at the post, to the Little Osage village to bear witness to the death of both innocent and guilty. "Nothing can be added to the submission of those Petits Osages; their rectitude surpasses everything that can be expected of a savage nation."

Submissive also were the Big Osages, "who are as haughty as the Petit Osages," for they had just suffered an unexpected set-back. They had been in continual warfare with the Panis-Noirs and Pani-Picques; and these nations, one of whose villages had been wiped out by an epidemic of measles and smallpox, begged assistance of the Laytanes, "a nation in the neighborhood of the Spaniards." Moved by the Panis' desperate condition, the Laytanes joined them, and together they came to a village of the Big Osages "at a time when their people were at the *Cerne* [surround] killing animals; the allies fell upon them and so sharp was the attack that the Big Osages lost twenty-two of their chiefs, while the others left twenty-seven of their people on the field of battle." This disaster caused the Big Osages

---

[105]D'Orgon to Vaudreuil, Natchez, October 7, 1752, printed in Pease and Jenison, *op. cit.*, 735-740, esp. page 738.

[106]Benoît to Captain Raymond at Fort Miami, Fort de Chartres, February 11, 1750, printed in *Wisconsin Historical Collections,* XVIII, 58-59. See also *Ibid.*, XVIII, 33, 60, 82, 86. Captain Raymond said that he prevented the conspiracy from being carried out (*Ibid.*, XVIII, 95-96). In 1749, says Parkman, French writers, with alarm and indignation declared that some bold and enterprising English traders had crossed the Mississippi and traded with the distant Osages (*Montcalm and Wolfe* [reprint, Boston, 1926], I, 46.).

[107]At that time a chief and fifteen men of the Missouri nation were present at Fort de Chartres; they revealed the mistake and confessed that they had positive knowledge of it.

to reflect, and they accordingly went to see the commandant at Fort Chartres to weep for the death of their chiefs. The commandant gave them a small present to console them. In reporting this incident Vaudreuil said:

The Grand Osages left no effort untried to induce the Illinois to join them to go to avenge the death of their people, but Monsieur de St. Clin, to prevent their solicitations having any effect, represented to the Illinois that the Panis-Noirs and the Picques and the Laytannes were allies of the French,[108] as they were; that they could not find fault with people who, after being long attacked, endeavored to avenge themselves; and finally succeeded in inducing the Illinois not to listen to the Grand Osages, but representing to them that if they wished to go to war, they should direct their efforts against the Chikachas, that the blood of their fathers and that of the French, still flowed on the lands of that nation, and that everything urged them to avenge their death.

The Grand Osages were surprised at seeing the Laytannes. They dread them greatly. In fact, that nation says it knows not what it is to retreat, and that it always attacks, whether it be weak or strong. The Laytannes are armed with spears like the ancient Spaniards; they are always mounted on caparisoned horses, and their women go to war with them.[109]

Regarding the general conspiracy of the Indians against the French Illinois posts, Benoît made a strong report to Vaudreuil. In relaying the information to the Minister, Vaudreuil stated that the Illinois country was "on the point of suffering a revolution on the part of the savage nations which are leagued against them in order to strike the different posts of this continent." Benoît was hard at work securing protection. The English had distributed collars and other presents among the Indians of the Wabash, the upper Mississippi, and among the Osages and Missouris; the English had attempted also to induce the Arkansas to join, but this was prevented by the prudent and wise action of Delinó, commandant of that post.[110]

In 1751 occurred the assassination of De la Barre, commandant of the Missouri, by one of his own men.[111] The murderer was a friend of the

---

[108]Margry, *Découvertes et Éstablissements,* VI, 455-462 taken from A. N. Colonies, F³24, folios 387-391 *vo.*

[109]La Jonquière to the Minister, Quebec, September 25, 1751, A. N. Colonies, C11A, vol. XCVII, folios 82-89, printed in *Wisconsin Historical Collections,* XVIII, 85-94. Further reports include the fact that the commandant at Fort de Chartres had effected an alliance with the Panis-Maha who promised to fight any enemy or rebellious "children" of the French. "This alliance is a very advantageous one, and, by maintaining that nation in our interest, we shall be master of the front and back of the Missouri country."

[110]Vaudreuil to Minister, New Orleans, October 10, 1751, A. N. Colonies, C13A, XXXV, folios 167-172. In a letter of the Minister dated Versailles, October 2, 1750, Delinó was mentioned as commandant at Arkansas.—A. N. Colonies, B91, folios 405 *et verso.* Vaudreuil to Macarty, New Orleans, September 9, 1751, Pease and Jenison, *op. cit.,* 333-334; 369-380; and 402.

[111]La Jonquière to Rouillé, September 25, 1751. A. N. Colonies, C11A, vol. XCVII, folio 82-89, printed in Pease and Jenison, *Illinois on the Eve of the Seven*

Indians to whom he had given brandy in contradiction of orders; and he himself was drunk when he committed the murder.[112]

Major Macarty was appointed Commandant at Illinois in 1751, his instructions being drawn up at New Orleans on August 8.[113] He was ordered to detach such garrisons as seemed proper to the outlying posts at Missouri and Vincennes. Since the trade of the Missouri post was secured to its commander, the concession was held by Portneuf (successor to Deruisseau's concession which had expired in May 1750), who was also responsible for its expenses. The continued existence of the Missouri post seemed to be a problem since the Indians moved from its vicinity. In addition the new commandant was to redress the complaint of the Illinois Indians that the best goods were carried by the traders to the post on the Missouri.[114]

Macarty from Kaskaskia, January 20, 1752, wrote to Vaudreuil[115] that on December 16 he had received a letter from Sr. Larche (dated at Grand Manitou, on his way to the Kansas, on December 10), reporting difficulties between the Little Osages and Missouris and Iowas. Macarty told his superior that he was leaving M. de Portneuf at the Missouri and would send some soldiers there; he inquired whether he should collect the one-hundred *pistoles* gratification paid by the *voyageurs* to the commandant of the Missouri post, or if the commandant should have an exclusive trade region.[116] From another letter of Macarty's it is clear that traders from Canada went regularly to the Missouri by way of the Illinois settlements.[117]

On March 18, 1752, Macarty had written Vaudreuil, reporting that he had permitted M. Despins to go to the Missouris and had instructed Portneuf to raise some war parties among the Missouris to attack the Piankesaws. He said that where Portneuf was located there were no longer any Indians and that Portneuf's fort was useless, since he did not see and hence could not control any of the *voyageurs* who went to the Missouri to trade during the winter season. It would be best to make his post lower down nearer the villages of the Missouri nation or even higher up. Port-

---

Years War, 356-368 (p. 368); and Vaudreuil to Rouillé October 10, 1751, A. N. Colonies. C13A, vol. XXXV, folio 173, printed in Pease and Jenison, *op cit.*, 410.

[112]The French commandant in the Missouri country, De La Barre, was killed by one of his own soldiers who was forthwith courtmartialed and executed. The perpetrator of the deed was a friend of the Indians who gave them brandy in contravention of orders and was drunk when he committed the act. As a matter of fact the French fort on the Missouri had probably been built by Vaudreuil in order to check the lawlessness on the part of the *coureurs-de-bois*. De La Barre was assassinated February 24 and his assassin shot on March 18.—Vaudreuil to Minister, New Orleans, October 10, 1751, A. N. Colonies, C13A, vol. XXXV, folios 173-173 *verso*.

[113]Instructions to Macarty, printed in Pease and Jenison, *op. cit.*, 293-319.

[114]*Ibid.*, xl-li.

[115]*Ibid.*, 432-469, see page 443.

[116]*Ibid.*, 467-468.

[117]Marcarty to Rouillé, February 1, 1752, A. N. Colonies, C13A, vol. XXXVI, folios 307-308 *vo*; Pease and Jenison, *op. cit.*, 478-483, see page 481.

neuf had been ordered to descend to Illinois with a party of his garrison; when plans were settled he would return to the Missouri. On March 10, the *voyageurs* from the Missouri began to arrive.[118]

On March 27 Macarty wrote again. Portneuf had sent three men from his garrison to get provisions and to inquire if the governor had decided to rebuild the fort, which, together with the barracks, was in a state of decay. If so, Portneuf wanted to acquire the wood. He repeated the information about the fort's now useless location and desired to build a new fort at a better site. He thought it best that all Frenchmen who traded in the area should do so only at the fort. "Even the Indians ask it to avoid the uproar of the *voyageurs* who snatch a beaver pelt from each other." Portneuf spoke of the gratification which had not been levied on the *voyageurs* that year. Since Portneuf would be forced to rebuild the fort himself, inasmuch as the King would not grant the funds, some advantage must be allowed him; Macarty asked the governor to decide the matter.[119] The Illinois commandant expected to see Portneuf before the end of April; meanwhile he had instructed his subordinate to stir up the Missouri tribes to take up arms for the French and also to rebuild the *enceinte* or fort which Bertet had made. Undoubtedly, the fort would soon be finished.[120]

In replying, Vaudreuil, on April 25, 1752, approved of Macarty's leaving the *Sieur* de Portneuf in command of the Missouri. The latter was in a position to keep those Indian nations in the interest of France and "to make them function under the present conditions." Vaudreuil told Macarty that there was no difficulty in paying the commander of the Missouri post the yearly gratification of one hundred *pistoles* from the *voyageurs*. That was a simpler and better plan than to grant the commandant an exclusive trade, as Governor La Jonquière had previously instructed Benoît.[121]

On April 28, 1752, Vaudreuil urged Macarty to gain securely the friendship of several tribes including the Big and Little Osages and others of the Missouri. With respect to the Missouri post, it was for the officer in command there to make arrangements not only for the rebuilding of the fort but also for its removal to the place Macarty deemed best adapted to the good of the service. But the King should not share in that expense; such had been the rule for that post. The traders, along with the com-

---

[118]Macarty to Vaudreuil, Kaskaskia, March 18, 1752, printed in *ibid.*, 506-536, see pages 529-530, 535.

[119]Macarty to Vaudreuil, Kaskaskia, March 27, 1752, printed in *ibid.*, 536-566, see esp. 548-550. Portneuf's post was three days march from any Indians, near present Leavenworth. He wanted to build a fort at a better site with reference to the Kansas and Missouri rivers. Portneuf complained that the *voyageurs* who entered the Kansas river avoid seeing him and cause trouble.

[120]*Ibid.*, 555.

[121]Vaudreuil to Macarty, April 25, 1752 printed in *Ibid.*, 590-611, see pp. 601-602.

47

mandant, should contribute to the completion of the fort and to its annual repairs.[122]

Another statement from Macarty complains that the difference in the price of merchandise between the English and the French had caused a great deal of trouble. If the French would sell merchandise at the same price as the English, it would "put our rivers and our distant posts under shelter. Thus this contagion would not spread to the Missouri river, from which much peltry was drawn this year."[123]

When Portneuf again left Kaskaskia on July 4, 1752, Macarty urged him to be tactful with the Missouri tribes and to induce them and the Osages to send some parties against the Miamis without passing Kaskaskia. If Portneuf encountered any unlicensed traders in his area, he should send them to Macarty. Portneuf was ordered to have the fort re-established by the *voyageurs,* as the Kansas had returned to their old homes. Macarty also desired accurate information about the latest violent incident with the Indians. He had received information from the corporal at the Missouri that, after Portneuf had left, a woman was wounded near the fort and a cow killed; that the Missouris came to steal horses and two were killed; and that a windstorm had blown down all the chimneys and damaged the buildings. On August 23, the chiefs of the Big Osages came to inform Macarty that they had been attacked by the Ietan and several other Spanish tribes. The Osages lost twenty but killed thirty of the enemy; they came to beg Macarty to send Frenchmen to them.[124]

Late in 1752 Portneuf informed Macarty that the Pawnees had made peace with the Ietans. Macarty wrote to Portneuf about repairing Fort Cavagnolle and the expenses to be borne by the *voyageurs,* promising that Portneuf should be paid the gratification due him for the past two years. Portneuf reported that two Frenchmen of whom he had no news might have been killed at the Oto village (near modern Omaha) by the Little Osage. The commandant still complained of difficulties with the *voyageurs* from Canada. Macarty admitted that many *voyageurs* through devious means (by leaving their goods at Cahokia) got trading permits from him at Kaskaskia and then, among other violations of regulations, went to the Missouri and dispensed brandy. Macarty forced the *voyageurs* to contribute the gratification to Portneuf and ordered him to search for mines, since there were mines already being worked in other parts of the present state of Missouri.[125]

---

[122]Vaudreuil to Macarty, New Orleans, April 28, 1752, printed in *Ibid.,* 615-626, see p. 621. This was in reply to Macarty's letters of March 18 and 27 summarized above.
[123]Macarty to Rouillé, June 1, 1752, A. N. Colonies, C13A, vol. XXXVI, folios 309-312 printed in Pease and Jenison, *op cit.,* 635-644, esp. p. 641.
[124]Macarty to Vaudreuil, Kaskaskia, September 2, 1752, printed in *Ibid.,* 654-699, esp. pp. 662-663; and 678-679.
[125]Macarty to Vaudreuil, Kaskaskia, December 7, 1752, printed in *Ibid.,* 746-777, esp. pp. 770-771.

Macarty wrote Rouillé on May 20, 1753, that four men who had deserted from the Missouri post had been killed by the Wichita. The Ietans, he said, "numerous and wandering tribes between our post and the Spaniards, have asked by Stabaco, chief of the Skidi in the western part of the upper Missouri, permission to come to see me." Macarty sent word that he would receive them. He added that Spanish convoys had recently gone to places where the Spaniards had been defeated some years earlier.[126] "I will try to settle these [Ietan] Indians at some place on the Missouri. It is claimed that by that river you can reach the Sea of the West, passing the Crest of the Mountains on which you can find a river which falls into that part of the sea. But private persons are not in a condition to undergo expenses of this sort." Interest in the search for a route to the western ocean, it is clear, still lingered on.[127]

Duquesne, now Governor-General of New France, believed in free trade but could not harmonize that view with the practical situation; he had therefore given some exclusive grants, against which many Indians had complained. He wrote Rouillé that he was going to grant freedom of trading, which would encourage *voyageurs* to undertake discoveries. He had decided that the Illinois trade should be opened to all in 1755. That of the "Sea of the West" [Missouri River] post, however, would not be made free until 1756 in order to avoid ruining those to whom exclusive trading privileges had been granted (for it was in the third year only that the trader was able to re-coup the prodigious advances and credits given to the Indians during the first two years of the concession).[128]

On December 17, 1754, Governor Kerlérec of Louisiana reported to the Minister that Macarty had informed him on August 28 last that the inhabitants of Vincennes and the Illinois were very discontented with exclusive trade privileges which Duquesne had granted for both the Missouri post and Vincennes and they were thinking about abandoning both these posts. The question of abandoning posts had been in the air at the time of Kerlérec's arrival in Louisiana, and he had discussed it with his predecessor Vaudreuil, who believed that abandonment by the governor of Canada would be contrary to the good of the service and of the colony. Enclosing copies of the exclusive trade privileges granted by Duquesne, and the representations of the inhabitants of Post Vincennes, Kerlérec asked for orders and for permission to stop *coureurs-de-bois,* vagabonds, and vagrants, who under the pretense of hunting were guilty of trading with

---

[126]Villasur defeat. See references in note 53.
[127]Macarty to Rouillé, Kaskaskia, May 20, 1753, A. N. Colonies, C13A, vol. XXXVII, folios 188-190 *vo.* printed in Pease and Jenison, *op cit.,* 820-821.
[128]Duquesne to Rouillé, Quebec, October 26, 1753, A. N. Colonies, C11A, vol. XCIX, folios 103-109 *vo,* printed in Pease and Jenison, *op cit.,* 832-838.

savages without the permission of the governor. Kerlérec pleaded for free trade but left it up to the minister to issue orders to Duquesne.[129]

We know that the French maintained soldiers on the Missouri, for Captain de Moncharvaux, cadet soldier Jean Bte. Monchauvaix, and four gunners were listed as serving there during the year, 1757.[130] In the list of salaries for the officers of the government in Illinois was included a M. Dulonpré, who was paid 250 livres for his services as interpreter for the Osages who were going to war against the English.[131] And on February 14, 1758, the Minister wrote to Vaudreuil approving what he had done in the case of the murder of two Frenchmen shot in the Missouri Country. Vaudreuil had apprehended the murderers and had granted some favor.[132]

Meanwhile the events leading to the final struggle between the French and English for control of the heart of the continent were all-absorbing, though very little information about the Osages and the Missouri is available. In general, the French policy was to keep the Indians of the Mississippi and the Missouri valleys at peace and friendly. For example, working among the Sioux was the younger Marin, who aided in making peace among the Indians of the upper Mississippi valley.[133] Obviously affairs west of the Mississippi river during the critical years of the French and Indian War could not have engaged very full attention of the French authorities. I have been able to collect only one or two items relating to the Osages during that period.[134] Although Bougainville never visited the area, he obtained information at first hand from the Canadian officers who knew the region well. Speaking of the Missouri region he mentions the Osages and Missouris, whose trade, including their neighboring tribes, in an ordinary year "amounts to eighty packs of deer and bear skins, few other peltries." From the fort among the Kansas (Cavagnolle) the French obtained a hundred packets of skins, chiefly beaver, deer, and bear. The Otos and Iowas furnished another eighty packets.[135]

Finally, on December 12, 1758, Governor Kerlérec gave a full list of the Indian nations which had relations with the French in Louisiana

[129]Kerlérec to Machault, New Orleans, December 17, 1754, A. N. Colonies, C13A, vol. XXXVIII, folios 118-119 verso, printed in Pease and Jenison, op. cit., 920-924.
[130]A. N. Colonies, D² C51.
[131]December 21, 1757. A. N. Colonies, D²D10.
[132]Minister to Vaudreuil, Versailles, February 14, 1758. A. N. Colonies, B107, folios 285-286 verso.
[133]See Margry, op. cit., VI, 648-655; Wisconsin Historical Collections, XVIII, 133, 158, 195-196, etc.
[134]The Minister wrote Vaudreuil on February 14, 1758, approving what Vaudreuil did concerning the murder of two Frenchmen on the Missouri. "As they had delivered the murderers promptly, your action will have a good effect and ought to make you loved and respected by those nations" (A. N. Colonies, B107, folios 285-286 verso). In 1756, Bossu saw some Osages, bearing as their manitou, a dried serpent of a monstrous size (Travels, II, 245).
[135]Wisconsin Historical Collections, XVIII, 177-178. De Bougainville's Mémoire also in Rapport de l'Archiviste de la Province de Quebec pour 1923-1924. See also Illinois State Historical Society Journal, XXIV (1931), 578-584.

and Illinois at the time. The French village of Cahokia, fifteen leagues from Fort de Chartres, was the *entrepôt* of all the *voyageurs* from Canada who came *via* Michilimackinac to the upper Mississippi and Missouri rivers; there, in exchange for merchandise, they procured skins which they carried back to Canada, the governor of which had supplied the traders with licenses.[136] The Indians of these rivers were far distant from the French posts; they often insulted the French flag and sometimes even killed Frenchmen. Distant as they were, it was not easy to avenge such acts. The only way of restraining the Indians, therefore, was for the French to deprive them of their necessities and their commerce with the traders. Of the Missouri river, Kerlérec wrote, that "almost all of the savages who had gone the farthest assure us that it has never been possible to find the source of it." His description of the Indians of this region follows:[137]

The Big Osages number 700 men bearing arms and are 200 leagues from Fort de Chartres.

On the left bank (of the Mississippi) ascending, and twenty leagues from Fort de Chartres is the mouth of the Missouri river. At its junction with the river, it runs east and west, but at about thirty leagues the Gasconade river is found qui court cet air de vent, and the Mississippi to the Northwest. Ten leagues above the Gasconade river is the Osage river. After having ascended it one hundred and forty leagues, one finds the Big Osages, with whom our traders trade skins, horses and mules. It is the elder branch of the Arkansas, the Little Osages and the Kansas of which I shall speak. They have the same language and customs, with a few differences in accent and pronunciation. It is very important to us to manage this nation. They are naturally good, and pass as being stupid among the other nations. Continuing to ascend the Missouri, forty leagues on the lower bank, is found the Missouri nation established on the bank of this river.

---

[136]Kerlérec spoke of the evils of this method and suggested that all *voyageurs* should be forced to appear at Fort de Chartres for examination of passports. The dependence of Illinois upon New France is well illustrated by the fact that in 1754 Governor Duquesne made a grant of exclusive trade in the Missouri valley and also of the trade of Vincennes. See Alvord, *Illinois Country*, 233. The inhabitants of Illinois and Vincennes complained against this privilege as granted by Duquesne. Vaudreuil and Kerlérec declared it was contrary to the well-being of the colony and would lead to inhabitants leaving the colony. Letter of Kerlérec, December 17, 1754, A. N. Colonies, C13A, vol. XXXVIII, folios 118-119 *verso*.

[137]A. N. Colonies, C13A, vol. XL, folios 135-140; 142-144 (entire is folios 135-156). See also *Congrès Internationale des Américanistes, XVe Session, Quebec, 1906* (Quebec, 1907), 61-86.

The Missouris number about 150 men and the Little Osages 250 men; and are 100 leagues distant from Fort de Chartres.

The Little Osages are about one league inland, and about forty leagues distant by land from the Big Osages. These nations likewise trade with the French and are very attached to us. They are very friendly with the Iowas and Octotatas, speaking the same language. I will make mention of them [the latter] in the proper place.

The Kansas number about 300 men bearing arms and are 150 leagues from Fort de Chartres.

Fifty leagues further up are the Kansas, where Fort Cavagnolle is located, which consists of a circle of piles [an enclosure of stakes][138] which encloses some bad cabins and huts [cabannes en loge]. The officer there commands seven to eight garrisoned soldiers and some traders. These Kansas were very numerous, but the wars that they have had with the Pawnees and small-pox have extremely weakened them. There remain today only two hundred and fifty to three hundred men. They are very attached to the French. They speak, as I have already said, almost the same language as the Arkansas, the Big and Little Osages. It is on their lands that there are found quarries of red stone from which are made the calumets for all the nations.

The Octotata and the Ayowais are 230 leagues from Fort de Chartres. The former number 100 men and the latter 200 men.

The Octotata are about eighty leagues further up, situated on the bank of the Missouri à la bord. The Ayowais are also located ten leagues further. These two nations live together, speak the same language, which is that of the Missouris, and also trade with the French.

The Panis-Mahas number 600 men bearing arms and are 330 leagues from Fort de Chartres.

The Pani-Mahas are established on the Platte River, which empties into the Missouri, and eighty leagues from the Kansas. They are located twenty five leagues from its mouth. They also trade with the French and are very numerous.

The Mahas number 800 men and are 410 leagues from Fort de Chartres.

The Mahas are eighty leagues further up than the Ayowais, ascending the Missouri. They would be little known if it were not for some French coureurs, who report that they number forty villages, extremely populated, as well as other nations of which we have very little knowledge.

---

[138] un entourage de Pieux.

The Kikara nation, according to reports which have been made by some slaves of this same nation, is more numerous than that of the Mahas. These same slaves assure that they have always heard it said in their nation by the elders [anciens] that the sources of the Missouri are not known, but [there are] many more numerous nations.

Continuation of the details concerning the savages of Louisiana—descending the river and leaving the Wabash.

Arkansas

The Arkansas number about 160 men and are 250 leagues from New Orleans and the same distance from Illinois.

The Arkansas nation, without doubt the bravest of all those nations which are dependents of this continent, commenced to be attached to the French as soon as they knew them, and never varied in their attachment to us. In vain did the British solicit their attachment to them; presents, promises, intrigues, plots of all sorts, all were useless. This Arkansas nation is still the only one which has never soaked their hands in French blood. They glory in all their harangues and do not cease to repeat them to their young men from the time they commence to be warriors. We live among them without defiance.

This nation is about two hundred and fifty leagues from New Orleans on a river which bears their name. It is the first that one meets on coming from Illinois to New Orleans and after having passed the mouth of the Wabash. It joins the river on the right, on descending. When Monsieur Cartier de la Salle came to reconnoitre the Mississippi, he found the Arkansas situated on the bank of the river, thirty leagues above the river where they are today. The gracious welcome that this nation gave him upon his passage made him hope from then on that some day it would be very useful for the execution of his project.

This nation was then very numerous, divided as it still is today into three divisions, composed of brave warriors, as capable of attacking as of defending themselves against any nation which might attempt to disturb them. They maintained themselves for a long time in this establishment, despite the losses they experienced. At last, solicited and pressed by their women and children, and more weakened by maladies than by war, they left the banks of the Mississippi. At first they went only a few leagues distant from the river, in order to be able always to observe their enemies, and to make war on them, but as their new establishment was too low and often inundated during the times when the river was swollen, being on the verge of damaging and often losing their harvests, they were obliged to move again and to go to seek higher lands, always observing not to separate themselves at a too great distance from the French established on the same river, over whose safety they watched.

In all the wars that the French have had to sustain against the different savage nations, the Arkansas have been a great aid to them. They were especially distinguished in the Natchez war, and it was they who defeated the Yazoos and the Courrois, two nations who have mixed in the conspiracy of the Natchez, and who, imitating them, massacred all the French established among them.

In the very last war which we had with the Tchaktas, the Arkansas, although very weakened in number, did not fail to be very useful to us by their continual incursions, which they made on their [Choctaw] lands— now burning the wheat, now falling upon some wintering hunters or fighting with some detachment of war, always with the intrepidity known to them, and very often with success.

Today, even though this nation is reduced to a fistful of people and formerly so numerous, they do not fail to go to war against their enemies and ours, and continue to make themselves feared and respected.

The Chikasaws, repulsed by continual losses that they suffered, and the mortal uneasiness caused to them by the Arkansas, were forced recently to ask for peace, but the latter replied that they would never make it with the enemy of the French, and since then have repeated it to them[?].

Although proud and haughty with their enemies, the Arkansas are good, affable and in full accord with the French. Nothing is easier than to hold them in their attachment to us. They are sensible of the confidence that we have in them, of the esteem in which we hold their valor, and of the remembrance which we keep of their exploits and those of their fathers. They will march everywhere where the need of the service requires. Jealous of their liberty, they will not suffer anything that might diminish it or place limits on it. It is for this reason that the chiefs of this nation have scarcely any authority over their warriors, and moreover, we remark that any French officer who knows how to succeed easily in bringing them where he wishes, has only to recall to them their former valor and to animate them with the hope of conquering. Their councils are good and very well composed. The chiefs and the old men sincerely and quite generally attached to the French do not cease to speak therein of the obligations which their nation has, for services that they have received from them [the French], their wives and their children. It is with these sentiments that they ordinarily hold together their young warriors. If by chance there is found in their villages some mutineer or malcontent, the old men put everything to use in order to bring them back or even to see them despoiled of that which they hold most dear in order to stop their rage.

Interested as the savages in general are, the Arkansas are sensitive to the slightest injustices. It is necessary to give them faithfully what they have been promised or what they have earned. They differ, however, from any other nation; they are paid within reason, since one can make them see the impossibility of furnishing them certain merchandise in time of war or in times of scarcity. One might say in praise of this nation that inclination plays more a part than their interest in the services which they render us. It is in general a brave nation, which merits friendship and bounties from the French.

One finds several other savage nations coming from the Arkansas to New Orleans. Some of them and nearly all were very numerous a long time after the arrival of the French. The Courrois *and the* Yazoos *have been entirely defeated by us and our savage allies—in punishment of their black treason.*

What action, if any, the Missouri tribes took during the war years is not definitely known. Possibly the Missouris and Osages may have been present at the defeat of the French near Niagara in 1759.[139] We do know that the Illinois Country was not lost in a military sense to the French during the war and that the Indians in general favored the French. In 1763 D'Abbadie granted the exclusive commerce of the entire Missouri valley to Maxent, Laclède and Company; and in a council held in Fort de Chartres in 1765, in the presence of English officials, the Missouris and Osages still strongly asserted their friendship for the French.

Throughout nearly the entire French régime the Osages were nominally the allies of the French, and yet, as Foreman says, the powerful Osages were probably more active than any other tribe in maintaining a state of warfare throughout Missouri-Kansas-Oklahoma area and preventing its peaceful occupation by either red or white men. They challenged practically all the tribes of Indians they encountered in the prairies and east to the Mississippi.

Thus by 1753 (when, for our purposes, the French leave our narrative, for the French and Indian War broke out in the following year, as a result of which war, France was expelled from North America) Frenchmen, be they *voyageurs,* traders, trappers, explorers (official or unofficial), Illinois or Canadians, had penetrated the whole trans-Mississippi West country and in a general way had made known the country contained in the watershed of the Mississippi-Missouri rivers. They had ascended practically every large branch of the Missouri to the mountains; they had set foot on most of the territory lying between the Mississippi and the Spanish border; they had reached the Rocky Mountains. But they lacked precise information concerning certain parts of that country. Not all the information procured by the explorers, traders, and trappers, either from Canada

---

[139]Villiers du Terrage, *Les Dernières Années de la Louisiane Française* (Paris, 1903), 106; *Wisconsin Historical Collections,* XVIII, 212-213.

or from the Mississippi Valley, was made known to the officials in Louisiana. Let us therefore glance for a moment at the extent of geographical knowledge concerning the Missouri valley at about the close of the French régime.

A good summary is afforded to us by Le Page du Pratz, whose *Histoire de la Louisiane* was published at Paris in 1758. Du Pratz wrote his three small volumes after a sixteen year residence in Louisiana. He had made a five month tour into the interior himself and had submitted his manuscript to men familiar with the colony. He also gives us a map[140] which bears the date 1757. We find that despite a few errors Du Pratz' map is fairly accurate for lower Louisiana. The three principal tributaries flowing into the Mississippi from the west, the Red, the Arkansas, and the Missouri, are reasonably accurate at their points of confluence with the Mississippi. The lower Missouri is also fairly accurately portrayed. Two of its tributaries, the Osage and the Kansas, are reasonably accurate, but the Missouri itself is shown running from the west in the fashion of a river taking practically the actual course of the Missouri-Platte. It was then commonly thought that the Missouri flowed eastward from headwaters near the sources of the Rio Grande, and therefore would serve as the best and shortest route between the Illinois country and New Mexico. (The same may be said of D'Anville's map which Villiers du Terrage reproduces in part. It is remarkably accurate but for Lower Louisiana only.)[141]

Du Pratz devoted chapter eighteen of his second volume to a discussion of the Indians residing to the west of the Mississippi river. He adequately describes the tribes of the lower Missouri, particularly the Osage and Missouri tribes, but beyond those tribes he names only the tribes living near the banks of the Missouri as far as the Sioux country.

We may conclude, then, that at the time of the cession of Louisiana in 1763 (despite proposals to explore the Missouri to its source), the French of the Illinois country had not reached a point much beyond the Platte river. It is true, however, that trade with the Sioux and other tribes living higher up on the Missouri was carried on from posts situated around the Great Lakes. And it is reasonably clear from the activities of the Veréndryes that the French had explored the Missouri from its mouth to the Mandan villages except for that stretch of river above the Platte and below the White or Cheyenne river. Moreover, many attempts had been

---

[140]Facing page 138 in volume I.
[141]*Les Dernières Années de la Louisiane Française*, 77.

made to reach Santa Fé from the Illinois, and at least one was successful. But many erroneous ideas yet remained, especially respecting the Upper Missouri.[142]

---

[142]LePage Du Pratz, *op. cit.*, I, 147, estimated the length of the Missouri at 800 leagues and averred that the French had penetrated it but 300 leagues at most. Chittenden in his *American Fur Trade of the Far West,* page 762, said that according to Du Pratz the Missouri had not been ascended for more than 300 leagues or about 825 miles. He probably meant the mouth of the Platte, for that was as high as fur traders went in those days and was regarded as the dividing line between the upper and lower Missouri. The distance is 650 miles or about 175 miles less than Du Pratz estimated. He estimated the length of the entire river at 800 leagues or about 2200 miles. The actual distance from its head at the three forks to its mouth is 2547 miles.

PART II

THE SPANIARDS TAKE OVER

Although Spain received the western half of the Mississippi by the treaty ending the Seven Years War, Spanish procrastination in taking possession, together with the set-back which Spain's first governor, Ulloa, received from the French of New Orleans in 1768, left the French actually in charge for some six years after the treaty. During these years affairs went on much as they had in French days.

Some notes intended to be used with a map of the Missouri region printed February 13, 1755, have survived in the French archives but without the map that should accompany them. They maintain that the sources of the Mississippi were unknown, that the Missouri extended westward as far as the mountains of New Mexico, as far to the west as the Ohio extends to the east. The Padoucas and Pawnees were regarded as the most numerous of the Indian nations estimated at between sixty and seventy villages. The map would indicate the route of the French via the Iowas and the "campagne de la Paducas"; it would show the fort the Spaniards had built in 1719 and soon thereafter abandoned, and finally it would mark out how far up the Missouri and the Mississippi the French had ascended.[1] Unfortunately, however, we must do without the geographer's reproduction of all this compactly indicated information.

Other *mémoires* of the period are more complete. An undated *mémoire* of C. Laudrain (?) states that to the north and west of the Illinois for a very considerable distance the French were established in *cabanages,* residences in which the *marchandes chasseurs* wintered in the cold countries and which rivaled the factories of the merchants of London on the most western lakes.[2] Another *mémoire* concerning Louisiana, 1763, evidently left for the Spaniards, recommended that presents be distributed to the

---

[1] A. E., Corr. Pol., Angleterre, vol. 438, folios 126-131.
[2] A. N. AF[IV] 1211, number 52. This probably refers, however, to a much later date.

Indians to favor the fur trade, and that a strong post be constructed at the entrance of the great Missouri river, staffed with a garrison of twenty-five men. The hinterland was said to abound in precious metals. Moreover, a number of Canadian settlers could be established at the garrison to prevent the English from crossing from the Illinois into Spanish territory. The author of this *mémoire* stated that he had founded a post two hundred leagues above the Red River in 1720, and, while endeavoring to penetrate to New Mexico, had gone inland to the northwest, crossing several mountains, and on the Upper Arkansas had come upon six fine Indian villages whose folk spoke different languages. In the environs of the Arkansas, a chain of mountains extended to the west-northwest. The Indians had told him of mineral wealth in that area between the Arkansas and the Missouri, and Dumont de Montigny, who accompanied him, found some grains of gold in the river.[3]

Thus the French made the geography known to their successors. In fact, little additional knowledge of the Missouri was acquired by the Spaniards until late in the eighteenth century. In 1774 Pedro Piernas reported that the "most distant nations of the Missouri" were the Mahi, Panis, Panimai (Pani-Noirs) and Otoes and "one recently discovered more in the interior than those mentioned," called Ricaras, who were attracted by the others and solicited Spanish friendship, communications, and traders. But Piernas complained that among the Missouri River nations a number of fugitive French traders had maintained themselves for a long time, long before Spain had taken formal possession of the Upper Louisiana Territory. They had caused the traders who ascended annually considerable harm and pillage by their counsel and by inciting the Indians. Piernas had threatened these Frenchmen, and most of them had come down to St. Louis.[4]

But that is getting ahead of the story. In 1763 Redon de Rassac in his *Plan pour rendre la Louisiane la plus riche et la plus puissante de toutes les colonies Françaises* declared that the post of Missouri, in the Indian nation of the same name and on the river of the same name, was inhabited only by the detachment from the Illinois. A great commerce in furs was carried on with those Indians. One of the best means of developing Louisiana would be to construct a small fort with a company in it two-hundred leagues above the post, following the ascending river. In addition nine other such posts should be built in the lands of the Missouris, Panis, Kansas, Cadodaquis, Opelouses, Attacapas, and along the frontier of New and Old Mexico, making ten in all, fifty leagues distant from one another, thus forming a chain of forts to protect the northern and eastern district

[3]A. N. Colonies, C13A, vol. XLIII, folios 357-364 *vo.*, see esp. folios 361 *verso—*364 *verso.*

[4]Piernas to Unzaga, St. Louis, July 13, 1774. Archivo General de Indias, (Seville), Sección, Papeles de Cuba, legajo 81 (hereinafter cited P. de C.).

bordered, neighbored, and enclosed by Louisiana. The plan also included ten other forts on the Mississippi. Redon de Rassac's geography of the Missouri is of course not accurate, but it indicates the existing geographical knowledge.[5]

Vilemont urged Grimaldi, Minister of War and Marine at Madrid, that the Spaniards send an officer to the Big and Little Osages on the Missouri to establish a post among the Missouris,[6] as the French had done, for the English were trying to woo these tribes. In place of the existing small *entrepôt* should be a strong *magasin* of all sorts of merchandise proper and suitable for the Indians to prevent their going to the English and the Illinois as they had been accustomed to do in order to trade with the Canadians. It was essential, said Vilemont, that this post never lack merchandise. In a supplementary *informe* Vilemont reported that the Big and Little Osages, Panis, Panis Piqués, Patakas, Ricaras, La Ventanes, etc., were all savages on the road to Santa Fé—some hostile to the Spaniards. It would entail little expense to the Crown to attach them to the Spaniards, for the trade and furs would defray the expenses.[7]

When Dabbadie arrived in Louisiana as director-general of Louisiana (June 29, 1763) he was very much concerned with the languishing state of the colony. Trade with the Indians was usually in whole or in part in the hands of the post commanders, who often interfered with other traders in order to derive more profit to themselves; numerous complaints against such practices remain in the annals of Louisiana. At times trade had been open to all licensed traders; at other times it had been granted exclusively to certain traders under control of the commandant. Both free and exclusive trading had advantages and disadvantages. Dabbadie talked over the matter with Kerlérec, Macarty, and other experienced officials in the colony. Kerlérec had previously believed in free trade. Dabbadie, however, thought that the colony would best profit by granting exclusive privileges for the various districts. Accordingly, in 1763, he granted to Maxent, Laclède, and Dée an exclusive trading right to the Missouris. Dabbadie himself did not profit from these arrangements.

These exclusive grants led to many heated arguments and complaints against Dabbadie from the New Orleans merchants. On June 6, 1764, the merchants delivered to Dabbadie a scorching denunciation of his methods with respect to finances, bills of exchange, and monopolies. They complained that the merchants, who had done so much for the colony, were

---

[5]A. N. Colonies, C13A, vol. XLIII, folios 377-389 *vo.*, folios used are 380-386.
[6]Three *informes* sent by Vilemont to Grimaldi; first one dated May 22, 1764, Archivo Histórico Nacional (Madrid) Sección, Papeles de Estado, leg. 3882, expediente 12 (hereinafter cited A. H. N. leg.).
[7]A. H. N., Est. leg. 3882. Vilemont urged that a fort garrisoned by troops would be necessary to hold the Missouris and that another fort or depot should be established on the Arkansas or Upper St. Francis river to take care of the tribes listed in the text. He urged that the Osages and Mahas be attached to Spain through trade.

poorly rewarded by Dabbadie, who gave all the commerce to four or five favored persons, cutting the others off from their promising business. They rightly[8] told Dabbadie that the king had granted free commerce to the inhabitants and that Dabbadie in granting the monopolies had followed a policy diametrically opposed to the King's desires. Such favoritism would ruin the colony. These complaints were signed by twenty-two merchants, nine of whom Dabbadie, in his reply, said had been residents of the colony for no more than one year.

Dabbadie forwarded the complaints to Paris on June 7, 1764, together with a full rebuttal, refuting the charges item by item. He denied that all the rights of commerce of the colony had been given exclusively to individuals; he cited growing of wood, cultivation of indigo, sugar, and cotton as open to all individuals, claiming that such production made up the "real branches of commerce." Only the Indian trade, which was the smallest object of Louisiana commerce, had been made exclusive, and that not permanently, since the privileges had to be renewed every three years. The exclusive privileges had been granted for necessary and worthy ends: safety to supply the needs of the savage nations, to maintain them in peace, to prevent unauthorized penetration among the Indians, and to curb the boundless liberty of an infinity of people dangerous for their cupidity and bad behavior. Known traders could supply the post at small cost; the officers and soldiers stationed at them could be supported by the goods with which the traders were forced to provide them to the extent of half their pay, according to a determined tariff. The only other favor he (Dabbadie) had given the grantees was to advance them some powder and some goods from the King's warehouse, which he would have been obliged to request from His Majesty by post, and which were paid back when goods arrived from France. By so doing he had saved expenses in the evacuation of the Illinois post.

Dabbadie further protested that before his arrival in the colony the trade had been on an exclusive basis through grants of other governors to private persons. He denied the complaints that the English would gain advantage from such a system of exclusive trade. The Minister could be trusted to decide whether the system of the merchants was preferable to that which the governor had established. He denied that the complainants had patriotic motives; they had, indeed, depicted the situation "with traits of insolence which deserve all your severity."[9]

---

[8] In a *mémoire* to serve as instructions to Dabbadie, dated, Versailles, February 10, 1763, His Majesty allowed the inhabitants of Louisiana freedom of trade with the savages; urged keeping the Indians friendly through presents; and granted Dabbadie the right to suppress or maintain distant posts. A. N. Colonies, B116, folios 571-573 *verso.*

[9] A. N. Colonies, C13A, XLIV, folios 61 *verso-62 verso;* 63-68.

Continuing the same controversy, Rivoire wrote on June 25, 1764, to Grimaldi, at Madrid, that some narrow persons, sacrificing the colony to their own selfish interests, might "insinuate to Your Excellency" that Spain should continue to follow the plan of granting to a few private persons the exclusive trade among the savages. Such narrow purposes had dictated the grants of the Illinois to Maxent, and of Natchitoches to Brau "aussi n'a-t-on pas tardé à s'apercevoir des suites dangereuses ques cet arrangement pouroit [sic] avoir—le commerce à fair," concerning which some representations in writing had been made to Dabbadie (Rivoire supposedly enclosed them, but they are no longer there). If Dabbadie persuaded the Spanish governor to follow the same plan, it would be very troublesome to the colony. Rivoire also warned that the English, who had free trade, would take advantage of this arrangement. He pleaded for free trade, the post commanders only taking care that strong liquor be not given to the Indians; for this purpose and to keep order, the traders should give bond.[10]

News of Dabbadie's policies was not well received in France. Writing to Dabbadie from Versailles on January 18, 1765, the Minister said he had just been informed that Dabbadie had established a company composed of five or six merchants and had accorded to it the exclusive privilege of commerce and trade of Negroes with the savages. The Commerce of France had complained against this and other of Dabbadie's measures. Expressing surprise, the Minister accused Dabbadie of irregular conduct and abuse of power. Dabbadie should have known that "any exclusive privilege is a derogation of the laws of commerce which, by destroying its necessary liberty, necessarily destroys itself; that His Majesty has reserved to himself alone the power to accord such when the circumstances absolutely require it."[11]

Before this letter arrived, however, Dabbadie had died. Foucault, the *ordonnateur,* replied to it on August 2, 1765. True, Dabbadie had granted exclusive trading privileges, but he had done so to alleviate the misery brought to the colony by years of war, to extend commerce, hoping thus to keep the Indians favorably disposed, to establish good order among the traders, to carry out the police regulations, to assure provision of the colony with the merchandise needed to carry on trade, and to reduce transport costs to the river posts for the government. He had consulted with Kerlérec, Macarty, Neyon de Villiers, Bobé, and many other experienced officials and traders, all of whom had agreed that exclusive trade grants were best. Moreover, exclusive trade grants had long been practiced in Canada. Foucault recited the various arguments that Dabbadie had marshalled, in order to counter the charges of the complaining merchants. Dabbadie,

[10]A. N. Colonies C13BI, n. p.
[11]A. N. Colonies B121, folios 670 et *verso.*

said Foucault, immediately after granting the monopolies had forwarded letters concerning them to the Minister, enclosing a copy of the "reglemens et autres pièces," and had asked for decisive orders whether to continue the policy or to abandon it. Foucault stated that the exclusive grantees had already shipped merchandise to Natchitoches and to Illinois and descended with the products, selling them in New Orleans or shipping them to France; all this had been done tranquilly.[12]

Meanwhile, however, as the Minister wished, the exclusive grants to Maxent and others were cancelled. Aubry, who had succeeded to the governorship upon the death of Dabbadie, hastened to write the Minister, on July 10, 1765, that he had done so, sending the orders and new regulations for trade to the interior post commandants. Aubry stated that as soon as he had read the Minister's letter of February 9 [sic] to Dabaddie he had assembled the merchants who had received such grants, and the complaining merchants as well, and informed them of the government's decision. He had written the commandants of Illinois, Natchitoches, and Opelusas, the only ones where exclusive trades were established, telling them that the Duc de Choiseul had abolished the monopolies. By the new rules, all "honest men can enjoy the liberty of commerce, as long as it will not be injurious to the tranquility of the savage nations, and to the advantage of the colony." The savages would be provided no liquor, and commandants would take care that all traders be men of recognized integrity, incapable of propagating bad feeling among the savages, and that the number of traders be reasonably limited.[13]

Although the grants were superseded, they led, among other things, to the founding of St. Louis. One of the grantees, Laclède,[14] had been entrusted with carrying out the grant which, according to Auguste Chouteau, had carried exclusive control of the fur trade of the Missouri and other tribes as far north as the river St. Peters[15]—perhaps all of the Indian nations west of the Mississippi. Laclède was assigned to select a site for a trading post. With an *armement* and accompanied by the young boy, Auguste Chouteau, Laclède ascended the river, leaving New Orleans on August 3,

[12]A. N. Colonies, C13A, vol. XLV, folios 128-136; same folios 200-204; and see also folios 137-142, and 143-151 *verso* to Choiseuil.

[13]A. N. Colonies, C13A, vol. XLV, folios 66-67. The Company itself formally dissolved on May 8, 1769, Laclède buying out the interests in Missouri from Maxent.

[14]When Laclède died, his brother, thinking that Laclède was a wealthy man who had made a fortune out of his exclusive trade of the Missouri, attempted to salvage his estate, since Laclède had not married. From this correspondence some information of the hearsay type has been derived concerning the exclusive grant. The correspondence includes, *"Mémoire* de Sieur Laclède," *Ms.* in part in B. N., n. a., vol. 9302, folios 269 et *verso*; and in full in A. E., Corr. Pol., Espagne, vol. 602, folios 226-227. Other material of this nature concerning Laclède's brother's attempt is in B. N., n. a., vol. 9302; A. E. Corr. Pol., Espagne, vols. 602, 603; and A. N. Colonies, C13C4; etc.

[15]Hunt's Minutes, [Manuscript in Missouri's Historical Society] I, 107, and Chouteau's "Journal" printed in *Missouri Historical Society Collections,* III, 349-350.

1763. The site selected was that of St. Louis, just below the junction of the Mississippi and Missouri rivers—the foundation of the settlement being made on February 15, 1764. To this post, after the formal cession of Fort de Chartres to the English, St. Ange moved and assumed control. Significantly, many Frenchmen followed him to St. Louis, which immediately sprang up as a commercial center for the fur trade of the Missouri and Upper Mississippi valleys.[16]

Ulloa was sent by Spain to take possession of the valley but actually did not assume full control; rather he chose to allow Aubry to continue in charge of administration. Shortly after Ulloa's arrival in the valley, the acting French governor accompanied him on an inspection tour of the posts. They visited the Iberville post of the English and others in the lower valley but did not ascend to the Arkansas or to the Illinois country. Aubry, however, considered the posts of Arkansas and Illinois as very important. He looked upon Illinois, then consisting of St. Geneviève and the newly founded St. Louis, as one of the keys to Louisiana and Mexico—the only one to oppose the English. He urged a strong establishment with Spanish troops to stop the English from ascending the Missouri.[17]

That St. Louis and the Missouri were important had by that time become evident. The sagacity of Laclède, who was the principal merchant-trader, the mild, paternal rule of St. Ange, the French aptitude for trade, and the good location of the town made it the important *entrepôt* that it was, even at that early date. That prosperity must have come to St. Louis immediately is amply illustrated in the correspondence of St. Ange, the remarks of Gordon, Pittman, and other contemporaries, and Dabbadie's journal, and by the many *batteaux* and pirogues heavily laden with merchandise which ascended the Mississippi from New Orleans. Laclède apparently confined his trade to the Missouri river, allowing private traders to go elsewhere. Indeed, it is my opinion that Laclède furnished the merchandise for a number of these traders.[18]

---

[16]A. P. Nasatir, "Trade and Diplomacy in the Spanish Illinois," *Ms.* unpublished Ph.D. dissertation (University of California) gives this story in full. See, A. P. Nasatir, "Ducharme's Invasion of Missouri," *Missouri Historical Review,* XXIV (1929), 3-25; 238-260; 420-439; also C. E. Carter, *Great Britain and the Illinois Country* (Washington, 1910) ; and C. W. Alvord and C. E. Carter, *Critical Period* (Springfield, 1915) ; *New Régime* (Springfield, 1916) ; and *Trade and Politics* (Springfield, 1921) for some published documents.

[17]Aubry to Minister, New Orleans, May 28, 1766 [wrongly dated or listed as March in Surrey, *Calendar*], A. N. Colonies; F³ vol. 25, folios 259-262; but see also Aubry's letter of March 28, in *Ibid.,* folios 249-258 *verso.* International rivalry was an important matter, for Spain and France were ever fearful of British traders intruding into their territory. Aubry and others urged the establishment of a stong establishment and troops in Upper Louisiana in part to stop the English from ascending the Missouri which excited the curiosity and cupidity of the English.

[18]Many accounts attest to these facts. See particularly Alvord and Carter, *Critical Period, New Régime,* and *Trade and Politics;* Dabbadie's "Journal" is only in small part printed in Alvord and Carter (*Critical Period* 162-204). Some parts are also printed in Marc de Villiers du Terrage, *Les Dernières Années de La Louisiane Fran-*

Out of St. Louis in the ensuing years trade and explorations of the Missouri region were carried on. The post had hardly been founded when the Indians began to come. Later, St. Ange held councils with those Indians, chiefly the Missouris and Osages. Aubry, on January 27, 1766, wrote the Minister that the Missouri was in general unknown, and that it would be of interest to make discoveries there, both for geography and commerce, and for beautiful, rare peltries.[19] Fear of British incursions gave further incentive for the settlement and fortification of the region. In fact, as early as 1765, the British had contemplated a fort of their own at the mouth of the Missouri to stop French and Spanish incursions to the east of the Mississippi.[20]

To check the British and keep the Indians west of the Mississippi loyal to Spain, Captain Don Francisco Ríu was sent by Ulloa on March 14, 1767, with lengthy instructions to construct two forts at the mouth of the Missouri and to plant a colony of Acadians. Supposedly St. Ange would be left in charge of St. Louis and Ríu be in charge of the area beyond the Missouri. Ríu was entrusted with the relations with the Indians and the regulation of trade. As commandant he was permitted to choose one trader with whom to trade for himself, but the trade was open to all under the proviso that each trader must obtain from the commandant a license, to be renewed annually. Thus the traders, forced to descend each year, would observe the regulations. Ríu always consulted with St. Ange, who was more experienced with Indian relations. Presents were to be distributed under St. Ange's direction. If the Indians were not friendly, the presents and also traders would be withheld from them. The fort was constructed at the mouth of the Missouri. As it turned out, Ríu was not a competent person; Piernas was sent to investigate, and dissensions broke out. The merchants of St. Louis demonstrated against Ríu's regulation and administration of trade licenses.[21]

From such trade licenses and the distribution of presents, the advance up the Missouri under the Spanish régime may best be illustrated.

çaise (Paris, 1903), 177-200 passim. It is in A. N. Colonies C13A, vol. XLIII, folios 249-282. Most of the remaining St. Ange and other correspondence is still in manuscript form. Gordon's "Journal" is printed in Alvord and Carter, New Régime, 290-311, and elsewhere; Pittman, Present State of European Settlements on the Mississippi, (ed. by F. W. Hodder, Cleveland, 1906).

[19]A. N. Colonies, C13A, vol. XLVI, folios 21-28 verso and printed in Alvord and Carter, New Régime, 138-149.

[20]Alvord and Carter, New Régime, 71, 231.

[21]By far the best account of Ríu is that by my former student, Miss Jacqueline Trenfel, "Spanish Occupation of the Upper Mississippi Valley, 1765-1770" (Ms.—unpublished M. A. dissertation). A few documents are printed in L. Houck, Spanish Régime in Missouri (2 volumes, Chicago, 1909). I have the full correspondence of St. Ange and Ríu in my collection of manuscripts. They were used by Miss Trenfel.

Ríu licensed traders for the Panis, Pani-Topage, Pani-Maha, Kansas, Utes (Otoes), Big and Little Osages, and Osages.[22]

The French had traded with all these tribes of the Missouri; hence the Spaniards had thus far not gone beyond the limits of their predecessors. One reason for this was suggested by St. Ange, who wrote, on April 18, 1768, that "it was not my thought to wish to attract new nations. I would rather never see them."[23] St. Ange's difficulties with regard to expenses and management of Indians and perhaps also his lack of authority (for he told the traders to apply the following year for licenses to New Orleans) caused this viewpoint. Ríu wrote to Ulloa, June 25, 1768, of developments regarding the Pani, Oto, Kansas, Petizó, and Missouri Indians, "who are the only nations with whom there is trade on the Missouri." Trade with these tribes, added to commerce with the Big Osages, constituted the extent of Spanish occupation. Ríu detailed the same complaints that St. Ange had made, and, although he did not specifically say so, apparently agreed that he too did not want to attract any new nations; this attitude alone would for the time being stop further advances up the Missouri.[24]

On May 2, 1768, Ríu forwarded the list of Indian nations whom it was customary to regale. His list adds no new ones; it includes the Petizó, Missouris, Kansas, Osages, and the Iowas, Sauteux, Foxes, Mascouten, Sioux, and others of the Upper Mississippi, and many from east of the Mississippi.[25] Chamard, on July 28, 1768, petitioned for permission to ascend with goods to the posts of the Big Osages and Otos "at the extremity of the Missouri."[26]

Maxent, on May 8, 1769, made a plea for a trading license, which act, incidentally, clears up a matter of vital importance concerning his former exclusive grant. It is herewith given in full:

To M. Don Antonio de Ulloa — Governor and Captain-General
of the Colony of Louisiana. . . . . . .

Gilbert Antoine Maxent, *merchant in this city has the honor of exposing to you, Monsieur, that the deceased M. Dabbadie, heretofore Commandant-general in this colony, shortly after his arrival here, had proposed and offered him the commerce and general and exclusive trade with the savages in the entire district of Illinois remaining to France after the last peace treaty, both in view of diminishing the expenses of the King in*

[22]Statement of Ríu, St. Louis, June 17, 1768, P. de C., leg. 109. Hubert's license to trade with the Little Osages was granted in New Orleans, August 4, 1768. Missouri Historical Society, *Mss.*, Bundle: Fur Trade.
[23]Précis of letters from Illinois written to Ulloa and Aubry by St. Ange, P. de C. leg. 2357.
[24]Ríu to Ulloa, June 25, 1768. P. de C. leg. 109. I have a number of the specific trade licenses granted.
[25]P. de C. leg. 109.
[26]P. de C. leg. 188A.

this district by charging the trade a part of it and by preventing access to these nations of an infinite number of vagabond traders and vagrants who would have been able to spoil the spirit of the savages and to turn them away from the union and tranquility which ought to result from peace. That the said Maxent for the greatest good of the service would have accepted the offers of the said Sr. Dabbadie under the conditions judged à propos to prescribe for him, and would in consequence have sent to Europe for the effects and merchandise proper for this trade for very considerable sums which he would then have had transported at great expense, as well as the effects of the King to the village of Fort des Chartres; *or with the certainty of the stability of this commerce he would have founded a very expensive establishment which would have been turned into pure loss for him.*

That the English having since taken possession of the said village of Fort des Chartres, *he would have been obliged to evacuate and abandon the said establishment to transplant himself to the possessions of France where he would have formed a considerable establishment at the place named* St. Louis, *which has since been the refuge of all the French who did not wish to remain under the domination of the English, and which has been the source of a village at present very numerous, and which is today the capital of the Spanish possessions in the said district, in which place he has pushed the commerce and the rivalry to the point that it sends down today annually to this capital twelve to fifteen hundred* paquets *of all sorts of skins, whereas heretofore it did not ordinarily send down one hundred to one hundred fifty* paquets.

That the exclusion of this trade was at last abolished because of the lack of support, by the liberty of commerce rendered general after the death of M. Dabbadie, and by the cession to Spain. And seeing himself consequently not only frustrated of advantages [profit] that he counted upon gaining by the exclusion, but even [finds himself] in great arrears, both because of the expenditures of an establishment which today has become useless to him as well as on account of the expenses to which he is liable in order to satisfy the conditions which had been imposed upon him by the said Dabbadie to the advantage of the King and of which he had not had the advantage of collecting the fruits, although he had faithfully fulfilled [all conditions]. That finding himself besides extremely wronged by the loss of a trial in which he was indispensably induced by the necessity of maintaining the privileges which had been accorded to him by a Commandant invested with the authority of the King and which [conditions] nevertheless the council did not judge it à propos to consider.

Exposing himself, acting both in his name and in that of Sr. Laclède Liguest, *his associate in the trading affairs of Illinois, he has recourse to your equity,* Monsieur, *in order that it may please you to accord him in the form of an indemnity for all the above damages and to recompense him for the good which resulted from his establishment in this district of Illinois, the trade of the Big Osages and that of the Otoes for the time that you judge convenient, submitting to all the orders and rules which it will please you to prescribe for this trade and to send there and give the* paroles *that it will please you to make for the good of the service; having the honor of observing to you, besides, that as this trade, if it takes place, will necessarily constitute new expenses of establishments, he begs you in this consideration to accord it to him for a term long enough so that he may indemnify himself for his expenses to find there the fruits of his labors, engaging himself to have the business carried on by men of good manners and conduct and whose proceedings and* paroles *will always tend towards the greatest good for the colony.*

Maxent [rubric]

Register of merchandise to send among the above mentioned nations for the year 1769[27]

40 pieces Limbourg cloth	*12 gross woodcutter's*
12 pieces flannel	*knives*
2,000 ls. [livres] *powder*	*6 gross French knives*
4,000 ls. bullets	*10,000 gun flints*
600 blankets	*150 gingham shirts*
100 guns	*100 ells printed calicoe*
500 ls. kettles	*30 pieces lace*
100 ls. brass wire	*150 picks*
	150 hatchets
	100 clubs
	150 ls. glass beads
	100 ls. vermillion
	10 ls. verdigris
	10 gross batfeu [sic]
	10 gross awls
	10 gross wad hooks
	10 gross bells

We the undersigned Maxent and Laclède in the presence of Mr. Delassize witness, forming the present private contract while awaiting its passage before M. Garic, notary, are agreed by our free will to come to terms and terminate finally short [and quickly] all business between ourselves concerning the commerce and trade with the Illinois and of which we have rendered to each other the accounts which we have allowed ourselves at one time or another.

---

[27]P. de C. leg. 188**A**.

In consequence of this we release ourselves from any responsibility of all transactions made heretofore, between ourselves and for the account of the said trade with the understanding that those which seem to have been paid by Mr. Maxent and carried to the debit of the account which I furnished on the date of fifteenth of April, last, on which account we have agreed, and which would be charged against me if these parties did not liquidate. Just as Mr. Laclède requires me also to pay the debts charged to the debit of the account I furnished to Sieur *Maxent dated May 31, 1768, just as the private [proven?] debts are charged to it. By means of which, I, Laclède, find myself in the same situation as the said* Sieur *Maxent possessed of the three-fourth interest which he had in the said trade, and I assume the interest which he had in the said trade, and I assume all aforesaid liabilities, which remain to be settled.*

On which we have agreed in good faith, and this by means of the price of 80,000 livres in silver having actual value in France which I shall pay to the said Sieur *Maxent or to his brother in four quarterly payments payable at New Orleans, and for which I shall give him my notes;—to wit: five notes payable in June, 1771, each one for 4000 livres, one note payable in June, 1772, for 20,000 livres, another payable June, 1773, for 20,000 livres, and another payable in June, 1774, for 20,000 livres. And by virtue of this arrangement I shall be undisturbed and sole possessor of the effects proceeding from and belonging to the said trade which consists in various merchandise which we have appraised at* ....22,000.

In actual debts carried for 10574-11-8
In paper 12230-10- in bills of exchange 62957-10-10

In furs which we have appraised at 25,000
In twelve slaves, some large, some small......................14,000
In horned cattle and horses 4,000
In pigs 1,000
In ploughs, implements for farm and blacksmith 1,000
In furniture, kitchen utensils and silverware 1,000
In houses, mill, barns, grounds, and generally everything belonging
  to the said trade 12,000

£80,000

To which we have agreed in good faith—mutually annulling all bills contracted at one time or another in debts antedating the present.

Done at New Orleans, May 8, 1769.

Delassize [rubric]   *Maxent [rubric]*
                                        Laclède Liquet [rubric][28]

[28]New Orleans, Archives 92826, copy in Missouri Historical Society, Laclède Collection.

On orders of O'Reilly, who took over the affairs of Louisiana, St. Ange, Ríu, and Piernas made lists and/or reports of the Indian nations of the Missouri. St. Ange reported May 2, 1769, Ríu on October 29, and Piernas on October 31. St. Ange listed the Missouris, Little and Big Osages, Kansas, Otoes, and Panimaha.[29] Ríu reported on the known geography. At the mouth of the Missouri on the west side of the Mississippi stood Fort San Carlos, and on the north bank of the Missouri was a block house. Eighty leagues up the Missouri was the Big Osage river, and seventy leagues up the Big Osage lived the Big Osages. Up the Missouri, one hundred and seventy leagues above the Big Osage, lived the Panimaha tribe, the most distant one to which the traders penetrated. Overland from the Panimaha at six to eight days journey were the Ayetan, and in another six to eight days one could reach New Mexico. The Kansas country yielded abundant beaver. Piernas' report was a brief resumé of his experiences in the Missouri area, including a much fuller geographical description than Ríu's. Both Ríu and Piernas submitted St. Ange's list of Indian nations.[30]

Piernas' report, dated January 4, 1771, of bread and maize distributed to the Indians who came to St. Louis to receive their annual presents lists no additional tribes from the Missouri area.[31] In fact, on June 12, 1771, Piernas wrote that, if retreat in the face of war with the English necessitated the use of the route of the Missouri, it would be eighty-five leagues from St. Louis to the nearest Missouri Indians and Little Osage, whose villages were not always fixed, and who were then under the influence of English presents. The other nations of the Missouri were one hundred eighty-five to two hundred leagues farther away.[32]

However, despite official frowning upon traders who ascended to more distant nations than the Panimaha, we may suspect that such more distant trading was actually carried on. Piernas reported on July 23, 1771, that a trader, operating against his strict injunction, had sent to him two children from the Patuca (Padouca or Comanche?) Indians, "who are found in the distant interior of Missouri."[33] Trade was good, and profits swelled.[34]

Our next complete report of the Spanish advance up the Missouri is provided by Cruzat, who in 1777 was ordered by Bernardo de Gálvez to send a list of traders to whom licenses had been given and an account of

---

[29]St. Ange's report is dated May 2, 1769, P. de C. leg. 2357, and is printed in Houck, *Spanish Régime*, I, 44-45, and also in *Wisconsin Historical Collections*, XVIII, 299-300.

[30]Original reports of Ríu and Piernas are in P. de C. leg. 2357, and are printed in Houck, *Spanish Régime*, I, 62-75. O'Reilly's list, giving tribes residing west of the river only, lists those which are contained in St. Ange's report for that district, P. de C. leg. 2351.

[31]P. de C. leg. 219.

[32]Piernas to Unzaga, St. Louis, June 12, 1771, P. de C. leg. 81.

[33]*Idem* to *Idem*, July 23, 1771, P. de C. leg. 81.

[34]*Idem* to *Idem*, July 2, 1774, P. de C. leg. 81.

the Indian nations. Again no new tribes are listed—just the Big and Little Osages, Missouris, Kansas, (Pawnee) Republic, Mahas, Panis, and Otoes. The Spaniards, we see, had gone little beyond the Platte River, or perhaps to the Niobrara, the limit of the French advance. Cruzat noted that the Otoes lived some two hundred and twenty leagues from St. Louis, about fifteen leagues from the Missouri River up the Platte, and that the Pawnees were fifteen leagues from the Otoes on a small stream branching off the Platte, and finally that the Mahas were two hundred and eighty leagues from St. Louis, about thirty-five or forty leagues overland from the Panis, on a tributary of the Missouri, about sixty leagues from the mouth of the Platte (Niobrara?)[35]

When De Leyba succeeded Cruzat as Lieutenant-Governor in 1778, the old familiar quarrel over exclusive or free trade arose. It was alleged that De Leyba granted licenses to those "who could afford to pay," that he granted all of the posts of the Missouri to MM. Chouteau, Labbadie, and Cerré, "pour une somme considérable."[36] No new tribes were added during De Leyba's tenure.[37] The war already in progress (the American Revolution) probably caused more Indian visits to St. Louis and consequently caused a demand for increased rations, which Gálvez did not wish to raise. It was becoming more difficult to ship materials to St. Louis.[38]

Little or no progress was to be expected from the Spaniards during the war years since they were interested in defending the Mississippi. The war brought no real results to the Upper Mississippi-Missouri valleys except the transfer of the territory east of the Mississippi from the English to the Americans. This was by no means reassuring to the Spaniards, who regarded the Americans as just as ambitious, restless, and threatening to their dominions as the English. During the war the Spaniards in St. Louis defensively confined their activities on the Missouri to keeping the loyalty of their Indians and preventing Indian outbreaks or treachery. Thus the Spanish Illinois country suffered economically, and in effect the English traders enjoyed a monopoly of trade on both sides of the Mississippi and began to penetrate to the Missouri from areas further north than St.

[35]Cruzat to Gálvez, December 6, 1777, enclosing reports dated November 15, 1777, and *Idem* to *Idem*, November 28, 1777, enclosing report dated November 1, 1777. P. de C. leg. 2358 and printed in Houck, *Spanish Régime*, I, 138-148; part of report on Indian nations is also printed in *Wisconsin Historical Collections*, XVIII, 358-368. A slightly differently worded report on Indian nations is in the Missouri Historical Society. Inaccurate copies are in the Bancroft Library. Panimaha, Panimacha, Pani-Mahans, Pawnee Loup, etc. This tribe was one of the four forming the Pawnee confederacy. Their traditional home is the Loup river in Nebraska. Bolton, *De Mézières*, I, 202 n.

[36]J. B. Martigny to *Monsieur* [Gálvez?], St. Louis, October 30, 1779, P. de C. leg. 113. Martigny had been denied a trading permit by De Leyba.

[37]De Leyba to Governor-General, St. Louis, July 21, 1778, P. de C. leg. 2358.

[38]*Idem* to *Idem*, July 21, 1778, and draft of reply of Gálvez attached thereto dated September 2, 1778. P. de C. leg. 1. See also A. P. Nasatir, *Anglo-Spanish Frontier in the Illinois Country during the American Revolution*, [Reprint from *Illinois State Historical Society Journal*, XXI (1928), 291-358] pp. 13-14.

Louis. Some Spanish traders, however, were sent to the Missouri and in 1780 reaped a good profit.[89]

In 1784, as names of Indian tribes and licenses to trade on the Missouri again begin to appear in the documents, we hear again only the names of the familiar tribes. Maxent asked that the trade of the Mahas and Panis be given to Cerré, the Otoes to LeConte, the Kansas and Missouris to the Sarpy brothers, and the Little Osages to Sanguinet. The governor [Miró] recommended that the post of the Pawnees be given to Francisco Marmillon, and in case of his death, to his companion, Claudio Mercier. Picoté de Bellêtre asked for the Kansas and Mahas in 1785. Cruzat wished to grant the trade of the Pawnees to Antonio de Oro, but as it had been granted at New Orleans to Mercier, Cruzat could allow de Oro only the remaining small trade of the Panimaha.[40] Chauvin reminded the officials of his request for trade privileges with the Oto and Panis nations, for in 1785 the prospects of the Missouri trade seemed bright.[41] The governor wrote DeVolsay in 1786 that he had recommended to Cruzat that DeVolsay be given the trade of the Kansas and Mahas, and since they were not then available, the trade of the Des Moines river. DeVolsay replied that the governor was misinformed, for the Kansas trade was reserved for Chouteau and the Mahas for Lajoye. Even the Des Moines trade belonged to Chouteau, but he had passed it on to Cerré.[42]

Cruzat was warned by Governor Miró in 1785 to be especially vigilant to take efficacious steps that no Americans introduced themselves into the Missouri to trade. Miró urged Cruzat to follow the earlier successful example of Piernas in keeping the English traders out of Spanish dominions.[43]

A document sent to the Comptroller-general from the French vice-consul, Toscan, at Portsmouth, December 31, 1787, gave the names of the different savages of North America and their population of warriors. It lists the Ajonis to the north of the Missouri, the Paducas to the west of the Mississippi, the Panis Blancs, the Panis Picotés, the Kansas, the Osages and Big Osages to the south of the Missouri, and the Missouri on the Missouri.[44]

[89]Draft to Cruzat, New Orleans, January 12, 1780, P. de C. leg. 117B. This story is in Nasatir, *op. cit.*

[40]Draft to Cruzat, March 11, 1784, P. de C. leg. 117B; Cerré to *Monsieur*, July 26, 1794, P. de C. leg. 203; Oro to Miró, Ste. Geneviève, July 26, 1784, P. de C. leg. 117A. Draft to Cruzat, New Orleans, March 8, 1785, P. de C. leg. 117A; draft to Bellêtre, New Orleans, March 8, 1785, P. de C. leg. 205; Cruzat to Oro, St. Louis, July 4, 1785, P. de C. leg. 177B; Oro to Miró, Ste. Geneviève, August 6, 1785, P. de C. leg. 11; draft of reply, New Orleans, September 13, 1785, P. de C. leg. 3.

[41]Cruzat to Miró, St. Louis, November 26, 1785, P. de C. leg. 11; Chauvin to [?], St. Louis, December 8, 1785, P. de C. leg. 2360.

[42]DeVolsay to Governor, St. Louis, July 18, 1786, P. de C. leg. 2370.

[43]Miró to Cruzat, New Orleans, March 8, 1785, P. de C. leg. 3; draft in P. de C. leg. 117A.

[44]A. E., Corr. Pol., États-Unis, Supplément, vol. XVIII, folios 16-32, especially folios 25-26.

A few other documents indicate the situation at that time. According to Vallière, who commanded the Arkansas post, the Pawnees were well served by the Spaniards. Pérez (at St. Louis) reported that trade was good on the Missouri.[45] Pérez had to admit, however, that the English traders had for a long time been using the savages of the Mississippi as go-betweens in trading with the Missouri in beaver and otter, the richest furs in the country. To ward off this practise, Pérez urged that more merchandise and presents be sent to the Missouri tribes, and later on, since he did not receive what he had requested, he suggested building forts at the Des Moines and St. Peter's rivers.[46]

The geography of the Missouri valley was described in an account of Spanish Louisiana, drawn up on December 12, 1785, by Governor Esteban Miró in response to a request from the *comandante-general* of the *Provincias Internas,* Felipe de Neve. This document, which opens our collection relating to the Missouri, was as full as available information could make it; it is hardly an exaggeration to say that the sum total of geographical knowledge of the Missouri valley and westward was no more than the French revealed in 1758. No one, said Miró, had been higher up on the Missouri than the Sioux,[47] about two hundred leagues from the mouth of the Missouri (yet later he mentioned the Arikaras). Miró speculated to give a picture which, somewhat over-simplified, would be the Missouri-Platte circling south-westward into the mountains and reaching near to the sources of the Río Bravo. As he unfolded his geography, mentioning various channels and rivers entering the Missouri, he was fairly accurate, except when speaking of streams flowing into other rivers. He was able to speak of rivers north of the Platte, namely the Sioux and Niobrara, but when he left the Sioux, he again ran into the realm of speculation. He rightly forecast that intruders would enter Spanish territory by the Des Moines river and the Iowa Indians. The Otoes, he said, were not obliged to trade with St. Louis because of their close friendship with the Iowas, and Miró feared that Americans might penetrate Spanish territory as far as New Mexico and also that they had already opened trade with the Iowas and Otoes. In discussing the Indian nations, Miró based his account on information supplied to him from St. Louis. He mentioned the Arikaras but gave no further knowledge than traders had given his lieutenant-gov-

---

[45]Vallière to Miró, no. 34, Arkansas, December 31, 1787, P. de C. leg. 13; Pérez to Miró, no. 11, St. Louis, April 18, 1788. Bancroft Library.
[46]Pérez to Miró, no. 56, and no. 58, St. Louis, November 19 and December 1, 1788, P. de C. leg. 2361. See A. P. Nasatir, "Anglo-Spanish Frontier on the Upper Mississippi," *Iowa Journal of History and Politics,* XXIX (1931), 168-170.
[47]The Spaniards had had traders trading with the Sioux but heretofore had considered the Sioux as belonging to the Mississippi Indians.

ernor several years before. He undoubtedly gave a true picture as far as the Niobrara river, which was the practical limit of true geographical knowledge in the French period.[48]

---

[48][Miró] to Rengle, December 12, 1785, printed in A. P. Nasatir "A Spanish Account of Louisiana, 1785," *Missouri Historical Review*, XXIV (1930), 523-536.

PART III

PRECURSORS OF LEWIS AND CLARK

1.

THE SPANIARDS ASCEND THE MISSOURI

As we have seen in the previous discussion, progress up the Missouri River during the first twenty years of Spanish rule was very slow. The Spaniards had busied themselves developing their trade with the neighboring tribes and fortifying their frontier against the encroachments of the British. They were doing their utmost to prevent the British, who were particularly active in the Iowa-Minnesota country, from entering Spanish territory and from engaging in trade with the Indians. However, Spain was to be forced to ascend the river, but she waited a while before undertaking that task. This is a little known chapter in her long story of defensive expansion.[1]

Meanwhile the British were steadily penetrating westward. By the Treaty of Paris, 1763, France was obliged to cede her territory east of the Mississippi and north of the Gulf of Mexico to Great Britain. The latter was temporarily prevented from taking possession of the Illinois country by the great Indian uprising led by Pontiac. When Great Britain succeeded in occupying the territory in 1765, her traders at once became active. They complained that the Spaniards, in conjunction with the old

---

[1] Part III of this introduction is taken from A. P. Nasatir, "Anglo-Spanish Rivalry on the Upper Missouri," which was published in the *Mississippi Valley Historical Review*, December, 1929—March, 1930 (XVI, 359-382; 507-530). I have made but very few revisions to this article. Many of the documents referred to in the notes of the original publication are printed in the present volumes but I have not here referred to those documents, in order to give a continuous and footnoted account of the entire story in this *Introduction*, comparable to parts I and II, documents for which parts are not included in these volumes. A number of documents not printed here are referred to in these notes.

French *habitants* and traders, were reaping the profits of the Indian trade which rightfully belonged to British subjects; they in turn seldom hesitated to cause irritation and loss in trade to the Spaniards and steadily and increasingly infiltrated the country beyond the Mississippi River—the international boundary line. Hence, we hear the Spaniards complaining to their government of the unlawful and illegal activities on the part of the British and the consequent dwindling of the profits which rightfully belonged to subjects of His Catholic Majesty. These British intrusions spurred the Spaniards to action and they increased the number of both posts and traders in the lower Missouri and the upper Mississippi regions.

The Revolutionary War did not directly affect the Missouri Valley to any marked degree, but indirectly it was responsible for the progress of the Spaniards up the Missouri. The close of that war had left the upper Mississippi Valley virtually an economic monopoly in the hands of the British traders.[2] Little, if any, effective effort to overthrow the British monopoly was put forth either by Cruzat or by Pérez during their respective terms as lieutenant-governor of the Spanish Illinois. True, they had written many letters proposing and urging the erection of forts at strategic points along the Mississippi to check the aggressions of British traders upon the territory of Spain. Particularly had they stressed the importance of erecting forts at the mouths of the Des Moines and St. Peter's (Minnesota) Rivers. But the Spanish Government, occupied at the same time with intrigues in the lower Mississippi Valley, preferred, for reasons of economy, to ignore all such propositions until the danger was more imminent.[3] And neither Cruzat nor Pérez had the resources necessary for the job without special help from the government.

The British traders from the posts of Michilimackinac and Prairie du Chien were not alone in reaching the Missouri. Other British subjects from the north began to follow the trail first blazed by the La Vérendryes in 1738-39. Traders from the posts of the Hudson's Bay Company and the North West Company began to turn southward in their own fierce struggle to extend commercial relations. They succeeded in developing a lucrative trade with the Mandan Indians, whose home was located near the "Big Bend" in the Missouri River. Again the Spaniards were stirred to action by this new threat. Not only was the Indian trade which should have been in their hands taken away from them, but a direct and distinct threat to Spanish control of the rich territory of New Mexico and Mexico loomed on the horizon. No wonder the Spaniards were frightened.

---

[2]A. P. Nasatir, "The Anglo-Spanish Frontier in the Illinois Country during the American Revolution, 1779-1783," *Illinois State Historical Society Journal*, XXI (1928), 291 ff.

[3]For events and intrigues in the lower Mississippi Valley, see S. F. Bemis, *Pinckney's Treaty* (Baltimore, 1926), and A. P. Whitaker, *The Spanish-American Frontier: 1783-1795* (Boston, 1927), *passim*. See, also, the present writer's "Indian Trade and Diplomacy in the Spanish Illinois" ms. in Library of the University of California.

From yet another angle came threats, if not actual encroachments, upon Spanish territory. The Russians were descending the Pacific Coast from the north. The British had been active for some time in the waters of the North Pacific and on the northwest coast of North America, while the Americans were beginning to come into that region in increasing numbers. The resulting "Swirl of the Nations" ended in the famous Nootka Sound episode, as a result of which Spain was forced to surrender her exclusive claim to the territory lying along the western shore of North America above the forty-second parallel. To protect herself against these two lines of approach—the Russians from the north and the British moving westward and then southward—Spain was forced to ascend the Missouri, in the hope of finding a direct passageway to the Western Sea. The Russians continued to push southward, and fear of their encroachment upon California, now a valued Spanish possession, was expressed by many Spanish officials. In the rushing advance of the Canadian fur traders to the west and to the south, Spain soon perceived a direct threat not only against her New Mexican but also against her Pacific possessions. Thus the best possible means of protecting the Spanish possessions was to establish a line of posts along the Mississippi highway from St. Louis to the sea. By doing this, fortified Upper Louisiana, still called by the Spaniards the "(Spanish) Illinois country," could serve as a barrier to the advance of both the British and the Russians, and at the same time hem in defensively and connect all the possessions of Spain in North America. Thus the northern (northeastern) frontier of New Spain, the "Spanish Borderland," would be safe. So dreamed many a Spanish subject of His Catholic Majesty in the last decade of the eighteenth century. But in order to carry out this scheme it was necessary to know much about the Missouri River.[4]

Even at so late a date as 1785, as has been noted previously, Spain had very little accurate knowledge concerning the Missouri River above the Platte. At the close of that year, information was dispatched to the Commandant of the *Provincias Internas,* Antonio Rengel, probably by Miró, which summarized the knowledge then current of the geography of the Missouri Valley.[5] According to this report, the source of the Missouri River was in the new kingdom of Mexico. "In all the time in which trad-

---

[4]See, especially, *Minuta del Acta del Consejo de Estado,* May 27, 1796, *Archivo Histórico Nacional (Madrid), Sección, Papeles de Estado* (hereinafter cited as A. H. N., Est.). A copy of this important document was procured for the writer by Dr. S. F. Bemis while he was in Madrid. It is printed in A. P. Nasatir and E. Liljegren, "Materials Relating to the History of the Mississippi Valley from the Minutes of the Spanish Supreme Councils of State 1787-1797," *Louisiana Historical Quarterly,* XXI (1938), 3-73. Trudeau to Carondelet, St. Louis, August 30, 1795, in *Archivo General de Indias* (Seville), *Sección, Papeles de Cuba* (hereinafter cited as P. de C. leg.) 211.
[5]Dated, New Orleans, Dec. 12, 1785, ms. in the Bancroft Library (hereinafter referred to as B. L.)—printed in Nasatir, "A Spanish Account of Missouri," in *Missouri Historical Review,* XXIV (1930), 523-536.

ing has been going on along the Missouri no one has ever gone higher up than the river of the Sius, about two hundred leagues from the mouth of the former." Later reports, however, said that the Arikara Indians had asserted that two hundred leagues beyond their villages were mountains. In fact, the Missouri was thought to cut the Rocky Mountains a little to the north of the source of the Río Bravo. The report discloses that the geographical knowledge of this region had made little, if any, advance beyond what was known in 1769, or, indeed, in 1758. One reason for this condition was the fact that the Spaniards had been concentrating their efforts upon the blocking of the passageways into their territory along the west bank of the Mississippi River. Officials of Spanish Louisiana were unceasingly demanding that forts be established at the mouths of the Des Moines and Minnesota rivers, the chief points of entry into Spanish territory used by the ever-increasing number of British traders. A short time later the Spaniards began to patrol the Mississippi in an endeavor to stop such inroads.

Meanwhile Pérez, in 1788, reported to his governor-general that the English and Americans for a long time had been looking for the means to penetrate the Missouri. Outbreak of war would result in the Missouri falling into their hands, for the Missouri had no means of successfully opposing them. If that should transpire it would inaugurate an epoch of vagabonds who would go into the province of New Mexico and pillage the mines. Pérez was working hard to maintain the friendship of the Indians of the Mississippi to prevent such a catastrophe; and for that purpose he had asked for more presents and, as we have pointed out above, asked for strategically located fortifications.[6]

Gardoqui from Philadelphia also reported to Floridablanca. He spoke of many enthusiastic Englishmen who had been in territory belonging to His Catholic Majesty. One of the Englishmen who visited the upper Mississippi and Missouri as far as the mountains had met Indians who had told him of a river flowing westward into the Pacific Ocean. He also had made a map. Gardoqui also heard of Lieutenant Lord Edward Fitzgerald, who was planning to cross the wilderness and the Indian nations as far as Mexico. Gardoqui pleaded for the Spaniards to reconnoitre the sources of the rivers flowing to the west as far as the Pacific Ocean.[7]

In most of the correspondence and speeches the Illinois was described as the key to Mexico; and as such its defense would make not only advisable but imperative the building of forts on the Missouri, Des Moines, and

---

[6]Pérez to Miró, no. 58, St. Louis, December 1, 1788, P. de C. leg. 2361; and Miró to Pérez in reply, New Orleans, January 14, 1789, P. de C. leg. 6. This is just an example of many other such letters. See Nasatir, "Anglo-Spanish Frontier on the Upper Mississippi 1786-1796," *Iowa Journal of History and Politics*, XXIX (1931), 155-232.

[7]Gardoqui to Floridablanca, *res.*, no. 25; A. H. N., Est., leg. 3893.

St. Peters rivers in order to keep the aggressive British out of the Spanish dominions. The English traders on those rivers were plentiful and had an abundance of merchandise which they could and did sell and exchange at cheaper prices than the Spaniards were able to do. Moreover, merchandise was available to them but not to the Spanish merchants.[8]

Paysá—the territory at the confluence of the Missouri and Mississippi rivers—was an area well known for colonial projects of settlement, land speculation, and as a jumping off place for entering the Spanish territory and the lucrative Indian trade.[9]

The project of ascending the Missouri was speculated upon and desired by foreigners. Lieutenant Armstrong and André Michaux, documents concerning whom are included in this volume, are well known examples.

During the Nootka Sound controversy period, when war seemed about to break out between Spain and England, the Spanish officials were fearful of a British invasion from Canada into the Spanish Illinois country with St. Louis as the principal objective. This also came at a time when Spain's relations with the recently installed government of the United States were far from cordial. Spain feared that the United States would grant permission to England to cross the newly organized Northwest Territory, in order to carry out her projected attack against Spain's Mississippi Valley possessions. That permission, although perhaps never officially asked for, was discussed in Washington's cabinet and this maneuver rather definitely aimed at forcing Spain's diplomatic hand in her relations with the United States. Hamilton favored such action if a sufficiently attractive *quid pro quo* could be obtained.[10]

For some years the Spaniards traded regularly with the Indians of the Missouri—at least as far as the Mahas. In 1791 Pérez reported that the

[8] *E. g.*, Dames of Illinois, *ca.* 1790, in P. de C. leg. 2362 and leg. 212B.

[9] *E. g., Report of the Canadian Archives, 1890,* 156-158 and many other documents among which the following may be cited: Mitchell to Hamilton, February 9, 1792, printed in *Mississippi Valley Historical Review,* VIII (1921), 264-266. Peyroux to Mr., Ste. Geneviève, April 9, 1790, P. de C. leg. 203. Carondelet to Aranda, no. 15 *res.,* New Orleans, October 1, 1792, A. H. N., Est., leg. 3398; Houck, *Spanish Régime in Missouri,* II, 144-147; *American Historical Association, Annual Report, 1896,* I, 1007; see also 1082-1084; Mitchell's autobiography in P. de C. leg. 208A; Viar and Jaudenes to Alcudia, Philadelphia, March 13, 1794, New York A. H. N., Est., leg. 3895 *bis.* See also Burt, *United States,* cited in note 10, below. On Mitchell see his autobiography, *op. cit.;* and letter of Las Casas no. 374 *res.,* Havana, February 21, 1794, *Archivo General de Simancas, Guerra Moderna,* leg. 7235. Santa Fé was reported as being but twenty-two days distant from St. Louis which frightened the Spanish officials for the safety of the Spanish Kingdom of New Mexico; especially because of the imminence of the Clark expedition, concerning which see Nasatir, "Anglo-Spanish Frontier on the Upper Mississippi, 1786-1796," *op. cit.;* Nasatir and Liljegren, "Materials Relating to the History of the Mississippi Valley," *op. cit.,* J. A. James, *George Rogers Clark* (Chicago, 1928), and E. R. Liljegren, "Jacobinism in Spanish Louisiana 1792-1797," in *Louisiana Historical Quarterly,* XXII (1939), 46-97.

[10] See in this connection S. F. Bemis, *Jay's Treaty* (New York, 1923), 72 ff.; W. R. Manning, "Nootka Sound Controversy," in *American Historical Association, Annual*

Otos had gone to trade with the English establishments on the Mississippi and that English traders from that area were going as far as the Missouri to trade with the Indians. Pérez suggested that forts be constructed at the mouths of the Des Moines and St. Peters rivers to prevent the introduction of the English smugglers—the objective of the English being to penetrate to the Kingdom of New Mexico.[11]

Pérez' successor, Zenon Trudeau, was instructed to maintain peace and good harmony with the English and the Americans, although the latter were at that time "more dangerous to the Spanish dominions than the English." Trudeau, however, was strictly enjoined not to permit traders, even English ones, in territory subject to His Catholic Majesty.[12]

When Arthur St. Clair was defeated by the Indians in 1791, they became so excited and so emboldened that some of them even threatened Spanish territory. They were made daring by support from the English whose avowed ambition was to obtain the commerce of the Missouri. The trouble the Spaniards had with the Osages even more complicated this intrigue, for depriving the Osages of goods and declaring war on them would throw them into the lap of the English.[13]

The British were looking with covetous eyes on the trade of the Upper Mississippi and Missouri river valleys. They reported to their government that up to that time the Spaniards had not attempted to stop English traders from any western river except the Missouri. The English openly coveted the trade west of the Mississippi.[14]

When Governor-General Carondelet assumed office in 1792, he decreed that the trade of the Missouri be thrown open to all subjects of His Catholic Majesty. This was directly opposed to the previous policy of

---

Report 1904, 281-478, see esp. Chapter X, pp. 412-424 *passim;* and Leavitt, "British Policy on the Canadian Frontier 1782-1792," in *Wisconsin Historical Society Proceedings*, LXIII (1915), 151-185. See also Diaries of George Washington (ed. W. C. Fitzpatrick, 1925), IV, 127; Robertson, *Louisiana under Spain*, I, 263, and W. C. Ford. *United States and Spain in 1790* (Brooklyn, 1890). Henry Cabot Lodge [ed.], *The Works of Alexander Hamilton* (12 volumes, New York, 1904), IV, 313-342. I am indebted to Dr. Gilbert L. Lycan of John B. Stetson University for this information. Dr. Lycan is now preparing a volume on Hamilton's foreign policy. For a discussion of this matter see A. L. Burt, *United States, Great Britain and British North America* (New Haven, 1940), 113-114, also 105.

[11]Pérez to Miró, no. 180, St. Louis, April 5, 1791, ms. in B. L. Las Casas to Carondelet, February 17, 1792, P. de C. leg. 2362, draft in *Ibid.*, leg. 1442; Houck, *Spanish Régime*, I, 332. See also Nasatir, "Anglo-Spanish Frontier on the Upper Mississippi 1786-1796," *op. cit.*

[12]Instructions dated March 28, 1792, P. de C. leg. 18; a slightly different version in *Ibid*, leg. 122A.

[13]Pérez to Miró, nos. 204 and 212, March 31, 1792, ms. in B. L. See Nasatir, "Anglo-Spanish Frontier on the Upper Mississippi 1786-1796," *op. cit.*

[14]Todd, McGill and Company, *et al.*, Montreal, April 23, 1792, enclosed in Hammond to Grenville, Philadelphia, July 3, 1792, Public Record Office, Foreign Office Papers F. O. 4/16; calendared in *Report of the Canadian Archives 1890*, State Papers, 325; *Michigan Pioneer and Historical Collections*, XXIV, 684; see also *Simcoe Papers*, I, 403. There are many letters concerning this matter in these last two cited works.

exclusive trade, but Trudeau, who dutifully published the decree, nevertheless exercised some control in the issuance of licenses to trade.[15]

In 1793 Trudeau reported at length concerning English trade. He carefully analyzed the conditions of trade, the superiority of English commerce over that of Spain, and listed the places where the canoes of the English traders from Michilimackinac wintered for the trade with the Indians. Therein he noted that traders entered Spanish territory from Prairie du Chien and from Rivière Pomme de Terre, via the St. Peters river—and that they went to the Upper Missouri, ten canoes going among the Sioux. Via the Des Moines river they penetrated to the Mahas and Pawnees, ten canoes going to the Sioux and seven to the Iowas. Via the Skunk river, three canoes went to the Sioux to winter. Via the Iowa river, four canoes went to the Iowas. Via the Grande Macoquité, two canoes went to the Sac and Fox tribes. In sum, thirty-six canoes traded with the Sac, Fox, Kickapoo, Loup, Shawnee, Mascutin, Puant, Illinois, Peorias, and other tribes.[16]

Upon being requested by Carondelet to acquire more information concerning the Mandans, Trudeau informed him on May 20, 1793, that he was unable to comply with his request—that he had called upon D'Eglise but the latter "is very simple and from a province in France of such a peculiar language [dialect] that nobody can understand him, and moreover he seems not to have made a single observation." But Trudeau hoped within a few days to see a well-informed Canadian *mozo* who had been visiting the Mandans, commissioned by the English Company. Trudeau also stated that some hunters from St. Louis had penetrated to the Mandans that year, and upon their return he hoped to be able to obtain and transmit more information about these Indians.[17] Thus we see a new period of activity in the Missouri River region undertaken from St. Louis and under Spanish jurisdiction.

Before long, however, there came further activity in this area. Undoubtedly British competition forced the Spaniards northward and westward, but it is also true that the increasing number of Spanish traders in St. Louis began to crowd the trade among the known tribes of Indians residing in the lower Missouri Valley. Hence, we find the Spanish traders beginning to spread out in search of new tribes with whom they might barter. In 1789, when Juan Munier discovered the Ponca tribe living on

---

[15]Proclamation of Trudeau, St. Louis, July 25, 1792, enclosed in Trudeau to Carondelet, no. 4, St. Louis, July 25, 1792, P. de. C. leg. 25A.
[16]St. Louis, May 18, 1793, P. de C. leg. 26; incomplete letter of Trudeau of same date in Bancroft Library, probably enclosed in Trudeau to Carondelet, St. Louis, May 20, 1793, no. 73, P. de C. leg. 26. The Iowas and other Indians went to Michilimackinac and received drink and gifts, oftentimes were drunk. Trudeau to Carondelet, no. 91, July 10, 1793, P. de C. leg. 26. See draft to Trudeau, January 3, 1794, P. de C. leg. 26 and draft to Trudeau, New Orleans, August 6, 1793, P. de C. leg. 124.
[17]Trudeau to Carondelet, no. 74, St. Louis, May 20, 1793, P. de C. leg. 26.

the Niobrara River, he petitioned for and obtained from the government the exclusive trade with these Indians.[18] A short time later two new names enter the chronicle of the Spanish advance up the Missouri. In 1787, Joseph Garreau, then twenty-three years of age, was sent by Don Andrés Fagot la Garcinière of St. Louis to hunt and trap on the upper Missouri. Just what occurred on this expedition, if it ever took place, is unknown to the writer.[19]

In August, 1790, Jacques D'Eglise obtained a license to hunt on the Missouri, and in his meanderings became the first Spanish subject to reach the Mandan and Tayenne Indian villages via the Missouri. According to D'Eglise, the Mandan resided on the Missouri about eight hundred leagues above its mouth. While among them, D'Eglise received authentic information from a Frenchman (Menard), who had been living among these Indians for fourteen years, that they were in constant communication with the British, who sent traders from their posts, located only fifteen days' journey due north. Moreover, the Mandan were in communication with New Mexico, for they had Mexican saddles and bridles for their horses. After persuading them of the greatness of the Spanish government and promising that he was going to establish a trade with them, D'Eglise returned to St. Louis to renew his stock of goods. Upon his arrival in October, 1792, he rendered a report of his journey to Zenon Trudeau, lieutenant-governor of the Spanish Illinois, who at once transmitted it to Governor-General Carondelet. On December 29, 1792, Carondelet replied that he was acquainted with all the information derived from D'Eglise, but asked that more extensive data concerning the Indians, their trade, habitats, customs, numbers, and other items of interest be sent to him.[20]

The following March, D'Eglise, accompanied by Garreau, with outfits advanced to them by Monsieur Collell and by Joseph Robidoux, set out upriver upon a return journey to the Mandan. They did not succeed in reaching their destination, due to the hostility of the Sioux and Arikara;

[18]On Munier see the documents translated in Louis Houck, *Spanish Régime in Missouri*, II, 1-3. All the documents therein published are from P. de C. leg. 2363. In addition, see the contract of partnership for trade with the Ponca Indians between Munier and Rolland, April 26, 1793; Munier and Rolland to Carondelet, St. Louis, October, 1794; and several depositions to the effect that Munier discovered the Ponca Indians (all mss. in B. L.). "Trudeau's [Truteau's] Journal," *South Dakota Historical Collections*, VII, 434-35, 443-44, 447, 451 ff. gives some references to Munier, who later sold or conveyed his monopoly to Clamorgan. Munier's claim to discovery of the Poncas was later proved false. Clamorgan to Trudeau, St. Louis, [April ?] 20, 1794 P. de C. leg. 28. Trudeau to Carondelet, no. 175, April 27, 1794, P. de C. leg. 28. Carondelet to Trudeau, New Orleans, May 25, 1794, P. de C. leg. 21. Trudeau to Carondelet, St. Louis, May 27, 1794 [or 1795?], P. de C. leg. 207-B. Trudeau to Carondelet, September 26, 1795, P. de C. leg. 211.

[19]John C. Luttig, *Journal of a Fur Trading Expedition on the Upper Missouri, 1812-1813* (ed. by Stella M. Drumm, St. Louis, 1920), 64; "Trudeau's [Truteau's] Journal," *South Dakota Historical Collections*, VII, 403-404.

[20]Carondelet to Trudeau, New Orleans, Dec. 29, 1792. ms. in B. L. A. P. Nasatir [ed.], "Spanish Exploration of the Upper Missouri," in *Mississippi Valley Historical Review*, XIV (1927), 58.

consequently their venture proved unprofitable. D'Eglise returned to St. Louis, but Garreau, who is painted by D'Eglise as a scoundrel, chose to remain among the Arikara rather than face his creditors. It is from this date, beyond any reasonable doubt, that Garreau's continued residence among the Arikara and other tribes of the upper Missouri began.[21]

To compensate him for his losses, D'Eglise petitioned the Governor-General for the exclusive trade with the Mandan and Tayenne nations for a term of four years, on the same terms as those on which Juan Munier had but recently obtained the trade of the Ponca. In support of his request, D'Eglise submitted sworn testimony of several well-known traders of St. Louis to the effect that he had discovered the Mandan and Tayenne Indian nations and justly deserved the reward of exclusive trading privilege with them. D'Eglise did not obtain his desire, for the grant requested would have conflicted with one which had just been made to the "Company of Explorers of the Upper Missouri." Notwithstanding, he made some additional sallies into the upper Missouri region; but before taking up his later attempts, let us take note of the proceedings in St. Louis.[22]

The information concerning the activities of the British among the Mandan and of the trade conducted by the latter with the Spaniards of New Mexico filled the officials of Spanish Louisiana with alarm. At the same time the competition of the British traders was being felt all along the western shore of the Mississippi River; not only were they snatching trade from the Spaniards, but they were even underselling the latter in their own territory. Moreover, the Indian trade of the lower Missouri, still controlled by the Spaniards, was dwindling. Whereas formerly profits of from one to three hundred per cent had been common, by 1793 the trade had so diminished that traders were satisfied with a profit of but twenty-five per cent. There were, in fact, too many traders for the small number of Indian tribes with whom the Spaniards were in contact. Hence, action was necessary, for the welfare of the inhabitants engaged in commerce and trade must be improved in order to contribute to the welfare of the colony and of Spain. Furthermore, the British must be taught to respect international boundary lines and to remain in their own territory. To carry out both these desires, one course was imperative; to ascend the Missouri, establish an acquaintance with the new tribes, and wrest their trade from the British.[23]

---

[21]For a sketch of Garreau see *Ibid.*, XIV, 50, and references there cited. In addition, see R. G. Thwaites [ed.], *Original Journal of the Lewis and Clark Expedition,* (New York, 1904-1905), I, 272-74; V, 355; Nasatir, "Jacques D'Eglise on the Upper Missouri," *Mississippi Valley Historical Review,* XIV (1927), 50-51; and Nasatir, "Spanish Exploration of Upper Missouri," *Ibid.*, 58-60.

[22]The material upon which this account of D'Eglise is based, together with a narrative concerning his activities on the upper Missouri, may be found in Nasatir, "Jacques D'Eglise," and "Spanish Explorations of Upper Missouri," in *Mississippi Valley Historical Review,* XIV (1927), 47-71.

[23]See *Minuta del Acta del Consejo de Estado,* May 27, 1796, A. H. N., Est., printed in Nasatir and Liljegren, "Materials for the History of the Mississippi Valley from the Minutes of the Supreme Council of State," *Louisiana Historical Quarterly, op. cit.*

Thus the British traders would be forced out of Spanish territory; for even if there existed no chance for pecuniary gain, the Indians might be persuaded to oppose if not actually to attack them. Then, too, fear and loss of money would soon keep the Canadian traders from crossing the Anglo-Spanish frontier. Without doubt the activities of the heretofore-unknown Jacques D'Eglise inspired trader and official alike to enact the final scene in the drama of Spain's dominion in the Spanish Illinois.

2.

The Formation of the Missouri Company

In an effort to make the trade of the Illinois country more lucrative to the individuals engaging in it, Carondelet, in 1792, decreed that all Spanish subjects who so chose might embark upon it, subject only to the restriction of obtaining permission from the Lieutenant-Governor, who, in turn, was instructed not to refuse except for certain obvious reasons.[24] However, such unrestricted freedom could not last for any length of time. Jealousies and competition usually result detrimentally to a government; and rivalry between subjects of the same power among the Indians led to bad conduct on the part of the latter.

Therefore, the merchants of St. Louis complained that the Indians of the Missouri were being corrupted by the English who had abundant merchandise and entered into the trade which the Spanish merchants could not meet. They complained against Carondelet's opening the trade to all. They wanted the trade restricted to merchants, traders, and others only on condition of their giving good security not to violate Spanish regulations.[25]

Carondelet followed up his proclamation granting free trade with a set of rules to regulate the trade of the Illinois country. According to these regulations, issued on July 20, 1793, the trade with the Indian tribes of the Missouri was to be divided among the merchants of St. Louis by lot. A year's residence and business with a New Orleans firm were laid down as

---

[24]Trudeau's proclamation, July 25, 1792, ms. in B. L.

[25]Genêt's plans and the activities of the French in the west against Spain caused a great deal of fear and anxiety to the Spanish officials. Mitchell writing to Genêt, September 17, 1793, stated that the Missouri trade produces a greater quantity of furs than any other river in the world. According to his plan of conquest the French could easily become masters of Spanish Louisiana. The details we cannot recount here. The key of his plan was the capture of St. Louis; this capture would gain for them a very considerable branch of English commerce which the latter then held on the frontier of the United States. See Mitchell's letter in Archives du Ministère des Affaires Étrangères, Correspondance Politique, États Unis, Supplément, XXVIII, folios 84-87 verso. See Nasatir, "Anglo-Spanish Frontier on the Upper Mississippi 1786-1796," op. cit. Experience had demonstrated the ease with which the Indians traded with the English. English traders penetrated Spanish territory via the Des Moines river to the Pawnee, Otos and Mahas. Even the Osages could communicate with them. Trudeau to Carondelet, St. Louis, September 28, 1793, P. de C. leg. 208A.

prerequisites for the procurement of a license. Foreigners were excluded from the trade, and a penalty was imposed upon anyone hiring for a voyage up the Missouri any man who had not resided for at least one year in Spanish Louisiana. From these merchants a "Syndic of Commerce" was to be chosen. It was further stipulated that the regulations must be submitted to the *Corps du Commerce* of the Spanish Illinois and must be voted upon article by article.

Lieutenant-Governor Trudeau submitted the proposals on October 15, 1793, and the St. Louis *Corps du Commerce* made a few changes, designed to secure a stricter enforcement of the ideas that inspired them and to make their activities accord with the seasonal business in which they were engaged. The merchants proposed, also, twelve additional articles and an addendum designed to regulate the conduct of the traders while they were among the savages, to control prices in order to prevent illicit trading, to encourage the employment of white people in preference to Negroes, half-breeds, or savages, and to stimulate closer cooperation between the traders and the government with respect to the conduct of the Indian nations. Article twenty-two provided for settling petty differences between traders. Article twenty-three is of such significance that we quote it in full:

> *May the central government be pleased to allow the members of the trade of this place [St. Louis] to make expeditions against foreigners who establish themselves on our land with merchandise to attract the trade of our savages, and also to authorize the merchants to confiscate their furs or goods, half for the profit of the members of the expedition and the other half to the profit of the association for the expenses undertaken by the group.*

Thus we have our first intimation of the economic motive combining with the patriotic to achieve the double objective of private pecuniary gain and the defense of the Spanish realm. To further their own motive, the financial one, the merchants of St. Louis joined to the foregoing articles an addendum in which they petitioned the central government for permission to form a "Company of the North West" with the exclusive privilege of exploiting the trade of all the Indian nations residing on the Missouri above the Ponca, which the company might visit, discover, or obtain information about. Moreover, to increase their profits and to facilitate their trade, the company asked for the privilege of purchasing goods in time of war from the British or from the Americans, because of the scarcity of merchandise in the Spanish Illinois.[26]

---

[26]Three copies of the drafts of the "Reglements pour la Traite des Illinois" containing only the original eleven articles are in P. de C. leg. 2362. A copy of these regulations in French interspersed with English translation is in the Missouri Historical Society, St. Louis, Spanish Archives, No. 90. The original, together with the com-

Thus the "Company of Explorers of the Upper Missouri" (referred to hereafter as the Missouri Company), had its inception on October 15, 1793. In accordance with the trade regulations, Jacques Clamorgan,[27] who had under its terms been elected syndic, applied to Lieutenant-Governor Trudeau on the succeeding April 5 to assemble the merchants and traders of St. Louis for the purpose of furthering and discussing the formation of the suggested company. On May 5 the meeting drew up a series of articles of incorporation which were approved by the Lieutenant-Governor. These were forwarded on May 31, 1794, by Trudeau to Carondelet for his approval. Carondelet must have been elated when he received the advices concerning the project; for he not only immediately gave his whole-hearted approval to it and granted the exclusive privileges demanded by the company, but in addition he offered a prize of $2000, later raised to the amount of $3000, to the first Spanish subject who should penetrate to the South Sea via the Missouri River.[28]

The directors of the newly formed company, being anxious to carry forward their program of work, without waiting for the formal approval of the articles of incorporation, drew up a long series of instructions, consisting of fifty-three articles, which were given to Jean Baptiste Truteau, who was chosen to head their first expedition. These required Truteau to proceed at once to the Mandan villages and there build a fort and establish an agency. He was given ample authority for action, fixing of prices,

---

ments of the merchants, the additional articles, and Trudeau's reply is in B. L. For further details see Nasatir, "Formation of the Missouri Company," in *Missouri Historical Review*, XXV (1930), 3-15. The scarcity of merchandise in the Illinois country during the Revolution was the cause of Spain's losing control over the Indians in the upper Mississippi-Missouri Valley. This scarcity, together with the superiority of the English trading methods and their cheaper prices, placed the Spaniards at a distinct disadvantage in the Indian trade of the upper-valley regions. See exposition of Lieutenant-Governor Trudeau on the English trade, in his letter of May 18, 1793, ms. in B. L. The beginning of this letter could not be found in the B. L.; consequently we are not sure to whom it was addressed, probably, however, to the Governor-General—See note 16 above.

[27]Nasatir, "Jacques Clamorgan: Colonial Promoter of the Northern Border of New Spain," in *New Mexico Historical Review*, XVII (1942), 101-112.

[28]Trudeau to Carondelet, St. Louis, May 31, 1794, No. 185, P. de C., leg. 2364, translated in Houck, *Spanish Régime*, II, 161-62. Carondelet to Trudeau, New Orleans, July 12, 1794, P. de C., leg. 2363, translated in Houck, *op. cit.*, II, 162-63. The Articles of Incorporation are in P. de C., leg. 2363, copy in library of Missouri Historical Society. It forms annex No. 2 to Carondelet's dispatch to El Príncipe de la Paz, New Orleans, Jan. 8, 1796, No. 65, *reservada*, A. H. N., Est., leg. 3900, translated in Houck, *op. cit.*, II, 149-57. The government of Spain did not formally approve the formation of the company until 1796 when its fortunes were already on the decline. Only nine of the twenty or more merchants assembled joined the company. Their names, together with some biographical comments concerning each, may be found in Mrs. N. H. Beauregard [trans.], "Journal of Jean Baptiste Trudeau [Truteau] among the Arikara Indians in 1795," *Missouri Historical Society Collections*, IV, 10 ff.; see, also Houck, *op. cit.*, II, 159 ff. For the names of the chief members of the St. Louis Board of Trade, see *Ibid.*, 150. See Nasatir, "Formation of Missouri Company," *op. cit.*, and A. H. Abel, *Tabeau's Narrative of Loisel's Expedition to the Upper Missouri* (Norman, 1939), 12, for comments.

and the regulation of trade. He was instructed to take note of the streams entering the Missouri and to mark their distance from St. Louis or from the Mandan. He was to keep a record of all knowledge and information that might come to him concerning the Indian nations, and in particular to inform himself concerning the Shoshonean tribe. He was requested to obtain information concerning the distance to the Rocky Mountains "which are located to the west of the source of the Missouri," and to maintain friendly relations with the Indians, especially those who resided to the west of the mountains, in particular the Snake. He was also to ascertain the distance from the Mandan to the Spanish settlements of New Mexico; but this provision in the instructions was struck out by order of Governor Carondelet. Finally, Truteau was to persuade the Mandan of the friendship and protection of the Spaniards and to stop them from trading with the British. The instructions were signed by Clamorgan, Reilhe, and Truteau, and were approved by Zenon Trudeau on June 30, 1794. They were not, however, approved by Carondelet until almost the end of the year. On November 25, 1794, two articles in the instructions were nullified by the directors in accordance with the orders of Carondelet.[29]

Truteau left St. Louis on June 7, 1794, accompanied by eight men in a pirogue, his objective being the Mandan villages. The party made fair progress, and on August 6 was but a short distance below the mouth of the Platte. On that day, Jacques D'Eglise, making his third sally up the Missouri, overtook Truteau and delivered to him certain supplementary instructions and some speeches intended for the Indians, which Zenon Trudeau had forwarded.[30] Despite pleadings on the part of Truteau that D'Eglise accompany him on the journey up the Missouri, the latter, acting

---

[29]The instructions to Truteau are in P. de C., leg. 2363. One of the copies in that legajo contains a sketch of the fort to be constructed. The instructions also form annex No. 3 to Carondelet's dispatch to El Príncipe de la Paz, No. 65 *reservada*, A. H. N., Est., leg. 3900. A copy is also in the library of the Mo. Hist. Soc. It is translated in Houck, *op. cit.*, II, 164-72. A short sketch of the expeditions sent out by the company is given in Trudeau's letter to Gayoso de Lemos, St. Louis, Dec. 20, 1797, ms. in B. L. This is given in full together with the missing parts in the documents. (The document in the B. L. is fragmentary, for the middle folio or folios of the document are missing.) The names of the men who accompanied Truteau on the expedition are given in "Trudeau's [Truteau's] Journal," in *South Dakota Historical Collections*, VII, 404. Trudeau reported to Carondelet in his dispatch No. 185, May 31, 1794, as follows: ". . . the Company has resolved to form its expedition immediately this year, and has done so; for an intelligent man to march with ten others in order to go to establish a station among the Mandan tribe; and to direct all their operations thence. In order to become acquainted with so vast a region, they will take three years for that first voyage. That expedition has caused an expense to the Company of eight thousand *pesos*, and in the coming year a like expedition will have to march to reinforce the first one, which must send minute reports annually of their discoveries and operations." P. de C. leg. 2364, copy in B. L., translated in Houck, *op. cit.*, II, 162.

[30]Did these supplementary instructions contain the directions to nullify the two articles in these instructions of which Carondelet did not approve?

as a rival trader,[31] refused, for, having a smaller contingent of men and a lighter load, he could travel more rapidly than could the expedition sent in the interests of the company, and could thus obtain the valuable trade of the tribes of the upper Missouri region before the arrival of Truteau.[32] D'Eglise's objective point was the Mandan villages but he was prevented from achieving it by the Arikara, among whom he passed the winter and obtained a good trade. As agreed, D'Eglise awaited the arrival of Truteau, and on May 24, 1795, in company with two of Truteau's *engagés* and the furs the latter had obtained from the Cheyenne Indians, he departed from the Arikara on his return to St. Louis, where he arrived in safety on July 4, 1795.[33]

Meanwhile Truteau was making progress up the Missouri. As it was the purpose of Clamorgan to extend the trade of St. Louis to the unknown tribes near the headwaters of the Missouri, Truteau attempted to pass the Indians of the lower Missouri without being perceived, for he feared mistreatment, should his purpose be discovered by them. The party succeeded in reaching the vicinity of the present Crow Creek agency in South Dakota, where it was stopped by the Teton Sioux, who helped themselves to Truteau's goods. Truteau thereupon decided to cache the portion that remained and proceed overland to the Arikara towns, which he thought to be nearby, in the hope of receiving aid. But the Arikara were absent from their villages, and Truteau was obliged to return to his cache. From that point the party proceeded down the river in search of a suitable wintering ground, which they thought ought to be located below the Sioux country but above that of the Ponca and the Omaha. At a place in Charles Mix County, South Dakota, a little above and opposite the site of the later Fort Randall, on the left bank of the Missouri, they began the construction of winter quarters on November 11.[34]

The winter was not an enjoyable one. Truteau, a schoolmaster by profession, was not a good trader, and the Omaha forced him to extend them credit. At the same time employees of Juan Munier, who had the exclusive trading rights of the Ponca, and another trader from St. Louis, Solomon Petit, were wintering in the same vicinity. Yet Truteau did

---

[31]D'Eglise had refused to join the company. See Nasatir, "Jacques D'Eglise," *Mississippi Valley Historical Review*, XIV (1927), 51-52.
[32]D'Eglise was burning with a desire to discover the route over the mountains to the Pacific.
[33]Nasatir, "Jacques D'Eglise," *Mississippi Valley Historical Review*, XIV (1927), 52-55.
[34]Annie H. Abel-Henderson, "Mackay's Table of Distances," *Mississippi Valley Historical Review*, X (1923), 441-46; Hiram Martin Chittenden, *The American Fur Trade of the Far West* (New York, 1902), III, 952. See also Aubrey Diller, "Pawnee House: Ponca House" in *Mississippi Valley Historical Review*, XXXVI (1949), 301-304, and at greater length by the same author "Maps of the Missouri River before Lewis and Clark," in M. F. Ashley Montagu [ed.], *Studies and Essays in the History of Science and Learning Offered in Homage to George Sarton* (New York, 1946), 505-519.

manage to obtain some furs during the winter by trading with the Sioux, the Omaha, and the Ponca.

On March 25, 1795, Truteau, departing from his wintering camp once more to ascend the Missouri, stopped among the Ponca in an unavailing attempt to secure payment for some guns and ammunition which they had obtained from D'Eglise but which rightfully belonged to the Missouri Company. Here his journal abruptly comes to an end. When it reopens we find Truteau among the Arikara, then residing near Grand River, having moved thence from their old home near the mouth of the Cheyenne.[35]

Among the Arikara Truteau found himself almost stranded. He had sent his big boat back to St. Louis in the early spring and had made his way from the wintering camp to the Arikara village in two small canoes which had been built during the winter. The Arikara had disposed of their furs to D'Eglise, and Truteau desired to go on to the Mandan towns, but he lacked the means of transportation. He sent his men in search of wood with which to construct a pirogue; but the venture proved unsuccessful, and he was forced to await the arrival of a boat which the company was to dispatch not later than April 15, 1795.[36] Of his later activities, definite information is lacking. As late as January, 1796,[37] according to Mackay, he was among the Arikara or Mandan.

During his stay among the Arikara, Truteau dispatched letters to Menard and Jusseaume, who were among the Mandan, in which he impressed upon them the fact that Spain would supply the necessaries of life to all the nations residing along the banks of the upper Missouri. For that

---

[35]See A. H. Abel, "Truteau's Description" cited in note 40.

[36]This account is based upon Doane Robinson's introduction to the translation of "Trudeau's [Truteau's] Journal," in *South Dakota Historical Collections,* VII, 403 ff. The sources for it are the "Journal of Jean Baptiste Truteau on the Upper Missouri, 'Première Partie,' June 7, 1794-March 26, 1795" (untranslated), *American Historical Review,* XIX (1921), 299-33 (from the original in P. de C. leg. 187); and the translation of the second part by N. H. Beauregard, "Trudeau [Truteau] among Arikara," *Missouri Historical Society Collections,* IV, 9-48. Both parts of the journal (but beginning August 25) are translated in *South Dakota Historical Collections,* VII, 412-74. Some additional information and documents may be found in *Mississippi Valley Historical Review,* XIV (1927), 47-71. See also, F. J. Teggart, "Notes Supplementary to any Edition of Lewis and Clark," *American Historical Association, Annual Report, 1908,* I, 189-90.

[37]Mackay to Evans, Fort Charles, Jan. 28, 1796, ms. in B. L. printed in Nasatir, "John Evans: Explorer and Surveyor," *Missouri Historical Review,* XXV (1930), 441-447. At about the same time, Mackay wrote in his journal, "Through my fear of arriving late next summer at the Mandans, I am going to send out a detachment within a few days under charge of Monsieur Even [Evans] until he meets Trudeau [Truteau] who must have already constructed his fort among the above-mentioned Mandans, if he has experienced no opposition on the part of the English, who have had the audacity to unfurl their banner there" (Houck, *op. cit.,* II, 192). See Trudeau's report concerning the Spanish Illinois, dated St. Louis, Jan. 15, 1798, *Ibid.,* II, 253-54. That document is probably the "Description of Spanish Illinois" listed in Roscoe R. Hill, *Descriptive List of the Documents . . . in the P. de C.* (Washington, 1916), 487, as in leg. 2365. The present writer failed to locate that document in the legajo cited during his researches in that archive during 1924-1925 and 1930-1931.

purpose a company had been formed, of which he was agent. He was expecting a pirogue laden with merchandise in July or August, and he informed the Frenchmen that he would arrive at the Mandan towns during the ensuing summer, at which time he would establish a trading post among them. He advised the Frenchmen to stop trading with the Indians in that vicinity and to maintain peace among those of the upper Missouri. In the meantime, he desired Menard to distribute some tobacco, which he was sending him, among the chiefs of the Mandan and Gros Ventres; and he stated that upon his arrival he would deliver to those Indians word from their Spanish Father.[38]

Success attended this venture of Truteau. On July 14, he received letters from Menard and Jusseaume informing him that they had distributed the tobacco to the chiefs, who had pledged their good will to the whites and were impatiently awaiting his arrival. A few days later several Cheyenne Indians arrived among the Arikara, with whom Truteau established friendly relations. As a matter of fact, he had summoned them in order to announce the words of the Spanish Father and to deliver some presents.[39]

This leads us to the question whether Truteau actually visited the Cheyenne at their home. From the words of his journal it appears that he did not, but in his "Description of the Upper Missouri" he tells us that in the summer of 1795 he had dealings with the Cheyenne, "where I saw and spoke to many chiefs and leading men." Doctor Abel conjectures that Truteau actually made the trip to the Cheyenne country and beyond. "Most probably," she further states, "it was followed by a visit of no short duration."[40]

Truteau's activities during the summer of 1795 and following months cannot be definitely stated. The journals of the Lewis and Clark expedition say that the Frenchmen wintered at the "Pawnee House" (Ponca House—Truteau's first wintering camp) in 1796.[41] Biddle expanded this time to include the winter of 1796-97.[42] However, the dates 1795-96 seem to fit the facts better; for Evans' journal contains no mention of Truteau,[43] and according to instructions Truteau was to consult with him. This would seem to indicate that Truteau was not in the region in the latter part of 1796. Trudeau speaks of Truteau having remained among the Arikara

[38]Trudeau's [Truteau's] Journal," *South Dakota Historical Collections*, VII, 465-66.
[39]*Ibid.*, 469-74.
[40]Annie Heloise Abel, "Trudeau's [Truteau's] Description of the Upper Missouri," *Mississippi Valley Historical Review*, VIII (1921), 154, 168. The writer has been unable to locate any corroborative evidence of that visit but he is inclined to accept Dr. Abel's conjecture.
[41]Thwaites, *Lewis and Clark*, I, 142. But see Diller's writings cited in note 34.
[42]Elliott Coues [ed.], *History of the Expedition under the Command of Lewis and Clark* (New York, 1893), I, 112.
[43]Milo M. Quaife, [ed.], "Extracts from Capt. McKay's Journal—and Others," *Wisconsin Historical Society Proceedings*, LXIII (1915), 195 ff.

for eighteen months, and it may be, as I am inclined to believe, that Truteau was back in St. Louis before the summer of 1796 was a month old.[44]

Before leaving our narrative of Truteau, however, it is necessary to mention one other item concerning his activities. One of the objects of the expeditions of the Missouri Company was to search for a route to the Western Sea. In his "Description of the Upper Missouri" Truteau mentions the fact that when he was among the Cheyenne, he asked all of the Indian chiefs with whom he came in contact whether they had ever discovered some river beyond the mountains, "the waters of which might possibly flow towards the setting sun." The Indians informed him of a large river and said that the Indians residing thereon had no goods coming from white men.

Although Truteau did not ascend the Missouri much above the Arikara villages, he procured a great deal of valuable geographical information. From the Indians and from Menard, he derived accurate information concerning the Yellowstone River. From the Cheyenne, he learned of the Comanche who roamed the banks of the Platte and of the *Hahitannes* who occupied the territory beyond the Platte and as far as the banks of the Arkansas. Accurate information of the Missouri from its mouth to the point of its confluence with the Yellowstone can be gleaned from Truteau's "Description," which, however, may have been written at a later date, Truteau probably being, as Doctor Abel plausibly argues, the *ancien traiteur* who accompanied Perrin du Lac.[45]

Meanwhile, the Company in St. Louis had not forgotten that it had sent a representative into the upper Missouri region. In April, 1795,[46] therefore, it dispatched its second expedition into the Indian country. The command of the expedition was put under the direction of one Lecuyer, who was instructed to join Truteau at the depot which the latter was supposed to have established for the company among the Mandan. Since the second party was stronger than was the expedition under Truteau's command, greater results were expected from it. Clamorgan and Reilhe, in a

---

[44]The writer can add but the following: "*Le Sr Truteau premier agent de la Compe du haut Missoury parti d'ici au printems de 1794. S'est vu forcé d'abandonner la nation Ricaras ou il etoit fixé depuis dixhuit mois pour y attendre les secours de la Compagnie que cell ci a fait partire en deux fois en 1795 . . . Le Sr Truteau m'a raporte que les Anglais S'en etre plus que jamais sur le haut du Missoury, et que toute l'hiver et Y'a un vas et vient des gens de leurs forts du nord. Chez les nations qui bordent cette Riviere, quils ont si parfaitement bien armés de fusils quils y Sonts infiniment plus connues que chez les nations plus bas que nos frequentons.*" Trudeau to Carondelet, St. Louis, July 3, 1796. P. de C., leg. 212. May not this fix the date of Truteau's arrival more definitely?

[45]This is the only indication the writer can recall of the slightest probability of Truteau's ever reaching the Mandan. Abel, "Trudeau's [Truteau's] Description," *Mississippi Valley Historical Review* VIII (1921), 175. See also *Ibid.*, 149-79, *passim*, especially 154. See also Diller, "Maps of the Missouri River before Lewis and Clark." *op. cit.*

[46]Trudeau said the expedition left in May. Trudeau to Carondelet, St. Louis, July 15, 1795, see Nasatir, "Spanish Exploration of Upper Missouri," *Ibid.*, XIV (1927), 70.

report upon the operations of the Company, made July 8, 1795, state that the expedition, dispatched ". . . under the command of a leader who was to shun nothing to remove all the obstacles from a thorny and difficult route, will be very fortunate if it reaches the Mandan nation at the end of fall, and before the severe cold, so as to be able to go overland to the Rocky Chain [Mountains] whither he has orders to go without delay in order to reach, if possible, by next spring, 1796, the shores of the Sea of the West."[47]

The total cost of Lecuyer's expedition amounted to 96,779 *pesos,* a sum more than twice as great as the entire expense incident to the dispatching of the first expedition. The second expedition met with difficulties and Antonio Breda was sent to its relief, but he arrived too late. It had been pillaged by the Ponca, and the *engagés* joined Mackay on October 27. The difficulties encountered by the expedition, however, may not afford the true explanation of its failure. Lecuyer was not a fit person to entrust with the responsibility of leadership, and to his misconduct Lieutenant-Governor Trudeau attributed the failure of the expedition, which did not ascend beyond the Ponca. Mackay, in a letter written on October 27 at a place "8 leagues above the Platte River," remarked that Tabeau, one of Lecuyer's enlisted soldiers, was an infamous rascal and should be severely punished in order to serve as an example to the future. "Lecuyer, the leader," continued Mackay, "who has not had less than two wives since his arrival at the home of the Poncas, has wasted a great deal of goods of the Company."[48]

Meanwhile, more accurate reports concerning the activities of the British traders in the Upper Missouri were coming into the hands of the officials in St. Louis. From the testimony of Juan Fotman and Chrysostome Joncquard, it was learned that for some time past a direct trade had been carried on with the Mandan by the Canadian traders, who had even built a fort on the Missouri, and also that the Mandan, the Gros Ventres, and other nearby nations were in communication with the Spaniards situated to the south.[49]

This information, coupled with what was already known concerning British encroachments upon the Spanish Illinois, undoubtedly hastened the government and the company to action. It also appears that the ill fate of the Lecuyer expedition was known to Director Clamorgan relatively soon

[47]P. de C. leg. 2364. This report, forwarded by Carondelet to El Príncipe de la Paz after the former had signed it, forms annex No. 7 in dispatch No. 65, *reservada,* A. H. N., Est., leg. 3900, translated in Houck, *op. cit.,* II, 176.

[48]Trudeau to Carondelet, St. Louis, July 3, 1796, P. de C. leg. 212. See also Mackay to Clamorgan, October 24-27, 1795, ms. in B. L. In 1798 Trudeau remarked that the company actually sent an expedition to aid Truteau, but that its leader managed it so badly that he was captured and detained by the Ponca tribe, who appropriated almost all of his goods. Trudeau's report, Jan. 15, 1798, in Houck, *op. cit.,* II, 253.

[49]Nasatir, "Spanish Exploration of Upper Missouri," in *Mississippi Valley Historical Review,* XIV (1927), 63-71; Nasatir, "Jacques D'Eglise," *Ibid.,* 49, and references there cited; and Houck, *op. cit.,* II, 171, 174-75. See also note 44 above, statement of Trudeau to Carondelet, July 3, 1796.

after its departure from St. Louis. All these factors combined with yet another to force the Company to dispatch a third expedition to the upper Missouri. Truteau's instructions stated that he was engaged for three years; yet Zenon Trudeau reported to Carondelet on July 15, 1795, that since Truteau had pledged himself to serve the Company for only two years, it was necessary to dispatch another man at once to replace him in order that he might retire before the return of the expedition from the upper country. "Since no native of the country," continued Trudeau, "has been found with sufficient intelligence to be entrusted with [the] important management of the discoveries that are proposed and the control of their interests, they have suggested to me, Mr. Mackay, a Scotchman, but a naturalized Spaniard, whom I have approved because of his honesty and intelligence. The Company will give him a part of its profits and four hundred dollars a year [besides] while the special privileges which you granted the company continues."[50] Mackay's appointment was formally approved by the Governor-General on December 10, 1795, nearly six months after his departure from St. Louis.[51]

3.

James Mackay Ascends the Missouri

The advent of James Mackay causes us to reflect upon the activities of the British on the Upper Missouri, for one of Mackay's specific duties was to drive the British from the Mandan towns and destroy the forts which they had established among them.

Between the visits of the La Vérendryes in 1738 and 1742 and the journey of D'Eglise to the Mandan in 1790-92, little that is certain is known of white contact with these Indians. It is known, however, that traders frequented the Mandan villages during this interval and engaged in active commercial relations with them. Menard is known to have been among them for a number of years. René Jusseaume, it was stated in 1806, had been an independent trader on the Missouri for over fifteen years, at least eight of which most probably were spent among the Mandan. Other free trappers from the north had visited and traded with the Mandan, notably Hugh McCracken.[52]

[50]Nasatir, "Spanish Exploration of Upper Missouri," *Mississippi Valley Historical Review,* XIV (1927), 70.

[51]*Ibid.,* 71.

[52]On the La Vérendryes, see Lawrence J. Burpee [ed.], *Journals and Letters of Pierre Gaultier des Varennes de la Vérendrye and His Sons* (Toronto, 1927) and part I of this *Introduction.* On D'Eglise, see Lansing B. Bloom, "Death of Jacques D'-Eglise," *New Mexico Historical Review,* II, (1928), 369 ff.; Nasatir, "Jacques D'-Eglise," and "Spanish Exploration of Upper Missouri," *Mississippi Valley Historical Review,* XIV (1927), 47-71. On Menard "Trudeau's [Truteau's] Journal," *South Dakota Historical Collections,* VII, 403-74; Abel, "Trudeau's [Truteau's] Description," *Mississippi Valley Historical Review,* VIII (1921), 149-79; L. J. Bur-

From the Red River to the Missouri ran two main trails: one from Pembina, west, the other from the Assiniboine, by way of the La Souris (Mouse), south. The latter was the one most used by the Canadian traders, who descended to the homes of the Mandan, Gros Ventres, and other tribes that inhabited the waters of the upper Missouri.

The Mandan trade of the North West Company seems to have been conducted from Pine Fort, but, when that fort was abandoned in 1794, due to the establishment of the Hudson's Bay Company and of other traders in that immediate vicinity, the North West Company continued its trade with the Mandan from La Souris River Fort.[53] McDonnell's journal refers to journeys of a band of traders from Fort Espérance to the Mandan in 1793,[54] and to another group which had just returned from the Missouri in May, 1795. During the year 1793, David Monin, the clerk whom Robert Grant had left in charge of Pine Fort, made a trip to the Missouri on the solicitation of three freemen (independent traders), Morgan, Jusseaume, and Cardin.[55] On the return journey Monin and Morgan were killed by a Sioux war party. Hudson's Bay Company men may also have gone from the Assiniboine to the Missouri at about this time, but no names or dates are extant.[56]

It was from the post on the Catapoi (Catapoye) or Qu' Appelle River, probably from Fort Espérance, that James Mackay set out in the beginning of 1787 on a journey which took him to the Mandan villages, thereby stamping him as one of the earliest of white men to visit these Indians. Mackay tells us that it was from that post, then the furthermost wintering post of the British traders from Canada, ". . . that the English Traders start to go

pee [ed.], "Journal of Larocque from the Assiniboine to the Yellowstone, 1805," *Publications of the Canadian Archives* (Ottawa, 1910), No. 3, 17; Beauregard, "Trudeau [Truteau] among Arikara," *Missouri Historical Society Collections*, IV, 36, and references there cited. On Menard's death see Coues, *Lewis and Clark*, I, 178, and Coues [ed.], *New Light on the Early History of the Greater Northwest* (New York, 1897), I, 311. On Jusseaume and McCracken see L. J. Burpee, *The Search for the Western Sea* (Toronto, 1903), 353; G. Bryce, *The Remarkable History of the Hudson's Bay Company* (New York, 1900), 136; Gordon C. Davidson, *The Northwest Company* (Berkeley, 1918), 93; Coues, *New Light*, II, 303; Thwaites, *Lewis and Clark*, consult Index; J. B. Tyrell [ed.], *David Thompson's Narrative and His Explorations in Western America* (Toronto, 1916); and Nasatir, "Jacques D'Eglise," and "Spanish Exploration of Upper Missouri," *Mississippi Valley Historical Review*, XIV (1927), 47-71.

[53]See David A. Stewart, *Early Assiniboine Trading Posts of the Souris-Mouth Group 1785-1832*, Historical and Scientific Society of Manitoba, Transactions No. 5 (New Series), July, 1930.

[54]See McDonnell's diary in C. M. Gates [ed.], *Five Fur Traders of the Northwest* (Minneapolis, 1933), 63-119, esp. 112-113 and note 105.

[55]Cardin may be Louis Cardin Jr., *voyageur*, mentioned in *Wisconsin Historical Collections*, XII, 93. See Gates, *Five Fur Traders*, 112 and consult index.

[56]Davidson, *op. cit.*, 46-47; L. R. Masson, *Les Bourgeois de la Compagnie du Nord-Ouest* (Quebec, 1890), I, 271-73, 283 ff.; also Gates, *op. cit.*, 112-113.

and make their unlawful Trade on the Missouri with the Mandaines and other nations that inhabit the Territory of his Catholic Majesty."[57]

Among the British traders who engaged in this illegal trade must be mentioned René Jusseaume, who led an expedition from La Souris Fort in October, 1794, to the Mandan villages, where he engaged in a profitable trade. While in this region he erected a fort, which was situated between the villages of the Mandan and the Gros Ventres. Joncquard was among those who made this trading voyage from Fort Espérance to the Mandan. There he met a certain Loison, the bond servant of Garreau, with whom he descended the Missouri River, and reached St. Louis in company with D'Eglise, where his conduct was investigated by Trudeau. Many like expeditions followed in rapid succession, but definite information about them has not yet come to light.[58]

Such information was sufficient to warrant the immediate dispatch by the Missouri Company of an expedition to put a stop to the wholesale violation of international boundary lines and the unlawful prosecution of the Indian trade in Spanish Illinois, and Mackay was chosen to lead the enterprise. But before taking up his expedition and the events which succeeded it, let us sketch briefly the story of the relations of the British with the Mandan Indians till the end of the Spanish régime.

The first detailed information we have of an expedition to the Mandan from the other side of the present international boundary line concerns David Thompson, who, accompanied by nine men, set off from the Assiniboine on November 28, 1797. Proceeding in a roundabout way in weather which ranged from zero to thirty-six below, his party reached the Mandan town at the close of December, having traveled a distance of two hundred and thirty-eight miles. During his stay of eleven days among the Mandan, Thompson vainly attempted to persuade the chiefs of the nation to hunt beaver and bring the skins to the posts of the North West Company on the Assiniboine. After making the "necessary" astronomical observations, Thompson set out on his return journey, and after experiencing "excessive bad weather," the party reached its destination on February 3, 1798. Other expeditions were sent to the Mandan villages and a regular trade was undoubtedly kept up between them and the posts on the Assiniboine, but we have no definite information concerning these subsequent

<hr>

[57]Quaife, "McKay's Journal," *Wisconsin Historical Society Proceedings,* LXIII, (1915), 191.

[58]Nasatir, "Spanish Exploration of Upper Missouri," *Mississippi Valley Historical Review,* XIV, (1927), 63-69. These expeditions were many and varied during the last decade of the eighteenth century because of the rivalry between the Hudson's Bay and the North West companies for the Mandan trade. Quaife, "McKay's Journal," *Wisconsin Historical Society Proceedings,* LXIII, (1915), 192-93. See Nasatir, "John Evans, Explorer and Surveyor," in *Missouri Historical Review,* XXV (1931), 219-239; 432-460; 585-608.

activities until the year 1804, at which time the Spanish régime in the Illinois country was terminated.[59]

James Mackay, to whom was entrusted the leadership of the new expedition, was born in Scotland, in 1759, of parents among whose ancestry were numbered several members of the Irish royalty, including one king. The date of Mackay's coming to America is unknown, but it was probably in 1776. During the fifteen years following, he seems to have been engaged in the fur trade of the Northwest. It is known that in the late 1780's he made trips to the Qu' Appelle River, the furthermost western wintering post of the Canadian traders; and from thence he made at least one trip to the Mandan villages on the Missouri. Carondelet reported to the Spanish minister, Godoy, that Mackay had been employed by the British with great success in the exploration of the Northwest, with the attempted purpose of opening a communication with the South Sea.[60]

About the year 1793, Mackay changed his allegiance and his abode, moving into the Spanish Illinois, where his ability and merit readily attracted the attention of his new compatriots.[61] In 1795, at a time when no native Spaniards with the requisite ability could be found for the proposed duties, Mackay, a Scotchman by birth but now a Spaniard by choice, was chosen to succeed Truteau as manager of the Missouri Company's affairs on the upper Missouri and to carry out the proposed discoveries in the interests of the Spanish government. Mackay was uniformly characterized by the officials of Spanish Louisiana as a man of ability, intelligence, prudence, loyalty, and honesty, a man "of knowledge, zealous and punctual," qualities which the Spanish government recognized after his return from the upper Missouri region, despite his failure to carry out to their ultimate conclusion the projects undertaken.[62]

---

[59]Tyrell, *op. cit.*, 209-40. McCracken seems to have made an expedition to the Mandan in 1798, *Ibid.*, 240-41. Among the later expeditions the following may be noted: Alexander Henry, 1806 (Coues, *New Light*, I, 285-483); F. A. Larocque, 1804-1806 (Burpee, "Journal of Larocque," Canadian Archives, *Publications*, No. 3; Masson, *op. cit.*, I, 299-313); Charles McKenzie, 1804-1806 (*Ibid.*, 317-93). A good summary of these expeditions is to be found in Burpee, *Search for the Western Sea, passim.*

[60]Houck, *op. cit.*, II, 182.

[61]Quaife, "McKay's Journal," *Wisconsin Historical Society Proceedings*, LXIII (1915), 187-88. A comment on a Spanish "plat" attached to a copy of Clamorgan's instructions to Truteau, in P. de C. leg. 2363, says: "*La linea puntuada en negro demuestra los numbros* [?] *qe observo MacKay en sus viages de descubiertos por el comercio ingles en 1784, 86, 87, y 88.*" Mackay was still in Europe in 1774, his uncle coming to North Carolina in that year. The biographical details concerning him are taken from a manuscript in the library of the Missouri Historical Society, entitled "Pedigree of James Mackay," but which in reality is a copy of a letter of James Mackay to his eldest son, John Zeno Mackay, written some time before 1822. The best published biography of Mackay is the short sketch by Judge Walter B. Douglas as an editorial footnote to Mrs. Beauregard's translation of Part II of "Trudeau [Truteau] among Arikara," *Missouri Historical Society Collections*, IV (1912), 20-21.

[62]Characterizations by Trudeau, Carondelet, De Lassus, Gayoso de Lemos, etc., Houck, *op. cit.*, II, 182, 253; Nasatir, "Spanish Explorations of Upper Missouri," *Mississippi Valley Historical Review*, XIV (1927), 70-71; Houck, *A History of Mis-*

The expedition was composed of four pirogues loaded with merchandise; one was intended for the Arikara, another for the purpose of "buying their way" past the Sioux, the third for the Mandan villages, and the fourth for the purpose of reaching the Rocky Mountains with orders to go overland to the Far West. The cost of the merchandise, totaling almost one-half the cost of the entire expedition, amounted to 50,000 *pesos*. The company thought that the work of the expedition would require six years, and Mackay was given a passport by Lieutenant-Governor Trudeau, approved by Carondelet, for this length of time.[63]

With an expedition whose total cost amounted to some 104,000 *pesos*, Mackay, accompanied by thirty-three men, set out from St. Louis about the end of August, 1795.[64] The object of the expedition, according to Mackay's own statement, was ". . . to open commerce with those distant and Unknown Nations in the upper parts of the Missouri and to discover all the unknown parts of his Catholic Majesty's Dominions through that continent as far as the Pacific Ocean." He was also ordered to construct forts wherever he should deem it necessary in order to protect the Spanish trade from encroachments on the part of the British.[65]

As it was late in the year, it was decided that Mackay should establish a fort and pass the first winter among the "Mahas" and continue his journey the following spring. Slow progress was made on the voyage up the river and it was not until October 14 that the village of the Oto, situated at the mouth of the Platte, was reached. A short distance above this point, Mackay built a house for some traders whom he left with the Oto. If the

souri, II, 70; *American State Papers, Public Lands*, VI, 718-20. See also, Abel-Henderson, "Mackay's Table of Distances," *Mississippi Valley Historical Review*, X (1923), 429-31.

[63]Houck, *Spanish Régime*, II, 178; *American State Papers, Public Lands*, VI, 720.

[64]Houck, *Spanish Régime*, II, 176, 178, 183. There is some uncertainty concerning the date of Mackay's departure from St. Louis. The date used in the text is the one given in Mackay's journal, P. de C. leg. 2364, and translated in Houck, *op. cit.*, II, 183. That date is also corroborated in Trudeau's letter to Carondelet, St. Louis, Aug. 30, 1795: "*La Compagnie de Commerce de la nation Mandana au haut Missoury vient de faire partir sa troisième expedition composée de trente-trois hommes bien munis*" (P. de C. leg. 211). André Michaux stated, "I was informed at Illinois that Mackay, a Scotchman and Even [Evans] a Welshman, started at the end of July 1795 from St. Louis to ascend the Missouri." ("Travels in Kentucky," Dec. 11, 1795, in Thwaites, [ed.], *Early Western Travels*, III, 79-80). Carlos Howard said the expedition left in July, Howard to Carondelet, St. Louis, May 13, 1797 (ms. in B. L.). Trudeau in a letter to Carondelet, dated St. Louis, July 15, 1795, said the expedition would leave the 15th of August (Nasatir, "Spanish Exploration of Upper Missouri," *op cit.*, XIV, 70). Mackay himself said he arrived at the Platte on October 14, after forty-four days of travel, placing the date of his departure from St. Louis about September 1 (Mackay to Clamorgan, Oct. 24-27, 1795, ms. in B. L.) Clamorgan stated the expedition would leave in July (Houck, *op. cit.*, II, 176). See also Teggart, "Notes to Lewis and Clark," *American Historical Association, Annual Report*, 1908, I, 191, and Nasatir, "John Evans," cited in note 66.

[65]Quaife, "McKay's Journal," *Wisconsin Historical Society Proceedings*, LXIII (1915), 193; Quaife [ed.], *The Journals of Captain Meriwether Lewis and Sergeant John Ordway, 1803-1806* (Madison, 1916), 19.

Company was to succeed in its trading operations, he informed Clamorgan, it would be necessary to obtain the good will of these Indians. This could only be done by agreeing to build a fort to protect them from their enemies, and by maintaining a supply of merchandise to prevent their resorting to British traders.[66]

Mackay remained eleven days with the Oto, devoting the time to cultivating their good will. Resuming his voyage, he arrived on October 27 at a point eight leagues above the Platte, where he was joined by six employees of the company, who had been among the Ponca and who had come up from St. Louis with Lecuyer's or Breda's expedition. On November 11 the expedition reached the Omaha village, headed by the great chief, Black Bird. Here Mackay endeavored to promote the Spanish interest by conferring several medals upon the chiefs, and by a generous distribution of gifts. Here also he erected a fort and passed the ensuing winter. Fort Charles, as it was called, was located about six miles below Omadi, Nebraska. While here, Mackay entered upon an alliance with Black Bird, who promised to avenge the injuries which had been perpetrated by the Ponca against the Spanish traders. Black Bird also offered to send emissaries to the Sioux and other tribes of the upper Missouri to induce their chiefs to visit Fort Charles in the spring with a view to securing peace and the free passage of the river. Black Bird further promised personally to escort Mackay to the Arikara.

In the meantime, Mackay was busily preparing for the resumption of his journey up the Missouri. Not having heard from the Arikara, and not being able to send word to them by water, he determined to dispatch a party overland to them to establish friendly relations and to procure for himself a peaceful passage of the river. The leader of this party was Juan Evans, Mackay's trusted lieutenant.

4.

ANGLO-SPANISH RIVALRY ON THE UPPER MISSOURI

Jean, Juan, or John Evans was a Welshman, who had crossed the Atlantic in 1792 in order to secure information concerning a tribe of Welsh Indians.[67] Precisely what he did upon his arrival here is not known, but it

---

[66]Mackay to Clamorgan, Oct. 24-27, 1795, ms. in B. L. Printed in Nasatir, "John Evans: Explorer and Surveyor," *Missouri Historical Review*, XXV (1931), 436-441. Abel-Henderson, "Mackay's Table of Distances," *Mississippi Valley Historical Review*, X (1923), 438.

[67]Evans may have been sent to America as an emissary of the several people in Wales, working on the subject of the Welsh Indians, one of whom was Edward William, whose letter to William Pritchard of Philadelphia, dated, London, Aug. 15, 1792, was forwarded by Evans. P. de C. leg. 213. See Nasatir, "John Evans," *op. cit.* A long erudite account of John Evans has just appeared in the *American Historical Review* January and April, 1949, issues. Jefferson, in a letter to Lewis, dated, Wash-

may reasonably be presumed that he visited Philadelphia and interviewed Mr. Pritchard, the bookseller, to whom he had a letter of introduction. Evans undoubtedly thought that the Welsh Indians were living in the Upper Missouri region; hence he made his way to the West, and early in 1795 we find him in the Illinois country. On March 10 of that year, a Mr. G. (?) Turner of Kaskaskia wrote Evans a letter in which he gave the latter some suggestions concerning his further journey. Turner had gathered his information from Mr. Chouteau who had himself traveled 500 leagues up the Missouri and who had assured him that the "Pacific Ocean can lie at no great distance from the Missouri's source." Chouteau had also imparted information concerning some "new" animals, which interested Turner, for he requested of Evans that the latter bring him a "couple of skins" of new and unknown species of animals in order to have them stuffed and placed on exhibition. After wishing Evans "all imaginable success" and having signed his name to the letter, Turner received word from Evans, probably asking him to write a letter of recommendation for him to Lieutenant-Governor Zenon Trudeau, a service which Turner had previously performed. Evans also desired to have a companion on his journey up the Missouri, which seems to indicate that it was more or less by chance that he entered the employ of the Missouri Company and became a member of Mackay's expedition.[68]

The purpose of Mackay in dispatching Evans was to ascertain the truth concerning a reported outbreak between the Ponca and the Arikara, and the trouble between the latter and the Sioux. He ascended the Missouri to the White River "about 80 leagues above the Mahas," where he came upon a band of Sioux engaged in hunting buffalo. He thereupon beat a hasty retreat—hotly pursued by the Indians, who had discovered the whites near their camp. Favored by the weather and by the approach of night, Evans made good his escape, returning to Fort Charles on January 6. Mackay now endeavored to placate the Sioux with presents, and in a conference with some of the chiefs succeeded in opening a communication

---

ington. Jan. 22, 1804, wrote: " . . . I enclosed you a map of a mr. Evans, a Welshman, employed by the Spanish government for that purpose, but whose original object I believe had been to go in search of the Welsh Indians said to be up the Missouri." (Thwaites, *Lewis and Clark*, VII, 292).

[68]Letters in P. de C. leg. 213. It seems that Evans, who we think left St. Louis with Mackay, had not begun his voyage by August 18, for on that day William Arundel addressed a letter to "Mr. J. T. Evans, Cahokia," in which we read: "Your intended journey will separate us for a long time but altho' at a Distance we may find ways and means of communicating and giving intelligence the one to the other. Which I am in hope will be always in your memory. My Level & your Square must strike the necessary Ballance and Best Rules in the World be the Guide amongst friends." Printed in Nasatir, "John Evans," *op. cit.*, XXV (1930), 411. Most of the Evans letters are here printed. On William Arundel see C. W. Alvord [ed.], *Cahokia Records, 1778-1790, Collections of the Illinois State Historical Library* (Springfield, 1907), II, consult Index. The writer believes that Evans left St. Louis in company with Mackay.

with that tribe. This done, he prepared to hazard another trial to penetrate to the west, and again the leadership of the expedition was entrusted to Evans.[69]

On January 28, 1796, Mackay issued a set of instructions to Evans "for crossing this continent in order to discover a passage from the sources of the Missouri to the Pacific Ocean, following orders of the Director of the company, Don St. Yago [Santiago or Jacques] Clamorgan under the protection of his Excellency Mgr. Le Baron de Carondelet, Governor-General of the Province of Louisiana, and Mr. Zenon Trudeau, Lieutenant-Governor of the Province of Illinois."[70] The instructions required Evans to keep a journal recording latitude, longitude, weather, and winds, and a second journal recording the extent and location of minerals, vegetables, plants, and animals, Indian tribes, and remarks descriptive thereof. "You will take care to mark down your route and distance each day, whether by land or water; in case you will be short of ink, use the powder, and for want of powder, in the summer you will surely find some fruit whose juice can replace both." He was instructed to consult Truteau, who was supposed to be either among the Arikara or Mandan; and detailed directions concerning the accuracy of his records, meetings with parties of Indians, and rules of conduct were prescribed. He was equipped with a supply of merchandise for distribution in placating the natives, who were to be informed that other parties of whites would follow him. He was directed to keep within the bounds of 40 degrees of north latitude until he arrived within the area between 111 and 112 degrees longitude, west; then he was to travel north to the 42nd parallel and thence due west. The distance from the Rocky Mountains to the Pacific Ocean, Mackay estimated at not more than two hundred and ninety leagues. Evans was told not to incur the jealousy of the Russians on the coast, but on his way thither he was to take possession of all territories traversed in the name of Charles IV, King of Spain, and the Missouri Company, inscriptions embodying both names to be carved on stones or trees as he passed from river to river. These were to serve as "unquestionable proof of the journey that you are going to make." Finally, Evans was instructed not to deliver nor show anything

---

[69]Mackay's "Journal," P. de C. leg. 2364, translated in Houck, *Spanish Régime,* II, 189. This journal was dispatched to Carondelet, accompanied by several other letters from Mackay, and by Trudeau's letter of May 1, 1796 (P. de C. leg. 193; Quaife, "McKay's Journal," *Wisconsin Historical Society Proceedings,* LXIII (1915), 194-95). On July 9, 1796, Carondelet wrote to Clamorgan saying that he had received the Mackay journal and the instructions given by Mackay to Evans (original in B. L.) : "I would be so much flattered should his last [expedition] succeed as it is confidently reported that a Spanish squadron has sailed from Europe in order to go and dislodge the English from Nootka Sound, and it would be a curious fact if our people were to reach the same point at the same time" (ms. in library of Missouri Historical Society).
[70]Ms. in B. L., printed in Nasatir, "John Evans," *op. cit.,* XXV (1931), 441-447. See also Clamorgan to Carondelet, April 15, 1796, P. de C. leg. 212.

regarding his discoveries to any person save Mackay, Clamorgan, or another representative of the company in the presence of the Lieutenant-Governor.

Although Evans' journal states that he left Fort Charles on June 8, 1796, evidence gathered by the writer seems to point to an earlier departure. Evans' instructions bear the date January 28, 1796, and in a letter dated Fort Charles, February 19, 1796, and addressed to Evans, Mackay wrote:

> I have found the time tedious since you left this [place] not withstanding my being constantly employed about some trip [?] or other, however, I begin to get accustomed to live Solletary I dare say that in the course of time hence I shall be happy alone as the Indian on the desert.[71]

In this same letter Mackay forwarded a sketch of the description of the Yellowstone which D'Eglise had obtained from the Indians, and Evans was authorized to refrain from visiting the Mandan should he find a navigable river lower down the Missouri. "Reveal your Plans & projects to no one whatever," continued Mackay, "not even to Mr. Truteau except what is necessary to forward your expedition & for your information you will at all events try to see the white people on the coast if it should answer no other purpose than that of corresponding by letters it will be of great service as it will open a way for a further discovery." Mackay instructed Evans to tell Truteau to make an inventory of what goods he might have on hand in the spring and have it forwarded to him. Truteau was to inform the Indian nations that Mackay was on his way up the Missouri River.[72]

Proceeding from Fort Charles, Evans was stopped at the Arikara villages, and while tarrying there met several chiefs of tribes living to the west, particularly the Cheyenne, who expressed their attachment to the Spanish standard. Resuming his journey with the assent of the Arikara, he arrived at the Mandan village on September 23. After he had distributed medals, flags, and other presents to the natives and delivered an harangue in favor of Spain, to which they readily gave their assent, Evans took possession of the fort belonging to the British traders and hoisted the Spanish

---

[71]However, James Sutherland, referring to Mackay's proclamation, wrote to Evans: "Your written declaration dated Fort Charles, the 27th of May last." Could Evans again have turned back and made a third sally from Fort Charles? Other factors also point to errors in Evans' dates as printed in his journal.

[72]P. de C. leg. 213, printed in Nasatir, "John Evans," *op. cit.*, XXV (1931), 447-449. Apparently Jacques D'Eglise was with Mackay at this time, for in this letter Mackay forwards D'Eglise's compliments to Truteau and to a certain Mr. Nourrow [Joseph Garreau?] who "is at the ricarras & tell him that Jacques [D'Eglise] wants him to come down with the Company's cajons [?] in the spring to help him up with his goods next summer." This bit of evidence concerning D'Eglise supplements the present writer's article on "Jacques D'Eglise," *Mississippi Valley Historical Review*, XIV (1927), 47-56; and Bloom, "Death of Jacques D'Eglise," *New Mexico Historical Review*, II (1928), 369-79.

flag. This measure not only gave the Spaniards control over the Mandan, but by closing the upper Missouri to the British traders, it promised to throw the trade of this region into Spanish hands.

Although Evans' first announcement of the arrival of British traders among the Mandan was under date of October 8, it is not unlikely that he had previously dispatched messages to the supply houses and forts of the Hudson's Bay and North West companies in Canada who were in control of the Mandan trade. On October 8, Cuthbert Grant, a "nor'wester interior leader," addressed a letter from his favorite residence, Rivière Tremblante Fort, stating that as he found "by Mr. James Mackay's letter that the Missisourie [sic] is chartered by a Company I wish to withdraw what little the N. W. Co. [?] has their [sic]." Grant complained that the company's business with the Mandan had been a losing proposition and that for some time he had wished to withdraw; and he entreated Evans to deliver "to the bearer" all the goods that belonged to Jusseaume that might be in his possession. Evidently Grant knew, or at least suspected, the capture and confiscation by Evans of the British post, together with its contents. Grant further informed the Welshman that Jusseaume would return to the Missouri during the ensuing month in order to settle his affairs. Moreover, it is probable that British traders were found among the Mandan when Evans reached that point, for on October 8 Grant wrote to Evans, "I am very much obliged to you for your kindness in lending a man to Mr. Mackay."[73] Grant requested Evans' assistance in the efforts of his company to find and apprehend deserters from their brigades, promising to reciprocate the favor should opportunity arise; he also requested Evans to make out an account of everything belonging to Jusseaume that he might deliver to the men.[74]

Evans tells us that on October 8, several British traders arrived at the Mandan villages. Not having a sufficiency of men, Evans did not attempt to oppose their entry nor object to their introducing the merchandise which they brought with them; but using other means, the Welshman outwitted his fellow Britishers, causing a hindrance to their trade and, some days after, forced them to take their departure. As these traders would necessarily return to Canada, Evans sent with them James Mackay's proclamation ". . . forbidding all strangers whatever to enter on any part of his Catholic Majesty's Dominions in this Quarter under any pretext

---

[73]From September 23 to October 8 is but fifteen days, approximately the amount of time required to travel to the Mandan villages from Cuthbert Grant's favorite post at that season of the year.

[74]Grant to Evans at the Mandan village, Rivière Tremblante, Oct. 8, 1796. P. de C. leg. 213, printed in Nasatir, "John Evans," op. cit., XXV (1931), 458-459. The Mackay referred to in the above letter and mentioned in the text is not James Mackay, but Neil or Donald Mackay, concerning whom some light is shed by Masson, op. cit., I, 282-95; Gates, Five Fur Traders, consult index. Letters are printed in Nasatir, "John Evans," op. cit.

whatever."[75] It seems that the traders to whom he referred were employees both of the Hudson's Bay and the North West companies, and on November 23 following, James Sutherland at Brandon House (on the Assiniboine six miles above [west] the mouth of the Souris)[76] wrote to Mr. Evans, "Trader at the Missouri," as follows: "Your written declaration dated Fort Charles the 27th of May last, prohibiting all British Subjects from trading at the Missourie, has come to our hands. This may effect the traders from Canada a little but nothing those from Hudsons Bay." Nevertheless, Sutherland inquired as to whether he could be permitted to visit the Missouri in order to trade horses, Indian corn, and buffalo robes "which articles we supose not to be conected with the Fur Trade and consequently expect you will have no objections."

However, the Northwesters were more aggressive. From the North West Company's post near or at the mouth of the La Souris River, in close proximity to Brandon House, John McDonnell addressed a letter to Evans which bears the same date as Sutherland's letter. McDonnell informed the Trader at the Missouri that he was sorry his company was obliged to trouble him (Evans) with *another* visit "much against our wills"—its purpose ostensibly "to fetch the dearly acquired debt of Mr. Jussaume." Jean Baptiste Desmarais was sent with some goods in order to bring back Jusseaume's furs. As winter was setting in, McDonnell found it difficult to get any of the "turbulent" French-Canadians to undertake the journey to the Mandan. He succeeded, however, after having been forced to advance some goods on credit to the men—a risky thing to do. McDonnell had warned the *voyageurs* that their goods were likely to be confiscated, but "they replied that they heard that Mr. Evans was a *bon garçon* and hoped upon asking leave to trade what little they brought that you [Evans] would not refuse them as they [had] so little that it would not injure your interest in the least." McDonnell entreated Evans to aid Desmarais "in apprehending Chayé [?] & conveying him back to his duty as he has three years of his time to serve the Company"; he also asked Evans' assistance in collecting something from Garreau, who was indebted to several members of the Company; and he forwarded a liberal present, including "two European magazines & a Guthrie's Geographical Grammar for your amusement." Before concluding, McDonnell informed Evans that La Grave had run away three years before at the Rivière Qu' Appelle, heavily indebted to him; he enclosed, also, Jusseaume's "will and power to

[75]Quaife, "McKay's Journal," *Wisconsin Historical Society Proceedings,* LXIII (1915), 197.
[76]Built in 1793 (Stewart, *Early Assiniboine Trading Posts of the Souris-Mouth Group 1785-1832, op cit.,* 12-14).

have his Peltries & little slave girl" delivered to the bearer, and thanked him for allowing one of his men to "accompany Mackay in his distress."[77]

That Desmarais reached the Mandan and delivered the letters addressed to Evans by Sutherland and McDonnell before December 20 is certain. His party returned to the La Souris River post on January 16, but on the first or second night out on their return journey they had lost their horses[78] and consequently had been obliged to leave their property behind, and it was now determined to send another party to the Missouri to recover it. Sutherland allowed two of his men to accompany this expedition (which was composed of Northwesters), "out of curiosity . . . to see the Mandan villages" and to attempt to purchase a slave girl. He also sent a gift to Evans and invited the latter to inform him of such news as when he expected "the gentleman from below at your post, what your Intentions are with regard to exploring further up the River, & and if your agent general be the same Mr. James Mackay who was formerly a Trader here in Red River. These perhaps you will say are tedious inquiries, but I suppose a gentleman of your ability's can have no objection to any communication which does not immediately concern the Company's affairs in so remote a country."[79] The party arrived at the Mandan villages on or before February 6 and returned to the La Souris River at 3 P. M. of the twenty-fifth of the same month.

On February 26, only a few hours after the return of the expedition from the Missouri, both McDonnell and Sutherland addressed replies to the missives it had brought them from Evans. These two letters, which indicate the intense rivalry between the North West and the Hudson's Bay Companies and which also afford an insight into Evans' activities among the Mandan, are of such importance that we shall quote extensively from both. Sutherland, writing in a pleasant mood, thanked Evans for his kindness to the "two English lads" whom the former had permitted to go to the Missouri:

I hear you have complaints against some of them the [Northwesters], and possib'ely not without reason, and I could say more on that head, had I the pleasure of seeing you, there is no harm however on your being on your guard against designing people: a word is enough to the wise . . .

[77]McDonnell to Evans, River La Souris, Nov. 23, 1796. P. de C. leg. 213, printed in Nasatir, "John Evans," *op. cit.*, XXV (1931), 585-586. "Chayé" may probably be Dubé, who left with Jusseaume on his trip to the Mandan in 1793-94. La Grave was also with Jusseaume on the same expedition. Masson, *op. cit.*, I, 286, 294. On Desmarais see Coues, *New Light*, I, *passim.*

[78]They had fallen into the hands of the Pawnee. McDonnell to Evans, River La Souris, Feb. 26, 1797, P. de C. leg. 213, printed in Nasatir, "John Evans," *op. cit.*, XXV (1931), 590-591.

[79]Sutherland to Evans, Brandon House, Jan. 21, 1797, Nasatir, "John Evans," *op. cit.*, XXV (1931), 587-588. This letter is addressed to "Mr. J. Evans Trader at Fort Makay."

You d need be under no apprehension of any more of our men visiting the Missourie, the exclusive trade to which being now in the hands of a foreign nation, nor are we permitted to act on [our] own account without the direct orders of our Company, who never as yet has been known to violate any law either foreign or domestic . . . I am obliged to you for the little information you have given me, your correspondence would be highly acceptable . . . I should be extremely happy to have the pleasure of seeing you in this or any other country, wher[e] perhaps something better than we can command at present would cheer our Souls and make us forgit our past cares, and each relate the adventure of the wandering Sailor (or rather soldier) for as well as you I have been appointed by providence to traverse the wild regions of America for several years past."[80]

John McDonnell, however, spoke in a different tone:

As you speak much of La France[81] *in your letter I have ventured to Send him with Jussaume, he could not be in better company, as you seem to be inveterated against the one as the other; they have an opportunity of vindicating themselves from your aspersions in your own presence. Let their conduct be what it will you would expose yourself in acting agreeable to your letter. British subjects are not to be tried by Spanish laws, nor do I look upon you as an officer commissioned to apprehend oth[er] people's servants, if you serve a chartered Comy. why not show the Spanish Governors Orders, declarations, denunciations or manifestoes, prohibiting others from frequenting that country. Then shall we leave you in peace: Be at bottom of it who will most certain I am that there is most complicated vilainy carried on this year at the Missouri in many respects witness the debauching of Chaye last fall, and the offering 200 dollars to the English men arrived yesterday if we were nearer neighbors than we are we could easily come to an understanding. It must give any sensible person no grand Idea of your Missouri Company making use of such Canaille as I have reason to think many of your Engagees are by judging of the remander by La Grave Garreau Chaye &c such as are not run aways from here are Deserters from La prairie du Chien & other places in the Mississippi La France goes with Jussaume to help the latter in bringing his family.*[82]

Jusseaume, accompanied by Baptiste La France, set out from the North West Company's post at the mouth of the La Souris River on or

[80]P. de C. leg. 213, printed in Nasatir, "John Evans," *op. cit.,* XXV (1931), 588-589.
[81]Jean Baptiste La France accompanied Jusseaume to the Mandan in 1793-94. Masson, *op. cit.,* I, 286-294. For other references to La France see Coues, *Lewis and Clark,* I, 301-302, 329, 332, 345, and Thwaites, *Lewis and Clark, passim.*
[82]P. de C. leg. 213, printed in Nasatir, "John Evans," *op. cit.,* XXV (1931), 590-591.

soon after February 26 and arrived at the Mandan villages on March 13. As we have now come to the end of our supply of letters from the Spanish archives,[83] we must rely upon Evans' own narrative to complete our account of his activities on the upper Missouri. He relates that Jusseaume brought merchandise to distribute as presents among the Mandan and the neighboring tribes, to wean them from their fidelity to His Catholic Majesty. Jusseaume and his cohorts attempted to induce the chiefs to enter Evans' house under the guise of friendship in order to murder him and pillage his property, but their loyalty defeated the dastardly project; instead, the chiefs informed Evans of it and promised to guard him against any attack. Jusseaume even attempted himself to take Evans' life but was frustrated through the alertness of the latter's interpreter.

According to Evans, it was the intention and purpose of the Canadian traders to spare no ". . . trouble or Expense to maintain a Fort at the Mandaine Village Not that they see the least appearance of a Benefit with the Mandanes but carry their views further, they wish to open a trade by the Missouri with the Nations who inhabit the Rocky Mountains, a Trade, that at this Moment is Supposed to be the best on the Continent of America."[84]

Just how long Evans remained on the upper Missouri is not known,[85] but before the end of the year (1797) he was acting as a surveyor in and about Cape Girardeau. Nor has any definite information as yet come to light concerning the operations of Mackay, whom, it will be remembered, we left at Fort Charles in February, 1796. Mackay himself says that he explored up to the Mandan; however this may be, he was back in St. Louis in May, 1797. It is quite likely that Evans descended the river shortly after, for Trudeau tells us that he took possession of the fort among the Mandan ". . . for an instant [only] as a short time after that he had to descend to this city."[86]

Mackay undoubtedly returned to St. Louis before Evans, for we read in Howard's letter to Carondelet: "McCay also informed me that before he came down the Missouri he had definite information that Don Juan Evans who had been sent to Explore a route to the Pacific Ocean had crossed the Mandan Nation successfully on the way to the *Montañas*

[83]P. de C. leg. 213. A number of letters concerning the later life of Evans are, however, to be found in this legajo. They are printed in Nasatir, "John Evans," *op cit.,* XXV (1931), 591-608.

[84]Quaife, "McKay's Journal," *Wisconsin Historical Society Proceedings,* LXIII (1915), 198.

[85]Evans left the Mandans on May 9 and arrived in St. Louis on July 15, 1797 (*American Historical Review,* LIV (1949), 524-525).

[86]Houck. *Spanish Régime,* II, 254. Howard to Carondelet, May 13, 1797, said: "With regard to the Mandan Nation, from the best information that I have been able to secure from the above mentioned persons as well as from several others and particularly Diego McCay [James Mackay] who returned a few days ago from the Missouri which he has been exploring since the month of July '95" (ms. in B. L.).

Relucientes, alias the White Mountains, alias the Rocky [*Pedrejosas*] Mountains and that once they were crossed he believed it would be easy to reach that sea."[87] However, in December Mackay was addressing a letter to J. T. Evans, surveyor at Cape Girardeau, and letters from various individuals similarly addressed are to be found in the Spanish Archives.[88]

Mackay, when petitioning for a position in the royal service, summarized his activities during the years 1795-97, and although he considers the work of Evans as his own, we quote:

I have but little merit to recommend me to my Sovereign or to your Excellency excepting that of being a Traveler from my youth, principally through the wild & unknown Deserts of this Continent Especially through that part of His Majesty's Dominions watered by the Missouri & its Branches, & agreeable to my Commission from Baron Carrondelete the then Governor Gen' of these Provinces, I omitted nothing in my Power to render my Services useful to my Sovereign & to my fellow subjects.

My Chief objects were, to pave the way for the discovery & Commerce of that vast Country on both side of the Missouri & across the Continent to the Pacific Ocean. In this enterprise I succeeded as much as could be expected from the resources & support I hade.

I Brought the Indian nations who were then at war to peace with each other & those of them who were at enmity with the white people of Louisiana (the Sioux of Grand Detour) I brought them to a sense of their Duty by Convincing them, how much it would be [to] their Interest to Traffic & live in perpetual friendship with the white Children of their Great Spanish Father [the King] to whom they owed the strictest alliance & attachment as well as to the Great Spanish Chief residing near the mouth of the mississippi, who from pity & regard for his red children wished to have the roads Clear for the purpose of sending the white people among them with the necessaries of life . . .

I also found means to drive the English out of His Majesty's Territories & took possession of a Fort which they built at the mandan nation on the upper part of the Missouri & broke off the Alliance that existed then between the said English & the nations of that Country I also took a Chart of the Missouri from its mouth to the wanutaries nation, which following the windings of the river is little short of 1800 miles.[89]

[87]*Ibid.* See also, Houck, *History of Missouri,* I, 334.

[88]P. de C. leg. 213. See Nasatir, "John Evans," *op. cit.* No definite information of Evans' going beyond the Mandan has been seen by the writer. Evans promised to return to the Mandan and bring them guns and ammunition, a promise which was never fulfilled. Thwaites, *Lewis and Clark,* I, 223.

[89]Mackay to Gayoso de Lemos, New Orleans, June 8, 1798, P. de C. leg. 2365. A copy is in the library of the Missouri Historical Society. For Evans and Mackay's contributions to geography and cartography see Diller, "Maps of the Missouri River before Lewis and Clark," *op. cit.;* A. H. Abel "A New Lewis and Clark Map," in *Geographical Review,* I (1916), 329-345, and Abel, *Tabeau's Narrative,* etc.

That Mackay's services were not unappreciated by the Spanish government is evidenced in his appointment as commander of the post of San André on the Missouri and by the extensive amounts of land that were granted to him by the officials of Spanish Louisiana. Trudeau, it seems, had promised Evans some land at Cape Girardeau in recognition of the service he had rendered to the Crown,[90] but whether he received it we have no knowledge. For some time he acted as a surveyor at Cape Girardeau. In a letter to Mackay on May 20, 1799, Governor-General Gayoso de Lemos, who had taken Evans into his household, says:

Poor Evans is very ill; between us, I have perceived that he deranged himself when out of my sight, but I have perceived it too late; the strength of liquor has deranged his head; he has been out of his senses for several days, but, with care, he is doing better, and I hope he will get well enough to be able to send him to his country.[91]

5.

THE SPANISH FINALE: THE IMMEDIATE PRECURSORS OF LEWIS AND CLARK

Despite the failure of Mackay and Evans to penetrate to the shores of the Western Sea, Spanish zeal for the enterprise was not altogether lost. Clamorgan reported in 1798 that despite the loss by death of Andrew Todd, "on whose resources we laid the foundation for the quick success of our enterprises for the discovery of the Pacific Ocean, we are still none the less moved by the same zeal and same ambition that we have always been to continue the course which should carry our business to the very source of the Missouri." Desire for profit now became the chief motivating purpose behind the Missouri Company. Efforts were made to develop the trade with the tribes residing along the Platte, and the slow ascent of the Missouri, tribe by tribe, was begun, gaining the friendship of each through trade and presents. Thus, direct attempts to penetrate to the Western

---

[90]Evans to Trudeau, Cap. a la Cruze, June 18, 1798, P. de C. leg. 213, printed in Nasatir, "John Evans," *op. cit.,* XXV (1931) 602-604.

[91]*American State Papers, Public Lands,* VI, 719. Quoted by Teggart, "Notes to Lewis and Clark," *American Historical Association, Annual Report, 1908,* I, 192, but with incorrect page and volume reference. An account of Mackay's later life is in the course of preparation by the present writer. For his appointment, see Houck, *Spanish Régime,* II, 245. Gayoso de Lemos considered Evans and Mackay invaluable to the service of Spain. He appointed Mackay to command at San André but having no place for Evans took him into his own household. De Lemos proposed using both in defining the land claims of the United States, England, and Spain in the north. Gayoso de Lemos to Saavedra, New Orleans, Nov. 22, 1798, ms. in library of the Missouri Historical Society. A summary of this letter is in P. de C. leg. 2365. Evans' instructions for surveying at Cape Girardeau and letters regarding his activities as surveyor at that place are in P. de C. leg. 213. See Nasatir, "John Evans," *op. cit.,* where documents relating to Evans are printed.

Sea seem not to have been undertaken during the next few years, although traders were being sent to the Ponca, the Sioux, the Arikara, and other tribes of the upper Missouri.[92]

Clamorgan operated in the Upper Missouri trade continually. His company reorganized many times and for a period was formally known as Clamorgan, Loisel and Company. As an example of their continuous trading activities let the following suffice: Francisco Derouin left St. Louis in August, 1796, in charge of the Missouri Company activities among the Octotatas. He returned to St. Louis in the spring of 1797. He experienced difficulties among the Kansas and Octotatas. He had no direct information of English trading but the Sioux had come to the Mahas to make war on the Kansas. The Octotatas were two hundred leagues from St. Louis.[93]

On the other hand, fear of a rupture with England and the consequent invasion of the Spanish Illinois from Canada caused Carondelet and other officials of Spain's possessions in the valley of the Mississippi to confine the greater part of their attention to effecting a better military defense for the Spanish settlements and to a military patrol of the Mississippi. Indeed, more than one military reconnaissance was made of the Upper Mississippi,[94] while spies were also sent into the interior, which, although technically belonging to the United States, was really in the hands of the British fur traders.[95]

Just how many Spaniards visited the upper Missouri after 1797 is difficult to say. Trade was being conducted in this region, but definite information concerning it is lacking. Some Spaniards certainly remained among the Mandan, for Garreau and others were met by Lewis and Clark when they ascended the Missouri in 1804. D'Eglise is supposed to have been in this region, although precise information concerning him has not come to light.

By the turn of the century, the Missouri River was well known to the St. Louis traders as far as the Mandan nation. Indeed, Truteau gives us an accurate description of the river up to its confluence with the Yellowstone. The same Truteau also possessed considerable information con-

[92]Clamorgan to Trudeau [?] June 18, 1798, ms. in B. L.
[93]Examination of Derouin, St. Louis, May 14, 1797, ms. in B. L. My former student, Betty Willets, wrote a B.A. thesis on Clamorgan. I am now preparing an account of the Missouri Company for publication. See Nasatir, "Jacques Clamorgan," op. cit. A number of illuminating documents are given in this volume.
[94]E. G. Caihol's reconnoitering expedition to Prairie du Chien, ms. in B.L., printed in Nasatir, "Anglo Spanish Rivalry in the Iowa Country 1797-1798," *Iowa Journal of History and Politics*, XXVIII (July, 1930), reprint, pp. 49-55.
[95]England, also, feared an attack upon Canada from the Spanish settlements. For illustrative documents on these points see *Wisconsin Historical Collections*, XVIII, 449, 456, 458, 464; Houck, *Spanish Régime*, II, 259, 289; and *Missouri Historical Society Collections*, III, 71. See Nasatir, "Anglo-Spanish Frontier on Upper Mississippi, 1786-1796," *Iowa Journal of History and Politics*, XXIX (1931), 155-232, and by same author, "Anglo-Spanish Rivalry in the Iowa Country 1797-1798," *Ibid.*, XXVIII (July, 1930), reprint pp. 3-55.

cerning the Yellowstone, although he admitted that none of his party had penetrated to it. Although the source of the Missouri was still unknown, the Spanish traders had a rough idea of the geography of the area watered by it. Mackay gives us a fairly accurate account of the Missouri from its mouth to its source.[96]

That trading activity on the Upper Missouri was going on continually cannot be doubted, for we have the testimony which gives us a few names and accomplishments. In 1801 Charles Le Raye left Canada with a view to conducting trade on the Missouri. Accompanied by six men, he attempted to reach the Osage country and engage in trade with that tribe. Hardly had he established himself upon the Osage River, when he was set upon by a war party of Brulé Sioux who made him a prisoner. The party was taken up the Missouri and after several detours arrived at the Arikara village on April 22, 1802. Here they encountered a Canadian trader among the Sioux, named Pardo, who was about to ascend the Missouri on a hunting expedition with a party of Gros Ventres. Pardo induced the chief who claimed Le Raye as his slave to permit the latter to accompany him on his expedition on condition that Le Raye should give the chief a part of the skins procured on the trip.

On May 27, the party, consisting of twenty-seven men, six women, and four children, crossed the Missouri and traveled in a northwesterly direction. They reached the Mandans early in June, where they remained eight days. Proceeding, they arrived at the villages of the Gros Ventres located on the Knife River on the thirteenth. On July 3, the party, now increased to forty-three, only twenty-one of whom were men, began its journey in earnest. On the fifteenth they reached the Yellowstone, and three days later the Powder River. Continuing up the latter river, trapping and hunting as they proceeded, they entered the mountains, reaching a tributary of the Big Horn on September 18. Four days later they reached an encampment of the Crow, where they rested two days. On October 5 they came to the Big Horn, where they paused to construct bull boats with which to begin their downstream voyage. Descending the Big Horn, the party arrived at the junction of that river with the Yellowstone on October 11. As the season was late, Le Raye and Pardo decided to winter on the Yellowstone. In March, 1803, they embarked for their starting point, arriving at the village of the Gros Ventres on April 24. On the ensuing fourth of May, Le Raye made a trip to the Assiniboine trading posts, where he tried to escape, but was prevented from doing so by the Sioux Indians who had accompanied him. Indeed, it was not until April 4,

---

[96]Abel, "Trudeau's [Truteau's] Description," *Mississippi Valley Historical Review,* VIII (1921), 174; Quaife, *Journals of Lewis and Ordway,* 24. Evans also gives a general idea of the Missouri from the Mandan to the mountains. Quaife, "McKay's Journal," *Wisconsin Historical Society Proceedings,* LXIII (1915) 198 ff.

1805, that he was able to make good his escape, succeeding, through the aid of a Frenchman named Paintille, in descending the Missouri to St. Joseph.[97]

Another traveler who visited the upper Missouri about this time was François Marie Perrin du Lac. Leaving St. Louis on May 18, 1802, he ascended the Missouri to the White River. Accompanying him was *"un ancien traiteur"* who Doctor Abel conjectures was Jean Baptiste Truteau. It is unnecessary to enter into the details of Perrin Du Lac's journey, since the geographical knowledge presented in his published narrative[98] adds nothing to that given by Truteau in his "Description of the Upper Missouri." Du Lac is of interest to us only in so far as he pointed out the extent of the British trade among the savages residing in territory belonging technically to France but still ruled by the Spanish authorities— a trade aggressively pursued by the British with the Indians despite Spanish prohibitions to the contrary.[99]

A perusal of the journals of the Lewis and Clark expedition reveals the names of a number of persons who were or had been engaged in trading with the Indians living in the upper Missouri region. Thus, Jean Vallé, a member of a prominent family of Ste. Geneviève, told the explorers that he had spent the winter of 1803-1804 three hundred leagues up the Cheyenne River in the Black Hills.[100] Many like references can be found scattered throughout the voluminous journals of this famous American undertaking. These references indicate that trade was continually being carried on upon the upper Missouri by men subject to, if not licensed by, the government of the Spanish Illinois.

For several years Clamorgan, Loisel and Company, in reality the successor of the Missouri Company, had been dispatching agents and merchandise to the Upper Missouri and particularly to the Mandan villages. But the competition of the British traders had a telling effect. Steadily the latter were strengthening their hold upon the trade of the Upper Missouri. With equal persistence but with more aggressiveness and success, the British traders with headquarters at Prairie du Chien were spreading westward, virtually monopolizing the trade of the Iowa-Minnesota coun-

---

[97]"The Journal of Charles LeRaye," *South Dakota Historical Collections*, IV, 150-80.

[98]Perrin du Lac wrote his narrative to convince the French that immense profits awaited those who would undertake to oust the British traders from the upper Mississippi-Missouri Valley and to capture the Indian trade of that region.

[99]Abel, "Trudeau's [Truteau's] Description," *Mississippi Valley Historical Review*, VIII (1921), 149-79. See also her *Tabeau's Narrative*. F. M. Perrin du Lac, *Voyages dans les Duex Louisianes et Chez les Nations Sauvages du Missouri* (Paris et Lyon, 1805), 195-240, 257 ff. Perrin du Lac's map is published in *Missouri Historical Society Collections*, IV, opp. p. 18, and in the German edition of his travels (M. Muller, ed., Leipzig, 1807), I, opp. p. 206. There are many documents given in this volume indicating the extent of British trade in Spanish territory.

[100]Thwaites, *Lewis and Clark*, I, 176.

try. They now began to capture the Ponca and Omaha trade, having established posts not only in the Iowa country but on the Platte River as well. So successful were they in this enterprise that practically every vessel sent up the Missouri by the Company was pillaged by these tribes. At the close of the year 1800 Clamorgan petitioned Lieutenant-Governor De Lassus to grant him the privilege of building stations and forts along the Kansas and Platte rivers.[101] Their purpose was to afford protection to a new route to the Mandan towns which would avoid the villages of the Ponca and the Omaha. At the same time Clamorgan pleaded with the Spanish officials to give him the one hundred militiamen which had been promised to him as early as 1796. He complained bitterly of the damage which the British traders were inflicting upon the agents of his company, exemplifying his statement by reciting the case of a *Monsieur* Héné (Hugh Heney), who led an expedition which probably left St. Louis in June, 1800, and which was destroyed by the British. This case was but one of many similar affairs which Clamorgan attributed to the British traders in the upper Missouri region.[102]

From the list of exclusive trading privileges granted by the Spanish officials for the Upper Missouri we find that in 1801 Sanguinet received the grant of the Mahas and Poncas; Clamorgan, the Panis République; Chauvin, the Panis—Bon Chef and Topage; Benito Vásquez, the Loups and Missouris; and Sarpy and Cabanné, the Kansas and Otos. In 1802 and 1803 Governor-General Salcedo granted all the trades of the Missouri above the mouth of the Kansas to Clamorgan, except the Panis which were granted to Chauvin. The men listed were well known merchants of St. Louis, but they usually supplied the merchandise on consignment or on other terms to hunters and traders who actually ascended the river. Very few of the men who ascended the river are known by name.[103]

We have evidence that D'Eglise made trips up the Missouri. He signed notes for goods, and it is understood that he had permission of the Lieutenant-Governor.[104] André Cayouga and Company obtained goods from Hortiz and probably traded in 1802-1803. Robidou signed notes for goods advanced by him for an expedition up the Missouri. Robidou

[101]As early as June 3, 1796, Carondelet had suggested to Godoy the formation of ". . . an expedition in Santa Fé to explore those districts more northerly than Nueva Mexico, and by driving the English from them by destroying the fortified post which they have on the Chato [Platte] River." (Houck, *Spanish Régime*, II, 182).
[102]Clamorgan to De Lassus, St. Louis, Dec. 1, 1800, P. de C. leg. 2366; Clamorgan to Salcedo, St. Louis, April 18, 1801. P. de C. leg. 218. Many documents concerning Clamorgan, Loisel and Company are given in the documentary section of these volumes. Abel, *Tabeau's Narrative* discusses this problem.
[103]Salcedo to Delassus, New Orleans, February 3, 1802, P. de C. leg. 2367, draft in P. de C. leg. 11; Delassus to Salcedo, number 142, St. Louis, May 13, 1802, P. de C. leg. 77.
[104]Notes in Missouri Historical Society, Stoddard Collection. Clamorgan advanced the goods, 1802.

himself probably sent or supplied traders; he most likely did not venture up the river himself.[105]

Fear of the invasion of Spanish territory from the north and dread of British and American penetration to New Mexico was frequently expressed throughout the period which we are reviewing, particularly so during the last decade of Spanish rule and administration in Louisiana. It was generally believed that the Missouri took its rise in the mountains, from which spot it would be a relatively easy task to descend to New Mexico. This notion struck fear in the hearts of the Spaniards, particularly so when, in 1804, several traders led by Lalande and equipped at the expense of William Morrison of Kaskaskia, the richest and most enterprising merchant in the West, were dispatched to Santa Fé.[106]

In 1803-1804, probably in 1804, Laurent Durocher[107] and Jacques D'Eglise departed from St. Louis with the intention of penetrating to New Mexico via the Missouri. Both men were recognized as *voyageurs* of much knowledge and experience; most likely the latter was connected with the operations of the Clamorgan Company. Casa Calvo expressed the opinion that, since D'Eglise had not returned, it was to be inferred that he had reached his destination. That this assumption was correct has but recently been revealed by the archives of New Mexico. While going through the records in Santa Fé and looking for documents relating to the life of D'Eglise, Lansing B. Bloom, late editor of the *New Mexico Historical Review,* brought to light the fact that D'Eglise did actually reach New Mexico, where he met with a brutal death, probably in 1806. In reporting this discovery, Mr. Bloom printed in the *Review* a number of documents, which, together with his introduction, bring out the names of several traders who penetrated to Santa Fé from the Illinois country and via the

---

[105]Note dated St. Louis, August 1803, Missouri Historical Society, Auguste Chouteau Collection.

[106]Chittenden, *op. cit.,* II, 490 ff. Other traders were also equipped by Morrison for the same purpose. See Houck, *Spanish Régime,* II, 356. Morrison placed his claims against Lalande in the hands of Pike when the latter made his memorable trip in 1806. *Chittenden, op. cit.,* II, 491; Coues [ed.], *The Expeditions of Zebulon Montgomery Pike* (New York, 1895), II, 602-603. For some additional light on Lalande see Bloom, "Death of Jacques D'Eglise," *New Mexico Historical Review,* II, (1938), 370 ff.; and I. J. Cox, *Early Explorations of Louisiana* (Cincinnati, 1906), 116 ff. James Pursley, a native of Kentucky, who had been among the Osage, ascended the Missouri as far as the Mandan Villages in company with a trader, probably from St. Louis. From the Missouri, Pursley made his way to Santa Fé, arriving there in 1805 (Coues, *Zebulon Pike,* II, 756 ff). The trail from Santa Fé to St. Louis was opened by Pedro Vial, whose journal of the expedition is translated in Houck, *Spanish Régime,* I, 354 ff. Houck's translation is from a copy in P. de C. leg. 1442 and leg. 2362. Vial's entire journal, which includes the diary of the return trip from St. Louis to Santa Fé, was found by Dr. Herbert E. Bolton in the *Archivo General y Público* (Mexico), *Provincias Internas,* Vol. 183. also in *Sección Historia.* Vol. 43. The return diary is printed by A. B. Thomas in *Chronicles of Oklahoma* IX (1931). 186-213.

[107]For an account of Laurent Durocher, see *Missouri Historical Society Collections,* IV, 10.

Missouri before or just at the close of the Spanish régime in the Mississippi Valley.[108]

Operating on the waters of the Upper Missouri at the opening of the nineteenth century was Régis Loisel, a trader and an explorer, who had been sent to the Upper Missouri on a voyage which was expected to last at least two years. Régis Loisel, a member of Clamorgan, Loisel and Company, applied for permission to ascend the Missouri and build a fort on the Upper Missouri. Clamorgan also applied for a similar grant. Both petitions were approved. This was in 1800. Loisel ascended the river and returned shortly thereafter. On July 6, 1801, Loisel entered into a two-year partnership with Hugh Heney, the latter having been active on the Upper Missouri.[109] After having been reported as assassinated, he returned to St. Louis. He had had some narrow escapes from Indians who tried to murder him.[110] Chouteau and Clamorgan outfitted him. Heney operated in the Upper Missouri among the Sioux and in 1804 went over to the Northwest Company. Loisel ascended the Missouri with Tabeau in 1802 and again in 1804.[111] Tabeau, who had been a trader for many years and had been with Lecuyer on the Upper Missouri in 1795, remained in the trade of the Upper Missouri for quite some time, going over to the Canadian companies after 1804.[112]

While ascending the Missouri, Loisel was stopped by the Sioux, and about 1800 built Fort au Cèdres[113] on an island in the river near the northern border line of present Lyman County, South Dakota. Loisel himself never went beyond Fort au Cèdres, being compelled by the change in governments to descend the river to St. Louis in order to adjust his business.[114] However, he dispatched an agent, Tabeau, with seven companions to continue the exploration of the Missouri. According to Loisel, it was discovered that one could travel by water from Hudson Bay to the mountains which surround Santa Fé, with the exception of a couple of short portages. He reported that the Platte River took its rise but a short distance west of Santa Fé, and although it was not navigable for the whole distance, travel overland was easy and open to Americans minded to penetrate as far as New Mexico. Foreigners could also go to New Mexico via the Cheyenne

---

[108]Bloom, "Death of Jacques D'Eglise," *New Mexico Historical Review,* II (1928), 369-79. See also Houck, *Spanish Régime,* II, 356.

[109]Loisel-Heney agreement is in Missouri Historical Society, Auguste Chouteau Collection.

[110]Delassus to Casa Calvo, number 108, St. Louis, September 29, 1801, P. de C. leg. 72.

[111]Loisel in his will stated that in 1805 "on arrival of my *cajeux* from the Upper Missouri," he would pay to Lisa, etc. Will of Loisel is in Missouri Historical Society, Lisa Collection.

[112]For a fuller account well substantiated see Abel, *Tabeau's Narrative,* Introduction, *passim.* Many of the documents referred to are given in this volume.

[113]See discussion of this in Abel, *Tabeau's Narrative,* 24-27.

[114]Compare Chittenden, *op. cit.,* III, 954, and Thwaites, *Lewis and Clark,* I, 160.

and the Yellowstone. The most effective means of preventing such pene-trations was to befriend the Indians along these routes and set them against the British and American intruders. This Loisel himself had been attempt-ing to do and would continue to do. Indeed, Casa Calvo proposed Loisel's appointment as Indian agent to aid in restricting the entrance of aliens into Spanish territory.[115]

At this critical juncture the negotiations in Paris between Livingston and Talleyrand came to a head, with the result that Spain's hold on the country immediately west of the Mississippi River ended somewhat abruptly, and President Jefferson dispatched Captains Meriwether Lewis and William Clark to carry out his pet project of exploring a route to the Pacific Ocean, which had been in his mind for twenty years or more.[116] Although the task of reaching the Pacific Ocean via the Missouri, attempted so enthusiastically by the Missouri Company, and encouraged by the officials of Spanish Louisiana, had not been accomplished, it is of interest to note that the Spaniards paved the way for the achievement of the Americans. It is reasonable to suppose that, had Spain continued its rule in the upper Mississippi Valley, the undertaking would before long have been ac-complished by her subjects.[117]

---

[115]Casa Calvo to Pedro Ceballos, New Orleans, Sept. 30, 1804, No. 47, *res.*, index and draft in P. de C. leg. 2368, also in A.G.I. Aud. Sto. Dom., leg. 2600, translated in Houck, *Spanish Régime*, II, 356-58; Loisel's memorial accompanying Casa Calvo's letter is translated in *Ibid.*, II, 359-64. This is a letter of Loisel to De Lassus, May 28, 1804. In James A. Robertson, *List of Documents in Spanish Archives* (Washington, 1910), it is listed under date of May 28 on page 309, but incorrectly listed on page 68. Robertson lists this letter as in A.G.I., 87-1-10. A copy is in P. de C. leg. 2368. In this connection See Abel, "Trudeau's [Truteau's] Description," in *Mississippi Valley Historical Review*, VIII, (1921), 152 and note, and more especially, Abel, *Tabeau's Narrative*, Introduction. Loisel descended to New Orleans in 1804 and delivered DeLassus' letter of August to the governor—see signed draft of Delassus' letter to Casa Calvo, St. Louis, October 3, 1804, ms. in Missouri Historical Society.

[116]Jefferson to Clark, Nov. 26, 1782, in J. A. James [ed.], *George Rogers Clark Papers* (Springfield, 1926), 155-156, also Jefferson letters in *Ibid.*, 250-251; Thwaites, *Original Journals*, VII, 193, 198, 202, etc. See also J. C. Parish, *Persistence of the Western Movement and Other Essays* (Berkeley and Los Angeles, 1943), 68 ff.

[117]The reaction of the Spanish officials to the Lewis and Clark expedition is given in several documents published in this volume.

DOCUMENTS
1785-1806

CHAPTER I

1785-1793

[Miró] to Rengel, New Orleans, December 12, 1785.[1]

My dear Sir: Under the date of July 12, last, Your Excellency enclosed to me a copy of a letter from Don Felipe de Neve, dated December 18, 1783.[2] In it he asks me for information that he thinks can be found in the archives of this capital in order to acquaint the commandancy-general with the Indian nations that border on these *Provincias Internas,* for the purpose of acting skillfully in the undertakings and projects which His Majesty has ordered put into practice, sending with the reports a map [*plano*] which may aid his better understanding.

I am very sorry not to be able to satisfy completely Your Excellency's desires to the full extent in the last matter since the French governor did not leave any map in this office, when he gave up this province, except those of the course of the Mississippi with the settlements that nation had made, but without any depth or explanation of the land on either sides, particularly on the west, which might have given information concerning the nations that border on the *Provincias Internas.*

---

[1]This is a draft written in Spanish of Governor-General Miró's letter to Antonio Rengel, *comandante* of the *Provincias Internas,* ms. in the Bancroft Library of the University of California. I have published this letter, fully edited, in the *Missouri Historical Review,* XXIV, (1920-30), 523-526, under the title, "An Account of Spanish Louisiana, 1785." I have made several changes in the translation from my previously published one. Since all places are identified in the published translation I have refrained from repeating my editorial notes here.

[2]I have published this original letter, a manuscript in the Bancroft Library, in English translation and edited in *Missouri Historical Review,* XXIV (1930), 521-522. Felipe de Neve was governor of the California 1775-1782; he was appointed *comandante-inspector* on July 12, 1782 and was *comandante-general* of the *Provincias Internas* from 1783 until his death in 1784.

119

However, I shall give Your Excellency a detailed report according to local knowledge and the information I have been able to acquire during the time that I have had the honor of commanding this province.

The mouth of the Missisippi is found at 29 degrees, 7 minutes, north latitude in the Gulf of Mexico; thirty-two leagues up the river on the east shore is New Orleans, capital of the province of Louisiana.

Sixty leagues further up on the west shore is found the Colorado River, by which one goes to Natchitoches, a district which borders on the province of Texas [the Texans]. From the entrance of the Colorado [Red] River it is not more than twelve leagues to the mouth of the Ouachita, which by way of the former [Red River] empties into the Mississippi. Between the Colorado and the Ouachita are the great and small Cados or Caudachos, Yatasés, Adaes, Natchitoches, Rápidos, Pacanás, Alibamones, Chactos, Ochanias, Biloxis and several others of less importance in the land of [the] Atak-apas and Opeluzás, which are the nations that border immediately on the aforementioned province of Texas on that side.

Continuing up the Mississippi from the mouth of the Colorado, a hundred and eighty leagues farther up stream we find the river of San Francisco de Arkansás on the same west shore. Twelve leagues up this river is the fort of Carlos III, between which and the Mississippi at varying distances are found the Arkansas nation divided into three villages, the Ogapás, the Otouy, and the Tulimas. Along the course of this river, over a hundred leagues up stream, the Little Osages have established themselves, who are the only nation that I know in this region which borders on the kingdom of New Spain.

Ascending the Mississippi to·its source there are no other settlements but those of Ste. Geneviève and St. Louis, five hundred leagues from this capital on the west shore, twenty leagues distant one from the other.

At St. Louis, by order of His Excellency, the Conde de O'Reylly, presents are given every year to the Sius, Big Osages, Ayues, Cancés, Panis Mahas, Sacs, Autocdatás, Hotos, Little Osages, Misuris, Renards, and Kaskakias.[3]

Further up is found the Missouri River, which having its source in the mountains of the New Kingdom of Mexico, it becomes necessary for me to give a detailed account not only of its course, but also of the rivers that flow into it.

The Missouri is a large river which flows from the northeast, one quarter to the East, and empties into the Mississippi five leagues above

---

[3]Many more tribes than those listed here received presents at St. Louis. Compare this list with that given in *Archivo General de Indias, Sección Papeles de Cuba, legajos* 2357 and 2358 (hereinafter cited A.G.I., P. de C., leg.), and printed in Louis Houck, *Spanish Régime in Missouri* (Chicago, 1909), I, 44-45; 141-148. Same in *Wisconsin Historical Collections*, XVIII, 279-301; 358-368.

St. Louis, the chief Spanish settlement of Illinois [located] at 40 degrees north latitude, more or less. It is extremely swift and full of falls everywhere. Navigation on it is dangerous for this reason and because the palisades which enclose these falls make the current swifter, so that there is hardly a passage in low water for a canoe in the rapids. Its channel changes every year.

In all the time in which trading has been going on along the Missouri no one had ever gone higher up than the river of the Sius, about two hundred leagues from the mouth of the former. Nevertheless, later reports of the Riis or Arricaras Indians assure that two hundred leagues beyond their villages is a rather large cascade which drops from a high mountain which they call "La Montaña que Canta" [the mountain which sings], doubtless because of the noise that the water makes.

Before going on it is necessary to bear in mind that the chain of mountains that starts [que toma] from Santa Fé, a little to the east [of it], and which goes to the province of Quivira, according to report, forms the high lands between New Mexico and this region. Many of the rivers that rise to the east of these mountains empty into the Arkansas River, of which I spoke above, and the greater number into the Missouri. Those that rise to the west [flow] into the River of the North [Río Grande], or Brabo which, as Your Excellency knows, empties into the Gulf of Mexico. The Missouri cuts this chain of mountains to the north of the source of the aforesaid River Brabo, verging towards the west, a quadrant to the northwest, and according to all signs, this is the region where the cataract or cascade is formed, of which the Arricaras speak. And passing these mountains, it should flow as far as the other chain of mountains which passes between the Colorado River and the province of Teguayo.

The rivers to the east of this mountain, to the north of Teguayo, must empty into the Missouri, which, as it seems, has its source here, because to the west of these mountains, the sea or the Bay of the West almost washes its base [baña quasi (sic) su pié].

Two leagues from the mouth of the Missouri is a place called Agua Fría. It is a cliff about a half league in width washed by the Missouri on the right. It must be about two hundred feet high and in spots has a fairly gentle slope. On its summit there is a meadow with land good enough to establish a settlement.

From Agua Fría to the Portage of the Sius they reckon two leagues. This place is a meadow a quarter of a league from the Missouri on the left shore, about a league and a half in width, which reaches to the shore of the Mississippi. It has good soil and is suitable for cultivation.

Two leagues from the Portage of the Sius there is a coal mine which can be exploited at little cost.

From the coal mine to Punta Cortada on the left short of the Missouri is another two leagues.

From Punta Cortada to the channel called by the French "Del Pensamiento," is reckoned as seventeen leagues. At this spot empties a river called La Lutra, navigable for canoes in the dry season for thirty or forty leagues. At the end of this aforesaid distance, there is found at ten or twelve leagues, the Haha [sic] river, at fifty leagues from St. Louis.

From the channel "Del Pensamiento" to the River Gasconade is reckoned as two leagues.

The Gasconade is a large river about thirty leagues from the mouth of the Missouri on the right shore, navigable in the season of the lowest water up to fifty leagues and in the highest water to more than a hundred and twenty. About thirty leagues from its mouth, it comes very close to the marshes of one of the branches of the Maramek (a river which empties into the Mississippi six leagues below St. Louis). From the Gasconade River to that of the Grand Osages is reckoned at ten leagues.

Forty leagues from the entrance of the Missouri on the right shore of the river is found the River of the Grand Osages, a fairly large river. It flows from the west, a quadrant to the northwest, and one can ascend it to the village of the Grand Osages located about a hundred and twenty leagues from the Missouri, but fairly high water is needed to do this, since in low water it is not possible to go beyond the River Niangá, which contributes a considerable amount of water to that of the Grand Osages. The current in this latter river is very rapid, a condition that arises from a number of islands and falls that are in it. The large number of rivers that flow into it make it subject to great freshets [avenidas]. Until it reaches its branch fifteen leagues below the village of the Grand Osages, where they end, there are ninety-eight islands.

Three leagues farther upstream than the River of the Grand Osages on the left bank is a small river called the Cedros [Cedar] from the fact of having that kind of tree, which regularly are two or two and a half fathoms [twelve to fifteen feet] in circumference.

From the River of the Grand Osages to the River of the Mine is reckoned as twenty leagues. This river is small and is on the right side of the Missouri. They call it the River of the Mine because of the many salt springs that flow into it [from the banks]. From the River of the Mine to the Charatón is reckoned as eight leagues.

They call the two equal-sized rivers that flow into the Missouri from its left side farther up, four leagues apart, Charatón. They approach very near the River of the Frayles [Des Moines] which empties into the Mississippi eighty leagues upstream from St. Louis, five hundred eighty leagues distant from New Orleans. From the Charatón to the Río Grande is reckoned eight leagues.

This [Río Grande] flows a distance of about three hundred leagues, parallelling [*costeando*] the Missouri at thirty or forty leagues, up to beyond the Arricarás. It comes very near to the River of the Friars, since from the large island [*grande isla*] that is eighty leagues up this river one can get in two days' marching to the Río Grande and from here in two more to the Missouri. From the Río Grande to the River de Cans or Cancés there are thirty-four leagues.

The Cancés is one hundred and eight leagues from the mouth of the Missouri, on its right bank. In high water one can ascend it to the village of the Republic [*Aldea de la República*] or Panis, which the Indians call Maniguacci or the "Eyes of the Partridge" [*Ojos de Perdiz*]. Farther on is the River Nichenanbatoné on the left shore of the Missouri near the River of the Friars. Ten leagues below that is another small river called the Weeping Water [*el agua que llora*].

The Chato River follows. This is more than half a league wide without being easily navigable. It is one of the largest [of the rivers] that empty into the Missouri and rises in the mountains of New Mexico. According to the Indians' reports, it has many good-sized branches, but we do not know it beyond the large island or eighty leagues from its mouth.

Fifteen leagues from the Missouri, on the right bank [of Río Chato], is found the village of the Auctocdatás, and twelve leagues beyond is that of the Panis on the same bank. Three leagues upstream from this last village on the left bank is the River de Papas or Lobos on which are settled the Lobos [Wolf] Indians, or the Panis Mahas, thirty leagues from its mouth.

Thirty leagues above the Chato River on the left bank of the Missouri is the River of the Sius. They claim that twenty leagues up this river is the quarry for the red stone of which the Indians make their pipes for their calumets. From the River of the Sius to the *Escarpado* [Rugged] River, or the River-that-Runs [Niobrara], it must be about a hundred leagues.

This river is about ninety leagues from the Arricarás. It is a large river but is not navigable. It goes dry in the summer but is very swift in the spring on account of freshets, which is the reason the Indians call it the River-that-Runs. It flows from the west, a quadrant to the northwest, and also has its source in the mountains of New Mexico. A league below its mouth and another league from the Missouri is a small river where the village of the Poncas Indians is. All the country between the Chato River and the River-that-Runs is like a meadow and of sandy soil [*guasi de praderías y tierra avenosa*].

Forty-five leagues above the Escarpado River is the Little Missouri, which is nothing but the first fork of the river of that name; it flows towards the west [sic], is not easily navigable, and has its source in the mountains of New Mexico.

The Pados or Toguibacós live near it, or at least have some small forts to which they retire. From the Little Missouri to the first village of the Arricarás is forty leagues. From the villages of these Indians to the River-that-Runs,[1] the soil is very sandy, almost without woods, full of sand dunes and small rocks. The sight is the most disagreeable that can be imagined. All this vast country beginning with the Arcanzas River to the shore-that-sings [costa que canta] is an immense prairie cut up and watered by the above-mentioned rivers. This prairie land is bound on the west by the mountains of New Mexico, on the east by the shore of the Mississippi; to the south by the river San Francisco de Arcanzás; to the north its boundaries are unknown because the Indians who have given this information do not go beyond the shore-that-sings.

In such a great extent of territory, the climate can not help being very uneven or varied and it is certain that nowhere does one find the kind one would expect judging from its latitude. The land near the Lakes of Canadá, the uncultilvated soil, and the immense plains do not put the least obstacle in the way of the north winds, which, together with other physical causes, make these regions much colder than the same latitude in Europe. The healthful quality of its water and the general excellence of the soil and the meadows, formed by nature, is the reason that they are covered with buffalo, goats, deer, does [bucks], etc. The woods [forests] are full of game and are especially stocked with all kinds of ducks, turkeys, pheasants, etc. The soil is suitable for the cultivation of flax, wheat and hemp.

This reported, I will pass on to relating the different tribes of the Indians who, as I have already mentioned, live on the shores of the Missouri or the rivers that flow into it.

The village of the Grand [Big] Osages is located a hundred and twenty leagues up the river of that name, two leagues from its mouth on a large prairie in a sort of natural and somewhat elevated platform. This is the most numerous of the nations of the Missouri, at least of those with whom we trade, and may have about four hundred or four hundred and fifty men capable of bearing arms. Generally they are good hunters.

The village of the Little Osages, of which those who have settled on the upper waters of the Arcansa River are a part, is located about eighty leagues from the junction with the Missouri on its right bank, a league inland in a large meadow on a hill which dominates it. They can put two

---

[1] The handwriting in the document changes at this point.

hundred and fifty men under arms and are skillful hunters. One must note in passing that all the wealth of the Indians on the Missouri consists in having many horses which they get from the Laytanes or Apaches and from the frequent raids that one nation makes on another. What is most surprising is that in spite of the large number of horses and mares that they have, they entirely prevent the raising of colts by loading the latter more than usual and making them run too much.

The boundaries of the hunting region of the Little Osages begin at the River of the Mine and extend to that of the Grand Osages. Their game [hunt] consists of the deer, geese, bears, mountain lions, beavers and otter.

The Missouris, who are one league from the Little Osages, have their villages on the bank of the Missouri. They must have about a hundred and twenty men capable of bearing arms. They are at peace with the Little Osages because of their proximity, and with the nations on the Upper Missouri in order to secure horses. The territory of the Missouris begins at the River of the Mine, extending to the Fire Prairie [*Prado del Fuego*], eight leagues below the River of Cancés, on both banks of the Missouri. Their game [hunting] is the same as that of the two former.

The Cancés have their villages about a hundred and forty leagues from the mouth of the Missouri on a very high cliff about two "avanzadas" from the shore of that river. They must have two hundred warriors [*hombres de armas*] and are unquestionably the best hunters on the Missouri. They maintain peace with the Little Osages and with the Missouris, and make war on the Panis in order to obtain horses. Their hunting land is up the River de Cancés as far as the River de Nimaha.

The Hotos live fifteen leagues up the Chato River on a small wooded hill [*montecillo*] in the middle of a prairie, and they have about a hundred men capable of bearing arms. The Hotos are the only nation on the Missouri who are not obliged to trade or carry on business with Illinois, because they are in close friendship with the Ayués, settled on the River of the Friars. This river might cause much trouble to the Upper Missouri and more to the towns of New Mexico, if the traders from the American district or the English continue to open up trails and trade with the Hotos by means of the Ayués. For this reason it is well to know that the Hotos hunt on the Grand River [*en el grand Río*], which is two days' march from the Missouri, and that from the Grand River to the large island which is in the River of the Friars, about eighty leagues from its mouth, only a two days' journey is necessary. Therefore, as was hinted above, traders from the other district need only a two or three days' journey to get to the hunting ground of the Hotos. In this case the trading would be all the more troublesome [*oneroso*] in the Upper Missouri because it could at-

125

tract the Panismaha nation and the traders could the more easily trade with the Ayovues.

While the Hotos are at war with the Sius, they prefer to trade with the Illinois, but it is always to be feared that the English may enter the villages of the Panis and Hotos, as they did in 1773 and 1777.[5] The extent of the Hotos hunting grounds is from the River of the Great Nimahá to that of Boyer.

The Panis are found about twenty-seven leagues from the Chato River, and consist of four hundred men capable of bearing arms. Their hunting grounds are on the tongue of land between their river and the Chato and extend from their village to the River of San Francisco de Arcanzás.

The Panimahás are found thirty leagues within [up] the River de Papas or Lupas [Lobos, Wolves]. They have three hundred and fifty men. They hunt from the left bank of the Chato River to the Padós river which is a tributary of the Papas.

The Indians of the Panis Republic, called Paniguacey or Eyes of the Partridge, [Ojos de Perdiz], live on the River Cancés about a hundred and thirty leagues from its mouth, and consist of two hundred and twenty men capable of bearing arms. It must be observed in passing that, since all these nations, or at least the majority of them, live by hunting, they are apt to divide themselves from time to time when they do not find enough animals on their hunts for the maintenance of their nation, and from the time [Punto] of the division they are enemies.

The Panimahás live about two hundred and eighty leagues from the mouth of the Missouri, and they hunt in the region that is between the Boyér River and their villages.

The Poncas have a village on the small river below the River-that-Runs. Nevertheless they are nomadic, naturally ferocious and cruel, kill without mercy those whom they meet on the road, although if they find themselves inferior in strength, they make friends of them and, in a word, although they are not more than eighty warriors, they only keep friendship with those whom necessity obliges them to treat as friends.

The seven villages of the Arricaras, or Riis, are located along the Missouri nearly four hundred leagues from its mouth. They have about

---

[5]See A. P. Nasatir, "Ducharme's Invasion of Missouri," *Missouri Historical Review*, XXIV (1929-30), 3-25, 238-260, 420-439; "Anglo-Spanish Frontier in the Illinois Country during the American Revolution 1779-1783," *Journal of Illinois State Historical Society*, XXI, (1928) 291-358 (reprint pp. 3-70.) See also *Iowa Journal of History and Politics*, XII, (1914) 358-359; and Houck, *Spanish Régime in Missouri*, I, 141-148.

nine hundred warriors, and although they occupy an extensive region, its dryness and barrenness does not supply animals with their regular pasturage, and they, therefore, lack them.

The Padós were in former times the most numerous nation on the continent, but the wars which other nations have made against them have destroyed them to such an extent that at present they form only four small groups [parcerías], who go wandering from one side to the other continually, which saves them from the fury of the other nations. They number about three hundred and fifty men, very skillful with the arrow and in running.

The Laytanes or wandering Apaches, like the Padós, are better known in your provinces than in this one. They inhabit the borders of New Mexico [las costas del Nuevo Mexico] and are considered the best warriors on the banks of the Missouri. They dominate all the neighboring tribes, and although divided into several war parties, or parcerías, they all live in perfect friendship.

The Sius, who extended from the River of the Friars to the source of the Mississippi are, like the Laytanes, the dominating nation on the left bank of the Missouri. In Illinois only those who trade on the River of the Friars are known. They are wanderers and live in several groups [parcialidades].

The Higadosduros [hard livers], or Pitacaricó, are settled along the Missouri higher up than the Arricaras. We consider them rather numerous since they consist of seven good-sized villages, but they are not known in Illinois except for their relations with the Indians, which accounts for the reason that the number of Laytanes, Sius, and Pitacaricos are not given here.

(There may be some differences in the names of the Indian tribes and of the rivers, but I give those that are known by the French who have been the masters of this province.)[6]

This is all the information which I can give to Your Excellency, and I shall be happy if this report will contribute aid to your undertaking and project for the purpose for which Your Excellency asked it of me.

New Orleans, December 12, 1785·

[Miró]

[To] Señor Don Josef Antonio Rengel,[7] Commandant of the Provincias Internas

---

[6]This seems to be an insertion and was probably added after this draft was first written.

[7]Rengel was comandante-general of the Provincias Internas, ad-interim, 1784-1785.

II

PEREZ TO MIRÓ, ST. LOUIS, DECEMBER 1, 1788[1]

NUMBER 58

I would believe myself failing in my duty if I did not inform Your Excellency of the events which are occurring or which may occur in the course of time because of the present situation of this country, because of the distance of your capital, because of its small population and because of its lack of strength, surrounded as it is by a great number of savage nations and the frontiers of the American and English, so that it is exposed to be the victim of the barbarousness of the one and the jealousy and envy of the others. This, in fact, is the true situation of the Illinois Country.

The good of the service incites me to give Your Excellency an account of what I regard as avoidable [sic—unavoidable] unless sure and prompt steps are taken to stop the evil in its beginnings. For a long time the English, and especially the Americans of some [torn] district have been looking for the means to penetrate the Missouri. The least appearance of war can place this country [which has at this moment no power of resistance] in the hands of one or the other, for which reason this loss can be regarded as [a consequence of?] the epoch of vagabonds who will go into the province of New Mexico, and thus [?] you will see that they [provinces of New Mexico?] are almost frontiers with the Missouri, from where [New Mexico] the principal rivers take their sources in the environs of the best mines of those provinces.[2] Conditions being as they are, one can believe that they will assemble troops of vagrants and will unite to go to pillage these mines, which, having no defense, they will have no difficulty in taking. They will commit disorders and insults before the government can take steps to force them to retreat. This reflection of mine will at the moment seem chimerical, but time alone will be able to tell.[3]

I see the good union and friendship which reigns between us and the nations of the Mississippi, and on the shore of the Maha and the Illinois, insensibly diminishing in some part, notwithstanding that I give all my

---

[1]Original written in Spanish in A.G.I., P. de C., leg. 2361. There is a copy from a copy in the Bancroft Library.

[2]The translation contained in this sentence is conjectural. There seems to be something faulty in my copy from the original. The Spanish is as follows: *La menor apariencia de Guerra puede meter este Pais (que no tendra en ese momento ninguna resistencia para oponerse) entre las manos de los unos ó los otros por lo que se puede mirar esta perdida como la epoca de bagamundos que iran en la provincia del nuebo Mexico, y equivara [sic] que son quasi fronteras con el Misury de donde las principales riberas ban a tomar su principio en las enmediaciones de las mejores Minas de esas Provincias.*

[3]This is an illustrative letter; there are many others like it. For the background

128

attention to maintaining it because I know the necessity we have of keeping them as friends. How can this union be maintained when there is scarcely the wherewithal to make them small presents, to which for many years past they have been accustomed, and which the neighbors offer to them in great abundance. How is it possible to do so with the scarcity [small amount] of goods which is sent for this purpose at present? An increasing number of parties of Indians are presenting themselves [now] in this town, the greater part of them numbering not less than forty to fifty men, without counting the women, and at the head of each of them a great chief [*considerado*] or a war chief always comes. It is best to give the same amount to each one, because, among themselves, they are regarded with the same authority. What present can be given them when the principal articles which are sent consist of only seven and one half pieces of cloth, seventy blankets, seventy-two guns, eighty-eight striped shirts, eighteen white shirts, five hundred pounds of powder and six barrels of *aguardiente* (these last, after having suffered the ordinary leakage of the trip and standing for a year, hardly come to four)? With such a small amount of goods which is almost two-thirds less than what was formerly sent, it is impossible to content them and give them proofs of our disposition to live in good friendship with them. Notwithstanding all the economy which I observed in the presents which I made, I was forced by dire necessity to let them see that I could not give them anything else because the city was totally burned;[4] at the same time I availed myself of the pretex of the loss of Mr. Sarpy's *batteau,* because I recognized by their appearances and replies that they would not be satisfied with what was given to them.

I am taking the liberty of informing Your Excellency that I find it indispensable, in order to maintain friendship and good relations with these nations, (and particularly with those of the Mississippi), and to enable them to oppose our neighbors in case of necessity, to increase the goods sent for gifts at least two-thirds above the amount sent this year, so that it will be possible to add something for them, and to keep them content, in order to avoid other greater expense and accidents which may happen.

---

for this letter see A. P. Nasatir, "Anglo-Spanish Frontier on the Upper Mississippi 1786-1796," *Iowa Journal of History and Politics,* XXIX, (1931), 155-232.

[4]New Orleans was burned on March 21, 1788, and 856 edifices destroyed. An account of the fire may be found in Charles Gayarré, *History of Louisiana, Spanish Domination* (New York, 1867), 203-205. Miró and Navarro's report on the fire dated April 1, 1788, is printed in *Louisiana Historical Society, Publications,* VIII, 59-62. Under date of September 30, 1788, Miró and Navarro informed the King that the loss caused by the fire reached $2,595,561.00 See A. P. Nasatir and E. R. Liljegren, "Materials Relating to the History of the Mississippi Valley from the Minutes of the Spanish Supreme Councils of State, 1787-1797," *Louisiana Historical Quarterly,* XXI (1938), 11, (reprint, p.11).

Your Excellency will likewise permit me to inform you that during my predecessor's[5] entire time, large presents were made to them by virtue of the great amount which was sent to him. Accustomed to these large gifts, they believe that our friendship is changing, as it has been necessary to reduce them [the presents] to a small number because of the reduction of two-thirds the total that was formerly sent to us.

May God keep Your Excellency many years.
St. Louis, Illinois, December 1, 1788.
Manuel Perez[6]
[rubric]

Señor Don Estevan Miró[7]

---

[5]Francisco Cruzat, lieutenant-governor of Upper Louisiana (Illinois Country) for the second time, 1780-1787. My student, Donald Barnhard, has written an excellent dissertation on Cruzat's second term.

[6]Manuel Perez, lieutenant-governor at St. Louis, 1787-1792.

[7]Miró replied on January 14, 1789, approving Perez' request. "It has been ordered that two-thirds be added to that which was sent to you last year so that you may be in a position of satisfying those nations with it. This will satisfy all that you propose in your cited letter [no. 58]". Miró to Perez, New Orleans, January 14, 1789, A.G.I., P. de C., leg. 6.

III

GARDOQUI TO FLORIDABLANCA, JUNE 25, 1789[1]
[EXTRACT]

Reservada, No. 25—One of the many enthusiastic Englishmen who roam [*corren*] these western countries of the King's dominions inhabited only by Indians has arrived here.

---

[1]*Archivo Histórico Nacional* (Madrid), *Sección Papeles de Estado, legajo* 3893 (hereinafter cited A.H.N., Est.). Written in Spanish.

Diego María de Gardoqui was born in Bilbao on November 12, 1735. His father's firm of "Gardoqui and Sons" had been the chief go-between through which Spain furnished secret military stores to the American revolutionists. Don Diego, however, separated himself from the business and embarked on an official carreer. He was elected as *regidor capitular* of Bilbao and served as *Síndico procurador and Prior del Ilustre Consulado* of Bilbao. He was educated in England; and served as *encargado de negocios* of Spain to the United States, 1784-1789. He later was appointed director of the commerce of the Indies and *secretario del despacho de Hacienda.* After several years of service in the ministry of finance and as a member of the *Consejo de Estado* he was appointed Ambassador to Turin and to Cerdeña. He died November 12, 1798. Gardoqui rightfully deserves a biographer. His stay in America and the negotiations with John Jay and the ill-fated Jay-Gardoqui Treaty have been treated in full in S. F. Bemis, *Pinckney's Treaty* (Baltimore, 1926), and in A. P. Whitaker, *Spanish American Frontier* (Boston, 1927), and elsewhere. A good deal of his correspondence when in the United States is in the A.H.N., and recently calendared in Miguel Gómez del Campillo, *Relaciones Diplomáticas Entre España y los Estados Unidos* (volume I, Madrid, 1944).

Don José de Moñino y Redondo, Conde de Floridablanca, son of a retired army officer, was born October 28, 1728. After a successful embassy at Rome he succeeded Grimaldi as first [Foreign] minister to Charles III. He retained this office until 1792, when through Godoy's influence he was dismissed and imprisoned. He re-

130

This person, although a young man, says he has traveled for nearly five years from the English establishment of Hudson Bay towards the west among various Indian nations, crossed the Mississippi and the Missouri and arrived at the cordillera of mountains which divide the waters [*arrojando por sus faldas*], some to this ocean and others to the Pacific.

He reports that the furthest nation he reached assured him that about 100 miles from that place there was a river which empties into the Pacific Ocean, and he adds that the distance to it was short.

He has made a map, *a su modo,* which I have seen and I have furnished means in order to obtain a copy.

By my son, whom I had make a voyage via the lakes of Canada to Quebec, I have learned that a Lord Edward Fitzgerald,[2] a young man, a lieutenant in the English army, left that city with the idea of crossing the wilderness and Indian nations as far as Mexico, guiding himself by the compass, as he did [crossing] the English wilderness to Canada.

Most Excellent *Señor,* would it not be worthy that His Majesty order reconnoitered the sources of those reported rivers and the country towards the west?

Perhaps in that country would be found the fur of which the traveler Cook[3] speaks, and the river where he refreshed his men, and which we have learned about from this first Englishman who has just arrived here.

What is certain is that we ought to fear all nations, and in particular the British. It is not rash judgment to believe that if the country of Botany-Bay, to which [British] prisoners have been sent, would prove fatal, then, the English would desire to establish a colony on some coast of our continent from which they could ship contraband goods to our ports which is the general purpose of everybody.

---

mained in seclusion until 1808, when he was nominated President of the Central *Junta* at Aránjuez. He died on November 20 of that same year. The best sketch of Floridablanca is A. Ferrer del Rio's biographical introduction to his *Obras Originales del Conde de Floridablanca* (Madrid, 1887).

This document is a short extract only. Omitted parts deal with: Sending duplicate of letter number 24 [in same legajo]; president wishing to retire due to illness; Gardoqui's conference with Major Dunn and the *pliegos* of Wilkinson; death of Hutchins; John Brown; Kentucky intrigues and separation; debates in Danville convention; navigation of Mississippi; stirring up Creeks. For the intrigues see Whitaker, *Spanish American Frontier;* Bemis, *Pinckney's Treaty;* and biographies and writings of Wilkinson.

[2]This English lord came down the Mississippi from Michilimackinac, visited St. Louis and Ste. Geneviève, and then went to New Orleans; some doubts about that trip have been held by contemporary and modern students. I have very little information about the details of that voyage. See Louis Houck, *History of Missouri* (Chicago, 1908). I, 359.

[3]Cook's third voyage, 1776-1779, excited the activities of the Spaniards and stimulated the interests of England in the Pacific coast of North America. The narrative of this voyage was published in London in 1785.

IV

LITERARY NEWS
ILLINOIS; AUGUST 1, 1790 *(Copy)*[1]

June 15, last, at two o'clock in the afternoon the lieutenant-governor, accompanied by Clerc and the most notable citizens of the place, left this post, forming quite a considerable committee to go to a distance of five leagues from here to assist in the benediction of a mission church of this parish. This benediction was pronounced at ten o'clock in the morning of the sixteenth with all the required pomp and solemnity. The Vicar-General, M. Pierre Gibault,[2] curate of Cahokia, officiated; the Deacon was R. P. [Rev. Pere] Jean Antoine Ledru,[3] *ad-interim* curate of this parish of St. Louis. Later, Father Ledru went to say the holy mass and the next day at *Petites Côtés* where they intend constructing another church which will be the second branch of this one. After all these ceremonies and having dined with all the guests at the house of the founder, they returned to this post without accident.

This country is becoming considerably populated; the harvest of this year has a good appearance, the season has been propitious for culture, but the lack of grain of past years has been the cause of the seed not being plentiful. The little wheat that has been harvested is very good.

Last year a stranger arrived here from the capital, who seemed to be a man of considerable importance. After he had been here two months, he requested permission to pass the winter at the village of the Big Osages, solely to learn the customs of the nations. By counsels and presents he stopped the savages from hunting and did not fail to do considerable harm to the trader who was with them. After having used up his merchandise, he [the stranger] descended here and left for Detroit in the month of March, saying that he would return here in the month of August. It

---

[1]Written in French. This is incomplete. A.G.I., P. de C., leg. 121.

[2]Father Pierre Gibault, concerning whose career in the Illinois Country see Rev. F. G. Walker, *The Catholic Church in the Meeting of Two Frontiers: The Southern Illinois Country (1763-1793)* (Washington, D. C., 1935) ; Sister Mary Doris Mulvey, *French Catholic Missionaries in the Present United States (1604-1791)* (Washington, D. C., 1936) ; "Correspondence between Abbé Gibault and Bishop Briand, 1768-1788," *Records of the American Catholic Historical Society*, XX, 406-430; J. P. Dunn, "Father Gibault: The Patriot Priest of the Northwest," *Transactions of the Illinois State Historical Society*, (1905), 15-35; P. L. Peyton, "Pierre Gibault, Priest and Patriot of the Northwest in the Eighteenth Century," *Records of American Catholic Historical Society*, XII, 452-498; J. J. Thompson, "Illinois' First Citizen—Pierre Gibault," *Illinois Catholic Historical Review*, I, 79-94, 234-248, 380-387, 484-494; IV, 197-214, 296-300; V, 154-159, 226-245; VIII, 3-29, 99-106; documents in *Collections* of the Illinois State Historical Society; C. W. Alvord, *Illinois Country* (Springfield, 1920) ; etc.

[3]In a letter to *Monseigneur* dated St. Louis, May 23, 1793 (A.G.I., P. de C., leg. 217) Ledru stated that he and Didier were dividing the church duties. The people of St. Charles and Florissant presented a memorial from Didier.

was said after his departure that among his papers had been seen a copy of a letter of exchange drawn on the bank of Venice; and that he was named Prince Bourbon, son of Condé. Whether or not he was a prince, he left here owing more than four thousand *piastres* and all the money that he used in merchandise to give and make presents to the savages in the name of the King of France. He paid these men with good reasons and promises [to be fulfilled] upon his return. It is certain that he gave all his suits and shirts. The savages regarded him as a God. He made a map of the country and of the Missouri without any one preventing him.

It was learned by some one who came from Canada that the English commandant of Detroit prevented him from crossing to New England, where he intended to go, and permitted him to go via Lake Erie. There the commandant of the fort [Erie] had him arrested, took inventory of his papers and sent them to the general of Canada, *Monsieur* Carleton. There are those who believe that his projects are supported by some power [country]. If that is so, one must conjecture that the Missouri will some day be the cause for the loss of a part or of the whole colony.[4]

The greater part of the inhabitants of this country are terribly disgusted with the ambitious means and the feebleness in all the dispatches of this commandant.[5]

He has had published at Ste. Geneviève the orders of the governor-general expressly forbidding the trade with the Big and Little Osages which [post] has never had it; and in this post from where the traders go out, the order has never been known and they send traders to other nations. However, it is evident that the Big and Little Osages will not be deprived of merchandise; because traders will go to the other nations and before

[4]Lord Dorchester, in a letter to Major Beckwith, dated Quebec, June 27, 1790, spoke of a subject of France named De Bon, who, after having passed some time among the Indians of the Missouri, lately passed from St. Louis to Detroit and thence to Niagara and into the United States. Dorchester asked Beckwith to investigate the man. *Canadian Archives Report,* 1890, page 144. Previously on May 5, Major Murray wrote Dorchester from Detroit concerning De Bon's arrival and character, enclosing a note from De Bon regarding his intended route from Detroit to Quebec and stating that De Bon's purpose was to see Quebec to satisfy his curiosity. De Bon's note is dated at Detroit, April 8. A letter from Lieutenant-Colonel Harris dated Niagara, May 16, related to De Bon. From Detroit May 5, Alexander McKee wrote John Johnson of De Bon's having passed through the Indian country but he did not know his purpose. On May 18 from Niagara, De Bon wrote Dorchester that, due to his ignorance of colonial laws, he had resolved to return to Europe through Canada, in order to avoid returning to New Orleans, and to see the province of Quebec and the Falls of Niagara. De Bon gave an account of his journey from the Illinois stating that he left there February 22; he was arrested at Detroit and sent to Fort Erie on the way to Niagara but was prevented from going there until orders were received from Dorchester. He begged Dorchester to give orders so that he be taken to Montreal, whence he would go to the United States or to Quebec as directed. *Canadian Archives Report,* 1890, "State Papers", pages 252-253. This was during the period of the Nootka Sound Controversy, and the Spaniards and Canadians were watching each other's moves on the frontier very closely.

[5]This sentence has been translated literally. It seems to imply great ambitiousness in making plans and extreme feebleness in carrying them out.

they return they will be stopped or [and] pillaged by these two nations. To bar the Missouri entirely would be a general good, but not for the commandant who, because of the two thousand *piastres* which the post of the Big Osages is worth to him and the others in proportion, does not fail to make a considerable sum.[6]

The permits of the merchants of Michilimackinac, although secret, [the merchants] do not fail to bring one hundred *piastres* each. In short, all we do is to make contributions [presents], and because of this, in time a revolt will occur which cannot be put down, because the English, ambitious for the Missouri, will not fail to support it. They are already saying as much, and they are introducing themselves as far as the Mahas, which is a nation in the upper part of this river.[7]

---

[6]The problem of the Osage Indians was a particularly vexing one. I have translated and edited the complete correspondence relating to the Osage Indians during the Spanish period. I hope to have that extensive work published in the near future, under the title *Imperial Osage*. I have cited this work a number of times in these editorial notes. See in this connection among many letters the one of the inhabitants of Ste. Geneviève to Miró, April 9, 1790, A.G.I., P. de C., leg. 7; Perez to Miró, no. 145, St. Louis, August 6, 1790, A.G.I., P. de C., leg. 16; the *Remarque* of the Dames of Illinois (undated but probably 1790), in A.G.I., P. de C., leg. 2362; and many others.

[7]See Nasatir, "Anglo-Spanish Frontier on the Upper Mississippi 1786-1796", *Iowa Journal of History and Politics,* XXIX (1931).

V

PEREZ TO MIRÓ, ST. LOUIS, AUGUST 23, 1790[1]

No. 148

Juan Bautista Pratte, having arrived at this town, I have given him the trade of the Maha nation, because of its being the best that remained after that of the Osages. With it he will be able to give some relief to sub-lieutenant of the militia Don Andrés Jago and, if he wishes, to pay at the same time something of the great amount which he [Jago] owes in this country.

This appointment, and our inability to send traders to the two Osage nations, which are the best of the Missouri nations for trade,[2] are the reasons that many persons have not been satisfied this year, and may be the cause of new complaints. Since you might wish each year to be by itself, the enclosed *relación* will inform Your Excellency of the subjects to whom I have distributed the trade myself. Although you have permitted me to take one of the best nations for myself, I have not wished to take more than one-half of the Kans, which will scarcely give me three hundred sixty to

---

[1]A.G.I., P. de C., leg. 16. Written in Spanish.
[2]Trade with the Osages had been forbidden.

four hundred *pesos*. In spite of my own arrears, it should be evident from this that I do not desire to prejudice others.

May God keep Your Excellency many years.   St. Louis, Illinois, August 23, 1790.

Manuel Perez [rubric]

Señor Don Estevan Miró

Note of the persons to whom the trade of the Missouri has been given this year:

Kansas................to the commandant and to Auguste Chouteau
Missouri......................to the commandant of Ste. Geneviève
Panis...to Pedro de Volsey
Otos......................................to Don Bentura Collell
Republic.......................................to Juan Bartélemy
Pani Maha ....to Benito Vazquez
Mahas.....................................to Juan Bautista Pratte

St. Louis, Illinois
August 23, 1790
Manuel Perez [rubric]

VI

LIEUTENANT ARMSTRONG'S EXPEDITION TO THE MISSOURI RIVER, 1790.[1]

[Henry Knox, as secretary of war, inaugurated this first official attempt to explore the Missouri River when he wrote his secret letter of December 20, 1789, to General Harmar:]

(Secret)   War Office, 20th Dec. 1789.[2]

Dear Sir: The subject I [am] about stating must be retained by you as a profound secret, and I depend on your honor not to communicate thereon now or hereafter, excepting with the Governor of the Western Territory [St. Clair] whom I shall refer to you.

[1]These documents are principally from an article based upon the Harmar papers in the William L. Clements Library of the University of Michigan written by Colton Storm, entitled "Lieutenant Armstrong's Expedition to the Missouri River, 1790" and published in *Mid America*, XXV (July, 1943), 180-188. To them have been added documents from R. G. Thwaites, [ed.], *Original Journals of the Lewis and Clark Expedition*, (Cleveland, 1904), VII, 198-201.

Captain John Armstrong was born in New Jersey, April 20, 1755. Having served with distinction as a commissioned officer in the Revolutionary War [Pennsylvania regiments], he was continued in the regular service upon the Western frontier, where he won a wide reputation as woodsman and explorer. In 1784 he commanded at Wyoming, in 1785-1786 at Fort Pitt, and 1786-1790 at the Falls of the Ohio (Louis-

135

It is important that the official information of all the Western regions should be as precise and as extensive as the nature of things will permit. You will thereafter exercise your mind in obtaining such information. Devise some practicable plan for exploring the branch of the Mississippi called the Messouri, up to its source and all its southern branches, and tracing particularly the distance between the said branches and any of the navigable streams that run into the Great North River which empties itself into the Gulf of Mexico. In order that you may better comprehend my idea, I send you a map of the said river and its conjectural relation to the Messouri.

You will see that this object cannot be undertaken with the sanction of public authority. An enterprising officer with a noncommissioned officer well acquainted with living in the woods, & perfectly capable of describing rivers and countries, accompanied by four or five hardy Indians perfectly attached to the United States, would, in my opinion be the best mode of obtaining the information requested. Could you engage two such parties, and send them off at different periods of one or two months distance from each other, it is highly probable that one if not both would succeed and return. I am not authorized to make any stipulations on this subject, but I pledge myself unequivocally that if the parties should succeed, that I will exert myself to the utmost that they shall not only be satisfactorily, but liberally rewarded, on their return. Endeavor therefore by all means to find suitable characters for this hardy enterprise. & having found them despatch them as soon as possible. I say nothing about their equipments or the manner of their being furnished, leaving that to your & the Gov-

---

ville). He was with Harmar's expedition against the Miami Villages in 1790 and was present at St. Clair's defeat. From the letters given in Thwaites, *Original Journals*, VII, 198-201, alone, it would appear that the expedition was not undertaken; the additional letters given by Mr. Storm found in the Clements Library prove otherwise. A biography of Armstrong in Cist's *Cincinnati Miscellany* (1845), I, 40, shows that he started on his tour in the spring of 1790, "and proceeded up the Missouri some distance above St. Louis, *not with an army to deter the savages, nor yet an escort, but alone.* It was his intention to examine the country of the upper Missouri, and cross the Rocky Mountains, but, meeting with some French traders, was persuaded to return in consequence of the hostility of the Missouri bands to each other, as they were then at war, that he could not safely pass from one nation to another." This is confirmed by Harmar's letter to Knox, dated Fort Washington, March 24, 1794 (in *Memoirs of the Pennsylvania Historical Society*, VII, 454, and quoted by Storm in his text), wherein Knox says, "I have received no intelligence, as yet, of Major Doughty, but have detached Lieutenant Armstrong to undertake the business recommended in your secret letters. No written orders have been given him upon that subject . . ." On returning to Vincennes, Armstrong immediately thereafter, with an escort of two friendly Indians, carefully explored the Wabash and its communications with Lake Erie. Armstrong made other important military explorations, and resigned from the army in 1793. He served as treasurer of the Northwest Territory, and later as a local magistrate, dying in Clark County, Indiana, February 4, 1816. Note in Thwaites, *Original Journals*, VII, 198.

²Original in Harmar Papers, Clements Library, vol. XI, 118; printed from transcript in Draper Manuscripts in the Wisconsin Historical Society, 2W133 in Thwaites, *Original Journals*, VII, 198-199.

ernor's judgment, & those to whom you may confide the direction of the enterprize. Pocket compasses would be necessary to their success, & pencils & paper to assist their remarks.

Were it practicable to make the operation with canoes, it would be most satisfactory.

> I am, dear sir, with great esteem,
> Your most humble servant,
> H. Knox.

Genl Harmar

(Private)[3]

Sir: In addition to my letter to you on the subject of exploring the country & waters on which you were to consult the Governor of the Western Territory, that the party employed on that business should be habited like Indians, in all respects, and on no pretence whatever discover any connection with the troops. Of course they will not take any written orders with them.

[*Knox's first letter was received by Harmar before February 20, 1790, for on that day Harmar addressed his orders to Lieutenant Armstrong, who was then at Fort Washington with his commander, as follows:*]

> Head Quarters, Fort Washington
> February 20th, 1790.

Sir:

I have already made you acquainted with the business which you have to undertake, provided the Governor of the Western Territory should Judge it adviseable—If not, You are to return from the Illinois Country to Post Vincinnes, & explore the Wabash river, & give me a particular report of its communication with Lake Erie, the depth of the Water, the distances ——— & if it can be done with safety, proceed to the Miami Village, in which case it will be necessary to have an Escort of Friendly Indians to accompany you—you will endeavor to return to Head Quarters by Land, after this business is effected.

I wish you a Safe Tour, & am with great Esteem & regard

> your hum, Servt.
> Jos. Harmar . . . . .

---

[3]Harmar Papers, XII, 8; Draper Manuscripts 2W177, printed in Thwaites, *Original Journals,* VII, 199.

From Headquarters, Fort Washington, January 14, 1790, Harmar wrote Knox: "Lieutenant Armstrong, I see, has been writing to the War Office about brevet rank. He is a valuable officer, but instead of troubling you upon the occasion, it is my opinion he should have represented his grievances, if any there were, unto his commanding officer." "Letters of General Josiah Harmar and others" in *Memoirs of the Historical Society of Pennsylvania* (Philadelphia, 1860), VII, 448-449.

[On the same day, Harmar wrote to Governor Arthur St. Clair concerning the projected expedition. Armstrong carried this letter with him when he set out to reach the "Governor of the Western Territory" at Kaskaskias.]

Fort Washington, February 20th, 1790[4]

Dear Sir: I have had the honor of receiving your letter from Fort Steuben, dated the 26ult., and observe that your detention so long there was occasioned for want of provisions. We have been upon the point of starvation here ever since my arrival. I have no great opinion of Major Doughty's mission, [up the Tennessee river] and another is on foot which I think to be really difficult and hazardous. The copy of the secret letter sent me from the War Office I do not think proper to commit to paper, for fear of accident, but Lieutenant Armstrong (whom I have ordered to undertake the tour, if possible) can fully inform you of the nature of the business, as the contents of the letter have been communicated to him, and he has taken notes in such manner as to be able to give you an exact copy of it. I have written to the War Office that I wished very much to have your Excellency's opinion upon this subject before I ordered the officer to proceed. I must, therefore, beg that you will be pleased to give it. It seems very much depends on the too adventurous establishment. If Your Excellency should be of the opinion that it is advisable for him to undertake it, be so kind as to afford him your advice and assistance upon the occasion, as it is impossible for me, at this distance, to make the necessary arrangements for that purpose. This is the subject that the Secretary of War has written you that we were to consult about. Mrs. Harmar desires to be remembered most affectionately to you and Major Sargent.

[As indicated in the preceding letter, Harmar had written to Knox earlier in the day. He was not sanguine about the success of such an enterprise.]

I shall shortly do myself the honor of writing to you again, as I am making preparations to endeavor to carry into effect what was communicated to me in your Secret letter of the 20th. December.—It will be a very difficult dangerous undertaking—I wish to have the Governor's opinion upon it, as he must now be at Kaskaskias; however if there is a practicability, it shall be attempted.— . . .

[On the fifth of March, Harmar received the second of Knox's two secret letters and three days later wrote to Armstrong the following supplementary orders:]

---

[4]Printed in W. H. Smith, *St. Clair Papers* (Cincinnati, 1882), II, 133, and in Thwaites, *Original Journals*, VII, 200.

Head Quarters, Fort Washington—
March 8th, 1790.

Sir:

Since the communication I made to you, another letter has been received from the War Office, dated the 16th. January last, & received the 5th. Inst. which mentions, "That the party employed on that business, should be habited like Indians in all respects, and on no pretence whatever, discover any Connection with the troops; of Course they will not take any written orders with them"—

Acknowledge the receipt of this letter, and govern yourself accordingly; you may then burn it— Persevere in the undertaking, if the Governor should judge it adviseable, as you find by this last Letter, that it is expected the business must Commence, & be pursued.

> I am
> > Sir
> > > with esteem
> > > your hum Servt
> > > Jos. Harmar. . .

[*Harmar recognized that Knox's orders on this matter were not to be taken lightly and he kept the Secretary of War informed as to Armstrong's progress whenever he himself received news. On the 24th of March, he wrote that he had "detached Lieut. Armstrong to undertake the business recommended in your Secret letters . . ."* And on the fifth of *April he added the tidbit that "Lieut. Armstrong left the Rapids of the Ohio on the 27th of February, to undertake the business ordered in your former Letters . . ."*

Armstrong reached Fort Kaskaskias on March 28 and delivered his dispatches, including the letter of Harmar, to Governor St. Clair.

The governor took his time about giving an opinion, for one of the numerous crises faced by the garrison at Kaskaskias arose about this time. Armstrong was put to work immediately upon his arrival trying to remedy a serious lack of supplies, and it was not until the first of May that St. Clair found time to give Armstrong his opinion. St. Clair wrote the first of his two letters regarding the expedition to Knox on May 1.]

Mr. Armstrong has been here for some time, in consequence of your communications to General Harmar, who made me acquainted with them by him. It is, sir, I believe, at present, altogether impracticable. It is a point on which some people are feelingly alive all over, and all their jealousy awake. Indians to be confided in, there are none: and if there were, those who would be most proper, and others, are now at war; but I have ex-

---

[5]Printed in *Memoirs of the Historical Society of Pennsylvania*, VII, 454.
[6]*St. Clair Papers*, II, 138, and Thwaites, *Original Journals*, VII, 200.

plained myself to Captain Armstrong for General Harmar's information, who will communicate it to you from a place whence there is less risk of dispatches miscarrying . . .

[*The following day (May 2) St. Clair wrote a similar opinion for Harmar.*]

I had the honor to receive your letter by Captain Armstrong, who also made some other Communications. — I have given him my opinion, that the Business, for the present at least, is impracticable, for the Reasons which he will inform you of.—I do not think it best to say anything about it in writing, but I have given the same information to the Secretary at War, and referred him to you for the particular explanation . . .[7]

[*Here the whole affair should have ended, but Armstrong went farther than Kaskaskias, although he did not, as his son claimed later (1844 and 1845), proceed "up the Missouri some distance above St. Louis." His report was written from Fort Washington, dated June 2, 1790, and reads as follows:*]

Fort Washington, 2.d June 1790.

Sir:

Agreeable to your Orders of the 20.th February I proceeded to Kaskaskias by way of the Rapids of the Ohio Post Vincennes & the Mississippi and reached Kaskaskias on the 28.th of March—having communicated to the Governor of the Western Territory the business on which I was detached after exercising his mind on the occasion he observed it was not only a difficult task, but one that in his opinion could be executed in the character of a trader only, and even in that there is a difficulty, as there are by Government fixed posts for Traders to assemble at and a certain quantity of Goods permitted to go to each Post The Spanish commandent knows the quantity of Firs that country produces yearly, and the quantity of Goods necessary for the Natives—As to Indians well attached to the United States I know not where they are to be found, but by making generous presents to some of those nations on the Missouri I have no doubt but in a Tour of eighteen Months or two years the necessary information might be obtained, promised rewards will not secure an indian to your interest—I presume the Governor has wrote you fully on this subject. it is a business much easier planned than executed, and should I again be called on to go on this Service I should chuse to be equipped for the Tour. the adventure ought to be furnished with a convenience made of Oil cloth for the purpose of securing his papers when traveling by Land, a half faced Camp or Tent of the same would also be necessary and is very portable—If it is a matter of consequence to the United States I am of opinion

---

[7] A different version, undated, is printed in *St. Clair Papers*, II, 144, and Thwaites, *Original Journals*, VII, 201.

there would be less difficulty in the execution at present than at an after-day—I have procured an invoice of the goods necessary for the Trade of that country, and conceive a connexion with some of the Traders might take place, and this business executed with very little expence to the Public— After visiting St. Genevive & St. Louis on the 2.d May I took my departure for post vincinnes from which I set out on the morning of the 13.th May in company with two Indians and after proceeding* two days on the course for this place one of my companions falling sick & the other being Lame they would proceed no ferther on that route, I then with much difficulty prevailed on them to take a course for the Rapids of Ohio assuring them I knew the way & that in four Suns we would reach that place where I arrived on the 25.th I found my companions attentive trusty fellows—

While at St. Louis I obtained some information respecting the country I was to have explored which is contained in the inclosed Notes—I also inclose you a map of the Missouri which I copied at St. Louis as also one of the Illinois River & its connection with Lake Michagon explained by remarks made by the drawer of the Original I am Sir with respect your ob.t. Servt

*I found from the hostile disposition of the Indians on the Wabash that it was unsafe to attempt exploring that & the Moami Rivers &c......

[Docket on verso:] Lieu.t Armstrong's Report

[*Among the Harmar Papers there are a few more documents which round out the story. Armstrong's expense account for the expedition is rather amusing, reading as follows:*]

Fort Washington 2d June 1790

D.r

The United States to Lieut. John Armstrong

To expenses for himself & Servant while on public Service from the 20 of February until the present date being one hundred and three days, *Amounting to Seventy* Dollars and thirty nine ninetieths of a Dollar.

$70 \frac{39}{90}$

To a Horse purchased for Public Service and delivered to Major *Hamtramck forty* dollars
40 dollars

Amounting in the whole to one hundred and ten dollars and thirty nine ninetieths of a Dollar Received the above Sum from General Harmar and gave duplicate Receipt for the same

June 5th 1790

John Armstrong . . .

[Harmar announced Armstrong's arrival at Fort Washington to Knox on June ninth as follows:]

Lieutenant Armstrong, whom I detached sometime since, to endeavor to carry into effect your Secret orders, returned to this post on the 2nd. Inst—After proceeding with the Governor from Kaskaskias to Cahokia, and informing him the business he was sent upon, the Governor was of opinion that it was neither prudent nor practicable to undertake it.—He has made several observations to me upon the Country, which he obtained from persons who had explored it for some distance, those notes & maps when arranged, I shall do myself the honor to transmit to you, together with an account of his expences.

[Knox's reply to Harmar's letter of the ninth of June contained the remark "I observe your information respecting the return of Lieutenant Armstrong and am satisfied therewith . . ." The final draft of the report with its attendant documents was ready by August 3, for on that date Harmar announced to Knox that "Lieut. Armstrong's report with observations that he made whilst on the Mississippi, Maps, &c, &c—I also enclose by this opportunity." To which Knox replied on September 14, touching on Armstrong's excursion for the last time, "Lieut. Armstrong's . . . reports shall be submitted to the President of the United States."

The draft of Armstrong's report retained by Harmar is accompanied by the original of the map which Armstrong secured in St. Louis.[8] It shows the Mississippi River and land east of that river to the center of Michigan and west of the Mississippi beyond the Rocky Mountains. Armstrong traced his map in pencil from the western half of Jacques Nicholas Bellin's "Carte de la Louisiane et des Pays Voisins . . ." (Paris) 1750. The Bellin map—famous in its day—was based principally on the travels of La Salle, according to the cartographer, with corrected observations by Le Sueur and de Lery. The tracing sent to Knox was probably a re-drawing of this original tracing. It is the first map of the country west of the Mississippi secured by a government-ordered expedition. Also found in the Harmar Papers are a two-page manuscript description of the Illinois River from Lake Michigan to the Mississippi River and a manuscript map of the Illinois River. Both the description and the map appear to have been copied by Armstrong from the notes and map of the explorer who made the trip.[9]]

[8]Printed in *Mid-America*, XXV (July, 1943), 187, but omitted here.

[9]Mr. Storm's concluding paragraph states that although the Armstrong expedition failed, nevertheless the Lieutenant seems to have been confident that he could have completed the task as laid out by the Secretary of War if he were given enough time and the proper equipment. Older and more cautious superiors prevented him from trying.

VII

PEREZ TO MIRÓ, ST. LOUIS, JANUARY 29, 1791[1]

No. 174

At the end of last month the savages killed two men, bachelors, while they were hunting in the Missouri thirty leagues from the establishment of *San Carlos de las Pequeñas Cuestas*. The savages, from what nation we have not been able to determine, took the scalp of only one of the two. It is suspected, however, that it was some party of *Puz* [*sic*], which was going in war against the Osages, and which perhaps had been unsuccessful in striking its blow, and that on their return they killed our two men who were hunting, in the manner regularly followed by the savages. When they cannot succeed on the first attack, the first one who has the misfortune of falling into their hands pays for it, since in that way they do not have to return to their nation without scalps. This incident proves it, since they took the scalp of only the one which had black hair and left the other one which had blonde hair.

May God keep Your Excellency many years. St. Louis, Illinois, January 29, 1791.

Manuel Perez [rubric]

Señor Don Estevan Miró.[2]

---

[1]A.G.I., P. de C., leg. 17. Written in Spanish.

[2]Miró replied, New Orleans, April 15, 1791 (A.G.I., P. de C., leg. 8), asking Perez to inform the Indians of the "bad that their Great Father will see in the one who stains the roads in blood"; that they should live in peace with everybody and "only look upon the Osages as their enemies on account of their well known perfidy".

VIII

PEREZ TO MIRÓ, ST. LOUIS, APRIL 5, 1791[1]

No. 179

Mr. Cadet Chouteau,[2] who was trading with the Kansas nation and who has just arrived, informed me that he had spent the winter very tranquilly with this nation, but that they had not traded with him all their furs because the savages of the Mississippi, sent as agents by some English traders, had taken part of the furs, notwithstanding all the efforts and steps which he had taken to stop it and to prevent the Kansas trading with them.

---

[1]A.G.I., P. de C., leg. 17. Written in Spanish.

[2]Pierre Chouteau. This complete story is contained in my as yet unpublished *Imperial Osage*.

He also informed me that on the first of March of this year about ninety or one hundred Big Osages, with all their chiefs and *considerados* at the head of the party had arrived where he was wintering on the Kansas river. They asked him why the [Spanish] traders had been prohibited from sending merchandise to their village. Chouteau says he told them that it was on account of orders which Your Excellency had given for the purpose of punishing them for the deaths, murders, and brigandage which they had committed on the lands and river of Arkansas. They replied angrily to this that such could not be the reason, for they had made all the reparations which had been asked of them. They had taken the aggressor to the commandant of Arkansas, because the crime had been committed on that river. In consideration of this submission and their promise to do no more wrong, the commandant, himself, pardoned them, cutting the cords with which they had bound the evildoer. At the same time he gave them flags and merchandise. In order to mark a reciprocal friendship, five Osages of the nation had descended to New Orleans to obtain medals from Your Excellency, whom they regard as the best of their Fathers. They will always remember and respect the name of Miró. They said that I was the evil father who, without Your Excellency's orders, had deprived them of merchandise, but that they would exceed themselves [revenge themselves?]. They then tried to pillage the little merchandise which remained of Cadet Chouteau's trade, in spite of the influence and power which Cadet Chouteau had over them, and in spite of the presence of the Kansas Indians. Had not the Osage and Kansas Chiefs opposed their actions they doubtlessly would have pillaged them, but after many discourses and compositions they kept their promise. This is what Mr. Chouteau assured me the Osages have told him, assuring that they will come here in a large party this summer to ask why they have been deprived of merchandise.

If what they have told Chouteau is true, I do not doubt that they will come as they have assured, and they will doubtless come in large number because of the war which they are having with the nations of the Mississippi. All I will be able to do is to receive them and placate them temporarily with something in order to prevent their doing greater damage to these districts which might be the result of my doing nothing, as they have strength enough to resist me if they are received badly.

May God keep Your Excellency many years, [St. Louis, April 5, 1791.]

Manuel Perez [rubric]

Señor Don Estevan Miró.[8]

---

[8]Reply dated May 13, 1791 (draft in A.G.I., P. de C., leg 122A). In his reply Miró sent a copy of his letter to Delinó, commandant at the Arkansas, which gave Perez fuller information about what had occurred with the Osages and of their delegation sent to New Orleans. Miró requested Perez to reprimand the Osages for their perfidy and refused to concede peace with them until full compliance with his stipu-

lated conditions: all trade and presents to the Osages were to be stopped, and other Indian nations influenced not to give munitions or goods to the Osages. Miró was in favor of reducing the Osages to peace by means of war, hostages, and deprivation of trade and provisions. The Osages were finally and fully subdued through the activities of Auguste Chouteau.

IX

PEREZ TO MIRÓ, ST. LOUIS, APRIL 5, 1791[1]

NUMBER 180

I have been informed by some traders who have come down the Mississippi that a large party from the Oto Nation of Missouri had gone to trade at the establishments of the English traders of the Mississippi, who, in order to tempt them to come, give them merchandise at a very low price [and] hope to recover their loss in the future. They are doing even more; they are going overland themselves as far as the shore of the Missouri in order to trade with the Indians. Other persons who likewise have descended the Mississippi have assured me that some Englishmen had left to trade with the Mahas and Panis, notwithstanding the fact that I have given your appropriate orders to the traders of these two nations to arrest any English trader who may present himself in their district. I fear this will not have any effect because the smugglers may be accompanied by savages from other nations who will not permit our traders to arrest them or do them any harm.

I must not fail to inform Your Excellency that it is time and more than time to prevent the introduction of the English onto the Missouri. To accomplish this I find no other means than to construct a fort at the entrance of the Des Moines river, and another one at the entrance of the San Pedro [Minnesota] River, and to take all possible precautions to oppose their introduction via the said rivers, which are very favorable to them for their purposes. If we do not do this we shall soon be forced to renounce the Missouri, and there will follow disorders on the frontiers of Mexico whither all our neighbors are continually desiring to go with hopes of acquiring great riches.

---

[1]Written in Spanish. Original in Bancroft Library; certified copy in A.G.I., P. de C., leg. 1442. Parts of this letter, translated in a slightly different manner, are printed in Nasatir, "Ango-Spanish Frontier on the Upper Mississippi 1786-1796," *Iowa Journal of History and Politics*, XXIX, (1931), 170, where the surrounding facts are detailed. The proposed forts suggested by Perez were to counteract and stop the great influx of English traders into the Upper Missouri, who gained all the rich and abundant trade and furs there.

The proposed forts were never constructed by the Spaniards at these points, although later on the Spanish traders went into the Iowa country and Spanish boats patrolled the Upper Mississippi. But these activities on the part of the Spanish had little permanent influence in stopping the Americans and English from entering Spanish territory and illegally carrying on trade there.

It is evident that the English and especially the Americans speak of nothing else than the Kingdom of Mexico, and strive to learn about it and to find a way that will give them some loophole for approaching it. Their introduction into the Missouri would make it easy for them, and if they once succeed in finding it, there is the risk that they will never cease following it because of the great zeal they have for this special desire.

May God keep Your Excellency many years. St. Louis, Illinois, April 5, 1791.

Manuel Perez [rubric]

Señor Don Estevan Miró.[2]

---

[2]Miró's reply, dated New Orleans, May 13, 1791, is in A.G.I., P. de C., leg. 122A. In it Miró simply stated that he would forward the information to the Captain-General. Las Casas' reaction is in Las Casas to Carondelet, Havana, January 17, 1792, A.G.I., P. de C., leg. 2362, draft in leg. 1442, and printed in Houck, *Spanish Régime in Missouri*, I, 332, and also in *Wisconsin Historical Collection*, XVIII, 441-442.

Perez' proposition to build forts at the mouths of the Des Moines and St. Peters Rivers was transmitted by Miró to Las Casas. Las Casas asked for more information. Carondelet, who had succeeded Miró as Governor-General, opposed the erection of the forts as useless and dangerous. Instead, Carondelet ordered Trudeau, Perez' successor, to strengthen the defenses of St. Louis. Carondelet to Las Casas, New Orleans, January 10, 1793, A.G.I., P. de C., leg. 1442, and enclosed in Las Casas to Minister of War no. 313, Havana, June 14, 1794, A.G.I., Audiencia de Santo Domingo, (hereinafter cited Sto. Dom.), 86-6-26 (old numbering), copy in A.G.I., P. de C., leg. 1484 [1442], printed in Houck, *Spanish Régime in Missouri*, I, 343-344. See also *Ibid.*, I, 342-349. See also draft [Las Casas ?] to Carondelet, Havana, June 19, 1793, and draft [Las Casas?] to *Inginiero Comandante* (Cayetano Payeto), Havana, May 18, 1793, A.G.I., P. de C., leg. 1442.

On September 20, 1791, Perez in his letter no. 186 wrote to Miró (A.G.I., P. de C., leg. 17) that in consequence of the governor's orders he had conceded the trade of the Osages to Picôté de Belêtre and that the latter had no right to complain since Cruzat had given him a trade and Perez himself had for two consecutive years granted him the trade of the Kansas and of the Mahas, each for one year. Picôté de Belêtre had written a very sad letter about his situation to Miró on December 9, 1790. Draft [Miró] to Belêtre, New Orleans, April 15, 1791, A.G.I., P. de C., 122B.

On the other hand, Andrés Fagot, to whom upon orders of Miró Perez had granted the trade of the Kansas, did not ascend to take up his trade, since he stopped with his goods at Ansa a la Grasa and was going to Cumberland. Therefore, Perez did not make the grant of the Kansas trade to him. Perez to Miró no. 188, St. Louis, September 20, 1791, A.G.I., P. de C., 17. This was in reply to Miró's letter to Perez, New Orleans, June 4, 1791, draft in A.G.I., P. de C., 122B.

X

[CONCHA] TO NAVA, SANTA FÉ, NOVEMBER 1, 1791[1]

No. 249

Because I furnished help to the Cumanches, Tupes, and Yamparicas, at the request of the Lieutenant General of the Paruananinuco Nation (of

---

[1]Written in Spanish. New Mexico Archives. Document 1164, Mss., Santa Fé, New Mexico. See several documents cited in R. E. Twitchell, *The Spanish Archives of New Mexico* (Cedar Rapids, 1914), II, *e.g.* nos. 1089, 1164, etc.

which I gave an account to the *Señor* Your Excellency's predecessor in official letter of July 6, last year, no. 171), to make their hunt against the Panana Nation, you warn me, among other things never to give distant and little known nations reason for approaching our frontier to look for the Cumanche Indians who have attacked them, but who are supported by our forces. [You also warn me] to give much more thought before granting such requests, bearing in mind that various articles of the Instruction of Sr. Cónde de Gálvez require us to urge[2] the allied Indians to destroy their enemies and ours, we trying not to take part in reciprocal offenses committed. It is further warned by the present Most Excellent *Señor* Viceroy, Cónde de Revilla Gigedo, not to provide escorts for the buffalo hunts[3] of those who live on the frontier of this province or at the four [provinces] which form the *Comandancia-General* of the [Oriente] East.

I agree with you in all these previous statements but I think that they authorize me to yield to the request in the following case which I am going to mention: The measures dictated by the present Most Excellent *Señor* Viceroy seem not to be directed to any other object than that of not harming the Cumanches, our faithful allies; as they were at the latter part of the past year. The escorts requested by the Apaches situated in the aforementioned districts were precisely for them to go safely protected against any harm they might receive from their nearest and only enemies, the Indians of the North. In order to avoid occurrences similar to those which have occurred in the past year Your Excellency should expedite such just and proper orders.

It is true that among the articles of the Instructions of Sr. Cónde de Gálvez, number 180, ordered us not to take part openly in the reciprocal offense between the Lipanes and nations of the North; but it also is true that numbers 177 and 178 warn clearly not to give the latter the least reason for complaint, and that their friendship must be maintained at all costs.

However rude the Cumanches may be, it would not be hidden from them that all the absolute refusals made of their requests were due entirely to our lack of good will and not to deficiencies, for at the time they began negotiations they did not see any specific pretext for our refusing to grant their request. These Indians constantly invite and present themselves to work either alone or united with our people against the Apaches, our common enemies. I have no doubt that if they were properly managed they would show the same vigilance against any other nation with which we might be at war. I know their manner of thinking, and I am certain

---

[2]"To require us" is my guess. The original says, *teniendo pres [ent]e q [u]e sobre conspirar varios art°ˢ de la Instruccion . . .*
[3]*Curneadas de Zibolo [sic]* which means something more than just Buffalo hunts.

that if we had not granted their request they would have developed a grudge which might have had regrettable results.

The little help which I supplied them and the admonitions in my Instruction to their commandant, a copy of which I remitted in the said official letter, appear to me to indicate sufficiently the clever way in which I conducted myself in this delicate matter. The sad effects which we experienced, and to which I refer in the same official letter, were caused by our regarding with indifference the Cumanches throwing out the Apaches, Lipanes, Lipiyanes and Llaneros from their territory, which I sought to prevent. I also consider them [these four nations] of some importance.

We should not look upon the Panana nation as an unknown one, for I know positively that they live in two *pueblos* at a distance of 160 leagues to the northeast of this capital, that their number reaches 700 armed men, that they are allies of the Huitauyrata who have 600 men and live in another village behind the former at a distance of a five-day journey. They are also allies of the Ricaras who have 1000 men, more or less, in seven villages all near our new establishments of the Illinois of this bank of the Missouri River.

These three factions are at war with the Sioux who are situated on the other side of the Missouri and are under the protection of our cited establishments. They are at war with the A. [*sic — apaches*] and with the Huachages, and also with our allies, the Cumanches and the Yutas Scihuahuanas; and so weighing these circumstances, and endeavoring to maintain the Cumanches, which is the only intermediate nation, as a barrier [defense] for our territory, we have nothing to fear from any effort made against them.

Notwithstanding all this, as my desires are directed to the success of the most useful service of the King, and as I do not consider myself well enough informed to act with the greatest effectiveness, I hope that Your Excellency will please dictate specific orders to me for the conduct which I should observe in similar circumstances in order that by observing them scrupulously the greatest advantages may be gained.

As soon as the Cumanches returned to these environs they brought to me all the firearms which I had given them for their campaign.
God keep you many years.

Santa Fé, New Mexico
November 1, 1791

Sr. D. Pedro de Nava[4]

---

[4]Pedro de Nava, *comandante-general* of the *Provincias Internas del Poniente.* Fernando de la Concha, governor at Santa Fé, was the writer of this letter.

XI

PEREZ TO MIRÓ, ST. LOUIS, NOVEMBER 8, 1791[1]

No. 194

Four *considerados* of the Osage nation having come to this post with a party of thirty-two men to speak to me for the entire nation and on behalf of the principal chiefs, I proposed to them, as Your Excellency has forewarned me, that they were not to hope for anything if they did not agree to send a chief and one or two *considerados* to your capital to serve as hostages and answer for any insults which their nation might commit, and if they did not give satisfaction for those insults. They replied that when those who had descended to your city returned, they informed the nation that Your Excellency had told them the same thing. However, they did not believe that a nation would ever consent to send down either a chief or a *considerado*. Because of this answer, I told them that as long as they did not agree to it [Your Excellency's request] they could not expect me to send them the traders they were asking for, and that I would not permit anyone to supply them any goods. I told them that they should return to their nation and tell the chiefs what Your Excellency was asking of them, since for my part I would not give them the slightest thing on any pretext whatever. When they saw that I was determined on this matter, and that I gave them absolutely nothing of what they were asking, they went away appearing discontented. I took the necessary precautions to prevent their doing any damage to the small establishments distant from this post and through whose vicinity they had to pass. This was happily successful, for although they were in San Carlos del Missouri, they did no damage; but after they arrived at their nation the chiefs led more than two hundred men to the Missouri, to await the traders who were to ascend to the other nations. They fell upon the pirogue which was ascending to the Kansas and Missouris, taking the greater portion of the merchandise, carrying it off on horseback and by land. Despite the fact that the traders made representations to them, threatening them that their Father would consider it evil if they did not allow them to pass with their merchandise which was destined for the Kansas and Missouris, it was not enough. To these representations the Chiefs replied that they were growing weary in vain, [at our actions] and they would not [permit our traders to] pass, since just as their Father was master in his town so they were masters here. They said that they [the traders] might go on, and they should be very happy that they were not robbed of everything. The traders were forced to follow

---

[1]Written in Spanish. A.G.I., P. de C., leg. 17. Certified copy in Carondelet to Las Casas, no. 36, New Orleans, February 26, 1792, A.G.I., P. de C., leg. 1441. Miró replied to this letter on May 10, 1792. See note 3 to Document VIII.

the Osages for the purpose of seeing if they could not recover their merchandise and not lose everything.

This incident makes it clear that the Osages are determined not to let traders pass to the other nations as long as they are deprived of them [traders], and it will not be possible to restrain them in any other way than by constructing a fort, as I have informed Your Excellency in my official letter Number 192.[2] This is the means which I find the easiest. To deprive all the nations of the Missouri of traders does not seem to me to be a means sufficient to restrain the Osages for various reasons: first, because it would be a motive for the English merchants to succeed in attracting these nations, as they desire and search for all possible means to succeed in it; second, this same privation would perhaps be a cause for not only the Osages but also the other nations to commit insults and robberies upon the hunters whom they might meet and perhaps even [to attack] the small establishments away from St. Louis. For the others to make war upon the Osages would not achieve any other advantage than [cause us] immense expense. The Sacs and Foxes, who are the strongest, and from whom something might be hoped, have recently made peace, and have sent a large party to the Missouri to hunt with them [Osages], after some Osages had been in the Sac nation, who gave them some merchandise obtained from the English merchants who are in the other district.

In view of what has happened it seemed to me indispensable to send another canoe with merchandise to the Kansas and Missouris in order by this means to prevent them, seeing themselves without traders, going to trade with the English merchants of the other district. This they could do without difficulty, since the English would look for means to achieve it. Once the English find the means by which the Missouri nations may trade with them, it will be difficult to take it away from them because of the advantages which they will have. This is the reason why the English are looking for every practicable means to gain this trade, availing themselves of the same savages of the Mississippi and even advising them not to make war upon the savages of the Missouri.

May God keep Your Excellency many years,

St. Louis, Illinois, November 8, 1791.

Manuel Perez [rubric]

Señor Don Estevan Miró[3]

---

[2]Perez to Miró no. 192, St. Louis, October 5, 1791, original in A.G.I., P. de C., leg. 2362; a contemporary copy is in the Bancroft Library; copy in A.G.I., P. de C., leg. 81; copy certified by Carondelet is in A.G.I., P. de C., leg. 1441. This entire story is given and documents presented in translation in Nasatir. *Imperial Osage.*

[3]In a letter written to Alexander Hamilton (Philadelphia, February 9, 1792, *Mississippi Valley Historical Review*, VIII, (1921), 264-266), M. Mitchell gave information about the Illinois country taken chiefly from Hutchins. He stated that the Missouri was navigated nearly 1200 miles and employed annually from 50 to 100 boats.

150

Mitchell complained of British goods and traders in the Mississippi valley and wanted to stop them, especially on the Wisconsin and Illinois rivers. His plans for stopping the British closely resemble the proposed plans of the Spaniards to combat the same evil; namely, use armed vessels, and erect a town at the mouth of the Illinois river (Paysá).

XII

Carondelet: Instructions to Trudeau, New Orleans, March 28, 1792[1]

Instructions which the New Commandant of the Post of St. Louis of Illinois Don Zenon Trudeau[2] must punctually observe.

First, You will try to treat with the greatest equality, kindness and justice [equity] all the inhabitants, carefully avoiding allowing yourself to be carried off by humor, preoccupation, or flattery.

Second, You will treat with attention and civility the *Padre Cura* bearing in mind that while you preserve the civil jurisdiction in good harmony with the Ecclesiastical, the town will be well administered and all the dispositions of government will be respected.

Third, You will protect agriculture and you will try by every means to increase the population without admitting into the towns, nevertheless, vagabond persons and persons of evil customs, corrupted in manners [*peste*] and outcasts of the nations, especially Americans or English.

Fourth, You will facilitate the departure and exportation of products from the country without requiring or permitting that they be molested in any manner. The commerce of the Missouri shall be free to everyone without exception. Upon this matter, you shall not admit any deceit.

Fifth, You will try to restrain the incursions of the Osages and protect the inhabitants against them and those of other savage nations, understanding that a fort is projected on the Arkansas River in order to restrain the Osages in that district, and to make war upon them if they do not cease their incursions.

Sixth, You will exert yourself to maintain peace and good harmony with the English and Americans but you must always bear in mind that the latter are much more terrible at present for the Dominions of His Majesty than the English. In this concept, you will try to maintain in the mind of the savages the fear and mistrust which they have conceived of the Americans and to live in perfect harmony with the English without, however, permitting their traders in this part of the River.

[1]Written in Spanish. A.G.I., P. de C., leg. 18. A signed copy in a slightly different form is in *Ibid.*, leg. 122A.
[2]Zenon Trudeau, lieutenant-governor of Upper Louisiana, July 21, 1792, to August 2, 1799.

Seventh, You will not give any passport or permit the English and Americans to cross the Mississippi River or introduce themselves into the Dominions of His Majesty situated to the west of that river.

Eighth, You will take the greatest care always to maintain your troop well disciplined, the fort in a state of defense, and the artillery ready for action. If any individual [of your troop] is malcontented, you will make it known to the government in order that his relief may be sent.

Ninth, *Reservada.*[3] In case of a war between Spain and the Americans, you will try to avail yourself of the English in order to maintain yourself in your post; and vice-versa in case of war against the English avail yourself of the Americans.

Tenth, With all possible promptitude, you will give this government information of everything that may occur between those two nations and particularly of all preparations for war and extraordinary assembling of troops which they may make, trying to discover their intentions. In case the English ask you for some aid of provisions or munitions you will permit the inhabitants to give them to them at current prices.

Eleventh, Having had the most bitter complaints against the monopoly which the former commandants have made of the trade privileges, selling them at excessive prices that have almost ruined an establishment which ought to be one of the most powerful of these provinces, I have determined that as soon as you arrive at your post you will make public by proclamation[4] in all the places dependent upon St. Louis of the Illinois, that all trade, without exception, is free and permitted to all vassals of His Majesty established in the said places without any limitation or restriction and without any further encumbrance than the fee of twenty *pesos* which each will pay to the said commandant of Illinois in order to obtain a license to trade wherever it might suit him best. These licenses shall be renewed annually, counting from the date of issuance and on renewal of the payment of the license fee. By virtue of this benefaction the commandants in the future shall not be able to reserve to themselves exclusively the trade of any nation nor can they refuse licenses applied for unless they may have well grounded reason for so doing, in which case they must without fail inform the government. (Having conceded the trade of three nations for the rebuilding of the Church of St. Louis, Illinois, a concession which is annulled by the said proclamation, the commandant shall require all the inhabitants to contribute in proportion to their ability to the said work and that those who do not have money will employ themselves, personally making up the amount of money which they should contribute by a few days work, calculated at the value of day laborers in the town.)[5]

---

[3]The word *reservada* is not in A.G.I., P. de C., leg. 18.
[4]See Document XIV.
[5]The words within the parentheses are in a P.S. in the copy in A.G.I., P. de C., leg. 122A (actually constituting the twelfth part in the instructions).

Twelfth,[6] The commandant will remit to the government the list of the licenses which he may have given during the course of the year with names of the nations, subjects and country of those who have profited from them up to the first of the following year.[7]

Thirteen,[8] The "commons" of the town have an extent of three leagues and these lands being the most fertile of that establishment, the Commandant shall proceed juridically to its reduction in such a manner that it may suffice for the pasture necessary for the cattle and nothing more. All the remaining land shall be divided among the residents of the town in equal shares with the necessary obligation of each one to cultivate his portion during the course of the following year and in case he has not done so the land shall be given to another new inhabitant.

Fourteen,[9] The commandant will observe punctually the instruction given by the former governor of this colony, Don Antonio de Ulloa, dated March 14, 1767,[10] from articles 38 to 77 inclusive, a copy of which should be in the archives of the said establishment (in everything which is not in opposition to these instructions), and in case it has been misplaced you will make it known to the government immediately.

New Orleans, March 28, 1792

El Baron de Carondelet [rubric]

[6]This is thirteenth in the copy in A.G.I., P. de C., leg. 122A.
[7]*E.g.*, see document XIX.
[8]This is fourteenth in the copy in A.G.I., P. de C., leg. 122A.
[9]This is fifteenth in the copy in A.G.I., P. de C., leg. 122A.
[10]See copy of Ulloa's instructions to Ríu, dated Balize, March 14, 1767, A.G.I., P. de C., leg. 2357, printed in Louis Houck, *Spanish Régime in Missouri* (two volumes, Chicago, 1909), I, 3-19, especially 9-19.

XIII

PEREZ TO MIRÓ, ST. LOUIS, MARCH 31, 1792[1]

NUMBER 212

The advantage which the savages obtained in the beginning of last November against the Americans, when the latter were defeated,[2] as I informed Your Excellency in my official letter number 204,[3] has caused many of the nations to become extremely insolent, as is evident in their

[1]Written in Spanish. Bancroft Library.
[2]Defeat of Americans by the Indians on November 4, 1791. St. Clair's own report is in *American State Papers, Indian Affairs*, I, 137-138; a British account is in *Michigan Pioneer and Historical Collections*, XXIV, 336-337. See also S. F. Bemis, *Jay's Treaty* (New York, 1923); Stevens, *Northwest Fur Trade*, (Urbana, 1928), 170 ff.; L. P. Kellogg, *British Régime in Wisconsin* (Madison, 1935); Whitaker, *Spanish-American Frontier* (Boston, 1927); and Smith, *St. Clair Papers*.
[3]No. 204 is dated February 16, 1792.

manner of speaking when they present themselves. There are some who threaten this district, as appears from various beads [collars] which are being passed continually from one nation to another for the purpose of uniting them and continuing warfare against the Americans. At the same time the English are animating them secretly and supporting them vigorously, and in the counsels which they give them, as has been explained to me, some chiefs drank so much that they were induced to renounce our friendship. And all this is [caused] only [by] the ambition which the English have to obtain the commerce of the Missouri.[4] It will not be very odd, should the nations win another victory like the preceding one over the Americans, that this district may not be very safe from their insults, and that the English themselves would take advantage of this opportunity to make the Indians believe that they have no reason to fear anyone, and that they are superior, not only to the Americans but also to the French and the Spaniards. This may prove very prejudicial to us, especially since the country is without forces able to resist them if they attempt to make any kind of an attack.

Up to the present time the nations of the Missouri are maintaining themselves quietly. The traders inform me that the Big Osages, notwithstanding the pillage which they committed upon the traders who were going to the Kansas and Missouris,[5] have conducted themselves well, having done no damage to the traders, who will be able to take out the value of their merchandise without loss. But the Indians have assured them that, if traders are not sent to them, they will seize those who may go to the other nations, take them to their own [villages] and provide themselves with what they need, although they will not do any harm to them. Because of this Your Excellency will please determine what I am to do in this matter. At the same time I am informing Your Excellency that if the means to be taken to deprive the Osages of everything is to entirely

---

[4]In the British Foreign Office Papers, 4/16, are some observations on the western trade enclosed in Hammond's letter to Grenville, dated Philadelphia, July 3, 1792: "It is a matter of immense magnitude that (according to the spirit of the late treaty) we should obtain a practical communication with the Mississippi, not only on account of participation of the *Indian trade on this side* but as an opening to the new sources of it on the West side of the River . . . [Our] Rivals on the west are only Spaniards who up to the present have not attempted to stop us from any *Western River but* the Missouri. The western trade will recompense us for losses in other parts." He describes the routes to the Mississippi, viz: via the Miami and Wabash rivers; via the Chicago and Illinois rivers; via the Fox and Wisconsin rivers. "We need Grand Portage." Isaac Todd and Simon McTavish, representing the principal houses carrying on the northwest trade, observed that most of the posts where the traders winter were within the limits claimed by the Americans with the exception of the trade of Grand Portage, and several of the trading places on the Mississippi were on the Spanish side of that river. *Michigan Pioneer and Historical Collections,* XXIV, 684. See also S. F. Bemis, *Jay's Treaty* (New York, 1923); W. E. Stevens, *The Northwest Fur Trade* (Urbana, 1928); and many other works. The *Simcoe Papers* abound with English trading activities in Spanish territory.
[5]See document XI.

forbid trade in the Missouri, it will not be possible by these means to force them to come to reason. On the contrary, it will do great damage, for it will cause the entire loss of the commerce of the Missouri. Moreover, other consequences worse for the country may result since the other nations, who will see themselves deprived of traders through no fault of their own, will go to trade with the English, who desire nothing else. The latter will provide them with all their necessities either directly or by means of the nations of the Mississippi, which they can do very easily without our being able to stop them. Moreover, the very nations who will be deprived of merchandise will perhaps commit insults and thefts, and we shall have them for enemies if they once become friends of the English, who will not give them advice favorable to us.

May God keep Your Excellency many years.

St. Louis, Illinois. March 31, 1792.

Manuel Perez [rubric]

Señor Don Estevan Miró.

XIV
Trudeau to Carondelet, St. Louis, June 25, 1792[1]

No. 4

I am sending Your Excellency a copy of the edict [*bando*] for the free commerce of the trade with the savage nations of this dependency which, according to my instructions,[2] I have had published in all the places of these establishments. The inhabitants are very grateful for the favor which Your Excellency concedes to them, which promises them the old happiness with which they lived formerly, by an equal and more abundant repartition of the benefits which the said commerce produces annually, in which many more people will now be employed and which will give to each family a share of its product.

May God keep Your Excellency many years.

St. Louis, July 25, 1792.

Zenon Trudeau [rubric)

Señor Baron Carondelet.

ZENON TRUDEAU — PROCLAMATION[3]
St. Louis, 1792

Zenon Trudeau, Captain of the 18th regiment of Louisiana, Commandant of the western part of Illinois.

---

[1] Written in Spanish. A.G.I., P. de C., leg. 25A.
[2] Document XII.
[3] Written in French. Bancroft Library.

This is to proclaim to all the subjects of His Majesty of the dependency and under the jurisdiction of our command in pursuance of an order of *Monsieur* the Baron de Carondelet, Governor General of the province, etc; having for its object the removal of all the obstacles which up until now have prevented persons from going freely to trade with the savage nations, that it is now permitted to all the subjects of His Majesty residing in the district of our command, without any distinction or restriction whatever, to go without limit or reserve to trade with such savage nations (of this western part of Illinois) as they see fit, on the single condition of paying 20 *piastres* for the licenses which they will need for a period of one year, reckoning from the opening of the trade to the expiration of the time, when those who shall desire to continue their trade will renew their fee.

Accordingly, the present announcement shall be proclaimed, published, and posted in every province, district, and dependency of this command in order that none will be ignorant of it and to make known to all the subjects of His Majesty residing therein the intention of *Monsieur* the governor general to promote and protect the trade of each individual equally.

Declared at St. Louis the 25th of July, 1792.

Zenon Trudeau [rubric]

XV

TRUDEAU TO CARONDELET, ST. LOUIS, JULY 25, 1792[1]

No. 6

This morning I spoke with the principal chief of the Osage nation, who has been here for two months awaiting my arrival. He has apologized for all the pillages which his nation has made up to now, accusing the Little Osages (their neighbors) of having committed the greater part of them. He said he had not been able to restrain his young men when they are separated from the chiefs and *considerados*. After some reflection, he decided to come alone to see me and to try to arrange for the new commandant to send out traders during the present year. He felt that his nation would be more willing to listen to his council, if it saw that we had granted him consideration, and that he had tried to obtain merchandise. Considering that it is impossible to entirely deprive them of the said merchandise, since they would surely take advantage of the traders going

---

[1]Written in Spanish. A.G.I., P. de C., leg. 25. The full correspondence relating to the Osage Indians is in Nasatir, *Imperial Osage*. Carondelet replied on August 30, 1792, approving Trudeau's actions. A.G.I., P. de C., leg. 18, draft in A.G.I., P. de C., leg. 123.

out to the other nations of the Missouri, except his, I have determined to concede to them the traders for which they asked. I have done this by virtue of Your Excellency's orders which rest in this archive, which permits such treatment whenever they show some submission (as this one has done). I have told him that this will be the last time, if they do any more damage to us. He has asked for the Indian of his nation who is in the calaboose. I have denied this request, insinuating that he would not be freed until the Osages return all the horses they have stolen. He realized my position, but he could not promise affirmatively that the horses would be returned, because very few are in his nation, and probably all will have been killed in the hunts which the young men are making. I gave him a small present and he will leave tomorrow, satisfied with having obtained some traders. He promises me and hopes for the best results, because he has gained the object he had in making the voyage.

God keep Your Excellency many years.

St. Louis, July 25, 1792.

Zenon Trudeau [rubric]

Señor Baron Carondelet.

XVI

Miró to Alange, Madrid, August 7, 1792[1]

[Extract]

Sixth and Last Point. Concerning the proposition which the Governor of Louisiana makes for the construction of a fort situated at 150 leagues

---

[1]Written in Spanish. A.G.I., Sto. Dom. 86-7-25 (old numbering). Copies in Missouri Historical Society, Papers from Spain, no. 84; British Museum, Additional manuscripts, vol. 17567, folios 65-96. This is from the *informe* relative to the political state of Louisiana, which was drawn up by Miró, ex-governor of Louisiana, while he was in Madrid, and which was presented to the *Ministerio de Hacienda de Indias*. The form of this *informe* is in reply to certain points suggested by Captain-General Luís de Las Casas.

Miró gave a description of the Mississippi Valley before taking up the points to be considered. He pointed out the importance of the Mississippi river and how easily the Americans could force their way. He urged that steps be taken to strengthen and preserve Louisiana. He suggested doing this by means of population so that the inhabitants could defend it, and secondly, by forming an alliance with Kentucky and the American west to serve as a barrier against the Americans. He described his intrigues with Wilkinson and urged delay in Spain's negotiations with the United States. Miró then took up the points and demonstrated how to postpone the negotiations. He urged use of Gayoso de Lemos and made observations and recommendations on the commerce of Louisiana. In reply to certain propositions relative to Louisiana Miró suggested: (1) force war vessels back which did not receive guards on board; (2) purchase a schooner to guard the coast from Bahía to Apalache; (3) be alert for a body of soldiers forming in Georgia and South Carolina to go against Louisiana; (4) reduce fort at Pensacola; and (5) take warning that McGillivray may deprive Creeks of a portion of their best lands to cede to the Americans.

from our settlement of Arkansas, two days' journey from the Osage Nation, as proposed by the Captain of that place, Don Josef Valière,[2] in order to repress the forays of those Indians and to serve as a refuge for the Spanish traders; the said governor supposes by reason of his knowledge of the country, that this is the easiest and least costly means of maintaining free the commerce with the Nations of the Missouri situated above the Ohio, which we have an interest in preserving, for if this commerce were hampered they would turn to the English, who by every means seek to attract them to their district.

Reply. According to my opinion there is a defect in this narration, for the proposed fort at 150 leagues above Arkansas could not in any manner conduce to preventing the English from entering into Missouri and trading with the Nations therein, for it empties into the Mississippi five leagues above our town of St. Louis, Illinois, and 250 from the River Arkansas, so that the said fort would be very far from the place where the English introduce themselves.

In regard to the projected fort serving as a protection and refuge for the traders of the River of Arkansas and as a restraint on the forays of the Osages, it is my opinion that it will only serve as the indicated refuge, as I will show.

I have written much about the Osages to the defunct Marqués de Sonora[3] and to the captains-general. This nation is on the upper Missouri, along which traders are sent to them from the district of Illinois. The Osages trade with them faithfully, but every year parties of young warriors break away from the body of the nation and descend to the neighborhood of the Rivers Arkansas and San Francisco, which empties [*sic*] into the former. If these young warriors encounter white hunters, they rob them of their peltries, and occasionally they have captured one of the hunters, who has never been seen again. The projected fort cannot remedy this damage, because they will pass between it and the existing fort in the 150 leagues mentioned which separate them, without the forty men which the governor indicates for its garrison being able to cover so extensive a country nor to go two leagues away from the fort without exposing themselves to be cut to pieces. Even though this plan should be completely successful, I am of the opinion that the cost of maintaining the necessary troops would be greater than the robberies that the Osages make annually. Perhaps it may be objected that the traders of Arkansas, being exposed to this danger, will abandon their trade. I am of the opinion that this, far from being detrimental to us, would force the above-mentioned individuals to be more useful, devoting themselves to the cultivation of

[2]Much of this correspondence is included in Nasatir. *Imperial Osage.*
[3]See *e.g.* Houck, *Spanish Régime in Missouri,* I, 233-257.

the land. There would be no failure in the supply of bear grease for cooking or peltries for the New Orleans trade, for the Indians would supply this demand and the people of Arkansas would have plenty of both staples from elsewhere. In order to repress the said Osages two years ago I ordered that no more traders should be sent to them. By the lack of trade I wanted to force them to suppress these parties of young warriors. In order to be sure that they would take this action, I repeated the proposition I had ordered made to them years before. This proposition, approved by His Majesty, was that they should send two of their chiefs to me at New Orleans, to remain there as hostages, with the understanding that they would be well treated, and could be exchanged every year. These hostages would answer with their heads for the murders and robberies which their nation might commit, it being well understood that if the guilty parties were delivered up the chiefs should not suffer. At one time they were almost agreed to this; but at the beginning of last year or the end of 1790 the commander of Illinois advised me that the chiefs of the nation, accompanied by many warriors, had been there and humbly begged him to restore the trade. They said they would do everything possible to restrain the young bad heads, but they refused to give the hostages. The commandant also remained firm and did not send the traders, but, a few days before, the commandant notified me that the said Osages had posted themselves upon the Missouri and had intercepted the traders who were going to other nations on the Upper Missouri,[4] obliging them to go to their towns to trade with them, but without committing any other acts of violence. Therefore I advised Carondelet to tell the Commandant not to enforce the demand for hostages, and to content himself with the promise of the body of the nation to repay the value of the robberies which their warriors might commit and to give satisfaction for any murder. I did this to keep the English from knowing of these dissensions and taking advantage of them to introduce themselves among the Osages, something which they have never yet done.

I will also say that the Commandant of Illinois likewise proposed to me to construct two forts on the Missouri.[5] These forts would certainly be better than the proposed one on the Arkansas to stop the clandestine commerce of the English, who could not then come up the river any more. It would be possible, however, for the English to reach the Missouri by way of branches of other rivers, which they follow from the upper Mississippi to near the Missouri, and detachments from these forts could apprehend whatever trader tried to make this passage. I informed the Captain General, Don Luís de Las Casas, that the evil was not of such conse-

---

[4] See documents XI, XII, XIII, XV.
[5] See document IX and especially note 2. See *e.g.* Houck, *Spanish Régime in Missouri*, I, 332 from A.G.I., P. de C., leg. 2362.

quence that he should incur the excessive expense which the two forts and the maintenance of their garrisons would cost.

I will have the greatest satisfaction if I have done well in these reports, if Your Excellency has not been bored by this long narration that it has been necessary for me to make in order that you may acquire a perfect knowledge of Louisiana and the position of its close dangers, and if the means which I have taken to save it give to Your Excellency sufficient light to enable you with your distinguished penetration to deduce what is proper to propose to His Majesty. May God keep Your Excellency many years.

Estevan Miró.

Madrid 7 of August of 1792.

XVII

Trudeau to Carondelet, St. Louis, September 24, 1792[1]
Number 24

On the 14th of the present month the Iowa Indians who inhabit the Des Moines River, which is 80 leagues distant from this establishment, stole 38 horses from the establishment of San Carlos del Missouri. They were the only horses which the poor inhabitants had for working their lands. This district of Illinois is sadly lacking in animals. Because of the bad harvest of wheat this year, flour is valued at eight *pesos* for *cwt.* and if it were not for the harvest of maize in Ste. Geneviève being good, the inhabitants would not have had anything to live on all this year.

May God keep Your Excellency many years.

St. Louis, September 24, 1792.

Zenon Trudeau [rubric]

Señor Baron de Carondelet.

---

[1]Written in Spanish. A.G.I., P. de C., leg. 25. Reply is document XX.

XVIII

Trudeau to Carondelet, St. Louis, October 20, 1792[1]
No. 33

The aforesaid Santiago de la Iglesia,[2] a Frenchman, has just arrived, who, having obtained a passport to go hunting on the Missouri from the

---

[1]Written in Spanish. Bancroft Library. Printed and edited in translation by A. P. Nasatir in "Spanish Exploration of the Upper Missouri," *Mississippi Valley Historical Review,* XIV (1927), 57-58. Reply is document XXI.

[2]Jacques D'Eglise. See A. P. Nasatir, "Jacques D'Eglise on the Upper Missouri," *Ibid.,* XIV, 48ff.

commandant, my predecessor, in the month of August in 1790, provided himself with some merchandise to trade with the Indians, and although the commandant had forbidden all trading with the nations we know, he has dared to make his way in his hunting more than eight hundred leagues up the Missouri. There he found eight villages of a nation about which there was some knowledge under the name of Mandan, but to which no one had ever gone in this direction and by this river. All were provided with English arms. A Frenchman[3] who has been with this nation for fourteen years, and who has gone with them to some English traders from the north of Canada, who are now established and fortified about fifteen days' march from the spot where the Mandans are, told de la Iglesia that the Mandans trade directly with the English.[4] This nation received the said man, de la Iglesia, well and welcomed him. They [Mandans] are white like Europeans, much more civilized than any other Indians, and always live in tribes fortified against the numerous nations of the Cius [Sioux] with whom they are perpetually at war. It seems that these Mandans also have communication with the Spaniards, or with nations that know them, because they have saddles and bridles in Mexican style for their horses, as well as other articles which this same de la Iglesia saw. As it seemed to him, the eight villages, which are a half league distant from each other, all on the bank of the Missouri, may have a population of four or five thousand persons. They have furs of the finest sort and in abundance. In sight of these villages there is a mountain with a volcano [volcanic mountain]. The Missouri flows always from a direction of west or northwest and has sufficient water for the passage of the largest boats on these rivers.

This is as much as I have been able to find out about this trip from an ignorant man who made no observations and who hardly knows how to speak his own French language. May God keep Your Excellency for many years.

St. Louis, October 20, 1792.

Zenon Trudeau [rubric]

To the Baron De Carondelet.

---

[3]Menard.
[4]Referring to the Northwest Company's fort or post at the confluence of the Assiniboine and La Souris rivers.

XIX

NUMBER 44

I am sending to Your Excellency the statement of the subjects to whom I have given permission to trade with the Indians of this jurisdiction. They are the only ones that can be sent out because the season is so far advanced. They are also the greatest number who can enter the Missouri. Because of the great amount of merchandise each trader carries, it would not be feasible to send more traders to the Missouri. We are not able to trade with the Indians of the Mississippi. This year it is full of Englishmen from Michilimackinac. At least 150 canoes from there each loaded with two to three thousand *pesos* worth of merchandise have been counted.

May God Keep Your Excellency many years.

St. Louis, November 12, 1792.

Zenon Trudeau [rubric]

Señor Baron de Carondelet.

[Enclosure]

List of the subjects to whom during this year, 1792, licenses have been given for the commerce of the Indians of the Jurisdiction of Illinois with statement of the nationality and country of each one and the number of persons employed by them.[2]

Dates of license	Subjects	Nationality	Country	Number of employees
August 1, 1792	Bacilio Vasseur	French	Illinois	4
Idem	Juan Beaudouin	French	Illinois	4
Idem	Joseph Hebert	French	Illinois	4
August 2	Don Pedro Montardy	French	Languedoc	9
Idem	Bapt\u00aa Mongrain	French	Illinois	4
Idem	Antonio Chouteau	Meztiso	Illinois	5
August 8	Juan Meunier	French	Illinois	7
Idem 9	Pedro Quenel	French	Illinois	6
Idem 29	Estevan de Rouin	French	Illinois	5
Idem	Eugenio Alvarez	Spanish	Madrid	4
September 17	Joseph Marié	French	Paris	8
Idem 18	Don Augustin Chouteau	French	New Orleans	14
Idem	Don Pedro Chouteau	French	New Orleans	14
September 19	Pedro Duchouquet	French	Illinois	6
Idem 19	Andres Andreville	French	Canada	7
Idem 19	Antonio Roy	French	Canada	8
Idem 26	Louis Bonpart	French	Illinois	6
				115

St. Louis, November, 13, 1792.

Zenon Trudeau
[rubric]

¹Written in Spanish. A.G.I., P. de C., leg. 25A. The reply is dated January 20, 1793. Trudeau was instructed to submit such lists annually. See documents XII.
²A.G.I., P. de C., leg. 25B. Most of these men are mentioned in Houck, *Spanish Régime in Missouri* (Chicago, 1909) and *History of Missouri* (Chicago, 1908).

XX

CARONDELET TO TRUDEAU, NEW ORLEANS, NOVEMBER 28, 1792¹

ANSWERED

In your official letter no. 24² you inform me of the raid made by the Iowa Indians, who live on the banks of the Des Moines River, 80 leagues from your establishments, in which they carried off 38 horses from the post of San Carlos del Misuri. These were the only animals which those inhabitants had for working their lands. This occurrence is all the more regrettable to me because it must be followed by the poverty which these inhabitants will experience because of the poor harvest of wheat and the small harvest of maize this year.

You, who are in command of these places, must see if there is any remedy for what has happened, or if the Iowas are a nation from whom the stolen horses may be reclaimed, in which case you will do it (recover them) and you will suggest to me the means which appear to you to be feasible.

May God keep you many years,

New Orleans, November 28, 1792.

Baron de Carondelet [rubric]

Señor Don Zenon Trudeau.

¹Original in Spanish in the Bancroft library; draft in A.G.I., P. de C., leg. 25B.
²Document XVII.

XXI

CARONDELET TO ZENON TRUDEAU, NEW ORLEANS, DECEMBER 29, 1792¹

In official letter number 33² you inform me that the trader Santiago de la Iglesia, while hunting, dared to go more than eight hundred leagues up the Missouri where he found eight villages of a nation known under the

¹Written in Spanish. Bancroft Library; draft in A.G.I., P. de C., leg. 17. This is the reply to document XVIII. I have edited and published this in my "Spanish Exploration of the Upper Missouri," *Mississippi Valley Historical Review*, XIV (1927), 58.
²Document XVIII.

name of Mandans, who trade with the English and also, as it seems, with the Spaniards or nations that live near them. I am acquainted with all this and I should be very grateful if you would get me the most extensive information you can, giving details as to the nations that live in or near these settlements, the spots in which they live, their rivers, their trade, the nations with whom they traffic, the number of people if it is possible, and also their articles for trade. You may send me this information in part or as a whole, as soon as it is obtainable.[8]

May God keep you many years. New Orleans, December 29, 1792.

El Baron de Carondelet [rubric]

To *Señor* Don Zenon Trudeau.

---

[8]See document XXVIII; but also see, *e.g.*, D'Eglise to Carondelet, St. Louis, June 19, 1794, Bancroft Library: Chapter II, Document XIII *below*.

XXII

André Michaux's Proposed Expedition, 1793
Jefferson's Instructions to André Michaux for Exploring the Western Boundary.[1]

(January, 1793)

Sundry persons having subscribed certain sums of money for your encouragement to explore the country along the Missouri, and thence westward to the Pacific ocean, having submitted the plan of the enterprise to the directors of the American Philosophical society, and the society having accepted of the trust, they proceed to give you the following instructions:

They observe to you that the chief objects of your journey are to find the shortest and most convenient route of communication between the United States and the Pacific ocean, within the temperate latitudes, and to learn such particulars as can be obtained of the country through which

---

[1]P. L. Ford [ed.], *Writings of Thomas Jefferson*, VI, 158-161; and R. G. Thwaites [ed.], *Original Journals of the Lewis and Clark Expedition* (Cleveland, 1904), VII, 202-204.

André Michaux, who was connected with the French intrigues in the west, had in 1793 made some general observations upon the French colonists, in which he stated that the present war with Spain and England was a most favorable opportunity for reestablishing France in its former possessions in North America. He advised against conquering it but getting people for it. He pointed out the ease with which France could repossess herself of Louisiana and recommended a town at the mouth of the Missouri as an entrepôt of commerce (like the British and Americans he had ideas of establishing a colony at Paysá). *Archives du Ministère des Affaires Étrangères, Séries Correspondance Politique, États Unis, Supplément,* volume XXVIII, folios 15-18 *verso*. See *American Historical Association, Annual Report 1903.* On Michaux see *Early Western Travels,* vol. III; J. A. James, *George Rogers Clark* (Chicago, 1928); and other works.

it passes, its productions, inhabitants, and other interesting circumstances. As a channel of communication between these States and the Pacific ocean, the Missouri, so far as it extends, presents itself under circumstances of unquestioned preference. It has, therefore, been declared as a fundamental object of the subscription (not to be dispensed with) that this river shall be considered and explored as a part of the communication sought for. To the neighborhood of this river, therefore, that is to say, to the town of Kaskaskia, the society will procure you a conveyance in company with the Indians of that town now in Philadelphia.

From thence you will cross the Mississippi and pass by land to the nearest part of the Missouri above the Spanish settlements, that you may avoid the risk of being stopped.

You will then pursue such of the largest streams of that river as shall lead by the shortest way and the lowest latitudes to the Pacific ocean. When pursuing those streams, you shall find yourself at the point from whence you may get by the shortest and most convenient route to some principal river of the Pacific ocean, you are to proceed to such river and pursue its course to the ocean. It would seem by the latest maps as if a river called Oregon, interlocked with the Missouri for a considerable distance, and entered the Pacific ocean not far southward of Nootka Sound. But the society are aware that these maps are not to be trusted so far as to be the ground of any positive instruction to you. They therefore only mention the fact, leaving to yourself to verify it, or to follow such other as you shall find to be the real truth.

You will in the course of your journey, take notice of the country you pass through, its general face, soil, rivers, mountains, its productions—animal, vegetable, and mineral—so far as they may be new to us, and may also be useful or very curious; the latitude of places or material for calculating it by such simple methods as your situation may admit you to practise, the names, members, and dwellings of the inhabitants, and such particulars, as you can learn of their history, connection with each other, languages, manners, state of society, and of the arts and commerce among them.

Under the head of animal history, that of the mammoth is particularly recommended to your inquiries, as it is also to learn whether the Lama or Paca of Peru, is found in those parts of this continent, or how far north they come.

The method of preserving your observation is left to yourself according to the means which shall be in your power. It is only suggested that noting them on the skin might be the best for such as may be the most important, and that further details may be committed to the bark of the paper-birch, a substance which may not excite suspicions among the Indians, and little liable to injury from wet or other common accidents. By the means of the same substance you may perhaps find opportunities, from time to time of communicating to the society information of your progress, and of the particulars you shall have noted.

When you shall have reached the Pacific ocean, if you find yourself within convenient distance of any settlements of Europeans, go to them, commit to writing a narrative of your journey and observations, and take the best measure you can for conveying it then to the society by sea.

Return by the same, or some other route, as you shall think likely to fulfill with the most satisfaction and certainly the objects of your mission, furnishing yourself with the best proofs the nature of the case will admit of the reality and extent of your progress, whether this shall be by certificates from Europeans settled on the western coast of America, or by what other means, must depend on circumstances. Ignorance of the country through which you are to pass, and confidence in your judgment, zeal, and discretion, prevent the society from attempting more minute instructions, and even from enacting rigorous observance of those already given, except, indeed, what is the first of all objects that you seek for and pursue that route which shall form the shortest and most convenient communication between the higher parts of the Missouri and the Pacific ocean.

It is strongly recommended to you to expose yourself in no case to unnecessary dangers, whether such as might affect your health or your personal safety, and to consider this not merely as your personal concern but as the injunction of science in general, which expects its enlargement from your inquiries, to whom your report will open new fields and subjects of commerce, intercourse, and observation.

If you reach the Pacific ocean and return, the society assign to you all the benefits of the subscription before mentioned. If you reach the waters only that run into that ocean, the society reserve to themselves the apportionment of the reward according to the conditions expressed in the subscription. If you do not reach even those waters they refuse all reward, and reclaim the money you may have received here under the subscription.

They will expect you to return to the city of Philadelphia to give in to them a full narrative of your journey and observations, and to answer the inquiries they shall make of you, still reserving to yourself the benefit arising from the publication of such parts of them as are in the said subscription reserved to you.

Synopsis of Proceedings of American Philosophical Society, in the matter of Michaux's Expedition

April 19, 1793—Society votes to solicit subscriptions "to enable Andrew Michaux to make discoveries in the Western Country".

April 30, 1793—"Resolved, that the President be requested to pay to Mr. Michaux such sum of the subscription as he hath or may receive;—not exceeding 400 dollars."

Dec. 16, 1796. The Michaux Committee reported that "Mr. Michaux's proposed plan . . . had failed."

Feb. 1, 1799—Treasurer instructed "to call on the Executors of David Rittenhouse & receive from the Sums contributed, and placed in his hands towards aiding the expedition of Mʳ Micheau."

Committee appointed "to report the proceedings which have been had with respect to the sums received on account of Mʳ Micheau's Expedition, and their opinion on the proper measures to be pursued thereon.—Collin, Peale, Wistar."

May 17, 1799—"A letter was received from the Treasurer satisfying the enquiry made in the minutes of 1st Feb. relative to a certain sum of money left in the hands of Mʳ. Rittenhouse."

April 4, 1800.—"Dʳ. Collin presented a Statement of sums received by him for the Society to aid Mʳ Micheau's projected expedition some years since; received previously to 25th April 1793, viz. Alex. Hamilton $12.50; Geo. Washington $25; John Vaughan $12.50; Walter Stewart, John Ross, J. B. Bordley, each $5; Wm. White $2.50; Robert Morris $20; Ewing S. Powell, McConnell, Nixon, each $2.50; S. Coats $2.25; B. Bache, Jared Ingersol, M. Clarkson, J. Dorsey, each $2; R. Blackwell, N. Collin, each $4; Thos. Jefferson $12.50— Total $128.25."

XXIII

Trudeau to Carondelet, St. Louis, March 2, 1793[1]

[Note of Carondelet][2]
All that was done is approved, but in a similar case it would be convenient to take a decorous course without allowing savages to avenge themselves and to inflict exemplary punishment on the Osages.

No. 48

At the end of January last, the Little Osages stole twenty some odd horses from the inhabitants of Ste. Geneviève who had them on an isle in

---

[1]Written in Spanish. A.G.I., P. de C., leg. 26.
[2]This marginal notation by Carondelet is in his reply dated May 5, 1793, A.G.I., P. de C., leg. 19; draft in A.G.I., P. de C., leg. 124.

the Mississippi where they were feeding them in shelter. This robbery has led fourteen of the most rascally chiefs and *considerados* of the nation to come to St. Louis to weep, as is their custom, and give up their medals and *golas*. They feigned the greatest sorrow about their being unable to stop the robbery nor bring the horses without exposing themselves to losing their lives. The savages said many other words of which it is useless to tell Your Excellency. I have not yet answered them, because it is the custom to do it the following day. On that day more than two hundred armed men of the Sac, Fox, Kickapoo, Mascouten, and Pus Indians were assembled,[8] either from those who were in the town or others who had to be called from the immediate vicinity. They surrounded the house where the Little Osages were quartered and staged a demonstration threatening to kill them. They surely would have killed them if I had not placed myself at the head of a guard in the house occupied by the Osages. This house was joined to the *quartel* of the troop. During the night I made them pass and hide in the loft of it. The following day I tried to make those who wished to kill the Osages believe that the latter had left, but they told me that they [Osages] were with my soldiers. All the best reasons could neither convince nor persuade them that I could not allow people who had come to give me their hand to be offended; and that first they would have to kill me and my troop as well as all the inhabitants before spilling other blood under the royal flag of my sovereign. I was in this position for the next ten days. Finally, with the help of some *aguardiente,* I succeeded in winning the chiefs whom I caused to come from the other bank of the river, where they were followed by the greater part of the others, who also wanted drink. Afterwards, having made those who had remained in the town drunk, I succeeded in taking advantage of the obscurity of the tenth night to have the Osages escape. Persuaded by the fear that I was sacrificing them, they told me that if one of them should perish, that would be sufficient for their nation not to allow any of the traders of the Missouri to return. To show them that they did not have anything to fear I accompanied them a league from the town, where they took the route which seemed to them most safe in order not to meet enemies.

---

[8]On October 24, 1792, Trudeau wrote to Carondelet (Bancroft Library) concerning a letter which several savages had written to him regarding injuries suffered by them by forays made by the Osages. Trudeau told them that Carondelet was preparing for war against the Osages and that no traders could have been sent to them had it not been so easy for them to go to trade with the English on the Des Moines. But since the Osages were at war with the Iowas, Sacs and Foxes it would not be easy for the Osages to go to the Des Moines. However, if traders were withheld from Osages, Trudeau feared attacks by them on Spanish villages and if several inhabitants are killed it might lead to migrations from here. Trudeau asked permission of Carondelet to permit him, if traders are withheld from Osages, to send traders to the other nations with a two year supply of merchandise and secretly, because then Osages would not be apt to stop the traders.

It seems to me that I could not conduct myself in any other way, for otherwise the many traders that there are on the Missouri would have remained exposed to a vengeance which could only fall again upon them and upon these establishments. Moreover, I must observe international law above all, protect those who are under the royal banner of His Majesty, making use of all the gentle methods used with the Indians before going to the extreme of making use of arms. This surely would have given cause for a war with some barbarians who do not know either the use or the customs and laws of civilized nations. All this I desire may merit the approval of Your Excellency.

God keep Your Excellency many years. St. Louis, March 2, 1793.

Zenon Trudeau [rubric]

Señor Baron de Carondelet.

XXIV

CLAMORGAN TO TRUDEAU, ST. LOUIS, APRIL 1, 1793[1]

Mr. Zenon Trudeau, Captain of the regular regiment of Louisiana and commander-in-chief of the western part of Illinois.

Sir:

During the more than ten years that the petitioner has made his residence in this place he has never ceased through his operations to render himself useful to the well-being of the people and to the advancement of commerce and agriculture.

The industry which he has loved and supported through enterprises, the emulation and encouragement which he has aroused in most of the farmers by receiving provisions from them in exchange, according to their needs, for the provisions which are to be consumed in the capital, [all these are] far from having supported the hopes which he had of giving reciprocal comfort to the district, far, I tell you, Sir, far from having enabled him to collect his modest recompense for his troubles and his hardships. On the contrary, he continually sees his expectations wither with no hopes of return.

Formerly the subjects of His Majesty did not have an equal right to carry on their industry among the nations of the Missouri without making themselves criminals in the eyes of the mercenary and the favored.

During this time, *Monsieur,* how many sacrifices, how many irreparable losses, did the business of the petitioner suffer? As the climax of disgrace today what a picture of sorrow and affliction is seen. The inhospitable

[1]Written in French. A.G.I., P. de C., leg. 26.

seasons, the cruel depredations of the savages, the often fruitless and often flooded sowings, the repeated losses of animals, leave for the future of the petitioner only the strength to have recourse to the extent of your kindness to take measures suitable to his position.

The petitioner is in debt for a large sum to the estate of the deceased Mercier whose heir is in Europe, and is desirous of meeting that debt.[2] Will he dare to demand of your justice the sacrifice of several families who are accountable [in debt] to him, will he dare to ask you that their lands, their houses, and their animals be sold to settle these obligations [due] to him? Without available resources where will the purchasers be? If there were any, Sir, the petitioner, always humane, would sacrifice only himself. The sale of his property would take place at once but here where circumstances destroy resources, here where everyone seeks to sell and no one to buy, what is one to do with property?

A salt factory that the petitioner established at great expense on the river Maramek for public use and need, will not bring today one tenth part of its value because of fear of the Osages and the lack of a purchaser.

If it were necessary to sacrifice only half of this same value in order to relieve, through an adequate delay, the unfortunates who owe him you would see him then bear in pomp the triumph of his hardships.

However, if the government, always looking after the happiness of its subjects, would found a colony on the banks of the Maramek able to resist the raids of the savages, this river where riches abound would offer an infinity of resources and innumerable provisions that the future would cause to circulate in the most remote places by means of the Canal [commercial channel?] of the Capital. This would then be an inexhaustible means of increasing without limit settlements useful to the state, some through their furrows increased twofold would give to human existence the sources of life and abundance; while others with their sharp pickaxes would tear without expense from the entrails of the earth the vast lead mines that it encloses, which a new branch of commerce would transport to the mother country.

These lands of an ever-renewing fertility would become in the future the inaccessible bulwark against neighboring ambition through repaying with interest the industrious tiller of the soil for his hard work. His domestic animals then sheltered from the depredations of the savages would

---

[2]Clamorgan had debtors in France. He had difficulty in selling property on account of the Osage war and he had accounts amounting to 20,000 *pesos* owed him upon which he could not at the time collect. He had to sell a house worth 6000 for 500 to be paid in two years (he could not sell it for 50 *pesos* cash). His saline on the Meramec cost him 6000 but he could not sell it on account of the Osage war. Trudeau to Carondelet, no. 62, St. Louis, May 16, 1793, A.G.I., P. de C., leg. 26, and Carondelet to Trudeau, New Orleans, July 9, 1793, A.G.I., P. de C., leg. 20.

become fat from the gifts of nature. Some would graze, gamboling about on the verdant grass, while others with comfort and without hardship would gather, while frolicking, in the rich presence of the oak, which bowed before nature, seems to offer in return its fruits that it has received from nature.

The petitioner perhaps goes astray, *Monsieur,* in the illusions of his dreams but he enters again the limits prescribed for him by his requests and by his dependence upon the kindness of the government so that it may graciously grant the petitioner a few years to put him in a position to reach a settlement with the estate of the deceased Mercier.

It is with this hope that the petitioner will not cease to offer his prayer to the Almighty for you.

Jacques Clamorgan[3]
[rubric]

St. Louis, April 1, 1793.

---

[3]See A. P. Nasatir, "Jacques Clamorgan: Colonial Promoter of the Northern border of New Spain," *New Mexico Historical Review,* XVII (1942), 101-112.
On October 4, 1793, Clamorgan sent to Carondelet a plan for populating Illinois, saying that it was necessary to increase the population of the province in proportion to its area, especially along the important frontiers, in order to prevent an invasion. Agriculturalists were especially needed and Clamorgan urged a very generous plan to bring in Germans and Hollanders, six thousand families at a cost of 174,550 *piastres,* which sum would be paid back in full within five years. Clamorgan's scheme was to strengthen the uninhabited parts of the Mississippi frontier and prevent the Anglo-Americans from penetrating New Mexico, since they could reach that area by land in fifteen or twenty days without trouble. He urged that the prospective settlers be brought from Europe to Philadelphia in neutral vessels and from there brought overland to the Illinois. Ms. in Bancroft Library.

XXV

Trudeau to Carondelet, St. Louis, April 10, 1793[1]

No. 50

Incite[2] the Indian nations to strike a general blow upon that same *pueblo* of Osages, guided by those hunters and traders who know the country, as is intended by the Arkansas, who ask for nothing but munitions, and who are taking many whites. Also give those Indians munitions for the account

Because our traders are still in the Missouri, and exposed to the anger of the Great and Little Osages, if the latter should now learn of Your Excellency's instructions taking [depriving] trade from them, and your decisions to make war on them, I have thought it well to postpone until the beginning of the

---

[1]Written in Spanish. Bancroft Library.
[2]This is a draft of the reply. A draft of the entire letter is in the Bancroft Library.

of the King. Finally, try to get together an expedition among those of New Madrid, St. Louis, Ste. Geneviève, etc., sufficient to destroy the *pueblo* of the Osages, cooperating with Don Thomas Portell. For this, Captain Don Zenon Trudeau is authorized to spend up to 1,000 *pesos*. An account must be rendered later as to how this [money] was used.

[Carondelet's rubric]

coming month of July[3] the publication of that measure, so that the traders mentioned may have time to withdraw, and to cause others to go and provide the other nations with arms and ammunitions before the Osages have learned of it, so that the war against them may be more general and successful.

I can assure Your Excellency that there are no nations in these territories who are not at war with the Osages, but with all one does not see any of them killing more than two Osages in a year; and they will never succeed in destroying them. With a population of 1,250 men, young men and warriors, they live all together in the same village in the midst of an immense prairie, an advantage which makes them formidable, and which will not permit in our [one] time the accomplishment of what is desired for the good of the province. Rather on the contrary, I fear and suspect that, if they begin war with these settlements, which are forty leagues distant from them, they will tire out and kill the poor inhabitants, who, not being able to

---

[3]In a letter to Carondelet, no. 57, dated April 16, 1793, Trudeau lamented the fact that the news of the war on the Osages had been made public in New Madrid and feared for the safety of the traders to the Missouri tribes. A.G.I., P. de C., leg. 26.

Carondelet ordered a war against the Osages, directing Trudeau to command a general expedition against them in concert with the commandant of New Madrid, Lorimier, and the commandants of Natchitoches and Arkansas. Dehault Delassus to Carondelet, no. 4, New Orleans, May 1, 1793, A.G.I., P. de C., leg. 214. The story of the "War on the Osages" is narrated and documents given in full in Nasatir, *Imperial Osage*.

On April 16, 1793, Trudeau wrote Carondelet that he had just learned that war on the Osages had been publicly announced at New Madrid and that he had lost hope of trying to send traders to the other Missouri River nations for the Osages, now informed of the war, would stop the traders and take away from them munitions, arms and merchandise. This may cause injury to our establishments and Trudeau was fearful of attacks by all the Indians, since they did not receive any traders. (No. 57— A.G.I., P. de C., leg. 26) See note 3 to Document XXIII. This is fully discussed in Nasatir, *Imperial Osage*.

cultivate their lands, will be obliged to emigrate to the other *towns* of the province or to the American side, as it is the nearest.

I am informed that the Loups have attacked a party of Osages on the Arkansas river, and that the first named had killed a half breed named Mongrain, who was reared in St. Louis, and who was engaged in trading with the Osages. This I learned through the merchant Don Augustin Chouteau, who was in the nation. The Osage relatives of Mongrain, wishing to take vengeance for his death, sought for the Loups, and, not finding them, killed two French hunters on the *Rio Blanco* and took another prisoner. The latter was rescued by the traders and will probably come to St. Louis. I have also been informed that they have robbed some Arkansas hunters.

May God Keep Your Excellency many years.

Zenon Trudeau [rubric]
St. Louis, April 10, 1793

XXVI

Trudeau to Carondelet, St. Louis, May 6, 1793[1]

No. 61

In case of robbery, it would be permissible for the inhabitants to punish the infractors severely, being justified to detain the de-

I have tried in every way possible to obtain from the "Nacion Ayoas", the thirty-eight horses stolen from the San Carlos establishment[2] and through my orders and words sent to the leaders, they have killed the man that had committed

---

[1]Written in Spanish. A.G.I., P. de C., leg. 26.
[2]See documents XVII and XX.

linquents who could be gotten from their country without maltreating them, but not setting them free until a suitable satisfaction from the country has been obtained.[a]

said theft, promising they would return the horses this spring, a promise which as yet has not been fulfilled and a fact which makes me feel like sending another order demanding an answer on the first day. If I succeed in getting said horses, it will be the first satisfaction of this nature which this rule has achieved from the Indians, who in general are thieves now more than ever. Six Pus, whom I had cordially welcomed, upon leaving my house with a gift, have just stolen two mares and a horse two steps from the town. This is the way these pests have always been and they will remain this way with no other remedy than a large population to punish these abuses from time to time.

May God keep Your Excellency many years.

St. Louis May 16, 1793
Zenon Trudeau [rubric]

M.[r] Baron de Carondelet

---

[a]Note of Carondelet.

XXVII

Trudeau to Carondelet, St. Louis, May 20, 1793[1]

No. 73

I remit to Your Excellency a report of the commerce made by our traders in the Missouri River during the entire last winter, which has been profitable, as Your Excellency will see by the report itself. The Indians have had much more merchandise than they are accustomed to and have gathered fewer furs; being able to buy cheaper, they have not worked at hunting and have become insolent.

I also remit the report that Your Excellency has ordered me to make

---

[1]Written in Spanish. A.G.I., P. de C., leg. 26.

of the English commerce with the Indians of this continent, with all the detail that I could.[2]

May God keep Your Excellency many years,

St. Louis, May 20, 1793

Zenon Trudeau
[rubric]

Señor Baron de Carondelet[3]

[Report on English Commerce With Indians]

The superiority of English commerce over ours in this continent is founded on methods which are not yet in use among us.

The first moving factor in their operations arises from their correspondence and relation with the capital. The greater part of the merchants of Montreal have commissioners and agents in England, and they are allied to rich men who cannot be incommoded by delay of their funds; while we, on the contrary, have no houses in Europe and few merchants in the capital doing business with them.

In Canada, which is the gathering place of the boats of the metropolis for the merchandise used in trade with the Indians, the merchant receives the goods on a deposit or on his own account, whether he afterwards sends them to the agent at Michilimaquina, who has ordered them in England, or directs them to the one who is limited to taking them from Montreal. In whatever way the operation is accomplished, the payment for the goods destined for Michilimaquina is not made in England until after two years, and those destined for the north at the end of three years, sometimes four years.

In our capital, on the contrary, nearly all the boats need their funds with which to meet the obligations which they have left behind them. It is a fact, then, that some wide-awake speculator takes advantage of the

---

[2]This report follows: It is an original document in the Bancroft Library but begins on page "2" (the first four pages or folios are missing in the Bancroft Library). It is dated May 18, 1793, and is followed by a list of the places where the canoes of the English merchants of Michilimackinac winter for the trade with the Indians and of the number of canoes of goods consumed by each nation which I found in A.G.I., P. de C., leg. 26. Concerning the subject of the British fur trade see G. C. Davidson, *The Northwest Company* (Berkeley, 1918); W. E. Stevens, *The Northwest Fur Trade* (Urbana, 1928); Nasatir, "Anglo-Spanish Frontier on the Upper Mississippi 1786-1796", *Iowa Journal of History and Politics*, XXIX (1931); L. R. Masson, *Les Bourgeois de la Compagnie du Nord-Ouest* (Quebec, 1889).

[3]On August 6, 1793, Carondelet replied, stating that he received the report of the trade and the other information and documents enclosed in Trudeau's letter no. 73. Carondelet added that he did not think that the unfavorable results of the year's trade was as bad as Trudeau thought it was "since the insolence of the Indians will be mitigated little by little and the competition will make them afterwards more tractable". Carondelet expressed satisfaction in receiving Trudeau's report of the English commerce with the Indians. Draft [Carondelet] to Trudeau, New Orleans, August 6, 1793. A.G.I., P. de C., leg. 124.

conditions which promise him a certain profit on his operations, even if he has to contend against the most active competition.

But in Canada the English merchant does not fear individual embarrassment, for the merchandise for which he asks is furnished to him on a profit, more or less high, which is rated by the London price; and there the price of merchandise, as well as that of the exchanges [in Europe], remains constantly the same with each banker at the same time. The same course is faithfully followed with the merchant of Canada in his relations with this continent; the price in Europe of the merchandise is placed upon the invoice with a certain percent of profit, and one and the other go on to their destination.

At the same time the penetrating vision of the bold and ambitious merchant rapidly runs over the entire globe; his profits are calculated beforehand; the remittance of his peltries to Europe, local or foreign consumption, the solicitations, more or less urgent, of remote nations, all form from that time the thermometer of his different prices; and the speculation of the rich and skillful man in Europe gives from that time a value to the peltries of which the trader here receives the first advantage.

Among us, on the contrary, the price of merchandise at the capital is always [unstable?] limited; the concourse and the abundance of [furs taken during] the season usually regulate the mark [procedure] of the merchant on the requisitions made for the merchandise by his agents, who receive here in exchange, peltries at a fixed and previously determined price.

From this state of affairs the advantage of the English commerce with the nations remains incontestably with that country, while on the contrary that which we do is totally for the advantage of Europe or for the capital. In order to enter into competition with the English in the commerce of the nations, it would be necessary that we should have in Europe rich agents who would be willing to direct their operations in[to] this part of the universe, and from that time we would obtain the superiority over a nation which has no surplus of persons in this continent.

Nevertheless there will be still remaining to them other advantages, as follows: the mass of their expenses is better handled than ours for the the transportation of merchandise from Europe to the capital; the said merchandise is manufactured expressly for the Indians, who on account of the frugality of their living, always give them the preference; the small number of sailors that they use on their ships; the rapidity of their expeditions; and the low price of their insurance. All these points must necessarily have an influence on the selling price of their merchandise.

But if we cannot come up to these methods, are we not well indemnified by the difference in convenience which we have in transporting our merchandise by water from the capital to the most remote nations, while

176

the English have more than a hundred portages to reach our possessions, where their merchandise is sold at a high price? What a difference in expenses!

We find that, although the economy with which they are introduced into our territory counterbalances our conveniences, the advantage will always be ours from the time that the government causes the territory belonging to it, and from which the English draw the greater part of their rich peltries, to be respected.

The merchandise of England, has to travel over a distance of fifteen hundred leagues to reach Montreal. Its transportation up to the place of disembarkation costing thirteen and one-half percent. Then it takes another road and goes to the places where it is to be consumed, loaded in canoes made of the bark of trees, under the direction of nine oarsmen, commanded sometimes by a factor and at other times by a conductor.

The canoes for Michilimaquina have to pass thirty-six portages, where the men are obliged to carry them on their backs in order to pass places impracticable by water and difficult by land. The merchandise destined for the north district, with which communication is made by way of Lake Superior in order to reach our territory (so as to pass above our territory), is also carried over impassable places more than a hundred times before arriving at its destination. These men of iron, who are hardened by the rigorous climate, have no food but unhulled corn, mixed with a little deer fat, and rare is the year when some of the men are not eaten on account of the lack of provisions. The extremely small wages of those who go from Montreal to Michilimaquina do not exceed three hundred or three hundred and fifty *livres* for what they call a "wintering." This "wintering" begins from the moment when they leave Montreal, which is in April or May [March ?], and terminates in July or August of the following year, covering fifteen months of struggle. For this they receive payment of their wages in merchandise, which is furnished to them at a price so high that these same wages never amount to half of the sum promised. If these hired men do not obey their factors of if they raise their hands against them, they lose their wages; and if they allow anything to get wet or spoiled, they pay for it. This severity and discipline do not fail to contribute to the success of the operations.

On the arrival of the canoes in Michilimaquina the men and merchandise are divided into two bodies, in order to form two different expeditions under two factors or conductors, and each starts for its destination.

Whether the merchandise is sold to the Indians by factors or by the proprietors, there are different methods of obtaining it, some receiving it directly from London, others from Montreal, and some from Michilimaquina. The first are simply charged with the freight, transportation, insurance, and commission; the second are made to pay from thirty to forty

177

percent, and the last from seventy to eighty percent on the price in England, so that a man of small knowledge in business may, among the English, carry on the same volume of operations as the most skillful merchant, nor can the one or the other determine his profit except in the same form and manner.

It happens nevertheless that this same merchandise is brought to us here clandestinely under the same conditions as to Michilimaquina, in spite of the passage of two hundred and fifty leagues, and a long portage which they have to make besides. But the purpose behind this operation is nothing but the object of making themselves owners of our peltries. The English make use of their merchandise to acquire our peltries, the same as we make use of our peltries to acquire their merchandise; the first can, then, regulate the movement of their operations on the purchase made by England of their peltries, while we are compelled to follow the regulations imposed upon us by the capital. From this difference in operation there undoubtedly arises a profit which makes the advantage of one the ruin of the other.

Before following further the operations of the English in this district, it is necessary to retrace our steps and observe the volume of their commerce in what they call the North, after having crossed Lake Superior to reach the sources of our Misuri.

Two companies, now united in one,[4] handle this rich trade; the merchandise destined for these uncommon profits goes from Montreal to be disembarked at the entrance of Lake Superior, fifteen [thirteen?] leagues from Michilimaquina. There it is re-embarked, to be scattered in various deposits which it has been necessary to place so that one part may take the direction of a road leading to Hudson Bay, while the others take an opposite direction leading them to the Upper Missouri, [which they reach] after traveling by water and land over territory belonging to His Majesty, where dwell a great number of different nations.

This company, which has its agents in London and Montreal, sends every year fifty or sixty canoes, of from fourteen to fifteen thousand *livres* (Tours money), to which it is necessary to add transportation, freight, and insurance to Canada (Montreal). This comes to the sum of seventy-two thousand *livres,* and afterwards to seven hundred and twenty thousand *livres* for the expense of the canoes, equipment, provisions, utensils, and nine oarsmen for each of the canoes which transport this merchandise to where it is to be consumed, after these same goods have been carried on their backs more than a hundred times in order to pass insuperable rapids and falls of the rivers, and also in order to cross portages separating one river from another.

---

[4]The Northwest Company.

For this journey, as long as it is painful, these men are given from one thousand to eighteen hundred *livres* for the "wintering," although they are more or less in the habit of consuming their wages in liquor [supplies], which is sold to them at forty *livres* the *alimete,* and the rest of their provisions in the same proportion. The sum total of the fifty [forty?]or sixty [fifty?] canoes, including all the expenses, up to the moment when they arrive among the savage nations, amounts to 1,692,000 *livres,* for which there are sent annually to England from this district alone sixteen to seventeen hundred bales of fine peltries, which can be compared to about twelve thousand bales of deer skins without hair. The sale in Europe of these peltries, under the worst circumstances, produces about four million *livres,* from which it is necessary to subtract the freight, insurance commissions, and duties, which may amount to four hundred thousand *livres,* so that there are left 3,600,000 *livres* to pay the principal fund, which is 1,692,000, leaving 1,908,000 clear profit for the proprietors of the stock.

It is necessary to turn again from the mountains of the north to the plains of the west to finish explaining the commerce of the English with the savages who live on the borders of the possessions of His Majesty. Retracing our steps, we find that Montreal despatches to Michilimaquina year after year, about eighty canoes, with the same number of men, in the same manner, and with about the same funds as those destined for the North; that is, eighty canoes of fourteen to fifteen hundred *livres* each, London prices, plus their expenses as far as Montreal, which amount to a total of 36,000 [96,000?] *livres;* and afterwards to 360,000 *livres* for those which it is necessary to cause to be brought from Canada in order to transport the merchandise to the place of consumption. Altogether it amounts to the sum of 1,656,000, with which is obtained the quantity of three thousand to thirty-four hundred bales of different kinds of peltries, which may be compared to nine thousand bales of deer skin without hair, of which the sale will produce about 3,500,000 *livres,* from which it is necessary to subtract the freight, insurance, commission, and duties, which may come to 300,000, leaving afterwards 3,200,000 to pay the capital of 1,656,000 *livres.* This will make 1,544,000 *livres* profit for the share-holders of this commerce with the different savage nations who dwell on our borders, of which it is necessary to give information, as well as of the particular consumption of each one, as is explained in the following list.

St. Louis, Illinois, May 18, 1793.

Zenon Trudeau
[rubric]

San Luis de Yllinois 18 de Mayo de 1793.

Noticia de los parages donde invernan las Canoas del Comercio Yngles de Michilimaquina para el trato conlos Yndios y consumo particular de cada Nacion.

179

	Sauteux	Otovoa	Poux	Mascutin	Kicapu	Folavoana	Puans	y Renards	Sioux	Ayoas
	Cans	Cans	Cans	Cans	Cans	Cans	Cans	Cans	Cans	Cans
Teritorio Americano en el Lago Michigan										
Le fond de la grande traversse	2	"	"	"	"	"	"	"	"	"
Laministre	"	6	"	"	"	"	"	"	"	"
Martigon	"	6	"	"	"	"	"	"	"	"
Grande Rivierre	"	4	"	"	"	"	"	"	"	"
Petit Calamec	"	2	"	"	"	"	"	"	"	"
Rivierre Blanche	"	2	"	"	"	"	"	"	"	"
San Joseph	"	"	10	"	"	"	"	"	"	"
Grande Colomi	"	"	2	"	"	"	"	"	"	"
Chicagou	"	"	2	"	"	"	"	"	"	"
Rivierre des Yllinois y los Pés	"	"	8	8	4	"	"	"	"	"
Petit fost	"	1	"	"	"	"	"	"	"	"
Miloaki	"	1	1	"	"	1	"	"	"	"
Les Deux Rivierres	1	1	1	"	"	"	"	"	"	"
La Baie Denoc	"	"	"	"	"	1	"	"	"	"
Rivierre Des Renards y Wisconsin	"	"	"	"	"	5	5	"	"	"
Rivierre Pere Mar Ket	"	2	"	"	"	"	"	"	"	"
en el Mississipi Territorio Español										
Praire du Chien	"	"	"	"	"	"	"	1	"	"
Rivierre Pomme de terre	"	"	"	"	"	"	"	2	"	"
Rivierre Sant Pierre por el qual se comunica en lo alta del Missuri									10	"
Rivierre Des Moins por donde se comunica con los Mahas y Panis									10	7
Rivierre Betes Puantes	"	"	"	"	"	"	"	"	3	"
Rivierre des Ayoas	"	"	"	"	"	"	"	"	"	4
grande Macoquité	"	"	"	"	"	"	"	2	"	"
Mississippi Partida Americana										
Rivierre des Sauteux	6	"	"	"	"	"	"	"	"	"
Lac Sant Croix	2	"	"	"	"	"	"	"	"	"
Aile de Corbeau	3	"	"	"	"	"	"	"	3	"
Rivierre Rouge	6	communica al Lago Superrior								
	20	25	24	8	4	8	5	5	26	11

30 Canoas sobre el teritorio Americano en los Contornos de Yllinois, con los Saquias y Renards, Kicapus, Loups, Chavanons, Mascutin, Puanti, Yllinois, Peorias, Cascaquias, y otras Naciones.

Totales de las Canoas 166 de que dos no hace mas que uno de Monreal a Michilimaquina.

San Luis de Yllinois 18 de Mayo de 1793

Zenon Trudeau

[rubric]

180

XXVIII

Trudeau to Carondelet, St. Louis, May 20, 1793[1]

No. 74

At the present time, I cannot give Your Excellency the least news of the Mandan Nation, as you ask me to in your official letter dated December 29 last.[2] The one named Santiago de la Yglesia whom I have called upon various times is so simple and from a province of France of such a peculiar language [dialect] that nobody can understand it, and moreover, he seems not to have made a single observation. But I hope to see within a few days a well informed Canadian *mozo* who has been in the said nation on discovery, and commissioned by *la Compañia del Comercio Yglés* [sic] of the North of Canada, who will facilitate me in remitting to Your Excellency on the first occasion the news which Your Excellency requests from me. Moreover, I know that some hunters of this jurisdiction have this year penetrated as far as the referred to Mandans, and whatever comes to my knowledge upon the return of hunters, as well as from the *mozo* that I am awaiting Your Excellency will be informed of immediately.

May God keep Your Excellency many years.

St. Louis, May 20, 1793

Zenon Trudeau [rubric]

Sr. Baron de Carondelet

[1]Written in Spanish. A.G.I., P. de C., leg. 26.
[2]Document XXI.

XXIX

Merchants of St. Louis to Carondelet, June 22, 1793[1]

To his Excellency *Monseigneur* Le Baron de Carondelet Chevalier of the Order of St. John, Colonel of the Provinces of Louisiana, and Intendant General and Inspector of the Veteran Troops and Militias of them, etc.
Monseigneur:

The merchants and inhabitants of St. Louis, Illinois, very humbly supplicate Your Excellency and hope to prove to you that they should be permitted to enjoy the advantages of liberty of commerce among the nations of the Missouri. They saw imperfectly the hope of regaining soon the considerable losses which they have suffered for many years. Courage, energy and industry had reappeared in their regions; they flattered themselves that under the benign influences of Your Excellency this colony would emerge from the state of stagnation into which it was plunged for

[1]Written in French. A.G.I., P. de C., leg. 188-3.

many years. In the middle of these sweet hopes, in the moment in which all are in the greatest activity, when all the capital was converted into objects of speculation, in which each one hastened to risk all or part of his fortune, the liberty of commerce[2] so long a time desired, so often solicited and which they had obtained from your justice, has been suppressed and limited to some [a few] persons, by virtue of the orders [which] have emanated from your authority.

The merchants and inhabitants are very much pleased with your kindness to them, very much persuaded of your equity, very much convinced of the lively interest which Your Excellency pleases to take in the prosperity of their establishments. They will never dare to form a suspicion which might alter in their hearts the respectful sentiments of confidence and gratitude which the wisdom of your administration has instilled there; on the contrary they are intimately persuaded that Your Excellency's decision to suppress this privilege had a plan of honoring under his protection especially the region of Illinois, by placing under suspicion all that might retard the aggrandisement and prosperity of this colony and alter the happiness and tranquility of these individuals.

May the merchants and inhabitants be permitted to represent very humbly that the plan which Your Excellency has conceived and put into execution, far from attaining the end which your justice and kindness had proposed, has on the contrary brought consternation, sorrow [chagrin] and desolation to the hearts of the majority of the citizens and prepared their future ruin on whichever side they look; they only see a chain of calamities which plunges their spirit into the depths of discouragement and abatement. Do they look towards their stores? They see their fortunes, without hope of bringing to them any interest, exposed to being perverted and altered by stagnation, even more so undermined because they have no means of bringing them out of the state of perdition into which the prohibition of carrying goods to the nations of the Missouri will infallibly reduce them. Formerly they could get along without this branch of commerce, but those fortunate times no longer exist. The nations with whom advantageous commerce upon the different rivers had been made no longer exist as they have been. [With the nations] tainted by the English, our neighbors, our traders hardly return with the merchandise which has been confided to them and which hardly returns the price of their goods; besides, the immensity of the merchandise which descends yearly from Canada to the different trading posts sets up a competition which the merchants of Illinois can not meet.[3] This sad position makes them unable to pay the

---

[2]Document XIV.

[3]See, *e.g.*, Document XXVII and Nasatir, "Anglo-Spanish Frontier on the Upper Mississippi 1786-1796", *Iowa Journal of History and Politics*, XXIX (1931), where fuller citations to sources are given.

debts they have contracted. When the petitioners consider the state of the mass of the citizens who carry on the trade, they see themselves and children exposed to the horrors of misery, as they have no other means of making subsistence for their families. If you consider them [as] together [with] the colony, they see the next dissolution occasioned by the obstruction of the channels which gave their livelihood.

Such, *Monseigneur*, is the frightful picture [situation] which the merchants and inhabitants dare to expose to your justice. They are persuaded that you will not consider such license and liberty which we have dared to take a crime; they have done so to enlighten the religion [mind] of Your Excellency upon the true interests of these countries, and the conditions under which they might be permitted, *Monseigneur*, to expose to your Excellency the remedies for such great faults [*maux*].

The merchants and inhabitants are agreed with your Excellency that it is time to restrain the insolence of the Osage nation, to make the flag of His Majesty respected and to assure the property and safety of his subjects who are near them. The declaration of war published the twelfth of this month was necessary; the interdiction of trade with this enemy nation was a natural step [result]. They never complained, because of this, they even desired it, and this prohibition will only cause them a small prejudice, but Your Excellency, in the fear that some people would be so unreasonable and so tempted by cupidity to carry merchandise to the Osage nation, has believed it necessary to abolish the liberty of commerce with all the other nations, and to forbid it to all except favorite persons, those chosen by *Monsieur* the commandant of St. Louis.[4] The merchants and inhabitants realize that the fears of Your Excellency were well founded, and that the first [principal] means which presented itself to Your Excellency was to restrict the commerce of the friendly nations to a certain few chosen individuals upon whom he could rely. Your Excellency had wisely judged the necessity of managing these nations on this occasion, but there was another means which has escaped Your Excellency, and which the merchants and inhabitants dare to submit to your examination which would not effectively interfere with the trade, but which would gain perfectly the ends of your wise administration. This would be to permit the individual liberty of trading in the Missouri, as Your Excellency had permitted last year, with modifications. These modifications might consist in giving permission to the merchants, traders and others, only on the condition that they give good and valuable security that they would not violate the order that nothing is to be delivered to the Osage nation. By this means those who may go to the trade, or those who send agents will

[4]Several references to the war on the Osages are made in the previous documents. These events are detailed together with the documentary evidence in Nasatir, *Imperial Osages.*

take such wise precautions, and will arm their *voitures* so that they can not be robbed by this nation. They would even prefer losing their merchandise by throwing it into the river to exposing themselves to the suspicion of having used this means of getting around [violating] Your Excellency's prohibition regarding the Osage. By this means the government could have persons among the friendly nations in whom they could place their confidence, and these countries would be on the road to prosperity.

Such are the first [just] representations which the merchants and inhabitants dare to take the liberty of making to Your Excellency as the means of abridging [shortening] the time of their calamity. They humbly present them to Your Excellency, begging Your Excellency to take into consideration and to have a look of pity on the poor families which are thrown into the paternal arms of Your Excellency and who wait [for] your justice and kindness—the reestablishment of commerce. They do not cease to invoke heaven for the prosperity of the Monarchy, for the conservation of the precious days of His Majesty, and that Your Excellency be accorded a long life, and success in all your enterprises and an unalterable happiness, which Your Excellency merits so justly. Such are the desires which the merchants and inhabitants of Illinois will never cease to form.

St. Louis, Illinois, June 22, 1793
[Signatures of persons.]
Cerré
Labbadie
Auge Chouteau.
St. Cyr
P. Labbadie
P. Chouteau
Laurent Durocher
Eugenio Álvarez

> [24 rubrics and 14 crosses with names written
> for them in circles. 38 all together.]

XXX

Trudeau to Carondelet, St. Louis, Illinois, July 10, 1793[1]

No. 91

I have received the most complete satisfaction from the chiefs of the Indian nation for the theft of the horses which the men of the same had

---

[1]Written in Spanish. A.G.I., P. de C., leg. 27B.

committed at the Post of San Carlos[2] and even though they did not return the same horses, they completed the number with the exception of one which they paid for. They came right away to see me. Because of the fine way in which they acted and because I need them to guard the River of *Des Moins*, I received them and feasted them well, giving them a full barrel of *aguardiente,* fourteen guns, and the rest proportionately, which is the best I have been able to do. But with all that, they still were not happy.

All these nations who trade with the English and go to receive gifts at Michilimaquinac are very given to drink and accustomed to receive the best of large gifts. They refused and mocked at the ones received from us, showing us what they have received in said Michilimaquinac in silverware, fine material, coats bordered with silver and gold, etc.

This Ayoa nation is at war with the Kansas, having entered this spring a camp of the said Kansas to buy horses from them. The latter went out to hunt in order to feed them and while they were gone, they killed, and took prisoner forty-eight women and children, and carried off all the horses. This is the reason why they do not dare send ambassadors to ask for peace and they have come to bring me five boy prisoners in order for me to make peace. I am keeping them in order to return them to the nation as soon as the occasion presents itself for that, and I will attempt to make peace if possible.

May God preserve Your Excellency for many years.

St. Louis, Illinois, July 10, 1793

Zenon Trudeau [rubric]

Sr. Baron de Carondelet

[2]See documents XVII, XX, and XXVI.

XXXI

TRUDEAU TO CARONDELET, ST. LOUIS, JULY 13, 1793[1]

NUMBER 96

Various chiefs of the different Indian nations have solicited from me some medals and other *patentes* [commissions] on account of their having lost theirs in carousals. I have always made them understand that I would solicit them from Your Excellency by which I find myself now somewhat annoyed with this promise which my predecessor had also made to them. If Your Excellency can remit to me some medals with the duplicate of commissions in blank, I will be very pleased, since the present circumstances require that they be pampered more than is customary on account of the war with the Osages. Without that [the war] Your Excellency might

[1]Written in Spanish. A.G.I., P. de C., leg. 27B.

think by this that it is my intention to create some new chief. [This is not so] since I see that their number is too great and that it would be better, on the contrary, to diminish them.

God keep Your Excellency many years. St. Louis, Illinois, July 13, 1793.

Zenon Trudeau [rubric]

Señor Baron de Carondelet

XXXII

REGULATIONS FOR THE ILLINOIS TRADE, ST. LOUIS, OCTOBER 15, 1793[1]

Desiring to make a definite regulation advantageous not only to the commerce but also to the inhabitants in general of Illinois who are engaged in the cultivation of the soil, the original source and fundamental basis of the true riches of every state, the workers who are indispensable to it, causing the profits of the Missouri trade to fall to all the business men and merchants of the said settlements who are in a position to contribute to the increase of this important branch of trade in such a way that the cultivator charged with providing subsistence to the merchants for the increase of consumption, which is a consequence of the comfort of the merchant, a very real benefit that all classes will enjoy, without thwarting [one another], a comfort from which they are really very far at present, I have resolved that the following plan be put before the eyes of all those who are interested and be discussed in an assembly of merchants and traders which will be presided over by the commandant Don Zenon Trudeau, who after having collected the votes of all present under each of the articles proposed will write in the margin the results of the vote and will send the said plan signed by all the representatives of all opinions present at this council and without any regard to the objections that any individuals may make against the majority of the votes.

Article 1.

Accepted unanimously. Only those shall be considered members of the

Only those who have at least a year of residence shall be counted as

---

[1]Written in French. A.G.I., P. de C., leg. 2363 (three copies). A copy in French interspersed with English translation is in the Missouri Historical Society, Spanish Archives no. 90. These copies contain only the eleven original articles as drawn up by Carondelet. The original, together with the comments of the merchants, the additional articles and addenda, and Trudeau's reply, is in the Bancroft Library. The additional articles were made at St. Louis on October 15, 1793. See A. P. Nasatir, "Formation of the Missouri Company", *Missouri Historical Review*, XXV (1930) 3-15; and "Anglo-Spanish Rivalry on the Upper Missouri," *Mississippi Valley Historical Review*, XVI (1929), reprint pp. 11-12. The translation here given is made from the copy in A.G.I., P. de C., leg. 2363, with the marginal notations and additional articles being translated from the document in the Bancroft Library.

St. Louis trade and that of its jurisdiction who shall be known to be carrying on trade, etc, there, and who have at least a year's residence by [and] actual ownership [of property] and maintain either direct or indirect trade with the capital or with merchants residing at New Orleans who themselves carry on trade between the capital and the Illinois, etc. This is to prevent any rich merchant in the jurisdiction of Illinois from establishing sham stores with no intention except to have so many storehouses which he will set up as stores [profiting from as many posts as there are storehouses]

members of the trade of St. Louis and its jurisdiction and those who have business relations with the merchants and traders of New Orleans, with those who carry on business there, or those who conduct it for themselves directly with the said capital.

Article 2.

Permission to go or to send agents to trade.

Permission to trade on the Missouri will not be granted to any hunter, citizen, trader, or *coureur-de-bois* who does not meet the conditions prescribed in the first article.

Article 3.

The trade humbly thanks the government general.

The entire Missouri trade shall be divided among the merchants and traders of the city and district of Illinois without the commandants having power to deprive any one of them of his privilege without good and well proved cause of being against the interests of the government, the said deprivation having been previously confirmed by the governor general of the Province.

Article 4.

The first of May instead of the first of July so as to make it easy for merchants to send out advantageously [early enough] to distant posts.

Of which the number shall be exactly equal to that of those present without prejudice to the one Mr. the commandant may desire to choose.

On the first of July of each year all the said members or their representatives in accordance with the first article shall be assembled by the syndic of commerce in order to proceed to a just distribution among themselves of the Missouri trade in such a way that each one interested may have a portion of the trade equivalent to any other. The commandant shall not be present, nor interfere in the arrangement of the lots or the divisions of the trade, which shall be exactly equal to the number of those present.

Article 5.

Each portion of the trade shall be drawn by lot in the presence of the commandant, who alone shall have the right to choose beforehand the portion of the trade which suits him best, without the right to change it afterwards for any other.

Article 6.

At the end of three days; it is better to say "in the interval of the month of May" as stated [changed] in Article 4.

"Sending it down to the city." In case that one of the merchants or several refuse to accept the bearers who would do to carry it [post they receive], the syndic shall employ one at the expense, profit and portion of the company [all].

The interested parties may exchange with each other the portion they have drawn by lot within the space of three days, after which each shall be obliged to keep what he has drawn and the syndic of commerce shall remit to the commandant the general list of the division of trades and he shall send a copy, signed by the said syndic, to the governor-general at the first opportunity for sending it down to the city.

Article 7.

[In a different hand from the others]
On the bill of lading for goods that goes to the Missouri or that region there shall be the name of each contractor, the syndic, the passport, etc.

The commandant shall give the necessary passports to those who ask him for them without the right to delay their dispatch [granting] and they [traders] will pay to the commandant [blank][2] *piastres* for this right each year.

Article 8.

The trader destined to a post on the Missouri will not be allowed to trade with any other under the penalty of having to return the peltries to the person or persons to whom that post was assigned.

Article 9.

After war shall be declared with a nation, a trader who trades with that nation shall be made prisoner and sent to the capital and his goods shall be confiscated, one-third for the profit by the royal treasury, one-third for that of the informer, and one-third for that of the commandant.

Article 10.

Insert after "and in case there is no public work coffer", "unless the Illinois district is short of man power in which case the traders shall be authorized to hire foreigners so as not to remove the agricultural workers from the country, provided that they inform the commandant, who will insert it in their passport and will allow it if it does not have the appearance of fraud."

The traders shall not employ foreign *engagés* for their voyages on the Missouri, including in this classification any one who has less than a year's residence in the jurisdiction of the Illinois under penalty of fifty *piastres* fine per head for *engagés* of this kind. This shall be paid by the proprietor of the boat; one half shall be applied to the profit of the royal treasury, and the other half to that of the informer, and in case there is none, to the public work coffers.

---

[2]Twenty-five *piastres*.

Article 11.

The syndic of commerce, who shall be elected the first of the year by a majority of votes, shall not have the power to convoke the assembly [of the traders] without the consent in writing of the commandant who shall never refuse it without very important reasons, of which he shall render a complete report to the governor general on the first favorable occasion.
New Orleans, July 20, 1793.

The Baron de Carondelet [rubric]

We, Don Zenon Trudeau, commander-in-chief of the western part of the Illinois, by virtue of the orders of His Excellency, the Baron de Carondelet, to assemble the traders of this city and communicate to them the plan of the central government for the exploitation of the Missouri trade, have, therefore, required them to assemble here today in the seat of our government to deliberate upon each article of the said regulation.

The merchants assembled proposed to us the remarks which we have put in the margin of the several articles, with the request that they be accepted by the central government since they are for the welfare of every individual.

We at once required the merchants there assembled to proceed to the appointment of a syndic. This resulted unanimously in the choice of Mr. Clamorgan.

Following the appointment of the syndic we [he?] laid some articles, additional to the plan above, before the assembly and they were adopted in our presence by a very great majority of the votes, as being necessary to the safety of the trade. We have the honor to submit these articles to you below, in the hope that you will be pleased to find them acceptable.

Article 12.

No intoxicating beverages are to be taken into the Missouri by any person whatsoever for the purpose of trading, exchanging or giving to any person whatsoever, free or slave, under penalty of a fine of one hundred *piastres,* of which one-third is to go to the profit of the informer, the rest placed at the disposal of the government.

Article 13.

No one is to advance to his employees destined for the Missouri more than half of their wages during the course of the trip under risk of losing the extra amount advanced.

Article 14.

In posts where there are several traders, all shall be forced to sell at the same price so that the savage nations may not be corrupted. This price shall be determined before opening the trade by the majority of the traders who are there, and in case there are an equal number in said post, then the oldest if there are only two or the two older men if there are four or more older men, shall determine the price at which trading should be carried on under penalty of a fine of two hundred *piastres* against the offender, always under the condition that there is not a majority opposed, in which case it would have the right.

Article 15.

From the month of July the traders or their representatives in the posts of the Missouri shall leave, ceasing to carry on trade with the nations where they or their employees are, or sooner if the traders of the following year appear before that time.

Article 16.

No trader may sell on the Missouri any merchandise to any white, half-breed, or savage, directly or indirectly to their profit or that of the trader, under penalty of a fine of two hundred *piastres* against the offender for each person that he employed or equipped.

Article 17.

The traders are not to use as couriers, if they need them, any but white men whom they have taken with them to the Missouri for the exploitation of their part of the post, under penalty of two hundred *piastres* fine for each individual employed contrary to this article.

Article 18.

It is forbidden to give to any hunter after his departure and during the course of his trip and hunting, anything but objects necessary for his operations. These they shall not give, sell or exchange, in order to prevent illicit trading that he might carry on, under penalty of two hundred *piastres* fine against the one who equipped him and the same amount against the hunter.

To avoid abuse the merchant who equips a hunter shall make two lists for him, which he shall sign and submit to the syndic for inspection, who will put his visa there. He will leave one in the hands of the syndic and the other will be for the hunter, upon which the commandant will deliver his passport to him.

Article 19.

The traders are not to take it upon themselves to employ on the Missouri either negroes or half-breeds or savages, free or slave. This is done to encourage the labor of white men already established or about to establish themselves in the district and to avoid the information and bad counsel they might give the nations.

Article 20.

No person whatsoever may trade, receive as a present, or exchange with nations of the Missouri, directly or indirectly, any branded horse so as not to encourage the savages to steal them from the whites. In case anyone has so traded a horse, the owner of the brand shall have the right to reclaim the horse, and in default of an owner the horse shall be sold for the benefit of the public works.

Article 21.

Since it has pleased the central government to give the members of the trade of this district the right to the Missouri trade, it is very important for our interests to have the Indians dwelling on our land absolutely forbidden to trade with the inhabitants of Arkansas. It is even more important for the safety of the traders, hunters, laborers, and other individuals who are forced every day to go far from the troops of the city, that the nations shall not be deprived of our aid, because in that way we should make these same nations hostile to us and turn them to foreigners. Then we should all be in fear for the safety of our lives and that of our property.

Article 22.

In order to spare the government from an endless number of small law suits, on the first of each year two commissioners should be appointed, one for the district above the city and one for that below, who should have the right to force the payment, regulate, or settle the differences between different individuals up to the sum of ten *piastres*. In the same way, they should be empowered to settle [assess] the damage or injury done by animals, regardless of the amount.

Article 23.

May it please the central government to allow the members of the trade of this place to make expeditions against foreigners who establish themselves on our land with merchandise to attract the trade of our savages, and also to authorize the merchants to confiscate their goods or furs, to be allotted half for the profit of the members of the expedition, and the other half for the profit of the association for the expenses undertaken by the group.[3]

May it please the central government to permit the corps of merchants [*Corps du commerce*] of this city of St. Louis to form a society under the name of the Company of Discoveries, authorized and licensed for the period of ten consecutive years for the Missouri trade, to extend above the nation known by the name of the Poncas, so that the said society may have the exclusive right to the entire exploitation of all the nations that it can visit, discover, or obtain information about; the company to be under the direction of a syndic, elected by a majority of the votes, who will make their resolutions in due form and in writing after approval by the majority in order to communicate them to the commandant who will make them valid by his approval.

In order to increase profits may it please the central government to permit the merchants of this place during the course of the war to procure from the country of the English[4] or from that of the Americans the articles necessary for the exploitation of the Missouri posts because scarcity of supplies and circumstances will not permit perhaps of their being secured from the capital, and because [of the circumstances] it should be urged upon the central government to grant and sanction this by a suitable decree for the welfare of each individual merchant.

Made and passed in the city hall of the city of St. Louis of Illinois by the merchants here present who have signed below with us, the fifteenth

---

[3]This was done immediately. See Trudeau to Carondelet, no. 142, St. Louis, October 21, 1793, A.G.I., P. de C., leg. 27B. See Nasatir, "Anglo-Spanish Frontier on the Upper Mississippi 1786-1796," *Iowa Journal of History and Politics*, XXIX (1931), 198 ff.

In September or early in October Trudeau received the Regulation sent by Carondelet. Trudeau called the meeting of the merchants on October 15, because the greater number of Merchants were ready to depart for their winter trade; otherwise he would have had to wait until the following spring. At that meeting the merchants voted on Carondelet's proposals and Trudeau placed their comments in the margin and added the additional articles. Each article was voted on separately. These were sent to Carondelet on October 20, 1793. Trudeau to Carondelet, no. 140, St. Louis, October 20, 1793, Bancroft Library.

It appears that Clamorgan, as Director of the newly formed company, had sent a *mémoire* to Carondelet who, adding his comments thereto, sent it to Trudeau for action. Draft [Carondelet] to Trudeau, New Orleans, November 9, 1793, A.G.I., P. de C., leg. 27B.

In replying to Trudeau's letter no. 144, Carondelet acknowledged receipt of Trudeau's letter and of the latter's being unable to put into effect the regulations or Plan of Commerce until June of 1794. Carondelet to Trudeau, New Orleans, December 23, 1793, A.G.I., P. de C., leg. 20.

day of the month of October, 1793, and the second [year] of the administration of His Excellency.

Boneventura Collell	R. Gengembre
Reilhe	J. Motard
Jn. Papin	Jn Lavallée
C. Yostiz	Cʰ. Sanguinet
Jh. Robidou	Benito Vasquez
Gʳᵉ Sarpy	Cerré
St. Sire	Antoine Roy
Guilaume Hebert	Andreville
Vincent	Louis Bonparé
Jq. Clamorgan	Dubreuil

[all rubrics]
Zenon Trudeau [rubric]⁴

---

⁴Trudeau in letter number 145 asked for and Carondelet approved "permitting the merchants of your establishment [St. Louis] to obtain from the English district without duty all the *merchandise of trade only, which is necessary for the consumption of the Indians*"—Carondelet to Trudeau, New Orleans, December 23, 1793, A.G.I., P. de C., leg. 20.

XXXIII

Petition of Juan Munier, September, 1793¹

Señor Governor and Intendant General:

Juan Munié, citizen of the village of Saint Louis, Illinois, and trader of the Missouri river in that jurisdiction, with due respect to Your Excellency declares: that when Captain Don Manuel Perez was civil and military commandant of those settlements, the petitioner discovered the Ponkas tribe, located on the upper part of the above named river and about four hundred leagues from the above-named settlements, at the cost of many dangers, hardships, difficulties and exorbitant expenses, and with no less sufferings, he opened up and established with that tribe a trade, which possessed not only the advantages of having them peaceful and well-inclined to the royal Spanish domination by making them understand who was the great Monarch of the Spains, the mildness of his government, and

---

¹Written in Spanish. A.G.I., P. de C., leg. 2363; copy in Bancroft Library; printed in Houck, *Spanish Régime in Missouri*, II, 1-3. I have corrected Houck's translation. See also contract of partnership for trade with the Ponca Indians between Meunier and Rolland, April 26, 1793, in the Bancroft Library and also in the same repository Meunier and Rolland to Carondelet, St. Louis, October, 1794. There are also in the Bancroft Library several depositions to the effect that Meunier discovered the Ponca Indians. These are given in Chapter II, document XIV. There are many references to Meunier in Truteau's "Journal," Chapter II, document XXII. Meunier later sold or conveyed his monopoly to Clamorgan. Meunier confessed presently that he did not discover the Poncas. See Chapter II, documents I, III and VI.

the especial favor with which he looks upon and treats the Indians, but also the fact that the traders who go up to their neighborhood to trade with them are able to do it with greater security. From this results an unfailing and considerable benefit to the trade of the above-mentioned settlements. By virtue of that, and as the supplicant designs to discover other more remote tribes for the increase of the above-mentioned trade, and in order to succeed in preventing them from continuing to live in that barbarity to which they are accustomed, as an indemnification for the exorbitant expenses which he has had, of the great expense which he will have to expend and risk, and of the small capital for his aid, he petitions Your Excellency to be so good as to grant him the exclusive trade with said Ponka tribe for ten years, as well as the trade with the other tribes whom he may discover.

In proof of the fact that he was the first to discover and pacify the above mentioned Ponka tribe, besides that which can be certified by the above mentioned Captain Don Manuel Perez, he duly presents to Your Excellency the subjoined document, at the bottom of which is a certification given by various persons, to whom all that he has said is well known.

He petitions Your Excellency to be so good as to grant him this favor which he hopes to gain by the approval of Your Excellency. New Orleans, September 16, 1793. Por la parte . . .

Marcos Rivero [rubric]

[Carondelet's decree]
New Orleans, September 17, 1793. Let Captain Don Manuel Perez report what he knows and what is evident to him in regard to the petition and request of the supplicant.

Baron de Carondelet [rubric]

[Perez's report:]
Señor-Governor General:

By decree of the 17th of the current month, Your Excellency was pleased to decree on the memorial presented by Juan Munié, a citizen of the village of Saint Louis, Illinois, that I inform Your Excellency of what I know and of what is evident to me in regard to the declaration and request made by the above-mentioned Juan Munié. In fulfillment of the said order, I must inform Your Excellency that I am quite certain that the said Juan Munié is the person who discovered the Ponka tribe on the upper Missouri in the year 1789; for I granted him a license to go hunting on said river. He having penetrated farther than he believed [possible] discovered that tribe unknown till then in Illinois. On his return, he informed me of his discovery, and what had happened to him among those Indians by whom he had been very well received. They were very well

195

pleased over his arrival at the tribe, for he made them understand as much as he declares in his memorial in regard to the Spanish nation. He gave me a peace-pipe which he told me had been given to him by the chief in order that he might give it to me. The chief requested me to send him annually some Spaniard with merchandise in order to trade. On that account, I permitted said Juan Munié to go up the same river the following year, in order to trade with that tribe. I gave him a banner to give to the chief, whom he was to tell that I sent it to him in token of my great esteem for his tribe, and that I recognized them as my children. He told me on his return that they had received that banner gladly, and that by this means we were assured of the friendship of those Indians towards the Spaniards, and the continuance of their trade, because of the advantages which result from it in favor of those Indians. Since they owe this benefit to the justness of the above-mentioned Juan Munié, as the first discoverer of the Ponkas tribe, and in consideration of the fact that he had carried himself so well, I allowed him, during the two following years of my residence at that post, to continue his trade with the same tribe, considering him entitled to it, as he had always borne himself well. I also consider the above-mentioned Juan Munié very capable, on account of his intelligence, of being able to make some other discoveries, which may be of great utility to the trade of that district especially. Will Your Excellency consider it advisable to grant him the favor which he petitions for what time may be agreeable to Your Excellency.

New Orleans, September 19, 1793.

Manuel Perez [rubric]

[Petition granted:]

In consideration of the good services and conduct of Juan Meunier, inhabitant of the settlement of Illinois, and of the good reports which the Captain of the regiment of Louisiana, Don Manuel Perez, has given me, concerning that individual, by informing me of the reality of his having discovered, as he represents, the Indian tribe of the Poncas, at a distance of four hundred leagues from the mouth of the Missouri: I have determined to grant him, as he requests, the exclusive trade of said tribe for the term of four years, which shall begin to run from the beginning of next year, 1794. Consequently, I order the commandant of the said settlement not to hinder him in his going to, stay with, and return to [sic] said tribe. The present given at New Orleans, September 21, 1793.

Baron de Carondelet [rubric]

196

XXXIV

In your official letter No. 91[2] informing me of the complete satisfaction given by the Ayoas Indians for the robbery of horses, which the young men [*mozos*] of the same nation made in the *Pueblo* de San Carlos,[3] animals which were all returned with the exception of one that they paid for, you tell me of the present which you gave them and which I approve of; likewise the step that you are thinking of taking to make peace between the said Indians and the Cances with the five boy prisoners which the former took from the latter.

With this motive in mind, I can do no less than recommend to you that under no circumstances should your inhabitants take Indian slaves, because it is forbidden by our laws under the severest punishment, and I find myself forced to maintain with the greatest rigor the observance of such laws, so just and conformable to humanity.

May God Our Lord keep you many years.

New Orleans, September 25, 1793

Baron de Carondelet [rubric]

Señor Don Zenon Trudeau

[1]Written in Spanish. A.G.I., P. de C., leg. 20.
[2]Document XXX.
[3]See Documents XVII, XX, and XXVI.

XXXV

Mon Général:

I did not wait for your last orders to make all my efforts to engage the savages to aid us in humilitating somewhat the Osages; making them understand that, war having been declared at their solicitation, they could expect nothing of us, but that, however, we would give them the munitions that were indispensably necessary to them for each expedition and not the immense presents that the English were accustomed to give to them which the latter used against the whites. After that they all promised me to join an expedition to go to the Osages at the beginning of August, the only favorable time for the success of a *grand coup*, because the nation at that time returns from the summer hunt and re-enters the village only in small groups which would facilitate the destruction of a large number without being greatly exposed. As our establishments are still too weak in white population for such an expedition, there are only the savages which we

[1]Written in French. A.G.I., P. de C., leg. 208A.

might use; but these unfortunates in this country are too enlightened and interested [mercenary], for one to be able to make them act without a large and great expenditure which it would be necessary to renew as often as one would want them employed. Therefore, it is the failure to make this expenditure which has made all the various nations merely pretend to make effective their promises, while even showing the willingness to make peace, in order to frighten us and to attract the immense presents which the English were in the habit of making to them on similar occasions—presents which I would never require of the government, I regarding them as even being fruitless when it is a question of destroying a numerous nation which might withdraw at the slightest signal of attack only to reappear later and render my expenditures without effect.

Seeing it impossible for me to act advantageously in the war that you have ordered, permit me, *Mon Général,* to sum up to you the inconveniences which might result from it. I have never been able to make them officially as I regard them as humiliating for a military man in whom you had confidence that he could meet obstacles which he would like to overcome but which, however, are joined to the same inconvenience which it is necessary that I make known to you.

If it were possible to reveal the physical appearance of the Illinois to your eyes, *Mon Général,* I think that you would see the great need that we have to humiliate the barbarous nations which surround us and particularly the Osages, and that with our local forces we are still far from being able to reduce and subject them. It would be necessary to form a combination with the neighboring powers, which might fix the safety and general tranquility of the civilized men who inhabit their vicinity. It would be necessary that the views of rivalry and special interests of each of these powers towards the others should never be used to excite discord among these enemy peoples.

Nothing is more easy for the Osages than to communicate with [reach] the Mississippi and to call new traders to them: What would be the means of avoiding it? We will deposit presents with the barbarians who perhaps would be interested in repelling them; but the English, ever watchful, would they not extend themselves again in order to open a communication for themselves?

Experience has already demonstrated this truth to us when they penetrated via the Des Moines river—to the Pawnees, the Otoes and the Mahas.[2] What means have we employed to repel them? Our forces have

---

[2]See Nasatir, "Anglo-Spanish Frontier on the Upper Mississippi 1786-1796," *Iowa Journal of History and Politics,* XXIX (1931), 155-232. Several references to the war on the Osages are given in the previous documents and all are given or mentioned in Nasatir, *Imperial Osage.* See *e.g.,* Trudeau's letter to Lorimier, St. Louis, May 1, 1793, A.G.I., P. de C., leg. 2365 and printed in Houck, *Spanish Régime in Missouri,* II, 50-51.

not allowed us any resistance and our weak establishments cannot yet support this burden.

The Osages, less distant from these same resources and accustomed to giving laws to their neighboring barbarians, would not fear stretching out beyond their limits to obtain their needs. However, their meeting here at the moment they came *en parole* is announced in a humble and submissive fashion, but they did not fear to say *that they only intended to fear the Chief alone to whom they spoke, that it was he alone whom they feared to offend.* There were at that time some Shawnees, some Kickapoos, Otawas and Loups in the village and not one of them dared to accept their challenge.

This imperious speech of the Osages, under the emblem of peace and concord, would perhaps be merely audacious if we were more powerful, but in the midst of dangers it is necessary for us to avoid the greatest.

The inhabitants of Ste. Geneviève, who have talked the loudest about punishing this nation, are today the first ones ready to sacrifice even the rest of their horses in order to have peace with them. Formerly they feared only robbers, today they fear assassins; and this danger, which is not without foundation, can easily render our fields uncultivated and deserted.

Experience has already shown us this truth and it has just been renewed a few days ago at the village of St. Ferdinand where three Pou savages slaughtered five persons in broad daylight about four *arpents* from their houses. Although after the attack had been made there should not have been any other risks,—this fact did not influence those who work the land; for some have already discontinued their fallow lands or ceased to cut hay; while the others intend to evacuate as the two brothers have done, one of whom lost his wife and the other his children.

Fears which have not been based upon any of these reasons for apprehension, but merely those of any nation against whom one has openly declared war, would be dangerous to agriculture and public tranquility, if they should take root among all the cultivators of each village of this province.

It is only necessary for one person to be killed by the Osages in the circle of our establishments to make them all relinquish work, even the most urgent work on the land. The distance from help when every cultivator is out in his field would not perhaps permit a person to save himself from danger;—a handful of savages adroitly hidden to surprise these laborers would perhaps slaughter them all before they would be able to fall back upon the forces of the village, and all the more easily because one-half of the population is without arms. So many evils, so many fears to apprehend for the people, can enter our reflections when we carry the tomahawk. As regards the barbarians, we must annihilate them or give up irritating them.

199

Maramec, formerly so well established, which was for so long the first market of the Illinois for bacon, tobacco, and maize, unfortunately shows today only traces of habitations, abandoned and left to devastation. These cultivators formerly scattered over an area one-fourth [?] league by one-fourth league have been obliged to evacuate in the course of time for fear of seeing themselves slaughtered after having been continually pillaged by the barbarians; and the sacrifice that they have made of their habitations and of their fortune, for the safety of their existence, is not a little to blame for the famine which they often experience and the need they have for the products with which they formerly flooded our villages.

This river which may be called *les galeries de Ozages* would have need of an establishment to stop their incursions there. The true and only means of rendering it respectable and diminishing the pride of the nations is to be able to oppose to them a body of population which might subject them.

However, if His Majesty wanted to make the sacrifices necessary to set against them nations who would sell themselves to our interests it might be easy to subdue them by harassing them. But such a war would be of long duration and expensive to the state, and not sure of success even after many expenditures, and we would be fortunate then not to be obliged to sue for peace.

It is then that we would have something to fear from these men who breathe only evil and vengeance, a secret war in reprisal which would become for us the most terrible plague of this country. The tomahawk of the savage that we would have hired would not be the one which would have struck them.

What would be, at this moment, the fatal situation of the Illinois if these uncertain means were put to use against a nation which could fall back a very long distance in order to protect itself from some hard blows which might be struck against it? But this distance would not hinder them from frequently edging in on our possessions and doing us an irreparable injury.

Since we have shown to them how many of our subjects have been irritated against them by continual robbery which they made of our horses and by the murders which they committed on the Arkansas River, they have excused themselves in the first place by blaming some bad men who only love evil and over whom the chiefs have not sufficient power to stop them from doing it; and in the second place, they give as their reasons that those who inhabit this river, being of mixed blood or allied to women of their enemies, they cannot be their brothers; that, moreover, the entire nation is far from thinking as one; that it is unfortunate for it that nature has not given it the rights that the other nations have for holding in check the mischievous ones among them; and that it is necessary that an entire nation often be the innocent victim of some of their individuals whose actions have always been disapproved of.

In any other position these excuses would be frivolous in our eyes; but if we look at the war between the Americans and the savages in the western part of the Illinois, who with their combined armies (and renewed every year) have not as yet been able to make any successful campaign,[2] what example will this be for us and what means must we employ to have a behavior agreeable to our local faculties and the security of our establishments!

After this proof, who would be able to serve us as an example. It seems to me that it would be well to overlook it sometimes when they appear to wish to excuse their conduct, until sooner or later we would be able to efface the total imprint of their existence.

Some deputies of the Little Osage nation, destitute and barefoot, have just presented themselves here *en parole* with tears in their eyes in order to soften my humanity upon the fate of their wives and children. Without the severity of your orders and of your intentions, I would have perhaps yielded somewhat to them because of the feeling which they inspired in me. It is sometimes good to waver opportunely. For our own good, it is often better to make a true merit of necessity or it might be perhaps better to subject ourselves to it than to let them see the resources which present themselves to them everywhere.

The Big and Little Osages are not the only ones of whom we have to complain. The other nations who frequent us every day have not fewer evil subjects among them who raise parties and go to strike without the nation holding itself responsible for the event. At this time when I have the honor to write to you, I am uneasy about a party of twenty men which has appeared at the village of St. Charles and of which I was warned by other savages who came to give me advice of it. However zealous *Monsieur* Tayon, commandant of the place, might be, it would be truly difficult to prevent them from taking some scalps with his having to leave the village. The empire [prestige] of the chief is only a frivolous title which does not give him authority over the nation except what it is willing to allow him to take. The only remedy is population and that is what we lack.

While awaiting this happy era, it is necessary to conceal the outrages against us and stop their progress by giving and withholding traders. This design is a means which has never been tried and which is, however, capable of repressing in large measure all the damage that we have experienced from the most powerful nation of this continent. Private interest is always opposed as you are going to see, *Mon Général,* by the certain fact which I beg you to permit me to report to you.

---

[2]Referring to St. Clair's campaign.

A commandant of this place having reproached the *Grand Chef* of the nation for a considerable robbery of horses which was made at the establishments, the chief told him that if he wished not to send merchandise as customary, he would promise him that the horses would be returned and, moreover, that no more will be stolen. The commandant seemed to consent thereto. With that conviction the chief left to announce the thing to his village, to the truth of which they did not at first pay great attention; but when hunting time arrived and not seeing the accustomed traders, each one hastened to complete the number of horses stolen in order to have them conducted by the chief to this post. At the time when they were going to leave, there arrived a loaded barge. Then the horses were taken again; and they even report that some savages say that, moreover, they will act good or bad in accordance with the way in which they are treated. The chief remained confounded, when they might have been able to win for him the greatest consideration and authority in his nation. This fact is attested to by all this village.

Having been at Ste. Geneviève several days ago to presuade the inhabitants to enclose their fields, I had the satisfaction of seeing there *Monsieur* Delassus who had just arrived and whom someone had told me had died. It is true that I found him in the most sad condition. The confidence that he placed in my ability to cure him made me play the role of a charlatan and I succeeded in cutting and stopping his fever. But he pointed out to me daily that he had relapses and did not gain any strength. I greatly feared that he might succumb and that his wife whom he expected next month would arrive only to witness the spectacle of his end which would place her moreover in a greater embarrassment not having here, yet, any arrangement or accomodation where she might await the moment to make another decision. The respect and the consideration which I have taken for this virtuous and unfortunate afflicted man will make me employ all that depends upon me to be useful to his family, if it should lose him, which I greatly fear may happen. I find them greatly discontented with *Monsieur* Peyroux—not for him but for the inhabitants of his residence whom he likes because they are really good—and because that commandant is annoyed without any other reasons than those of having abandoned a village where he has however only a wretched ruined house. Moreover be it said without slander this officer is somewhat presumptuous of his pretended knowledge and everything that he himself does not think of is never anything but very bad. *Monsieur* Delassus told me that he wants especially to return to the Illinois. His sojourn has entirely changed for him because of the change of commandant. Before that, the whole village appeared to be contented and happy and one might even say only formed a single and same family and that is what had determined *Monsieur* Delassus to remain among them as he told me and wrote me ten times.

202

Monsieur Le Dru wrote me that he was going to descend to the capital having all the while discontented these parishioners by an interest and a commerce which gave him lawsuits with everybody, vexing them further by additional fees in all the ceremonies of his ministry. He finished by unpolitely telling me of the reputation of the women and daughters of the village. The public demanded of me an inquiry of his conduct which I refused, imposing silence upon him. The priest, seeing the general outcry on his account, himself demanded this information. I took their statements and communicated with him about it. It seemed that he was not satisfied and that according to him, I am the author of the general discontent. However, if he wishes to be in good faith he could say that I had counselled him to remain tranquil in his parish and that I would appease the discontent effectively with a word. I had succeeded there and with time he would perhaps gain a confidence that he has never had. As I certainly believe him capable of making complaints about me without reason, I shall have the honor, *Mon Général*, to remit to you upon his departure the information which might confuse it a second time with me, as well as the letters about which I have previously spoken officially.

To tell you, *Mon Général*, the true difficulties which exist between Portell and Lorimier,[4] I see no other reason than the latter attracting the savages to him, and that he draws the greatest part of commerce from them. It is not, however, of great consequence and will exist only as long as Lorimier remains at Cape Girardeau with so much ambition. If this man goes to another place, the Loups and Shawnees savages will have soon followed him and these are the only ones who existed in this place who did not produce four thousand *piastres* a year, from which each one obtains his small share according to his finesse.

I am extremely pained to have received so tardily the demand which you made of me, *Mon Général*, for martin skins. As this object only comes upon demand, in the Upper Mississippi, the opportunities this year had already left when I received the letter with which you honored me. It will not be until next year that I shall have the satisfaction of fulfilling your desires.

I shall have the honor, *Mon Général*, of asking from you your protection and of pardoning a long non-sensible speech which I cannot make otherwise and which can only be excusable by the profound respect with which I say of myself, *Mon Général*,

Your very humble, obedient servant.

Zenon Trudeau [rubric]

St. Louis, September 28, 1793.

---

[4]One of my students, Robert Burch, has written an excellent dissertation on Louis Lorimier.

XXXVI

Trudeau to Carondelet, St. Louis, October 2, 1793[1]

Mon Général:

I have been informed by your confidential letter of May 10 last concerning the English commerce with our establishments. I have zealously carried out your intentions, and at the same time I have agreed with M. Portell to make a report to you if the troubles which are agitating Europe should cause us a scarcity of merchandise, particularly those of trade which it is important to give the savages at the price which our neighbors charge them, and which we will scarcely be able to do if we have to pay import and export duties, unless this merchandise be only for the Missouri. For the other nations it will not be possible to enter in competition with those which border our possessions and who will furnish merchandise to us.

The Americans trade only a little in their district. They have only the Canadians and English of Michilimaquinac as merchants. The latter by the cheapness of their merchandise attract all the savages who would come to us. They give them bad counsel as they have always done and take away from us the best furs.[2]

I read the sad end of the defense of Louis XVI, which was given me by M. Delassus, which affected all the old French here. If I dare, *Mon Général,* assure you of the fidelity of all the subjects of the king in this country, it is not because there never appears an incendiary paper in the Illinois, but it is because they are truly attached by gratitude to a sovereign who does not cease to spread graces on all these people.[3] They have already known the price in the year 1768[4] being the only ones in the province who behaved as submissive subjects in the unfortunate troubles which disturbed us then. Also I am assured of their obedience to the king and to all the orders which you will deem convenient to communicate to me in all the events.

My wife dares to present her respectful homage to Mme Carondelet begging her to kindly accept a small case of pears which Sergeant Sereyra

---

[1]Written in French. A.G.I., P. de C., leg. 211.

[2]See Document XXVII.

[3]See E. R. Liljegren, "Jacobinism in Spanish Louisiana, 1792-1797", *Louisiana Historical Quarterly,* XXII (1939), 3-53.

[4]Referring to the Revolution of 1768. See J. E. Winston, "Causes and Results of the Revolution of 1768 in Louisiana," *Louisiana Historical Quarterly,* XV, 181-213; and C. Gayarré, *History of Louisiana* (New York, 1867) *French Domination,* II, 284-359; and *Spanish Domination,* 1-41. More recently this has been discussed from the Spanish point of view in V. Rodríguez Casado, *Primeros Años de Dominación Española en la Luisiana* (Madrid, 1942).

will give her. These are the only ones that we have been able to procure in the place and which still will not be sold according to our wishes.

I have the honor of recommending myself to your bounties and to be with the most profound respect,

Mon Général

Your very humble, obedient servant,
Zenon Trudeau
[rubric]

St. Louis, October 2, 1793.

XXXVII

Trudeau to Carondelet, St. Louis, October 20, 1793[1]

No. 137

I am going to occupy myself immediately with the construction of the *quartel*[2] which, with approbation of the *Señor* Captain-General, Your Excellency in official letters of the 9th of July last authorizes me to build.

As the navigation of the Missouri is prohibited in the present circumstances, and as the workers whom I might employ to cut cedar wood along that river, where it is only found, may be harrassed by the Osages, I shall try to construct the said *quartel* with stone, if the 1500 *pesos,* which I have solicited and which has been assigned to me with reduction of the price and value in the country of the 600 pounds of nails which I have received as also the other implements, suffices.

May God Keep Your Excellency many years.

St. Louis, October 20, 1793.

Zenon Trudeau [rubric]

---

[1]Written in Spanish. A.G.I., P. de C., leg. 148.
[2]See J. B. Musick, *St. Louis as a Fortified Town* (St. Louis, 1941). The fear of the projected George Rogers Clark invasion was behind this strengthening of St. Louis.

CHAPTER II

1794

I

CLAMORGAN TO TRUDEAU, ST. LOUIS, [APRIL] 20, 1794[1]

Monsieur:

After the kindness of the general government to the Illinois trade its members have been pleased to appoint me their representative before you.[2] Today in fulfilling the duties that were entrusted to me I shall take the liberty of informing you of the events that gave rise not to the discovery of the Ponca nation but in the first trading that was done at the village of that nation.

During the administration of your predecessor two traders who sought the Missouri trade at the same time were not sure about the lot which fell to them before the time set for assigning them their share. Thus it was that one of them obtained beforehand permission to trade with the Ponca nation, which is on the bank of the Missouri about thirty leagues above the village of the Maha nation. These same Poncas usually come to trade their furs with the trader assigned to the Mahas' village without his having the trouble of going any farther.

This new enterprise was [a word made illegible by erasures] a violation of the usual trade which had formerly been made with the two nations, which are really only one nation, since the Poncas are nothing but Mahas who have left the tribe. Since this time a separate trade has been made of them.

---

[1]Written in French. A.G.I., P. de C., leg. 28. This letter was sent by Trudeau to Carondelet, see *infra* document III. The month is not given in the document, but it is April as is evident in document III.
[2]See Chapter I, document XXXII.

206

This is the reason, *Monsieur,* that it is important to explain to the government the falsity of this new discovery made by Jean Meunier,[3] who was not sent there at the proper time by the merchant who supplied his equipment but in order to anticipate and stealthily injure the one who was to carry on the trading with the Mahas' village.

Moreover, *Monsieur,* it is none the less advantageous to cause it to see the danger that it runs of destroying the confidence of the merchants who are obliged to sell their merchandise to a trader who could have had the means of obtaining a license for a post exclusively from the government.

The ownership of the Missouri trade by the merchants of the Illinois is destroyed in this case and such a wise and advantageous arrangement on the part of the government comes to nothing, unless in similar cases the favored individual is forced to supply himself from the syndic for the account of the general membership of the trade. Otherwise one finds himself favored in a market for his merchandise which gives him an advantage of which the rest of the traders are deprived. In addition it amounts to forcing these same traders to give credit to one who may not deserve it.

All these considerations demand, *Monsieur,* that you be kind enough to inform the general government so that it may not henceforth be surprised into granting favors and privileges.

It is with this hope that I take the liberty to call myself most respectfully, *Monsieur,* you very humble and obedient servant.

Jacques Clamorgan [rubric]

St. Louis, the twentieth of [April][4] 1794.
To *Monsieur* Zenon Trudeau.

---

[3]See Chapter I, document XXXIII.
[4]See note 1 above and document III.

II

TRUDEAU TO CARONDELET, ST. LOUIS, APRIL 24, 1794[1]

No. 173

The syndic of commerce of this city of St. Louis, M. Clamorgan, has solicited me by the enclosed letter to request Your Excellency to form [?] a Commercial Company among these [merchants?] in order to remove the English [who] usurp our [commerce?] on the Mississippi [and Des Moines] where they not only [gather] peltries but also [scatter bad rumors?] against us among the Indians as has happened a great deal more this year than in any other previous one. The English have penetrated via the *Grande Rivera* which falls into the said Des Moines which reaches very

---

[1]Written in Spanish. A.G.I., P. de C., leg. 125. This letter in almost entirely *polilla* eaten and is almost illegible. The reply to this letter is document V.

near the Missouri to where they have penetrated and traded their merchandise this year at such a low price that our traders have been robbed, maltreated, and ridiculed particularly in the nation *Des Machas* [Mahas] where I believe that no one from our establishments will dare to go to trade this year without exposing himself to losing all his merchandise [torn] as has happened to a great number of those who have just returned and who are ruined.

The chief of this nation has written to me asking me for a present amounting to about four thousand *pesos* and a medal six inches in diameter like one the English have given him, without which he says he will not allow any of our traders to penetrate in [to] his nation.

What M. Clamorgan proposes would be very favorable were it not for the circumstances of the war in which we are now engaged with France, because if we occupy ourselves at present [?] in disturbing the [— —] accustomed to trade [— —] not [?] from our particular merchandise [— —] they would not cease to [— —] against us in a time when we must have them at least quiet, now that we may not have them favorable which makes me believe that we must abandon M. Clamorgan's project until peace is concluded and then the government will be able to protect this country against the ambitions of our rivals.

May Our Lord keep Your Excellency's life many years.

St. Louis, Illinois, April 24, 1794.

Zenon Trudeau [rubric]

Señor Baron de Carondelet

III
Trudeau to Carondelet, St. Louis, April 24, 1794[1]
No. 175

I am sending to Your Excellency a letter from the syndic of commerce of this town, Don Santiago Clamorgan,[2] in order that Your Excellency may take into consideration what he faithfully exposes. I have gathered the most scrupulous information on this matter and have found it to be in conformity with what he exposes. Because of this I shall await what Your Excellency may dispose, setting free Juan Meunier for this year, because I can not expect in time [wait for] Your Excellency's determination on the subject.

God keep Your Excellency many years

St. Louis, April 24, 1794

Zenon Trudeau [rubric]

Señor Baron de Carondelet

---

[1]Written in Spanish. A.G.I., P. de C., leg. 28. Reply is document VI.
[2]Document I.

IV

Distribution of Missouri Trading Posts, May 1-3, 1794[1]

To *Monsieur* Don Zenon Trudeau, captain of the fixed regiment of Louisiana, lieutenant-governor, [and] commander-in-chief of the western district of the Illinois.

The syndic of trade has the honor to inform you that he desires to hold a meeting of all the members [merchants] of your government to proceed to a division of the posts of the Missouri, in accordance with the resolution taken before you on the fifteenth of the month of October of last year by the merchants who were there assembled as representatives of the whole.[2] This is the reason, *Monsieur,* why I beg you to order the meeting to be held on Saturday, the third of the present month, in order to determine the part and portion that shall fall to each one and *feres bien* [and see that it is done?].

St. Louis, the first of May 1794.

[signed] Jacques Clamorgan

St. Louis, May 2, 1794

Permission granted to hold the meeting tomorrow at eleven o'clock.

[signed] Trudeau

The third day of the month of May of the year one thousand seven hundred ninety-four; In accordance with the permission granted by *Monsieur* Don Zenon Trudeau, the lieutenant-governor, to hold a meeting of the merchants [commercial corps] for the purpose of dividing the trade of the Missouri, the syndic called the meeting to order and proceeded to the assigning of the amounts that could be taken in merchandise to each of the posts. The value of those to be carried was according to unanimous opinion the following:

The post of Grands Eaux,[3] estimated at	72 thousand *livres*
That of the Petits Eaux,[4] estimated at	24 thousand *livres*
That of the Kans, estimated at	24 thousand *livres*
That of the Republique, estimated at	6 thousand *livres*
That of the Othos, estimated at	14 thousand *livres*
That of the Panis Bonchef, estimated at	5 thousand *livres*
That of the Panis named Tapage, estimated at ...	5 thousand *livres*
That of the Loups, estimated at	5 thousand *livres*
That of the Mahas, estimated at	20 thousand *livres*
	175 thousand *livres*

[1]Written in French. This is a certified copy in the Bancroft Library. This was sent to Carondelet on May 31, 1794. See document XI.
[2]Chapter I, document XXXII.
[3]Big Osages.
[4]Little Osages.

The total sum for the exploitation of the entire trade of the Missouri amounts to one hundred seventy-five thousand *livres* cash which is to be divided among the number of twenty-five merchants of the city of St. Louis, three from Ste. Geneviève, and the share that belongs to our lieutenant-governor. Therefore the proportion for each one will be the sum of six thousand *livres* or thereabouts in merchandise.

For this purpose we have given:

to the Grands Eaux	12	portions of trade
to the Petits Eaux	4	portions of trade
to the Kans	4	portions of trade
to the Republique	1	portion of trade
to the Othos	2	portions of trade
to the Panis Bonchef	1	portion of trade
to the Panis Tapage	1	portion of trade
to the Loups	1	portion of trade
to the Mahas	3	portions of trade

29 portions of trade

After which and in the presence of the lieutenant-governor, we, the merchants here assembled, drew lots for the portions of trade which were to be ours, after *Monsieur* Don Zenon Trudeau had chosen for his portion a part in the Kans nation. They were as follows:

Grands Osages	MM. Coliere[5] Ceret Robidou Andréville Motard Dubreuil Cadet Chouteau Papin Chovin Sanguinet Clamorgan Boleduc of Ste. Geneviève	12 shares
Petits Osages	Roy Marié Lafleur Prat of Ste. Geneviève	4 shares

[5]Most of the names here listed are referred to in Houck, *History of Missouri* and *Spanish Régime in Missouri;* J. T. Scharf, *History of St. Louis City and County* (Philadelphia, 1883) ; F. L. Billon, *Annals of St. Louis under the French and Spanish Dominions* (St. Louis, 1886).

The Kans	Benito Basquez Beral Sarpy Durocher M. Zenon Trudeau	4 shares
The Republique	The elder Chouteau	1 share
The Othos	Reilhe Lavalé	2 shares
The Panis Bonchef	Yostie	1 share
The Panis Tapage	Le Conte	1 share
The Loups	Labadie	1 share
	Total	26 shares

The following are the shares in addition to the above twenty six shares.

The Mahas	Vincen St. Sire Hubardau of Ste. Geneviève	3 shares
		29 shares

It was thus agreed and passed in the council chamber of the government of the city of St. Louis in the presence of *Monsieur* Don Zenon Trudeau, lieutenant-governor, the third day of May, 1794.

[signed] Clamorgan
[signed] Zenon Trudeau

[This is] a true copy of the original on file in the archives of the government of the city of St. Louis. This same day and year as above.

Zenon Trudeau [rubric]

Absent from the city of St. Louis who have a right to trade on the Missouri.

MM. Gingembre
    Lajoye, fils
    Gratiot
    Socier

V

CARONDELET TO TRUDEAU, NEW ORLEANS, MAY 27, 1794[1]

I have received the proposition which the Syndic Clamorgan makes in favor of your commerce [corps of merchants] for establishing a Company of the Missouri to separate the English from the commerce which they are usurping from us.[2] This project seems useful to me but in order to put it into execution, it is necessary that the aforementioned syndic explain himself with more clarity, informing the government of the powers, means and opportunities [*proporciones*] of those who offer themselves to form the said company, upon which they hope to be able to sustain the competition with these English. In the meanwhile you will inspire your merchants to unite all their efforts so that the Indians, to have a greater trade with us, will separate themselves from the English. This must be done without violence, trying to make the commerce fall into our hands by means of good treatment and good faith in the exchanges. If it is possible choose traders and hunters of the best or at least of the most regular conduct, if such people may be found, since it is true that some better than others will be found, then the former must be preferred. You should avoid by all means sending people who may spread bad advice and influence against the peace and calm of these provinces.

May God keep you many years.

New Orleans, May 25, 1794.

El Baron de Carondelet [rubric]

Señor Don Zenon Trudeau

[1]Written in Spanish. A.G.I., P. de C., leg. 21.
[2]See document II.

VI

CARONDELET TO TRUDEAU, NEW ORLEANS, MAY 25, 1794[1]
Answered

I have seen and have reflected upon the letter[2] of the syndic of commerce of your establishment, Don Santiago Clamorgan, concerning the falsity with which Juan Meunier has pretended that he has discovered the Poncas nation when it is verified and your *informes* corroborate that you have considered the "so-called" Poncas nothing but a part of the refugee Mahas, and how by allowing the division of this trade, the notable prejudices which the syndic Clamorgan faithfully points out would be detrimental to the commerce of Illinois. You will withdraw and you will send to me the exclusive permission which I gave to Meunier for trading with

[1]Written in Spanish. A.G.I., P. de C., leg. 21.
[2]Document I. See also document VII.

212

the Poncas,[3] the latter remaining in the future included in the Mahas nation as formerly, and you will thank the said Clamorgan for his zeal, recommending to him that he continue to inform you and the government of the abuses which he might note. If we know them we will be able to correct them, and forsee the confusion which otherwise will be introduced against the tranquillity and calm of this province to the great disadvantage of your inhabitants. And in order to serve as an example to restrain others, as soon as Meunier returns from his trade you will put him under arrest for fifteen days, reprimanding his boldness for having dared to presume upon the good faith of the government and threatening him with the most severe punishment if he relapses into error.

May God keep you many years.

New Orleans, May 25, 1794.

El Baron de Carondelet [rubric]

Señor Don Zenon Trudeau.

---

[3]Chapter I, document XXXIII.

VII

Carondelet to Clamorgan, New Orleans, May 26, 1794[1]

New Orleans, May 26, 1794

I have read, Sir, with much interest the memorial[2] which you have addressed to me; it contains political views which do honour to your understanding and are in accordance with the ideas which I have laid before the Court two years ago; we are, perhaps, very near the moment when we shall see them realized, but, time and pains were needed to convince the ministers of their utility. The grand objects which, for the present, absorb all the attention of the different powers, will perhaps delay for some months, the approbation of this plan, but I do not despair to see it adopted before the end of the year.

Some Errors have crept in among your details, which, the enthusiasm for what is good, and too great a conviction in your own ideas, have hidden from you, but in the main, they are just and the means of execution well-combined.

I have the honor to be, with the most perfect consideration, Sir, your very humble and very obedient servant.

Baron de Carondelet
[rubric]

Monsieur Clamorgan

---

[1]Missouri Historical Society, Clamorgan Papers; printed in *American State Papers, Public Lands,* VIII, 234.
[2]This possibly refers to an earlier proposition mentioned in Chapter I, document XXIV, note 3.

VIII

Trudeau to Carondelet, St. Louis, May 27, 1794 [?][1]

Answered

Mon Général:

By this opportunity I am having sent to the commandant of the Arkansas the three carabines that the Osages stole on this river. It is the only thing of which I indirectly have knowledge and it was not difficult [to accomplish]; on the contrary, the chiefs as well as the considerables lent themselves to it with all possible interest and have banished from their councils the one who was at the head of the band which committed this theft. He did not resist their action. It is only imperceptibly that they [the Chiefs] will be able to succeed in restraining them from the evils they are doing—particularly the red men from whom they likewise experience the same vexations. Despite that, *Monsieur* Pierre Chouteau, once installed with them, will obtain very easily all that we can desire for our establishments and the neighboring nations. The two *Messieurs* Chouteau who should leave immediately will make them make peace with the Arkansas and Caddos. The fort will be finished the end of July. But there is no hope of being able to conduct there this year the artillery that you announced to me had been embarked in the *galeras* concerning which no one has heard anything. Their failure to arrive has retarded until now these men who desired to profit by the high waters in order to conduct it in a week. The *rivière des Grands Osages* will only be navigable enough for very average *pirogues*. It is very difficult for me to attract here Germans, Dutch, and French royalists as you desire. None have appeared in our environs. Only a few Canadians have come, deserters from boats which traded on the Upper Mississippi and the St. Peter, Skunk, Des Moines and other rivers in our district. These men all have a liking for voyaging and are definitely not cultivators. A few marry and settle down. That is the only increase that we have in population.

St. Geneviève, New Bourbon and St. Ferdinand are beginning to turn their attention to agriculture. Between the first two named villages, there is a superb location for a mill which could operate the year round. The remains of an old mill, which formerly was very advantageously located, may still be seen. These remains and the site belong to three different proprietors who because of contract interests, can never agree on its reestablishment. I am using your name to order these same people to work there or lose their property. However, I beg you (if you find it *à propos*) to speak about it to *Monsieur* Baptiste Vallé, who is descending to New Orleans to look for his sister, Madame Villar who [Vallé] has a share in

---

[1]Written in French. A.G.I., P. de C., leg. 207B.

this mill; he can tell his brother, the commandant, and *Monsieur* Pratte, who between the two have [the] three[third?] shares, that they should work on the mill as soon as possible. This work finished will be very lucrative to them, although not very expensive and of very great advantage to the public, who have always had grain, but who often lack bread because they have no way to grind the grain. *Monsieur* Chouteau has just sent grindstones to his mill which is today in condition to grind a one hundred *milliers* [one thousand weight] of flour a year, and this mill will certainly make as fine flour as the most superb in Europe when it has sufficient grain to keep it busy, winnowing it, cleaning it, and in short taking the precautions that millers are obliged to take in all countries. Moreover, the inhabitants in general have the habit of sowing their grains in the spring rather than doing it in the autumn. This gives them a double harvest of infinitely superior grain which should not be mixed with any other grains which blackens and spoils their flour.

The two associates Meunier and Rolland[2] will remain in possession of their trade with the Ponca nation which has not been very advantageous to them this year. For ten years Meunier has always been with this nation. Never has he been able to join the two ends of the advances [*avancés*] which have been made to him, which had put him into considerable debt. Rolland, his associate, who today sees that there is little or no profit to be gained in this nation, would this year have liked to have the whole of the Kansas [trade] divided into six portions as you will see by the repartition of the trade[3] that I am officially sending you. I have been obliged to make the portions very small in order that all the merchants who did not have any of it during the last years can participate in it this year. In spite of this there are many people who are jealous and discontented because there are several nations such as the Otoes, Mahas, Poncas being exploited by so many people, that they do not yield any particular profit. They [traders to them] have lost at least fifty per cent this year.

Monsieur Didier has had the very bad *grace* to inform you that the captain of the militia, commandant of St. Ferdinand, lived in public concubinage. Seeing that since he spoke of it to me and although certain of the contrary my counsel alone to this commandant has sufficed to make him send away a woman afflicted with epilepsy and who at first had only been welcomed by charity [torn]—being next rendered useful at a time when she had good health and a time when *Monsieur* Dunegan had just lost his wife who had the care of six orphans whom this good man was still rearing and carrying for, having however, only his arms as his total

[2]See Chapter I, document XXXIII, especially note 1; and this Chapter documents I, III. and IV, and especially XIV.
[3]Document IV.

215

wealth, and, to meet the expenses of a so-weighty charge this woman became necessary to him for the care of these same orphans and for the care of the interior of the house, from which he was continually obliged to separate himself for the cultivation of his land which was distant from it. *Monsieur* Didier never had in appearance a more cordial friend than *Monsieur* Dunegan, as long as he believed himself to have need of him. He had even promised him in marriage a girl who remained with him, before having undertaken the voyage from New Orleans. He [Didier] then ignored what should have been his [Dunegan's] but conditions had changed so much that he no longer needed the poor man who had nourished and sustained his house during his absence. He broke the projected marriage— in an outrageous manner for one who had made preparations for it. He vexed her, decried her, and for greater humiliation he summoned her publicly to appear as a disgusting woman, and one who only invoked pity. The outraged *Monsieur* Dunegan could not keep himself from reproaching the priest, with the fact that he also had girls at his house and that he ought to begin to show a good example. That is the only wrong of a man, simple, dull, but good, honest, religious, and infinitely charitable, since we count in our establishments eleven orphans whom he has raised at his own expense and the greater part of whom are still supported at his expense. *Monsieur* Didier would surely not have spoken to you of him if he had not made the plan of descending to New Orleans, but the priest believed it necessary to forestall him, as he had forged in his imagination accusations of a concubinage that no one would like to believe. I am absolutely obliged to justify the innocent. You see, *Mon Général,* that it is necessary to be quite prudent to be able to live in good harmony with a priest so inconsistent. I have, however, had the good fortune to do it. There are many times that he has prevented me from consulting you on a point that is important for me to have made clear. A few months ago there was an assembly of the notable parishoners to appoint a new church warden and to see the accounts of the one who had finished his charge, who according to the custom of the country has tried to collect the votes of the assistants. The priest was opposed to it, saying that that belonged to him. As president of the assembly no one disputed him. I only observed to him that the instructions formally say that the one who represents the *vice-patron* ought to be present at this assembly and that if I acted in this capacity [that] it would never be right that I be preceded by anyone since there was only I who could represent you. We agreed with friendship to enlighten you and certainly they [Dunegan and Didier] would not fail to write to *Monsieur le Proviseur.* That is why I ask you also to give me your advice.

There is absolutely nothing new in our establishments where we live in the greatest tranquillity. Permit me, *Mon Général,* to ask you for the continuation of your bounties and to testify to you the deep respect with which I am, *Mon Général,*

Your very humble, obedient servant

Zenon Trudeau [rubric]

St. Louis, May 27, 1794 [or 1795?]

IX

Articles of Incorporation of the Missouri Company, St. Louis, May, 1794

Rules[1] for the corporation proposed to the Board of Trade [*Comercio*] of St. Louis for the formation of a company for the Exploration of the Country West of the Missouri, on the 5th of May, 1794. Accepted and inaugurated by a number of merchants on the 12th of the same month and year, and approved by the general Government July 18, following. [Petition to Trudeau:]

To Don Zenon Trudeau, Captain of the Regular Infantry Regiment of Louisiana, Lieutenant-Governor and Commandant-in-chief of the western district of Illinois.

The syndic of the Board of Trade [*comercio*] of this jurisdiction, desiring that each one of its members may enjoy the advantages which trade with the Indian tribes of the Missouri may procure, has the honor of stating to Your Excellency that, having petitioned, with your aid and consent, from the Baron de Carondelet permission to form an exclusive Company for trading with all the tribes that are found farther up than the Poncas, in the hope of being able to open immediately a department of trade both important to industry and local necessity, the Syndic finds it necessary to have recourse provisionally to the kindness of Your Excellency, asking that you may be pleased to permit until the arrival of the decision of the Governor-General the convocation of all the merchants for

---

[1]Written in Spanish. Certified copy A.G.I., P. de C., leg. 2363. A copy certified by Carondelet is annex no. 2 to Carondelet to Prince of Peace, no. 65 *reservada,* New Orleans, January 8, 1796, A.H.N., Est., leg. 3900; photostat in Library of Congress, copy in Missouri Historical Society, Papers from Spain. Printed in Houck, *Spanish Régime in Missouri,* II, 148-167. I have carefully rechecked and corrected the printed translation. There is an original of Clamorgan's letter to Trudeau of April 5, 1794, also in A.G.I., P. de C., leg. 2363, and a copy of the articles of incorporation with Trudeau's rubric on every page and at the end of the document is his signature. The articles of incorporation are in French, but there is an unsigned copy in Spanish translation in the same legajo. See Nasatir, "Formation of the Missouri Company", *Missouri Historical Review,* XXV (1930), 10-22, and by same author, "Anglo-Spanish Rivalry on the Upper Missouri", in *Mississippi Valley Historical Review,* XVI (1929), reprint pp. 11-14.

the purpose of learning the particular opinion of each one, and taking the measures suitable for so vast an undertaking.

St. Louis, April 5, 1794.
Clamorgan

[Permit:]

I permit the Syndic to assemble the merchants today at nine o'clock in the morning in the Assembly Hall of the Government. St. Louis, May 5, 1794.

Zenon Trudeau

[Articles:]

It was resolved unanimously at the meeting held in the Government Assembly Hall, in the year one thousand seven hundred and ninety-four, on the fifth day of the month of May by virtue of the permission granted by the Lieutenant-Governor to convoke the members of the Board of Trade, these hoping that the Governor-General will grant the permission requested for the formation of an exclusive Company for the trade or commerce which may, now or in the future, be had with the tribes who live farther up than the Poncas, who are located on the upper part of the Missouri and in other places in which trade may be carried on, that, in order to begin the formation of the above-mentioned Company [already] provisionally created, (except that all contrary matters [in the provisional company] shall be amended), until the arrival of the approval of the Governor-General, for the Director to dispatch traders beforehand to the distant tribes, from the general funds of those who should become incorporated in the above-mentioned Company.

In consequence of that, Messrs. Reihle, Papin, Yosty, Motard, Sanguinet, Benito Vasquez, Bernardo Sarpy, Cerré, Roy, St. Cire, Le Conte, Endrevil, Vincent, La Fleur, Dubreuil, Manuel Marié, Labadie, Chouteau, Sr. Robidou, Chauvin, Collel, Durocher, Lavallée, La Joye, Chouteau, Jr., Gratiot, De l'Or Sarpy, Clamorgan, all members of the Board of Trade, being present and represented by virtue of the edict made by our Lieutenant-Governor at the last Assembly held on the third of the present month, citing them to appear in person or by their proxies—which was renewed on this same day [i.e., May 5] with each one in particular by the Syndic of the body, so that no one might allege the pretext of ignorance:—the Syndic explained about this Company, and submitted to the opinion of each one of those present the following articles, so that, by a plurality of the votes of the members of the Company, what appeared to be important to the Board of Trade in general and to its individual members in particular, might be accepted or refused.

ARTICLE I. The conditions, rules, statutes, and wishes of the general government for the exclusive handling of the trade, petitioned for ten years, shall be incident to the present articles of incorporation, for which they shall serve as the base and foundation.

ARTICLE II. As soon as all the members of the Commercial Company are assembled, one Director and one Substitute shall be appointed by a plurality of the votes of those present. They shall be chosen, necessarily, from among those members, in order that they may take charge of the interests of the said Company. The duties of both men shall begin May first, one thousand seven hundred and ninety-five, and shall last three whole consecutive years beside the present year, which is no more than provisional.

ARTICLE 3. Two Directors and Substitutes appointed for the duties of the present year shall continue for the first three years, beginning with the first of next May.

ARTICLE 4. Every three years at the same time, a new Director and a new Substitute shall be appointed, or the same ones shall be continued in the management of the interests of the Association. That shall be determined by a plurality of votes in the Assembly which shall be convoked.

ARTICLE 5. If the Director shall be replaced [before the completion of his term], the Substitute, whom he shall have had during his term, shall succeed him; and at that time no other than the Substitute necessary for the new Director shall be elected.

ARTICLE 6. It shall be the duty of the Director to arrange for the necessary expeditions and to receive the returns. He shall keep an open account of those returns for the liquidation of the interests of each member. The expeditions from this town shall be made annually in April, at the latest, unless that is prevented by the greatest obstacle.

ARTICLE 7. In case of the absence, sickness, or death of the Director(s),[2] the Substitute shall perform his duties *ad interim*. In that case a member of the Board of Trade shall be appointed who shall also fill the place of the Substitute.

ARTICLE 8. The Substitutes shall not be allowed to refuse their services to the Director in the occupations that concern the interests of the Company. In the contrary case the individuals of this Company shall appoint another Substitute in his [their?] place when the refusal is verified at a meeting for which the fitting notification must have preceded.

ARTICLE 9. Every member incorporated in the Company shall be required to supply his share in merchandise in accordance with the written notification which the Director shall hand him. The Director shall make

---

[2] The "s" is in the Library of Congress copy.

a careful and detailed statement of each article in the account of the one supplying it, in order to enter it in the general fund.

ARTICLE 10. Each member shall have the right in his turn to supply the Association through the Director with his share of remittances for the dispatch of the expedition, which that Director shall make, if he is careful to give him advice thereof at least a fortnight before the departure of the *pirogues;* for in any other way, the Director must not pay any attention to it.

ARTICLE 11. He who shall wish to resign his membership in the Association, may do so by refusing, in writing, to supply his share, without the need of any other formality; although it will be the duty of the Director to inform the members of the Company, which will make a record thereof in the presence of the Lieutenant-Governor.

ARTICLE 12. Under no consideration can the members of this Company be allowed to refuse to supply their share, quota, or portion, during the first three years, under penalty of being deprived of their membership [in the Company]. That deprivation shall be ratified in a meeting of the Company which shall be called by the Director.

ARTICLE 13. If it should happen that any of the members of the Company should refuse, during the second or third year, to supply the share which he should owe, or ought to supply, he shall not therefore be deprived of the return which belongs to him, for the share which he shall have contributed before.

ARTICLE 14. Every member incorporated [in the Company] may demand at will permission to inspect the employment of his goods, the expeditions, and the returns, whenever he thinks it suitable. The Director shall not refuse such inspection, in order to justify his administration.

ARTICLE 15. The Directors and Substitutes shall take the means which they believe advisable for the future prosperity of the Company. They may make stations [deposits], take salaried clerks, or other persons, or means useful and necessary for the passage or despatch to the districts possible on the Upper Missouri for the discovery of unknown tribes, either to the north of the said river or to the south, and in any distance at all for the formation in the future of a fur-trade with the most remote tribes.

ARTICLE 16. In the face of events which may happen on account of the preceding article in the fruitless explorations, it is established that every member incorporated in the Company at present shall supply and give bonds of one thousand *pesos* to cover the trifling and burdensome expenses which might result from the various expeditions which might be made without other success than that of discovering tribes, and for reaching which there may have been caused great expense, both in presents, which it might be necessary to make to them, in order to get their good-will, and in opening up communications with even the more distant tribes.

ARTICLE 17. In consideration of the preceding article, the signers shall sign as interested and incorporated members in the said Company, and after their signatures shall place the names of those for whom they shall be bondsman, of such and such an one.

Then all their goods of the present and future shall be especially reserved and as pledges for the security of said bond.

ARTICLE 18. The lack of bonds shall essentially prevent incorporation [into the Company]. The bonds thus designated shall be recognized as true and valid, and there shall be no need of any other formality.

ARTICLE 19. If it should happen during the space of ten years for which the present Association or Company for the discovery and exclusive trade of the Upper Missouri must last, as was previously stated in Article 15, that any of its members wish to resign, he cannot do it directly or indirectly in favor of any person; but his portion must revert to the Company.

ARTICLE 20. In case of the absence of one of the members because of business or because of sickness, he shall appoint a proxy to represent him, so that the absent one may always be considered and reputed a resident and proprietary citizen and of the jurisdiction of St. Louis.

ARTICLE 21. When the first three years, which shall only begin to run from the first of next May, one thousand seven hundred and ninety-five, have expired, the lack of a representative in the meetings or the lack of share or quota in the expeditions, shall cause a tacit resignation from incorporation in the Company; but it shall deprive the person of the benefit that he may have been able to have or obtain for his share, both in the meetings and in the remittances of money which shall be made during his absence in behalf of the Company, without prejudice to what is stated above in Article 12.

ARTICLE 22. In the explanation of Article 21, preceding, it must be understood that the meetings of the Company, that are called, shall not prejudice the claims of absent members, who have been previously recognized as members in the Company.

ARTICLE 23. On the arrival at St. Louis of furs, as return for the goods despatched by the Directors at the account of the Company, immediate division shall be made to each one of the members, in proportion to the shares or portions of each one, after having paid the expenses which were incurred before the division.

ARTICLE 24. Although it is not to be understood by the preceding article than any of the members has the right to contribute more funds than another in the general sum in the expeditions which shall be made by the Director at the account of the Company, nevertheless, the amounts contributed may be less by half, and in no other way, in order that it may

221

be continued so and may be proportional to the wealth of each one interested. And then, and henceforth, the Directors shall pay or divide the excess to the account of the Company in general.

ARTICLE 25. In case of the death of one of the members, his heir shall enjoy the same rights, prerogatives, and advantages as the deceased, as soon as he shall present himself to the Director in order to make himself known, either by power of attorney, or by means of his guardian or custodians. This shall not be considered as done until the Director shall have given his signature in order that it may so appear. The Director shall not be able to evade it or refuse it, when he who petitions or makes the representations shall have any grounds for it.

ARTICLE 26. The Company shall not be able to be dissolved even by a plurality of votes; nor shall the exclusive privileges which it has petitioned from the general government for the regulation of the trade of the Missouri, accepted on the 15th of October of last year with the addition of the notes of the body of the Board of Trade, be changed or diminished because from that time the advantage of this Board of Trade [comercio] to each one of its members was unanimously recognized; as was the fact that if it should ever happen that a contrary opinion should be presented either at the present or in the future it would be for no other reason than because of intriguing spirits who were attempting for private ends by secret means to combat the general opinion, in order to procure its ruin.

ARTICLE 27. Notwithstanding Article 11, which states the liberty of resigning one's membership in the Company whenever that may be judged suitable, the bond given by him who shall retire, shall remain during the administration of the Director in whose time the resignation shall have been made, and to the end of his term. That term must run for three years, and the bond shall be freed from fees, but without any prejudice to the capital which shall belong to each retired proprietor, if at the time of the division, any funds should be owed to him or belonged to him.

ARTICLE 28. Resignation from the Company shall be made without any return to the Director. The latter shall give information thereof at the first meeting which shall be held, according to Article 11, at any time in the existence of the Company.

ARTICLE 29. The Director shall keep an exact register of all the meetings relative to the Company, which shall contain the results of the deliberations which, in time and place, must serve as a rule and regulation.

ARTICLE 30. He shall also keep the books of his operations, according to the rules of the Board of Trade, in order that he may carry the accounts of his Company. In that book each person interested and each one employed in its service shall have an open account of the receipts and disbursements of his exclusive property.

ARTICLE 31. Accounts shall be kept of goods sent to the Missouri for traffic among the tribes discovered and those accounts shall be balanced with the returns.

ARTICLE 32. An account of every kind of fur which is bought shall also be opened, so that it might be known at any instant what is the condition of the receipts for each kind [of fur] at the account of the Company.

ARTICLE 33. The agent sent to the tribes of our exclusive trade shall also send annually to the Director the report of the goods remaining to be sold, in the manner that may be possible; and every three years he shall be absolutely obliged to send a detailed account of everything under his direction and management, sending in the furs so that the Director may adjust his accounts and render them to the Company, before the nomination of his successor.

ARTICLE 34. Each Director, at the end of his administration, shall strike the balance of all the business which shall have been done by the Company, and shall give a succinct resumé to every one of the members who shall demand it, and, especially, to his successor.

ARTICLE 35. The registers, although made at the expense of the Company, shall remain in the possession of the administrators, who shall have made and kept them. The latter shall aways be obliged to show them whenever necessary to illustrate the future by the past.

ARTICLE 36. The Directors and Substitutes shall make no expedition until very one of those interested in the Company shall have furnished, and placed in the hands of the Directors of the Company, with date and signature, the report of the goods supplied, in the following manner: The Company of the Missouri owes to N. "—— all on one sheet of paper."

ARTICLE 37. A special rule shall be made by the Directors and Substitutes for the treatment and support [food] of the rowers when the latter leave here to go upon their voyage and during their stay among the tribes, so that the report of expenses may approximate to that which the English have in their trade in the North, in order that an equality of competition may be preserved with them.

ARTICLE 38. Another rule shall also be made for the subordination of each trapper or rower to his leader, superior, chief, or any other person entrusted with the leadership and command, in regard to what concerns the interests of the Company.

ARTICLE 39. Any person who shall be in the employ of the Company and shall commit fraud or shall wilfully cause any damage or injury during his voyages, or in any other manner, shall lose his wages or salary when the offense has been proven, without detriment to the restoration or compensation of the value of the thing. If the injury is the result of his negligence, he shall not lose his wages or salary, but shall repair the loss or damage which he shall have occasioned.

ARTICLE 40. The leaders, chiefs, or superiors, who shall pillage or allow the pillaging of stations during their voyages, belonging to whites or Indians, shall lose their wages, or salaries, just as do the rowers or trappers who shall have committed the offense, and they shall further be obliged to make restitution for the value of the theft. He who shall declare, on their arrival here, such a deed, shall receive the wages or salary of him who shall have committed the theft or done the damage.

ARTICLE 41. The Directors of the Company shall receive two per cent commission on the whole sum or general capital of the operations of receipts and expenditures which shall pass through their hands on the account of the Company, so that they may be recompensed for their troubles and the continual cares which they shall be obliged to employ. This right may not be taken away from those who shall exercise this duty.

ARTICLE 42. In accordance with Article 5 of the regulations for the traffic of the Missouri, proposed by His Excellency, July 20, 1793,[3] one share shall belong to our Lieutenant-Governor in the formation of the present Company, if it suits him to take it.

ARTICLE 43. The passports which it may be necessary to ask for from the Government, for the different expeditions which may be made shall be placed at the foot of the invoices of their goods, and shall be certified by the Director without their being for any reason subject to the different precautions taken beforehand for the plan of trade of the Missouri proposed by His Excellency, as above said, July 20, 1793.

ARTICLE 44. The same thing shall be true of every kind of trouble or obstacle mentioned by said rules of commerce, especially, in Articles 10, 12, 13, 16, 17, and 19, with the exception of the present reservations of Articles 7 and 9 of the above-mentioned rules, which alone shall have place in the present Company, in consideration of the fact that the renunciation of the other articles follows by right, by the reunion of the body of commerce which is formed at present into one single corporation, one single individual, and one single interest, composed of many heads which have no other consideration than the same means, the same resources, and the same advantages under the special administration of one of the members of the Board of Trade acting for the members in general.

ARTICLE 45. The Directors must convoke the members of the Company whenever they judge it necessary for their interests, after having obtained the consent of the Lieutenant-Governor of these settlements. [Adjournment:]

---

[3]Chapter I, document XXXII.

After each member of the meeting had been instructed concerning the articles proposed by the Syndic of the Board of Trade, it was resolved and determined that the meeting should be adjourned until the Monday following, on the twelfth of the present month, so that each article might be reflected over maturely, thus facilitating to the body of the Board of Trade the approbation or disapprobation of whatever might be the general interests. Thereupon this action which took place before the Lieutenant-Governor, Don Zenon Trudeau, May five, one thousand seven hundred and ninety-four, was concluded at two o'clock in the afternoon.

Santiago Clamorgan
Zenon Trudeau

[Articles of Incorporation Approved:]

In the year one thousand seven hundred and ninety-four, on the twelfth of the present month, after a discourse pronounced and directed to the body of the present Board of Trade by the Syndic in regard to the validity of the claims of each one of the members of the town of St. Louis who compose the Board, the session was opened with the deliberations of the fifth of the present month, in order to again state to the individuals of the Company newly convoked and assembled the articles proposed by the Syndic for the formation of a Company.

In consequence, it was unanimously resolved and decided that all and each of the preceding articles to the number of forty-five should be allowed and executed in all points and should serve as the articles of incorporation for the Commercial Company of the Missouri, for trade with the Indian tribes farther up than the Poncas. Those articles cannot be altered or added to without the consent of the majority of the Association. Therefore, supplication was made to the Lieutenant-Governor to procure the sanction of the whole by the approval of the Governor-General, being pleased, meanwhile, to lend hand to the execution of each one of the articles which are contained in the articles of incorporation. Petition is made to have it passed to a vote so that by a plurality of the votes, a Director and Substitute may be elected, both of them being chosen from the body of the Association that was formed and created on this day, and which was composed of Messrs. Durocher, Reylhe, Robidou, St. Cyr, Sanguinet, Dubreuill, Motard, Benito Vazquez, and Clamorgan. Those are the only gentlemen of the Board of Trade who have wished to try and risk their fortune in an undertaking of so much cost and danger for the discovery of the remote tribes. All the other members of the Board of Trade who are present have duly represented at the moment of the conclusion and formally declared that they have no remarks to make in regard to the resolution taken upon the matter thus renouncing incorporation in the Company for the

Exploration of the Missouri. A record was made of it by our Lieutenant-Governor in the presence of all the incorporated members of the Board of trade, in order to certify the validity and legality of the resolutions of each one of the members who have signed, all in accordance with the intention of Article 17. So that everything may be executed according to these articles except whatever may be contrary, the Governor-General is petitioned to prohibit all other associations, companies, or private persons, from being able to claim any right to injure or harm the present Company in the trade which it is endeavoring to attract to this place in order to extend that trade to the capital [i.e., New Orleans]. Having been made and passed in the Government Assembly Hall in the town of St. Louis on May twelfth, one thousand seven hundred and ninety-four, it was signed by those interested in the Company, with the individual Syndic of the Company before the Lieutenant-Governor, with the exception of Jacinto St. Cyr, who had his wife sign, as was his custom.

REYHLE,[4]
   A. Reyhle, bondsman for Dubreuil.
MOTARD,
   Bondsman for Durocher.
DUROCHER,
   Bondsman for Clamorgan.
BENITO VASQUEZ,
   Benito Vazquez, bondsman for St. Cyr.
JOSEPH ROBIDOU,
   Robidou, bondsman for Sanguinet.
SANGUINET,
   Bondsman for Robidou.
HELENA ST. CYR,[5]
   Bondsman for Benito Vasquez.
DUBREUIL,
   Dubreuil, bondsman for Reyhle.
CLAMORGAN,
   Clamorgan, bondsman for Motard.

                                            Zenon Trudeau.

[Petition:]

To Baron de Carondelet, Governor and Intendant-General of the provinces of Louisiana and West Florida.

The Director of the Commercial Company for the upper part of the Missouri, has the honor to inform Your Excellency that a number of the

---

[4]Short biographical sketches of these persons may be found in *Missouri Historical Collections*, IV, 10ff., see also Houck, *Spanish Régime in Missouri*, II, 159.
[5]St. Cyr's wife.

members of the Board of Trade of this town have not become incorporated in the Association for exploration, because some of them fear to incur heavy expense without any result, and others with the intention of harming, if they can, in the future, the enterprise of those who today compose the Association, and whom the zeal for industry causes to risk[6] cheerfully the dangers of a most costly enterprise and perhaps one very fruitless in its beginning. The general funds of the Commercial Company, in whose name the Director has the honor of addressing to Your Excellency this request, rated at a capital of fifty thousand pounds of authorized bonds, respectively, which will, perhaps, be consumed in expenses like the capital of the first expedition which will amount to about forty thousand pounds, demand that the Company implore your kindness for the grant and consent of its petition, and the conclusions set forth in the record of the Articles of Incorporation of this day, in order that said Company may not, in the future, be exposed after considerable hardship and expense, to lose and destroy the credit to which many of the members of the Company will be obliged to have recourse in order to support themselves and continue this famous enterprise, which has been feared for such a long time [to undertake] because of the immense expense which must be incurred during the first years without other hope than that of a very distant prosperity. Therefore, the members of the Company that has been formed, being on the eve of adventuring everything for the discovery of distant and unknown tribes, after Your Excellency shall have had the goodness to approve and sanction the Articles of Incorporation passed this day before this Lieutenant-Governor with his consent, petition Your Excellency to please to guarantee and preserve for the members of the Company alone the right of exclusive trade for ten consecutive years. That time shall run from May first of next year, one thousand seven hundred and ninety-five, and said trade shall extend to all the tribes who may be found above the tribe of the Poncas. This supplicant, in the name of the members composing the above-mentioned company, will not cease to pray Heaven for the preservation and prosperity of Your Excellency. St. Louis, May twelfth, one thousand seven hundred and ninety-four.

Santiago Clamorgan

[Decree:]

New Orleans, July 18, 1794, in consideration of the advantages which result generally to the province and especially to the settlements of Illinois from the establishment of the Commercial Company of the Missouri, whose Articles of Incorporation and Instructions I approve in the terms which appear from the official letters to the Lieutenant-Governor of Illinois, Cap-

---

[6]Word is *anotar*—to note.

tain Don Zenon Trudeau: I, making use of the powers which His Majesty has conceded to me, approve the exclusive privilege of its trade for ten years as is petitioned.

Baron de Carondelet.

[Certification of copies:]

I, Don Zenon Trudeau, Captain of the Regiment of Louisiana, Lieutenant-Governor of the western settlement of Illinois, attest that the preceding copies are made exactly according to the originals, which are conserved in the archives under my charge, and that they are made in order to send them to the Secretary of the General Government of this province. St. Louis, November twenty-nine, one thousand seven hundred and ninety-four.

Zenon Trudeau [rubric]

X

TRUDEAU TO CARONDELET, ST. LOUIS, MAY 31, 1794[1]

Number 185

I send herewith to Your Excellency for Your approbation the Articles of Incorporation[2] made by the merchants of St. Louis for the discovery of new Indian nations as far as the source of the Missouri River. That is a corporation in which I have agreed to take part in order to induce others to do the same. For I am sure that if trade does not become profitable in the said territory, a country of which various reports are given can at least become well known. An old man who has just come from the Panis tribe where he has been for ten consecutive years has assured me that he has gone overland with the Patucas [Paducahs] nation to the source of the said Missouri where at a certain distance from it, there exists and he has seen a large river whose current flows toward the west. That will be verified within a few years if Your Excellency will approve the above Company which will exert all its efforts for it. Consequently, I send Your Excellency a petition of the Syndic of the said Company.[3] This petition requests the exclusive privilege for ten years of trading with all the new nations which may be discovered, so that they may indemnify themselves, if possible, for the heavy expenses indispensable on such an expedition, in which a single person cannot pledge himself without danger

---

[1]Written in Spanish. A.G.I., P. de C., leg. 2363; copy and transcript in Bancroft Library; printed in Houck, *Spanish Régime in Missouri*, II, 161-162. I have retranslated and checked the printed translation with and from the original, and my translation differs slightly from the version which is found in Houck. The reply is document XIV.

[2]Document IX.

[3]Document IX.

of ruining himself. As I have not seen any objection to the discovery of a territory very far from New Mexico, not only do I hope for the approbation of Your Excellency in the terms in which the Syndic *Monsieur* Morgan [*sic*] requests it, but I have persuaded the Company to form its expedition immediately this year, and it has sent an intelligent man together with ten others in order to go to establish a station among the Mandan nation; and to direct all their operations from there in order to become acquainted with so vast a region.

They will take three years for that first voyage. That expedition has caused an expense to the Company of eight thousand *pesos,* and in the coming year a like expedition will have to march to reinforce the first one, which must send minute reports annually of their discoveries and operations.[4] May God preserve Your Excellency many years.
St. Louis, May 31, 1794.

Zenon Trudeau [rubric]

Señor Baron de Carondelet

[In margin. "Approved (Carondelet's rubric)."]

---

[4]For a discussion of the expedition under Truteau's command see Nasatir, "Anglo-Spanish Rivalry on the Upper Missouri", *Mississippi Valley Historical Review,* XVI (1929), reprint pp. 13-19. For Truteau's "Journal" see document XXII.

XI

TRUDEAU TO CARONDELET, ST. LOUIS, MAY 31, 1794[1]

Number 186

I am sending Your Excellency a statement which shows the distribution of that amount of trade carried on along the Missouri which in this year has fallen by lot to the share of each merchant of this town of St. Louis and of the village of Ste. Geneviève.[2] All has been done in accordance with the form ordered in the new regulation,[3] and after the merchants themselves have apportioned [equalized] the trade among the posts in the best possible manner. This has served to prevent any complaint or dissatisfaction.

Your Excellency will see by the report itself how small is the value of the commerce of Missouri, which yearly decreases more and more. The introduction of merchandise increases imperceptibly, but the amount of peltries taken out by traders grows less and less. They are satisfied

---

[1]Written in Spanish. Bancroft Library.
[2]Document IV.
[3]Chapter I, document XXXII.

now if they get twenty-five per cent when in times past they obtained as much as three or four hundred.

May God keep Your Excellency many years. St. Louis, May 31, 1794.

Zenon Trudeau   [rubric]

Señor Baron de Carondelet.[4]

---

[4]In discussing the Kentucky intrigues with Harry Innes, Wilkinson, Lacassagne, and others, and the negotiations between Spain and the United States concerning the navigation of the Mississippi, Carondelet stated that, "Louisiana has a branch of immense commerce which the United States lacks; scorned or unknown until now by Spain; and that the English of Canada are strengthened enough to usurp from us, *the Commerce of the rich furs of the Missouri*, capable of enriching separately all the Province, and of attracting an immense population at [to] its borders, this can be favored, and extended without any force, and only with the open commerce of this Capitol with all Nations, which benefitting equally of its advantages will be found interested in which Spain conserves the navigation and the domination of the Mississippi river". Carondelet to Alcudia, no. 36, *res.*, New Orleans, June 3, 1794, A.H.N., Est., leg. 3899.
    Carondelet feared that the project of the Americans (and Britishers) to establish a city or colony at the confluence of the Missouri and Mississippi rivers would eventuate in the loss to the Spaniards, "of our rich Missouri fur trade, for a long time the object of the ambition of the English". They would proportion to the Americans (and/or British) "the trade with the savage nations situated on both banks of the Missouri, which we are beginning to discover, having formed a Company for this reason in St. Louis, Illinois"; they would open up an easy avenue "to the rich mines of California and to the Interior provinces without the latter being able to offer sufficient force to people accustomed to running two hundred leagues and maintain themselves five or six months in the woods without any more aid than their carbine and a little corn meal". Carondelet to Alcudia, no. 38 *res.*, New Orleans, July 9, 1794, A.H.N., Est., leg. 3899 with enclosures; covering letter alone is printed in *American Historical Association, Annual Report, 1896*, I, 1065-1067. Enclosures include proposals to establish a town on western bank of the Mississippi north of the Missouri river (from A.G.I., P. de C., leg. 2363; translated and printed in Houck, *Spanish Régime in Missouri*, II, 144-147) and letters of Simcoe to Carondelet, April 11, 1794 (in various publications of which the most available is *Simcoe Papers*). Same enclosure in Carondelet to Las Casas, no. 119 *res.*, New Orleans, July 16, 1794, A.G.I., P. de C., leg. 2363 (answered August 5, 1794, *American Historical Association, Annual Report, 1896*, I, 1082-1085.). See Nasatir, "Anglo-Spanish Frontier on the Upper Mississippi 1786-1796," *Iowa Journal of History and Politics*, XXIX (1931), pp. 177-178. See also Carondelet to Portell, New Orleans, July 20, 1794, Bancroft Library. I am engaged in collecting the full documentation on this project of Paysá.

XII

Trudeau to Carondelet, St. Louis, June 8, 1794[1]

Mon Général:

I received your letter of March second, last, as well as all of your official letters up to the same date, and it is with the greatest satisfaction that I have seen that our province is maintaining itself in duty and fidelity to our Prince. I admit that I was at one time very alarmed because of the poor harvest which was reported to be expected here, which would have placed me in a very critical situation especially before receiving your orders

---

[1]Written in French. A.G.I., P. de C., leg. 209.

of the second of January, last. However I had already taken steps to facilitate my retreat. I would perhaps have been very undecided if I had found myself in the necessity of carrying it out. Moreover your order gave me the tranquillity which I lacked before the time of my receiving it.

It has been a long time since the country has enjoyed such a great tranquillity. I find the inhabitants truly satisfied with the fact that the French expedition never appeared to have taken place. However, it has been reported that they have disembarked an army of twelve thousand men in Virginia and that they have money in great quantity which is scarcely probable at a time when they have enough to occupy themselves in Europe and where, I am persuaded to believe, according to what you have written me, they are, if not conquered, at least in a desperate situation.

May God grant it and thus give us peace, so sweet. Their comfort is making them seek peace and tranquillity; nevertheless, they are the only barbarians upon whom we can truly count for help. I have not had difficulty in persuading the Loups to return. A large party of them embarked this morning, and the others will not delay in doing likewise. They would have liked to leave their wives at St. Louis, but I did not wish to consent to it because I lacked food and there is no resource from which to procure it, the country being very destitute. If Lorimier had told me in time of the emigration, I do not doubt at all that it would have taken place and that I could have avoided the expenditures which I could not help incurring by feeding at least eight hundred persons who gathered at the same time. The gathering exhausted the remainder of the food and also ruined the harvests by killing a large number of animals. It was not possible to restrain them from killing the animals.[2]

Monsieur Didier, after having taken possession of the curacy of St. Louis which he had scorned, appears to be willing to conduct himself as a good pastor. Both for my repose and the welfare of the community I hope he continues to do so. If he had acted in the same way upon his arrival, he would have made a very auspicious beginning but he has caused offence in wishing to root out by force what he would have obtained through the generosity of the inhabitants. I am on very good terms with him and will be always if he leave me without annoyances. The one from Ste. Geneviève is not as zealous for his ministry but despite that he is

---

[2]For events alluded to, *e.g.,* Clark's projected invasion, see Nasatir, "Anglo-Spanish Frontier on the Upper Mississippi 1786-1796", *op. cit.;* Liljegren, "Jacobinism in Spanish Louisiana 1792-1797", *op. cit;* James, *George Rogers Clark;* Bemis, *Pinckney's Treaty;* A. P. Whitaker, *Spanish American Frontier* (Boston, 1927); F. J. Turner [ed.], "Correspondence of Clark and Gênet," in *American Historical Association, Annual Report 1896,* volume I; etc.

The manuscript correspondence of Carondelet and Trudeau on these events is voluminous. My former student, Frances Coughlin, has dealt with this problem in her excellent dissertation entitled "Spanish Galleys on the Mississippi River 1792-1796".

loved by the inhabitants and for the goodness of humanity and tranquillity by all the nations.

Monsieur Menard, associate of the company of *Messieurs* Delassus and Tardiveau, has just told me this moment that he had seen the copy of a letter of an officer of the army of General Wayne who is marching towards Detroit, which says that this army had received orders to withdraw in order to unite with another considerable corps of troops and of militia who are marching to lay siege to Quebec. It seems evident from all that has been said for a long time that the war between England and the United States is inevitable. As I am not a clever enough politician to disentangle the role that we are going to play with our dear ambitious neighbors it delays me infinitely—while waiting to receive your first letters in order to regulate my conduct in accordance with your orders. I have just found myself quite embarrassed by the reception of the letter enclosed herewith—from a magistrate who is coming to the eastern part of the Illinois to administer justice there, as is the custom at certain times. You will see, *Mon Général*, what he demands, and please accord me your approbation for my having taken all the means that are practiced in order to restrain the savages as far as it is in the power of a commandant to do. I have likewise written to *Monsieur* Portell to engage him to aid me, which he will certainly do, in that I do not suppose him to have more extensive instructions than mine, and, animated as he must be with the desire of manifesting to the Americans that we have no part in the war which the savages are making upon them. It is still less our character to permit them [Americans] to be hostile in a navigation which we share, especially after they have solicited our influence among the nations in our territory.

The Loups and the Shawnees have abandoned Cape Girardeau in order to come to the environs of St. Louis. Portell believed himself justified in thinking that they have been won over by the traders or by other counsel, and consequently he sent here Don Domingo Bouligny to try to discover the true authors of their emigrations of which no one warned me in sufficient time to stop them. However, I first employed the two Vallé brothers who have used all sorts of entreaties to keep them at St. Geneviève, but all their influence only served to further their desire to leave. When they arrived at St. Louis, I tried my best to find out why they had come here. The Shawnees told me that they were fleeing from the Loups, who, despite Lorimier, had done wrong on the Belle Rivière and that their great chief of Detroit had sent them word to place their wives under the protection of this village. This is verified by the fact that I myself have received *collars* from this chief who begged me to give assistance to the nation and to save the women and children, whom he begged me to place above the Illinois river,—seven leagues from St. Louis. This was in order to then make use of the men to wage war at the entrance to the Belle Rivière. From there if they were repulsed they would be able with greater facility to rejoin and conduct their wives to Detroit, whose inhabitants could help them in arriving there without accident. I am ready to acknowledge that this recommendation is partly responsible for their step, but the true cause is that for savages they are rich—they have horses, cows, pigs, and poultry, they love to cultivate land. They have no commerce, as is to be expected; they are very generous in this regard and it is very easy for their emoluments are paid in lead, wheat or maize. With that they procure their needs. They make money moreover when they can and it is, doubtlessly, what might be called commerce.

The man[3] named Jacque de Léglise, the same person who discovered the Mandans of the Missouri, arrived today from his second voyage after an absence of fifteen months. He was obliged to stop one hundred leagues below [the Mandan] having encountered the Ricara and Sioux Nations who kept him from making profit. With difficulty has he brought back the wherewithal with which to pay for his equipment, and the man named Garro [Garreau] who had been with him consumed one [equipment] of sixteen hundred *pesos*[4] which *Monsieur* Collell advanced to him. The latter remained among the Ricara nation where he could not help but be very pernicious with his advice.[5]

I fear, *Mon Général,* becoming very annoying to you, that is why I beg you to excuse me and to believe me to be with the deepest respect,

     Mon Général,

       Your very humble, obedient servant

          Zenon Trudeau   [rubric]

St. Louis, June 8, 1794

To *Monsieur* le Baron de Carondelet

P.S.: *Monsieur* Morgan has just remitted to me a copy of the instructions which was brought by the person in charge of the affairs of the Company of the Upper Missouri. I have had the honor of sending it to you as it was proposed to me in order that you may have the goodness to make remarks thereupon which you might believe necessary and convenient and which I have not been able to forsee.[6]

---

[3]This paragraph is published in Nasatir, "Spanish Exploration of the Upper Missouri" in *Mississippi Valley Historical Review,* XIV, (1927) 59.

[4]Collell says two thousand *pesos fuertes.* See document XVII.

[5]See Truteau's Journal—document XXII.

[6]Document XVIII or perhaps document IX is meant.

233

XIII

D'EGLISE TO CARONDELET, ST. LOUIS, JUNE 19, 1794[1]

Señor Governor-General:

Jacobo L'Yglisse, a citizen residing in the city of St. Louis, Illinois, with all due respect informs Your Excellency that in the year one thousand seven hundred ninety-two, the deponent having proper permission for the usual practice of hunting on the Missouri River, and going in this way as far as the nation of Mahan, met there a trader, Don Pedro Montardy, lieutenant of the militia in this aforesaid port of St. Louis, from whom the deponent bought some goods for trading with the Indians. With them and two hookers he set out in search of some of those nations with whom there was no trading or commerce at that time. When, indeed, he had finally traveled for a space of two months, more or less, he came upon the Mandan and Tayenes nations, about three hundred leagues distant from the Poncas. He established a truce with them for trading, at that time not at all advantageous to the deponent because he did not have sufficient goods for it; however, after he had used up what he had, and had persuaded those Indians of the advantages that would come to them from the commercial dealings he was about to establish with them, explaining to them the greatness of the Spanish nation and the wise rules of its government, he promised to return to them the following year with the articles that were necessary for carrying it out and to give a report concerning them to the commandant of these settlements. This he did the year just past, reporting it to Sr. D". Zenon Trudeau,[2] now commandant, who gave the deponent the permission necessary to return and to put into effect what he had agreed with those Mandan and Tayenes nations. He was accompanied by a man named Gareau, each one with a pirogue loaded with the articles and oarsmen necessary for their enterprise. The bad conduct of this Gareau, his turbulent and dissolute attitude put the deponent in danger of losing everything completely among those nations, because he distributed the articles that were entrusted to him for trading to improper uses other than those intended. In this situation the deponent was obliged to return down stream to these settlements with the articles and furs he had been able to collect to satisfy his creditors. He had, therefore, not accomplished anything but pacifying to some extent the savage character of those nations and having

---

[1]Written in Spanish. Bancroft Library. This document was written by some one other than D'Eglise, probably Eugenio Álvarez. It is signed in another handwriting "Jacques D'Eglise". Printed in Nasatir, "Spanish Exploration of the Upper Missouri" in *Mississippi Valley Historical Review*, XIV, (1927) 59-61. See also Nasatir, "Jacques D'Eglise on the Upper Missouri" in *Ibid.* XIV, (1927) 49-50; and also Nasatir, "Anglo-Spanish Rivalry on the Upper Missouri", *Ibid.*, XVI (1929), reprint p. 9. This petition was forwarded with document XX.

[2]See Chapter I, documents XVIII and XXI.

been the first to establish trade with them as the enclosed certificates prove. It is well known in these settlements that the deponent wasted his time and his labor and lost the profit he might have had from this trading by the bad conduct of said Gareau, who abandoned him and remained among those Indians after he had used up entirely all the merchandise he took with him, without rendering him an account for the least thing.

In view of this said deponent humbly begs that it be deemed right to grant him the exclusive trade with those nations for the term of four years on the same terms that Juan Meunier enjoys for the discovery of the Poncas nation,[a] to the end that in this way he may recover to some degree the losses he has suffered in the discovery of these nations. The hardships that he suffered were that at every step he ran the risk of losing his life and that in such trading, past losses are irreparable by any means. He also begs permission to buy his merchandise anywhere without being obliged to procure it at a predetermined depot, promising as he should, not to enter into any secret trading or act offensively to anyone, thanks to which he hopes to deserve your great favor.

St. Louis, Illinois, June 19, 1794.

Jacques D'Eglise [rubric]

We, the undersigned, certify to the best of our ability and as there is occasion, that Jacobo L'Eglise discovered the Mandan and Tayenes nations, as is well known in these settlements of Illinois, and that it may be known to whomever it concerns, we give this statement and the petition of the same man, at St. Louis on the nineteenth of June of seventeen hundred ninety-four.

J. H. Robidoux [rubric]
witness
Jn. Lacombe [rubric]
witness
Eugenio Álvarez [rubric]
Montard
Pierre Quenel
Witness

---

[a]Chapter I, document XXXIII and this Chapter, document XVI.

XIV

CARONDELET TO TRUDEAU, NEW ORLEANS, JULY 12, 1794[1]

I have received the *reglamento de Sociedad* [Articles of Incorporation] made by the merchants of St. Louis to discover new nations of Indians as

---

[1]Written in Spanish. A.G.I., P. de C., leg. 2363; printed in Houck, *Spanish Régime in Missouri*, II, 162-163. I have retranslated this document from the original.

far as the source of the Missouri which meets my approval as well as everything else mentioned in [your official letter], number 185.[2]

I am returning to you with my decree the memorial of Don Santiago Clamorgan[3] granting to the Company the exclusive privilege for ten years which he solicits and I beg you to thank all of them in my name for the zeal with which they are encouraging the public welfare of those establishments and I charge you very particularly to procure the entire and exact fulfillment of everything contained in the said *reglamento* and the Instructions,[4] doing everything possible to discover the source of the Missouri River and to penetrate as far as the South Sea, upon whose shores are to be found the new Russian establishments formed above California, bringing with you some certain proof of having penetrated and communicated with them. His Majesty will give a prize of two thousand *pesos*[5] to the discoverer and his zeal and merit will be especially heeded. A certification from the Russian commandants will be the most authentic proof which can be produced; it being written in that language.

May God Our Lord keep you many years.

New Orleans, July 12, 1794.
El Baron de Carondelet [rubric]

Señor Don Zenon Trudeau

[2]Document X.
[3]Document IX.
[4]Truteau's instructions is document XVIII.
[5]Later raised to 3000.

XV

Carondelet to Clamorgan, New Orleans, July 22, 1794[1]

I have indeed received, Sir, the political memorial which you have addressed to me under the double cover which you mention. The letter [which] was annexed to it for Mr. Delassus, was also delivered to me at the same time, and suspecting some mistake, as also conjecturing what might be the contents of it, I threw it in the fire.

I have already had the honour to tell you my sentiments on one part of the contents of your memorial, which I have read with the greatest interest. Let us wait until the storm which agitates the political atmosphere be somewhat dissipated and then we shall see, according to the situation in which Europe will remain, what we will be able to do for the welfare of Louisiana, which, I do hope, will advance more in the last five years of this century than it has done since the beginning of it, to the period of my coming into the province.

[1]Missouri Historical Society, Clamorgan Collection; printed in *American State Papers, Public Lands*, VIII, 234.

Your views, Sir, are in perfect accordance with mine. True riches lie in agriculture, and this requires a competent population and easy outlets: Louisiana is susceptible of all these advantages, but present circumstances are not favorable to our views; let us then have patience for a while, and by remaining attentive speculators of what passes, we may seize on the first opportunity of success.[2]

I have the honor to be with the most perfect consideration, Sir, Your very humble and very obedient servant

Signed: Le Baron de Carondelet

Monsr. de Clamorgan

---

[2]See in this connection Clamorgan's memorial, Chapter I, document XXIV and notes thereto.

XVI

Meunier and Rolland to Carondelet,

St. Louis, September, 1794[1]

To *Monseigneur,* the Baron de Carondelet, Chevalier of the order of Malta, Colonel of the armies of His Catholic Majesty, Governor, Intendant, Vice-Patron of the provinces of Louisiana and West Florida, sub-inspector of troops and militias of the same, etc.

Monseigneur:

Jean Meunier and Rolland, merchants and traders at St. Louis, Illinois, very humbly beg you and again call to your attention that by an act of your kindness, Your Excellency saw fit to grant to the said Jean Meunier the exclusive right to trade with the savages called the Poncas for four years,[2] as due to [as a reward for] the courage that he showed in penetrating into the country of these barbarians, where no one had yet gone. As a result of this generous act of yours the petitioners have entered into an act of partnership, having supplied their stores with goods suitable for trade with this nation for the duration of the time of their license. The said Jean Meunier had left on his first expedition and the said Rolland remained in St. Louis to attend to the correspondence and send supplies. The petitioners then learned with surprise of the revocation of their license.[3] They have not hesitated to address Your Excellency and dare to point out to you, *Monseigneur,* how very prejudicial this revocation is to their in-

---

[1]Written in French. There are two copies of this document in the Bancroft Library only one of which is signed. There is no difference in meaning between the two copies, which are evidently intended to be exact reproductions, but the spelling is frequently quite different. Most likely one is a draft. This petition was forwarded to Carondelet with document XX.
[2]Chapter I, document XXXIII.
[3]See document VI. See also documents I and III and also VIII.

terests since they have made the purchase of merchandise suitable for trading, which would not be desirable for any other nation except that one. All their goods have remained unsold which makes it impossible for them to discharge their affairs with honor. The petitioners are firmly convinced that if Your Excellency personally revoked this license it was done for the general good, but they are equally persuaded that some one has taken advantage of Your Excellency's trustfulness and Christianity in order to make a false statement of the public welfare, while those who have applied for this revocation had nothing in mind but their own individual advantage. Under this consideration, *Monseigneur,* they dare to hope that, bearing in mind the entreaty of two unfortunates, Your Excellency will be willing to grant again the same license. They hope for your kindness and your justice and they do not cease to pray for the preservation of your precious life.

St. Louis, this day of September,⁴ 1794.

Jean Meunier and Rolland⁵
[rubric]   [rubric]

[Second copy]   Certified Copy:

Contract of partnership between Jean Meunier and Jacques Rolland.

Before me, Don Zenon Trudeau, Captain of the fixed regiment of Louisiana, Lieutenant-Governor, Commander-in-chief of the western district of the Illinois, lacking a notary and in his place, there appeared *señores* Jean Meunier and Jacques Rolland, two merchants and traders, residents of St. Louis, who have voluntarily made the agreement of partnership which follows, namely, that they have entered upon their association for the time and space of four years beginning with today to four years hence, for trading on the Missouri among the nation of Poncas. Said association is to end upon their arrival in this city in the year of 1798 and during the said time of four years is to make its profit and share the injuries that it may please God to send upon their business.

Article 1. The said Jean Meunier promises to leave as soon as possible to go to the said village of the Poncas, as soon as the said partners have supplied him with merchandise suitable for the trade at that post.

Article 2. The said Jacques Rolland shall remain to make the necessary arrangements for their spending the winter as well as to make provisions for the requirements in merchandise that will be necessary to them during the time of their association, which he promises that he will furnish

---

⁴Neither of the two copies has the day and the second copy has October.
⁵The second copy only is signed.

and seek. Wherever it shall be necessary he shall charge the bills to the partnership, having paid the necessary amount to take them where they are needed and give notes that he will make on the security of the above-mentioned partnership. He will then go to join the said Jean Meunier at the above-mentioned post with the merchandise that he will have for this purpose and the said Jean Meunier promises to trade with them and exchange them with the aid of the said Rolland.

However, the said partners are not to be held for each other's debts contracted before their partnership. If any are found, they are to be paid by the one of the two who made them, without the other or his goods being held in any way. They shall be totally apart from this partnership.

The above-mentioned partners have agreed that on the return of one of the two, the debts for the sums expended for the said partnership shall be paid and settled in the name of the said partnership.

The said Jacques Rolland has agreed to pay the said Jean Meunier, his partner, the sum of a thousand *livres* in deer skins for each year that the said partnership [endures], the amount [equal to] of two thousand *livres* in silver which shall be paid from all which he may have or claim in the said partnership and from all his property, present and future, without any reference to the said partnership. If it happens during the period of four years that either of the partners becomes ill, he is to be cared for, treated, and doctored from the common funds of said partnership.

It is agreed between the said parties that a clerk is to be hired to keep the account book of the said association, who for each year that he manages their accounts said clerk shall be paid at the expense of the said association; in case any question arises between them they promise to abide by the decision of two arbitrators whom each of them shall name. Thus the said parties have agreed, and otherwise they would not have assented to the agreement herewith contained, promising, binding themselves, and waiving claims. Done in St. Louis in the government hall, the twenty-sixth of April of the year seventeen hundred and ninety-four in the presence of *Sieurs* Clamorgan and Mathurin Bouvet whom we have called in as witnesses, and who have signed the original with me the lieutenant-governor, with the exception of Jean Meunier and the said Jacques Rolland who have declared that they did not know how and who have made their ordinary marks and thus signed the original. J. Cla Morgan. Mathurin Bouvet. Jean Meunier, His mark of a cross. Jacques Rolland, his mark of a cross below.

Zenon Trudeau.

I, Don Zenon Trudeau, Lieutenant-governor, Commander-in-chief of the western district of the Illinois, certify and attest that the present copy is in the conformity with the original on file in the archive of our government, in evidence of which we have given the present at St. Louis, the same day and year as the above.

Zenon Tudeau [rubric]

The Baron de Carondelet,[6] Knight of the Order of San Juan, Colonel of the Royal Army, Governor, Intendant-General, Vice-Patron of the Provinces of Louisiana, West Florida and Inspector of the Forces, etc. . .

In view of the good services and conduct of Juan Meunier, citizens of the settlements of Illinois and the good report that the captain of the regiment of Louisiana, Don Manuel Perez, has given me of this person, having proved to me the certainty of his having discovered the Indian nation of the Poncas, four hundred leagues from the mouth of the Missouri River, I have just granted him, as he requests, the exclusive trade with this nation for the period of four years, which are to begin from the beginning of the coming year, 1794. I therefore order the Commandant of those settlements not to put any obstacle in the way of his going to, staying at, or returning from that nation. Given at New Orleans on the twenty-first day of September, 1793

The Baron Carondelet
[rubric]

Andrés López Armesto
[rubric]

[Series of statements that Jean Meunier is the only trader known to the Poncas.]

I, the undersigned, certify that I have never known any other trader [among the Poncas] except Jean Meunier who was the first trader who made his way to the Poncas. He is an old Missouri trader. Not knowing how to sign my name I have made the ordinary sign.

Mark
Joseph   X   Hébert
of
Louis Dorion, witness
[rubric]

St. Louis, September 12, 1794.

---

[6]This is also in document XXXIII of Chapter I.

I the undersigned, certify that I have never known any other trader [among the Poncas] except Jean Meunier, who was the first trader to make his way to the Poncas, and who is an old Missouri trader.

> Mark X of
> Basille Vaseur
>
> > Joseph La Brosse, witness
> > [rubric]

St. Louis, September 11, 1794

I, Pierre Quenel, certify that I have never known any other trader among the Poncas except Jean Meunier. Likewise, I have never seen nor heard it said that there was any doubt.

> Pierre Quenel, Missouri trader.

Pierre Marujuy to the Governor:

The bearer of the present letter is a citizen of the Illinois who has been recommended to me by his associate, *Monsieur* Vossay [Volsay?]. Knowing that your happiness is the pleasure that you get from doing service to those who deserve it, I take the liberty of addressing you, begging you to aid him kindly by your wise advice in a matter in which he seems to me to be right. Pardon me for the liberty I take. Your gracious character, which is especially well known to me, bids me be importunate. If I should be so happy as to be of use to you in anything, command me with the confidence of one who is held in the most perfect respect.

> Your most humble and obedient servant,
> Pierre Marujuy [rubric]

November 28, 1791

XVII

Bonaventura Collel to Governor-General [Carondelet], St. Louis, October 20, 1794[1]

To the Governor-General:

Don Ventura Collel, citizen and resident of this city of St. Louis, Illinois, with all due respect calls to your attention the fact that during the past year, 1793, for the purpose of encouraging trade and urged by certain

---

[1]Written in Spanish. Bancroft Library, printed in Nasatir, "Spanish Exploration of the Upper Missouri", *Mississippi Valley Historical Review*, XIV (1927), 61-62. This memorial was sent to Carondelet on November 26. Document XX.

persons for that reason, he provided for the necessary equipment in a pirogue loaded with goods suitable for the Indian trade, of which there were signs and which were ready to be discovered at that time, so as to establish a regular commerce with them and give them the advantages which would come to them from their having a thorough knowledge of our government in general and of its wise regulations. For this purpose two suitable persons were chosen,[2] who were considered capable, one by José Robidoux, a merchant in this city, and the other by the deponent. They started with their men and the necessary supplies for their enterprise, which was successful until they arrived at their destination, without any bad accident on the whole voyage. After their arrival José Garreau, in charge of the deponent's goods, inspired by a troublesome and wanton spirit, used them up for other purposes than those for which they were intended, with the result that from this bad conduct there was a considerable loss to the deponent who secured nothing from his capital, which amounted to more than two thousand *pesos fuertes*.[3] He himself remained among those savages, giving himself up to them after having thus used up all the goods that had been consigned to him, as the other trader, the one sent by the aforesaid José Robidoux, explained on his return to this city,[4] thus occasioning to the said trader considerable losses by his bad conduct.

Therefore the deponent humbly begs Your Excellency in view of so considerable a loss as he experienced from the conduct and evil practices of the said José Garreau, and because the deponent was urged to undertake this expedition only by patriotism and to inform those Indians of the greatness of the Spanish nation and the wise laws of its government, he begs that he be granted the exclusive right to trade with the nation of the Kances, by way of compensation for his loss, for such time as Your Excellency's wisdom finds desirable so that by this means he may recover from said loss. The deponent has set forth nothing that is not true and well-known in these settlements of Illinois, wherefore the deponent has begged the present commandant, Don Zenon Trudeau, to be pleased to authorize by his signature all that the deponent has set down concerning this matter to the end that Your Excellency may be informed of what actually happened on this expedition. This favor the deponent hopes to obtain from your well known kindness and abolute justice.

St. Louis, Illinois, October 20, 1794.

Bonaventura Collel [rubric]

---

[2]D'Eglise and Joseph Garreau. See documents XII and XIII.
[3]Sixteen hundred *pesos*, according to D'Eglise. See document XIII.
[4]See documents XII and XIII.

XVIII

CLAMORGAN'S INSTRUCTIONS TO TRUTEAU, ST. LOUIS, JUNE 30, 1794[1]

Instructions according to the designs of the Company, given to *Señor* Truteau, who is in charge of the *pirogue* destined for the Mandanas Nation, by the Director Don Santiago Clamorgan, concerning those things which he must observe from the moment of his leaving this town, and while he has in his care the interests of the said Company with the nations of the Upper Missouri, whither he is going; these instructions must also be followed by him who by some unforseen accident may succeed him.

1. *Señor* Truteau on leaving this town shall proceed, with all possible foresight, to his destination, the Mandana Nation, on the Upper Missouri to make there a settlement or establish an agency [*factoria*] for the Company.

2. He shall cause to be constructed, upon his arrival among the Mandanas, a building [*cabaña*], thirty feet long and fifteen feet wide, built of logs placed one upon another in English fashion, the corners joined and fitted by a kind of mortise; on the inside he shall have a partition made in order that one part may serve as a storeroom and the other as a lodging.

3. He shall cause to be constructed another building, or *cabaña* in the same manner, for his men, opposite the first, with a distance of fifty feet between them. He shall have the doors and the windows of the two *cabañas* made exactly opposite each other and only on the sides facing each other, but no opening must be made on any of the other three sides.

4. He shall cause to be constructed a fort,[2] one hundred feet by eighty, which shall be so arranged as to enclose the two *cabañas* above mentioned, according to the plan on the margin, on the highest place in the (small) village, and as near as possible to the Missouri, so that the water may be near; he shall do this under the pretext of giving protection to the women and children in case of an attack. There shall be only one door to enter the enclosure, which shall be opposite the space or yard between the two

---

[1]Written in Spanish. There are several copies of these instructions in A.G.I., P. de C., leg. 2363. One of these copies contains a sketch of the fort to be constructed and has marginal notations. A copy of the instructions certified by Carondelet forms annex number 3 to Carondelet's dispatch no. 65 *reservada* to the Prince of Peace, New Orleans, January 8, 1796. A.H.N., Est. leg. 3900; photostat in the Library of Congress. There is a copy in the Missouri Historical Society, Papers from Spain. The instructions are printed in Houck, *Spanish Régime in Missouri*, II, 164-172 and as such are reproduced with a number of corrections here. I have collated and checked Houck's translation with the copy in A.H.N., Est. leg. 3900. The copy in A.G.I., P. de C., leg. 2363, contains a sketch map showing the route of Makay's voyages in 1784, 1786, 1787, and 1788; a pencilled tracing of which I made in Seville is reproduced in this volume.

[2]The model of the fort was drawn in the margin. It is here reproduced from the photostatic copy in the Library of Congress.

cabañas. The stakes of the fort shall project seven feet above the ground, if possible, with strips of wood fastened above by nails; the stakes of the garden shall be only five feet.

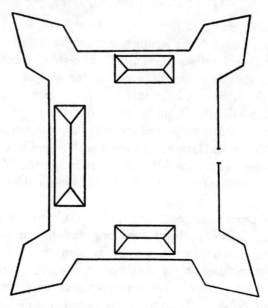

5. *Señor* Truteau shall take with him little trees, fruit seeds or stones, and other seeds in order to have an orchard and garden.

6. The next year *Señor* Truteau shall cause to be erected a shed, fifty feet long, and from 15 to 16 feet wide, in front of the gate of the fort, and it shall be in the interior as is shown in the plan drawn above, taking special care that the whole be solidly built in order that it may last a long time.

Nations[*]   7. It shall be the aim of *Señor* Truteau to keep the Indians in their simplicity of character, giving them counsel and advice only favorable to our commerce, animating them to increase their hunting and to improve their furs and skins in a suitable manner, well flayed to give them form and renown.

Merchandise   8. He shall fix a very high price on everything, keeping in mind that the prices of the armament are excessive and that without this precaution, the Company would sustain a loss.

---

[*]Marginal headings taken from photostat in Library of Congress.

Merchandise Nations	9. The price which *Señor* Truteau shall fix for the Mandana Nation shall always serve as a standard and norm for all other nations, when they come to deal with him; but he shall raise said price for the nations to which he is obliged to send the goods.
Information [*Conocimientos*]	10. He shall obtain all the knowledge and information possible concerning the separation, distance, and direction of the nations which he may see or of which he may hear, referring to the plan which I deliver to him in order that he may know his whereabouts, and to change or correct the location of the nations and rivers, adding those that are found and not yet on the plan.
Information	11. Going up the Missouri he shall take note of the large rivers [*Ríos grandes ó caudalosos,*] which are found on the south or on the north of that one, marking their distance from here to them, or from the Mandana Nation.
Nations Information	12. He shall inform himself concerning the Chionitones [Shoshones] who are on the Missouri far above the Mandanas and he shall send someone to gain knowledge of them and to inform himself concerning the rivers which may be found on one and the other side of the Missouri on ascending that stream.
Information	13. He shall inform himself of the distance to the Rocky chain [Mountains] which are located west of the source of the Missouri.
Nations Information	14. He shall attempt to have friendly relations with the Indians who live on the other side of the Rocky [Mountain] Chain, on which there are numerous nations, known under the name Serpientes [*i.e.* Snakes] and to find out from them, if they have any knowledge of the Sea of the West [*Mar del Ouest*] and if the waters of the rivers on the other side of the Rocky [Mountain] Chain flow westward.
Nations Information	15. He shall inform himself of the habits and manners of all the nations, their laws, their gods, their customs, their vices, their origin, and their food; and whether these nations are increasing or decreasing in population.
Nations Peace	16. He shall try to find out and become acquainted with the friends and enemies which each nation has, taking special care to show them his desire that all of them

live in peace; he shall speak to them of the Lord of Life as their guide with this object: in short, he shall establish peace everywhere.

Hunt

17.   He shall strive to ascertain the foibles or propensities of every nation to attract them everywhere to the thing which flatters them as the case may be.

Nations

18.'   It shall be the duty of *Señor* Truteau to locate the Pelé nation or Motilones, who must be south of the Mandanas, to whom one may go by passing through the territory of the Panis and he shall act in such a way that they will know there will continually be a warehouse where they can trade, reserved for them, in the Mandana nation, in order to establish friendly relations with them.

Information

19.   He shall try to ascertain the distance from the Mandanas to the nearest Spanish settlements which are located south of said Indians.

Nations

20.   He shall send messages to all the nations whom he may be able to reach, informing them of the motive which directs him, in order that as many Indians as possible might come to trade with him.

Nations
Information
Merchandise

21.   When he has the opportunity he shall take note of the articles most desired by each nation, that is, bagatelles and things of little value, since it is not desirable to cause them to wish for goods that are dear, and which transportation for a long distance will make still more dear.

Information
Merchandise

22.   If he suspects that his information is insufficient to give us a good idea of the cheap articles most salable, he shall send us patterns or samples so that we shall make no mistakes.   He shall also instruct us in regard to the favorite colors of each nation, as well as those that are disagreeable to them, and he shall not fail to inform us if the neighboring nations have the same tastes.

Salaried
persons

23.   At whatever time it may be, if anyone, receiving a salary from this Company, or any other individual shall trade with the nations above the Poncas, *Señor* Truteau shall confiscate their goods; he shall take their merchandise and furs, and shall immediately instruct the Director, Don Santiago Clamorgan, on the first occasion that pre-

---

'Articles 18 and 19 were annulled by order of Carondelet.   See Chapter III, document VIII.

sents itself; and he shall not be permitted to protect those persons who might be known, for which he alone shall be responsible.

Engagés

24. The Director, Don Santiago Clamorgan, shall be informed by *Señor* Truteau, [of] the faults and acts of disobedience of the engaged men, under penalty of being held personally responsible.

Engagés

25. He shall keep an account of what he furnishes to the enlisted employees, to whom he shall sell, in the territory of the Mandanas and above that of the Poncas, at the same price as he would sell in the same places to the Indians of the Mandanas nation; but below the Poncas he shall sell at fifty per cent above the price of the equipage to said employees, if they may have need of any merchandise, which shall be charged against their salaries, provided it does not exceed half of what is due them, according to the article below, which shall speak more definitely about the matter.

Engagés

26. *Señor* Truteau shall keep a duplicate of the accounts with the employees to whom he may have furnished anything, which he shall send yearly to the director, Don Santiago Clamorgan, with the boats that may come down the river, in order that he may be able to settle their accounts on their arrival here.

Information

27. He shall also keep a duplicate of his discoveries [explorations] and of everything worth knowing with information as complete as possible.

Engagés

28. He shall always send the employees who owe least to the Company on expeditions to explore to the north, and those who owe most, to those on the south and on the west; however, he shall not be authorized by this to advance more than half the wages of each man, including that which he may have obtained in Saint Louis.

Occurrences
[Events]

29. If *Señor* Truteau should happen to die during his administration, in that case *Señor* Periche [Pierre] Berger shall take charge of the management of affairs according to the same instructions.

Information

30. At the expiration of the three years, the period of the engagement of *Señor* Truteau, he shall make a careful, detailed report of all that remains in his possession and belonging to the Company, in order that the Director may present it to the members.

Damage to the Company	31. If *Señor* Truteau should be pillaged by the Mahas nations, on his trip on the Missouri, and, if the nation does this in order to avenge the damages and injuries which Santiago de la Iglesia and Garau have caused them on going through their village,[5] it shall be his duty to notify promptly the Director, Don Santiago Clamorgan, on the first occasion, in order that he may know the loss to the Company.
Engagés Voyage	32. He shall not advance any merchandise to the employees before arriving in the territory of the Mandanas, and in case that that may not happen this year, because the Mahas or the Poncas may prevent it, and that he is obliged to deal with them, then he shall advance to his employees as much as half of their salaries, including that which was advanced to them in St. Louis by the director, Don Santiago Clamorgan, which account with them shall be attached to the back of the engagement which is delivered to *Señor* Truteau for his guidance.
Nations Merchandise *Engagés* Voyage	33. If *Señor* Truteau is obliged to deal either with the Mahas or the Poncas, he shall traffic only in blue cloth or woolen blankets, saving the rest, if it is possible, in order that when it thaws he may continue his way with several men until he reaches the Mandanas.
Engagés Voyage	34. He shall take there the men whom he may need for his safety, acting according to the manner indicated in the preceding articles, in order to establish among that nation the agencies which we propose.
	35. During the voyage or immediately after his arrival at his destination, *Señor* Truteau shall remove all the obstacles which might oppose the plans of the Company, treating kindly all nations that he may meet, and all those to which he may send an exploring party even to the most remote regions.
Nations Merchandise Voyage Return	36. Before his departure, *Señor* Truteau shall arrange with the trader of the Mahas, or of the Poncas in whichever of these nations he may stay, to send down the river with the remainder of their employees the furs of the Company, which shall bear the mark C D M, with a detailed statement of the quantity and quality of the peltry.

---

[5]This is a typical matter in French, a fact overlooked by Houck in his translation.

Nations Information Voyage	37. If *Señor* Truteau should be detained by the Ottos, Poncas, or Mahas, he shall send a courier, if it is possible, to *Señor* Clamorgan in a light canoe which may be able to reach here from the fifth to the tenth of April, 1795, in order to inform us; and if he sees that this man cannot arrive here at the time set forth, he shall not send him, since when he will arrive the boats will be on their way, which we propose to send the 15th of April of next year at the latest, to the Mandanas subject to his orders, in which case, the information that he would bring us would be useless.

38. By means of presents of cloth and blankets *Señor* Truteau will be able to induce the nation that may detain him to permit him to continue his way to the Mandanas; he will do well to select this means although onerous; but it is proper to make some sacrifices to attain success.

Voyage Merchandise Return	39. Should he have the good fortune to pass without being detained, he shall send the Company the following year all the furs possible and as soon as possible in order that they may be here by the tenth of June; he shall keep some men with him among the Mandanas and shall send the rest with their bundles to *Señor* Clamorgan.
Memoria Return	40. *Señor* Truteau shall remember to send to me from the Mandanas, four well scraped skins, very large and well mottled, variegated in colors by the first boat, of a new style altogether, from different nations, if it is possible, to send to Spain; two of the skins shall be of ox skins with fringes of porcupine, one of the other two, in the same way, shall be of beaver, and the other, of any other animal except the otter, but all shall be made up in rare style and new, to announce a different fashion and a more elegant mode than that of the nations whom we frequent.
Memoria Merchandise Privilege Purchase Return	41. By virtue of the passport of the *Señor Comandante*, he, *Señor* Truteau, shall stop the trading of Santiago de la Iglesia and of Garau,[*] if they are still there, or anyone else in their place, if they trade or cause trade to be carried on with the Mandana nation, or with any other, even though it be with the whites, who may be encountered

---

[*] See Nasatir, "Anglo-Spanish Rivalry on the Upper Missouri", *Mississippi Valley Historical Review*, XVI (1929), reprint. pp. 9-15; and Truteau's "Journal", document XXII.

there. If the articles which remain in the hands of Santiago de la Iglesia and Garau are useful to the Indian nations in that region, *Señor* Truteau shall ask for them, so that *Señor* Clamorgan may give to them in Saint Louis the same quantity and quality, or their value in cash with a profit of ten per cent upon the price of the stock in Illinois for the Missouri, which shall be arranged or settled on their arrival here, they having a receipt which will show the quantity and quality of the merchandise which they have turned over to *Señor* Truteau for the Company.

Diary of
All
Occurrences

42. *Señor* Truteau shall keep a daily record of all that may be done for the Company, in which he shall give information of the daily operations: as, an exploring expedition; a treaty with one or the other nation; the arrival of foreign Indians; works of the establishment; a circumstance which is worth the trouble of being written down; finally everything that may happen to be done and ordered on each day by *Señor* Truteau for the benefit or detriment of the Company, in chronological order. He shall send every year a copy to *Señor* Clamorgan, and keep the duplicate.

Drink
Prohibited

43. He shall bear in mind that there are heavy fines against those who ship *aguardiente* in their boats for the Missouri, and he shall inform *Señor* Clamorgan if anyone should ever introduce drinks.

Voyage
Purchase
Merchandise

44. When *Señor* Truteau shall be ready to depart for the Mandanas, supposing that he should be stopped by the Poncas or the Mahas or in any other place, he shall ask the traders who may be in any of these nations, for the cheap articles which they have, if they are useful to the Mandanas where he intends to go, provided that we are not obliged to pay them here one hundred and fifty per cent above the price in England; that is in case *Señor* Truteau believes it to be necessary for the good of the Company.

Voyage

45. Should he have the good fortune to pass the Mahas and the Poncas, without being seen, and should he be obliged to put up for the winter on the way he shall fortfy himself well during the winter in order to be secure from unforeseen enemies.

46. He shall not make use of, nor shall he permit any of his employees to make use of the tin dishes intended for the trade, because this might make less valuable and discredit this line of merchandise.

Information

47. He shall ask all Indians, whom he believes in a position to answer satisfactorily, what kind of minerals there may be in that locality, or in some other, having specimens of each kind sent to us at the first opportunity and keeping a memorandum of the place or locality of every kind of mineral, in order to be able to go there in case of necessity; he shall do likewise in regard to the fruits, and the most abundant species of animals, concerning which he shall inform us.

Flag
Medal
Tobacco

48. He shall take with him three Spanish flags, for three different nations that he may see; with each banner he shall give a carrot of tobacco; the most beautiful of the banners is intended for the chief of the Mandanas, with a medal which the Governor sends him in order that he may make strenuous efforts to establish peace with all neighboring nations and to live in friendship with us.

Friendly
Relations

49. He shall secure for the Company the friendship of the white people who may be among the Mandanas, doing them favors inasmuch as he may be able, without causing harm or damage to the Company, affecting that these people transact their business with us, if it is agreeable to them, it being our intention to be useful to them, and we also desire that they be useful to us.

Merchandise
Preference

50. He shall remember that if the whites who are among the Mandanas purchase some goods from the English for their needs, he ought to persuade them to take from our Company all that with which the English are able to provide them, in order that the preference of the fur-trade may be given us.

Consejo
of the
Nation

51. On his arrival among the Mandanas, he shall proceed to convoke a council among the chiefs, which he shall hold in the name of the Chief of the Spaniards, announcing to them that the latter sends them a flag of his nation, and a medal which bears the likeness of His Majesty, the great Chief of all the Spaniards, protector and friend of all red men, who loves the beautiful lands, free roads, and a serene sky; he shall tell them that the flag

251

which they receive is the symbol of an alliance and of the most sincere friendship which he is able to give to the Mandanas nation, and that the medal ought to be the symbol of an eternal memory, that the Chief of the Mandanas ought to believe in the sincerity of the Chief of the Spaniards; finally, that the sons of the Mandana chiefs are also the sons of the Chief of the Spaniards, that he will ever protect them from all those who may wish to harm or injure them.

52. He shall invite the white people who are among the Mandanas to be present at the council in order to give more weight and solidity to the motive of the convocation, and each one shall cement the peace and friendship respectively (the chief of the Mandanas being at the front), with the calumet of peace.

53. *Señor* Truteau declares by these presents to accept and to find agreeable these instructions given by *Señor* Clamorgan, which are conformable to the wishes of the Company, to put them in observance and execution at all times, unless by contrary orders from him, or from any other person representing him, he nevertheless being free to act alone in an unforeseen case, in a manner which shall be the most advantageous for the Company, for the interests of which he is held accountable by the charge and direction which has been entrusted to him, but he shall not ignore the aforementioned articles to the numbers of fifty-three and this one included, being likewise most essentially obliged to execute every new order or instruction, which *Señor* Clamorgan may issue for the Company, in whatever manner that may be, without being able to ignore it.

Drawn in duplicate in St. Louis of Illinois in good faith, the 30th of June, 1794, in the presence of the Lieutenant-Governor of this province.

Santiago Clamorgan, Antonio Reyhle, Juan Bautista Truteau. Examined and approved by us. Lieutenant-Governor Zenon Trudeau.

Today, the 25th of November, 1794, we, Santiago Clamorgan, Antonio Reyhle, Directors of the Company of the Missouri, have come to the hall of the Governor, where *Señor* Don Zenon Trudeau, Lieutenant-Governor, has communicated to us in writing the intentions of *Señor* Baron de Carondelet concerning Articles 18 and 19 of the instructions given by us to the agent of our Company for the upper Missouri, as the consequence of which the said articles are null and void, it being forbidden to put them into execution, as this is essential for the security and tranquillity of the new kingdom of Mexico, against which the nations with which we might have commercial relations would perhaps turn their arms.

SANTIAGO CLAMORGAN
REYHLE
ZENON TRUDEAU.[7]

[7]The A.H.N., Est., leg. 3900 copy contains the signature of Carondelet.

XIX

Carondelet to Las Casas, November 24, 1794[1]
[Extract]

Most Excellent Sir: Complying with the order of June 16 last, by which Your Excellency ordered me to give you in the greatest detail all the information that may be gathered concerning the condition and consistency of Louisiana; and the respective location of its places, forts, and suitable ports, and other points, the knowledge of which is necessary for the plan of defense adaptable to the circumstances of this province be examined by a board of generals: in accordance with His Majesty's wishes, I have ordered the accompanying map prepared,[2] which has been drawn from the most trustworthy plans that could be obtained since I have taken possession of their government. For all the maps printed both in England and in the United States and in France, are absolutely false, especially in regard to the course of the Mississippi and Missouri Rivers; besides which the settlements, both Spanish and American, which have grown up since the printing of those maps, could not be noted therein.

[1]Written in Spanish. This is Carondelet's military report on Louisiana which is found in many places, viz: British Museum, Additional Manuscripts, volume 17567, folios 22-63 verso; Carondelet to Aranda, no. 129 reservada, New Orleans, November 24, 1794 in A.H.N., Est., leg. 3897; enclosed in Carondelet to Alcudia, no. 48 reservada, New Orleans, November 24, 1794 in A.G.I., P. de C., leg. 2354 (there is a supplement to this report in this same legajo), etc. It is printed in English translation in J. A. Robertson, Louisiana under Spain, France and the United States (Cleveland, 1911), I, 294-345; extracts published in Houck, Spanish Régime in Missouri, II 9-17; and in its entirety but inaccurately by F. J. Turner in the American Historical Review, II, 475-505. The translation here given is taken from Robertson op, cit. See Nasatir, "Anglo Spanish Frontier on the Upper Mississippi 1786-1796" Iowa Journal of History and Politics, XXIX (1931), 183-187.

[2]Carondelet in his dispatch no. 48 reservada, to Alcudia, dated New Orleans December 1, 1794, says he was remitting a map of the Provinces of Louisiana and West Florida to accompany a copy of his military report. Draft in A.G.I., P. de C., leg. 2354.

Louisiana, which extends from twenty-nine degrees north to more than fifty degrees comprehends some thousand leagues between the mouths of the Mississippi, or the ocean, to the source of that river. This is the boundary unquestionably recognized by England in Article 6[VII] of the treaty of peace of 1763. In virtue of that treaty Spain may contest with the English and Americans their commerce with the savage nations who live above forty-four degrees. But I consider that the attention and efforts of Spain should be limited to the conservation of the dominion of the Mississippi to the St. Peter [San Pedro] River, located in the same latitude so long as the increase of the population of the settlements of Illinois, which are yet to be considered as in their infancy, does not permit of competition with the English of Canada, and especially with the Americans. The latter, advancing with an incredible rapidity toward the north and the Mississippi, will unquestionably force Spain to recognize the Missouri as their boundary within a short time, and perhaps they will pass that river, if the plan which I proposed to His Majesty in my secret despatch, number thirty-six, of June third last, and directed to the ministry of state, is not adopted.

Supposing that Louisiana extended no farther than the Missouri, it would be sufficient to glance at the map in order to recognize its importance with respect to the preservation of the internal provinces of New Spain and the kingdom of Mexico, which the Mississippi and Missouri Rivers encircle from the gulf almost to the South Sea. At least from the relations of various traders and travelers, who have lately entered by way of the Missouri, among savage nations of whom we have scarcely any information, it must be inferred that that mighty river, which is navigable in all parts, takes its rise a short distance from a very lofty chain of mountains not more than forty leagues from the South Sea. It is even inferred that another large navigable river is found at the foot of the same mountains, which empties into the above-mentioned sea. I trust that information in regard to this particular will soon be extended by means of the efforts of the company of discovery which has just been formed at St. Louis of the Illinois, and the reward which I have promised to him who penetrates to the above mentioned sea by way of the Missouri, and brings back definite information of its location, and the strength of the Russian settlements in case they are near that part of the coast.[3]

St. Louis of the Illinois

I have left until now to treat of the post of St. Louis of the Illinois. It is the capital of the other towns of that district. Wherefore, I shall note

[3]See documents IX and X, and Nasatir, "Anglo Spanish Rivalry on the Upper Missouri" *Mississippi Valley Historical Review,* XVI, (1929).

that, located on the west bank of the Mississippi, five leagues from the Missouri, and five hundred leagues from the capital, it is supplied by several industrious merchants, who are comparable to those of the capital. They would have an immense fur trade with the nations of the Missouri, if they were favored with free trade with the capital and against the English of Canada, who usurp that trade and daily introduce themselves in greater number upon said river and among the nations living near it.

A fort garrisoned by fifty men on the St. Peter [*San Pedro*] River, which is one hundred and twenty leagues from St. Louis,[4] and another fort on the Des Moines River, forty leagues from the said St. Louis, could entirely cut off all communication of the English with the savage nations of the west bank of the Mississippi, and of the Missouri—a trade so rich that notwithstanding the enormous distance of five hundred and more leagues of wilderness to cross with their merchandise and the furs which they receive in exchange, the London Companies which engage in it do not fail to reap profits of a hundred percent.

If the two forts above mentioned were established, many settlers would flock to their vicinities, both from our settlements and from Canada, and from the banks of the Ohio. Within a few years they would have several posts in those districts more populous than that of St. Louis at present, and could serve to protect the part of Louisiana higher up on the Missouri from the usurpation of the English and Americans.

The commerce and trade of the Missouri would produce—without imposing any burden on the royal treasury and without extraordinary effort—immense wealth for Louisiana, and would afford the most solid wealth of all to the state, in a considerable product founded on the agriculture, industry, and consumption of a large population. Such advantages do not require or expect more than the protection of the government, and above all else, a free trade with New Orleans. The latter place must necessarily become some day the trade center of a very vast continent with the other nations of the world.

Since the town of St. Louis of the Illinois is surrounded by very brave savage nations, who are more industrious than ours of Lower Louisiana; and since it is open to the assaults of the Americans and English, in case of a rupture with them; and since it is at the same time the trade center of Upper Louisiana; it ought to be encircled by a good stockade, with its banquette and corresponding glacis. The first should be defended at the two angles which look on the camp of the quadrangle, by two good redoubts faced with stone; and at the center by the small fort now in existence. A portion of its inhabitants being men [capable of bearing] arms would serve for its defense. Consequently, I consider that if four companies be detached

---

[4] These forts had been suggested earlier by Perez and Miró.

from the battalion of New Madrid for St. Louis, and from which detachments would be provided for the St. Peter and Moine [i.e., Desmoines] Rivers, they would suffice to cause the dominion of Spain to be respected throughout Upper Louisiana. And should His Majesty consider it proper for those detachments to be recruited from foreigners who should offer to serve five years in them provided that a constant ration be promised them, and who should be married or should marry and devote themselves to the cultivation of the soil for another five years during which they would be compelled to serve as militiamen, I am convinced that the battalion would always be full. That would obviate the great difficulties and save the great expenses necessary to transport the troops by the river to places so remote.

XX

TRUDEAU TO CARONDELET, ST. LOUIS, NOVEMBER 26, 1794[1]

Number 202

I am sending Your Excellency three memorials from that number of traders requesting exclusive trades with the Indian nations of the Missouri; one of them, Santiago de la Iglesia[2] is certain that he has discovered the Mandans and that for this reason he deserves the favor that he asks. However, this would be going against the Missouri Trading Company which has decided to place its first establishment in this nation where nevertheless the discoverer might be permitted to enter with whatever goods he wished and as he did this year, with articles that the Company advanced and supplied him with. In addition the Company has offered him the opportunity to take an interest in all its operations.[3] The memorial of Meunier and Roland[4] who point out the losses they will suffer from voiding their licenses to the Ponca nation for four years, which was made void on the just representations of the Commissioner of Trade [sindico del comercio], does not deserve attention unless Your Excellency wishes to look with compassion on the expenses they have incurred for the four years, because they counted on this consideration; that they might be granted a license for the coming year, so that they will not lose too much.

The third memorial, that of Don Bentura Collell,[5] for the Kansas nation, points out the loss he suffered with the said Garro and this is a

---

[1]Written in Spanish. Bancroft Library, printed in Nasatir, "Spanish Exploration of the Upper Missouri" in *Mississippi Valley Historical Review*, XIV (1927), 62-63. For the reply see Chapter III, document II.
[2]Document XIII.
[3]See Nasatir, "Jacques D'Eglise on the Upper Missouri" in *Mississippi Valley Historical Review*, XIV (1927), 51-52.
[4]Document XVI.
[5]Document XVII.

fact. If it is a sufficient reason or not, you will decide, but the other traders would find themselves deprived of the small profits that the Missouri yields.

May God keep Your Excellency many years. St. Louis, November 26, 1794.

Zenon Trudeau [rubric]

To the Baron de Carondelet.[6]

---

[6]In dispatch no. 204, dated November 26, 1794 (A.G.I., P. de C., leg. 30) Trudeau again asked for nine *patentes* and nine small and large medals for "two *pueblocillos* of the Ricara nation and seven of the Mandan nation, where the Missouri Company will have dispatched its second expedition at the end of the coming March". The new model *patentes* granted to the Osage chiefs by Carondelet had created envy among the chiefs of other tribes. The relation of *patentes* and medals for the chiefs of the Big and Little Osages, dated November 17, 1794 is in A.G.I., P. de C., leg. 127, but was most likely enclosed with Trudeau's letter no. 204 cited above. Carondelet replied on January 28, 1795, sending Trudeau the *patentes* solicited by the Osage chiefs, and nine blank commissions for the Ricaras and Mandans and flags for which Trudeau had asked the governor. Carondelet to Trudeau, New Orleans, January 28, 1795, A.G.I., P. de C., leg. 2364. See Chapter III, document IX.

In Trudeau's dispatch no. 209 also dated November 26, 1794 (A.G.I., P. de C., leg. 30) the lieutenant-governor proposes the appointment of Antoine Soulard as surveyor and remits some maps drawn by Soulard among which was a map of the Missouri river, a photostat of which is in the present editor's collection.

XXI

REMARKS ON THE MANNERS OF THE INDIANS LIVING HIGH UP THE MISSOURI

[BY J. B. TRUTEAU][1]

. . . They have a singular kind of polygamy among them. If a man take a woman to wife who has several younger sisters, it is common for him to marry them all in succession, as fast as they become old enough. I have seen several who had as many as six wives, and all these sisters.

A young Indian seldom however lives long with his first wife. This is so much the case, that by the time he is thirty years old, he has perhaps cohabited with ten different women, and abandoned them. After that age, they usually grow more permanent in their attachments. The men generally are allowed the liberty of divorcing their wives when they please, and of marrying again. The women have not the freedom of doing this until

---

[1]Translated from a manuscript of Jean Baptiste Trudeau [Truteau] put in the possession of Doctor Mitchill by Mr. Nicholas Boilvin and published in *Medical Repository*, second hexade, VI, (New York, 1808), 52-56; 120-124 (parts here published, pp. 121-124). See also Truteau's "Description of the Upper Missouri" in *Ibid.*, III, 313-315 (November 1805-January 1806) and A. H. Abel [ed.] "Trudeau's [Truteau's] Description of the Upper Missouri" in *Mississippi Valley Historical Review*, VIII (1921), 149-179; *infra*, Chapter IV document I. I have several photostats of the several articles printed and/or reprinted in the *Medical Repository*, a file of which periodical is in the Lane Medical Hospital Library of Stanford University located in San Francisco. The account here given is taken from the reprint published under the editorship of G. Hubert Smith in the *American Anthropologist* n.s. XXXVIII (1936), 566-568.

after they have been deserted by their first husband. Then they have full range and power to act as they please. Accordingly these women take new husbands as often as their curiosity or convenience prompt them. After a woman becomes more advanced in life, she attaches herself to some one man, and he is commonly that one by whom she has had the greatest number of children. If a man quits a woman by whom he has had a number of children, he only takes away his arms with him; but the horses and other things remain with the wife.

When a young woman has lost her husband by wars or otherwise, and there are surviving brothers of the husband, one of them marries the widow, or rather has the right to do so. It must be observed, however that this takes place only among the savages who value themselves most highly in keeping up an observance of their ancient customs. The Indians to whom we relate the circumstances of our marriages, are wholly at a loss to comprehend how white men, possessing so much understanding and knowledge, should be so blind as not to see that marriage is a source of pain and torment to them; they look upon it as a monstrous thing for a man and woman to be so indissolubly bound together as never to get loose. In short, talk to them as we please, they remain unalterably persuaded that white men are the slaves of women. There are few Indian females who are constant and faithful to their husbands, but are much given to intrigue and incontinence. This is however not equally the case with all the nations; for among some of them, the women are more reserved and chaste.

The Panis, Mandanes, Ricaras and Bigbellies, are somewhat more than ordinarily indifferent as to their women.—No such sentiment as jealousy ever enters their breasts. They give this reason for it, that when a man dies he cannot carry women with him to the regions of the dead; and that they who quarrel, fight, and kill each other about the possession of a woman, are fools or mad-men. They are so firmly convinced of this, that many of them take a pride in treating some of the considerable men among them with their youngest and handsomest women. So true is this, that husbands, fathers and brothers, are importunate with the white men who visit them, to make free with their wives, daughters and sisters, particularly those who are most youthful and pretty; and in consideration thereof accept a few baubles or toys. Indeed both the girls and married women are so loose in their conduct, that they seem to be a sort of common stock; and are so easy and accessible that there are few among them whose favours cannot be bought with a little vermillion or blue ribbon. This kind of commerce is carried on to a great length by our young Canadian traders. The consequence of these libertine manners is the venereal disease. This is very frequent among them; but the Indians cure it by decoction [concoction] of certain roots. I have seen some that were rotten with it, cured in six months.

258

When menstruation happens, the woman goes out of the hut, makes a fire by herself, and cooks her food alone. No person takes any of her fire on any account, not even to light a pipe with, for fear of bringing some misfortune upon himself. Their war-mats and Physic-bags are at these times carried out of the house, and suspended from the end of a pole in the open air, until the operation is over. While the women are in this situation they are very careful not to enter any cabin where there is a sick or wounded person; lest the patient's recovery should be retarded. When a woman finds herself with child, she receives the embraces of her husband no longer, but abstains from them entirely until thirty days after her delivery. There are, as may be supposed, exceptions to this: but such women are considered as behaving foolishly, and endangering both the lives of mother and child. When a pregnant woman finds her labour approaching, she withdraws to the hut built for the lying-in business, at all places where they have a stationary settlement: some old women follow her and give her all the help they can. But parturition is effected without the aid of a midwife; for they bring forth their young ones with a facility of which our civilized ladies have little idea. The term of their confinement seldom lasts more than two days. And if the party should find it necessary to march, the woman's lying-in never detains them half a day. For the mother, as soon as the child is born and swaddled, travels with the assistance of some of her friends, the whole day's journey to the place of encampment. And the next day after the infant is brought into the world, she plunges and washes it in water, both winter and summer. Then she wraps it in a piece of Bison-skin and ties its back to a plank about three feet long. The women nurse their children themselves, and as they never wean them, they suck as long as they please.

XXII

JOURNAL OF TRUTEAU ON THE MISSOURI RIVER, 1794-1795[1]

This first part of my journal will inform you truthfully about everything that happened to me from my departure from Illinois until my arrival at the Poncas to betake myself from there to the nations further up.

---

[1]This is Truteau's journal of his trading trip to the Upper Missouri. The first part, June 7, 1794-March 26, 1795, of his journal is in A.G.I., P. de C., leg. 187, and was well edited by J. F. Jameson in *American Historical Review*, XIX, (1914) 299-333. This part was sent to Carondelet on June 4, 1795 (Chapter III, Document X). The second part (actually the third part) of his journal from May 24 to July 20, 1795, has been translated and edited from a copy in Washington, D. C. by the late Mrs. N. H. Beauregard in the *Missouri Historical Society Collections*, IV, 9-48. Both parts of the journal, but beginning with August 25, are found in English translation in the *South Dakota Historical Collections*, VII, 412-474. I have here printed the entire in English translation. I have translated the first portion from the French text in the *American Historical Review* and have carefully checked the translation of the remainder of the first part of the journal. It is not necessary here to fully edit the entire journal as that has already been done, except to suggest that Truteau's "Descrip-

I have marked my route exactly, the number of larger rivers from the mouth of the Missouri to the Ricaras nation and their distance. Instead of seeing there a happy and favorable beginning to your enterprise, you will find there only disenchantments and circumstances to the detriment of the Company.

The loss of a part of your merchandise at the hands of the Poncas and the Sioux, the insults and violences that I underwent from the Mahas and Poncas chiefs, the excessive expenses I had to make to feed nine men among the harshest nation of this whole river, bring a considerable damage to the Company. I have added at the end of the journal the inventory of the [skins, illegible word] and utensils that I am sending you.

You will have a journal written incorrectly, and dirty. Overwhelmed the whole winter by the savages, who crowd in our cabin from morning to evening, I can only write at night when I [illegible].

It will be easy [for you] to judge, *Messieurs,* [illegible] concerted project, and [illegible] in surety orders and instructions of the conduct given for their [illegible] easier to dictate on the [project] than to carry out.

Journal of the agent of the Company of Upper Missouri
on his route to betake himself to the Mandan nation.

I embarked the 7th of the month of June, 1794, at the city of St. Louis of Illinois, in a pirogue equipped with eight oarsmen, to betake myself to the Mandan nation, situated on the upper part of the Missouri and to make an establishment proper for the fur trade with all the nations that I might discover beyond the Poncas nation, entrusted with the interests of the Company of Upper Missouri, represented by Mr. Clamorgan its director, with the permission of Mr. Don Zenon Trudeau, lieutenant-governor of Illinois.

On the 8th I arrived at St. Charles on the Missouri. Some business delayed us the next day the whole day long. The 10th I left and camped some leagues higher up. The 11th, 12th, 13th, and 14th, little progress because of contrary winds and rain.

The 15th of the month I camped at the Gasconade River.

The 16th five leagues further up. The 17th on Bear Creek. There we were stopped on the 18th by the rain and the wind. The 19th, camped several leagues further up than the Great Osage River.

---

tion of the Upper Missouri" (Chapter IV, Document I) be used in connection with the journal. I have summarized Truteau's activities based upon his journal and many other letters in Nasatir, "Anglo-Spanish Rivalry on the Upper Missouri" in *Mississippi Valley Historical Review,* XVI (1929), reprint pp. 13-19. This account of mine, revised in the light of but little additional material, is contained in part III of the INTRODUCTION to this volume. Several letters and documents relating to Truteau are given in this and succeeding chapters. Truteau's instructions is document XVIII.

The waters began to rise rapidly. I will not mention here the route for every day until the entrance of the Kansas River. I have been delayed so often by the force of the waters and the continual rains, that the details would be too lengthy.

I will simply mark only the names of the outstanding rivers and their distance from the entrance of the Missouri to the entrance of the Kansas river.

The Gasconade River is 30 leagues away, the Grand Osage 40; 20 leagues further up is the Mine River, all three to the left in ascending. One finds five leagues further up the two Chariton Rivers and nine leagues from the latter the Grand River. To the right of the Missouri, 6 leagues further up have been living since several years ago the nations of Missouri and the Little Osages. The former have been almost entirely destroyed by the nations situated on the Mississippi. The latter took refuge higher up on the Great Osage River. 20 leagues higher up to the left, one discovers a vast prairie, called the Prairie of fire, which is estimated to be 100 leagues from the mouth of the Missouri. 10 leagues from there the Kansas river empties. On the same side, this river in the spring is navigable for more than 100 leagues from its mouth. It abounds in beaver, otter, and other wild animals. 80 leagues from the mouth is the village of the Kansas; good hunters and good warriors.

10 leagues further up issues [illegible] which the Republican Pawnee inhabit.

I passed the Kansas River the 12th of July. The 13th I camped on the Little Platte River, 5 leagues further up to the right of the Missouri River. The 14th I camped on the Parques. The 15th the first old village of the Kansas, 12 leagues from the entrance of their river.

The 16th, 17th, and 18th stopped at the same place by a heavy rain, which did not cease until the 19th in the morning. I thought I would perish by the water that time. I spent that day drying out skins for covering, already well damaged by the rains and the excessive heats we were undergoing.

I shall say in passing that everyone who embarks on long trips, in the summer season, should take precautions with good tarpaulins to cover their equipment and not with deer or ox [buffalo] skins, which, in spite of all possible care and the time which one spends in drying them, rot promptly in the heats of summer and expose the merchandise to being damaged by the ravages of the weather. This is a thing which the director of the company had not well provided for, having made me leave with bad skins, half spoiled and small, old, torn tarpaulins.

On the 20th I left this place and I traveled the whole day. The 21st I camped at the 2nd old village of the Kansas 12 leagues from the first one. The water rising every day with force, reaching waist high [demy écorres (sic) possibly á demi-corps] my oarsmen were overcome with weariness, being constrained, from morning until evening, to row with all their strength without stopping. The 22nd, we camped on the great bend. The 23rd, stopped by the rain. The 24th, 25th, and 26th traveled. The 27th, rain. The 28th, 29th, and 30th, en route. The 31st I discovered a recently abandoned summer hunting encampment, along the Missouri, of the Otoctatas nation.

I was very much afraid of meeting them on my route for it is certain they would have detained me.

Their great chief, called le Sac de Médécine, having gone to the Illinois, and not having yet returned, his people would have held me until his arrival.

This chief would have absolutely prevented me from going further, for I found out afterwards that on his return he had sent couriers to the Mahas and the latter to the Poncas, to have me pursued, exhorting them not to let me reach the nations of the Upper Missouri. The delays that the rain and the force of the waters caused me on the way made me avoid falling into their hands, for they had spent the months of June and July on the banks of the Missouri.

The 1st of August, wishing to let the savages, whom I was afraid of meeting, go further away, and my people have several broken oars, we spent the day there in the same spot making oars.

The 2nd, 3rd, and 4th of the month I traveled. The 5th, stopped by the rain. The 6th I dried our skin covers. That day Mr. Jacques d' Eglise arrived, coming from Illinois. He rendered to me the parole of the commander of Illinois, consisting of four letters for two chiefs of the Ricaras, a Sioux chief and a Cheyenne chief, three medals, a flag, four carrots of tobacco, a barrel of powder and the bullets, to add to the three flags and a medal with which I had already been entrusted.

He also handed over to me the letters and the new instructions that the director of the Company was sending me, in which I was enjoined to give to Mr. Quenneville, at the entrance of the Kansas River, the 26 trading guns which were entrusted to me. I was not able to do it, being nearly 100 leagues away from him. I offered them to Mr. Jean Monier even as I had been asked to do. He did not want them. I proposed to Mr. Jacques d'Eglises to accompany us in traveling. He answered me that being late in the season, he could suffer no delay without injuring himself greatly. That he had provided himself with four men, he making five, a small not very heavily loaded canoe to betake himself promptly to the beaver hunting grounds: that being provided with good tarpaulins for covers, he could travel during the rain, which I could not do, that with his little pirogue he would easily pass the villages, even at night and also the back passages which are on the way; that finally it was impossible for me to follow it [d'Eglises' pirogue] and for him to wait for me, that when they will have arrived at the Arikara village, where he well expected to be detained until my arrival, he would send some Frenchmen and savages with provisions to me. The next day, 7th of the month, we set out together. He slowed up his pace that day for me. I saw very well, by the lightness of his load, he being able to avoid the big bends that I was obliged to frequent, that I could not follow him. I begged him three hours after stopping to think about means by which I could save my guns from the hands of the Otos, Mahas, or Poncas. The month of August is the month when these nations usually return to their villages after the summer hunting.

I strongly doubted that I could pass them before their return. Thus the seizure of the guns by either the ones or the others was inevitable. Mr. Jacques d'Eglise had a great deal more hope of avoiding them than I did. I consulted him on the subject. I asked him if he wished to take them up to the Ricaras in his canoes and then return them to me on our first meeting. Mr. Jacques d'Eglise told me, that in order to render service to the Company he would take them willingly, but without incurring any risk, that he would bring them to the villages of the Arikara and further if it were necessary, without requiring any payment for his carrying and service; that if he delivered them successfully he would sell them for the Company's account; that in case I cannot betake myself this autumn either to the Ricaras or the Mandanes, he would deliver to me the proceeds the first time he saw me. Having told me that the guns were not very valuable among the nations of the Upper Missouri, I urged him not to sell them at less than 10 big beavers or otters; which he promised me.

Thus, *Messieurs,* I thought I did well, by all the reasons I have mentioned above, to dispose of the guns into the hands of a man whose merit you yourself have recognized.

The 8th day of August we traveled. I was camped at the entrance of the Platte River. Mr. Jacques d'Eglise left us. I saw them no more.

The Platte River empties into the Missouri 200 leagues from the Illinois. From the Kansas River to this river one finds three others which are navigable only in the springtime, when the snows melt and for a short distance from their mouths.

The first, named the Great Nemaha, is 50 leagues further up than the Kansas River; 10 leagues from the latter, the Little Nemaha; both on the left ascending. 15 leagues further up to the right empties a river called the Nishnabotna.

The Platte River empties into the [Missouri(?)] on the left in ascending; it is very wide, not very deep. It runs rapidly; its bottom is full of moving sand; it is not navigable except with very small hunting canoes.

12 leagues from its mouth lives the Otactatas nation, good warriors and good hunters. 25 leagues further is situated the village of the great Pawnee, cowards and poor hunters; 30 leagues from there, on a river which empties into the Platte River, live the Panimahas, good warriors and not hunters. The traders who barter furs with the Pawnee nations are obliged to have their merchandise transported on horseback from the entrance of the river to their village and to bring down the furs that they obtain from them in the spring in ox skin canoes to the Missouri, where they usually have pirogues in reserve.

The skins they obtain from them in exchange for the merchandise are beaver, otter, wolf, fox, and cat skins, robes and withered cow skins, in abundance.

The 9th, 10th, and 11th, I traveled. The 13th, strong wind, little progress. The 14th, 15th, and 16th, on the road with fine weather. The 17th stopped by the rain. The 18th I camped on the Little Sioux River 50 leagues further up than the Platte River. Here we find the waters more shallow, and the currents less strong. The 19th, on the march until noon; some storms, added to contrary winds, stopped us that day. I traveled the 20th and 21st. The 22nd and 23rd contrary winds, little progress. The 24th I approached the village of the Mahas with caution, afraid of being discovered by someone of that nation, who would have prevented me without fail from going further. The policy of the savages of this river is to prevent communication between us and the nations of the Upper Missouri, depriving them of munitions of war and other help that they would receive from us if we made our way there easily. They keep these distant people in a continual fear of their fire arms.

Thus they kill them, massacre them for no reason, make them slaves, chase them from their own territory, without their hardly daring defend themselves, having no resource but flight; so much do they fear the nations provided with fire arms. This is an advantage which the former know how to profit from very well, and keep, by closing the ways to us as much as they can.

I therefore passed this village at nightfall, I camped about 2 leagues further up; the darkness prevented me from going further.

We saw on the banks of both sides of the river a number of tracks of men who had crossed several days earlier. I learned later that they were Sacques who had come there *en parole*.

The village of the Mahas is situated in a beautiful prairie at about a league's distance from the Missouri and 280 leagues from the Illinois. From the Platte River to this village, the waters of the Missouri run less rapidly than in the lower part of this river. The turns are long and frequent, so that a man on foot can travel a distance of land in one day that a well equipped pirogue could not make in 4 or 5 days by water.

There are no important rivers from the Platte River to the village of the Mahas.

The[2] 25th [August, 1794], I embarked at dawn of day and went into camp at the Big Sioux River, on the right of the Missouri six leagues above the village of the Omahas [Mahas].

This river is able to carry only hunting canoes. We found this day a very swift current and many bad passages because of short sandbars. The 26th, rain, very little travel.

The 27th I camped above the great bend estimated at twelve leagues from the Omahas [Mahas].

The 28th I proceeded until noon. The rain stopped us the rest of the day and it continued all night. The next day, the 29th, we dried our blankets a part of the day. The 30th and 31st of August and the 1st of September advanced in beautiful weather. The 2nd and 3rd rainy weather, little travel. I set out and camped three times the same day. The 4th in the morning our hunter, Noel Charron, killed a deer at the mouth of the James River, on the right of the Missouri. This river is forty-five leagues above the village of the Omahas. It is navigable only in little boats.

I spent a part of the day drying over the fire the flesh of the deer which would soon spoil, a necessary precaution not only to avoid fasting but in order not to be obliged to fire our guns in dangerous places. For more than ten leagues below the village of the Omahas, we had carefully extinguished our fires and every morning we threw the wood of our leanto into the fire, taking great care to leave as little trace as possible. The 4th [5th] advance until two or three hours after noon. The rain obliged me to camp on an island, named Chicot Island, at four leagues above the James River. The 6th of the month I caused our blankets to be dried on another island named Bon Homme Island at three leagues above the first. The 7th I advanced the entire day. The 8th, 9th, and 10th, little travel on account of contrary winds. The 11th I embarked in the early morning; our hunter this day killed a deer which gave us great succor.

Having for food only about a *minot* and a half of maize and fifty pounds of flour for nine men, I have yet over a hundred leagues to make in order to reach the Arickaras, constantly impeded by bad weather. I camped this day below the Niobrara River. The mouth of this river on the left of the Missouri, is estimated at seventy leagues from the great village of the Omahas, and also distant from the mouth of the Missouri three hundred fifty leagues, according to the reports of the savages. This river is the

---

[2]Here begins the journal as printed in *South Dakota Historical Collections,* VII, 412.

most abundant one in the entire continent of beaver and otter, but the waters are so swift that one is not able, so to speak, to either ascend or descend. The village of the Poncas is situated a league above, near the Missouri. The trade in pelts with this nation would be advantageous were it not that the Omahas, although their allies, offer an obstacle hindering the traders from reaching there in the autumn, suffering them only rarely to go in the spring to make the exchange of such merchandise as remains after they have taken out at least the better part.

They never failed to try to persuade the French that it was for the conservation of their profit and the safety of their lives that they detained them saying that this people called the Poncas were not civilized, that they only think of robbing, striking, or killing those who entered their country because of the great friendship which they had for the French they did not wish any evil to befall them; false talk which they gave us. The real motive which urges them to act is their own interest, for in depriving this nation of a direct commerce with us they would obtain all the best pelts, beaver and otter, for a mere bagatelle, which they sold again very dear, and they exchange these same pelts either with us or with nations situated on the Mississippi for good merchandise which they obtain very cheap.

The night of the 11th and 12th of September we were surprised by a furious tempest of wind, hail, and rain which forced us to unload our *voiture* in the darkness of the night. The 12th the rain continued all day. The 13th the weather was cleared by a strong wind from the west. I had some of the merchandise dried which had been soaked while unloading it in the night. The 14th I set out, approaching the village of the Poncas with suspicion. About three or four hours after noon I hid myself behind an island which reaches their village. I set out at the falling of the night and proceeded as late as we could, but having run on to flat sandbars [*battures*] we spent the night on the aforesaid without fires. This village is very difficult to pass without being seen, for besides there being prairie on both sides of the Missouri near their lodges there rise up hills from the tops of which they can watch up and down the Missouri for three or four leagues.

The 15th I set out in the early morning and I came to camp at a place called the tower at six leagues from the village of the Poncas.

The 16th camped on the *Isle aux Basques* five leagues above the tower. The 17th I advanced until noon. The wind from the west arose with such force that I was unable to proceed. Our food is diminishing, we are not killing anything in the lower part of the Missouri, the rain and the mountains of water have retarded us very much here. The furious and frequent winds in the vicinity of the prairie are holding us back.

I am in continual fear of some evil mishap, perhaps a lack of food, perhaps a meeting with some nations which will oppose us. The 18th I camped on the Isle of Cedars, twenty leagues above the *Rivière qui Court*

[Niobrara]. The 19th stopped a little farther up because of contrary winds. Our hunter killed for us today a roe. The 20th little travel because of the contrary winds and the bad shoals [battures].

The 21st we set out again. We killed this day a deer and a buck which give us an abundance of food. The 22nd I camped about two leagues below the White River on the left bank of the Missouri, estimated at fifteen leagues above the Isle of Cedars. In this length of journey are to be found many islands well covered with wood and abundant with wild game. The 23rd and the 24th stopped by a great wind and rain. The 25th little advance, 26th little progress, rainy weather. The 27th I advanced the entire day. We discovered a smoke which arose on the banks of the Missouri above us. My men thought that this might be the French and the Arikaras who had come before us and had built the fire, that it would be proper to respond to them, which fortunately I did not wish to do.

The 29th stopped by contrary winds. One of my men who had gone on a hunt reported to me that he had seen the track of a man who had passed the day before.

I went myself to find out. Having reached the place where the fires had been built I found the trail of a band of Sioux who were marching ahead of us. There appeared to me to be about ten or twelve lodges. I was very glad that they had not discovered us. The 30th I set out, and having crossed to the other bank I stopped at three leagues above to give the savages time to get away.

The food failed absolutely, after the White River we found nothing to kill, the Sioux having passed so recently. This band marching before us placed me in an embarrassing position. I feared, with just cause of falling into their hands. I was informed of the bad treatment which they had just received among the Arikaras at the hands of Lauson and Garaut, who had shot them. I know that the greatest satisfaction of the savages is for revenge. I was afraid of becoming a victim and in spite of all my suspicions and my precautions I was not able to avoid being partly their victim and by a narrow escape from being fully their victim.

Believing myself not far from the Arikaras, according to the indications which Quenneville and Jacques d'Eglise had given me, I determined to send two men across country to this nation as much to seek food as to invite them to come to me to guarantee me from the insults of the Sioux.

The men Pierre Berger and Joseph la Deroute whom I was sending to the Arikaras having supplied themselves with shoes and with some biscuits for their trip, were just rising up to start out when we heard a cry from the other side of the Missouri.

I saw many savages who were descending the opposite side toward us, shouting in the Sioux tongue who we were, where we had come from and where we were going. I replied in the same tongue that they could easily see that we were French.

They yelled this information immediately also to a number of others who arrived up and down the bank of the river.

In this occasion my embarrassment was not small. Flight was difficult and dangerous in this place, the wide sandbars which filled the Missouri, the waters being low at this season, the channel being narrow, which we were obliged to look for and which we found where the savages were, hindered me in doing it in safety. To continue going up they would have joined me again very quickly. To hide myself in this place in order to resist by arms would have been for a very little time only. We were needing food, and besides they were stronger in numbers and we would all perish there. In this extremity I pondered for some time over the course which I ought to adopt. My men were very much afraid. It was a little reassuring that I had some knowledge of this nation, of which I possessed the language passably, a fortunate resource for travelers in dangerous happenings.

I decided then to speak to them, but before approaching them I made sure that my arms were in good condition. I floated a flag on the rear of my pirogue. I had three shots of the blunderbuss fired and my men fired a volley with their guns. During these preparations they asked me without ceasing to come to them. I did not wish to do so without assurance of what nations of Sioux they were, if they were a war party or a hunting party, if they had some notable chief among them. I asked them these things in their own language. They were not a little surprised to hear me speak after this manner.

The spokesman rose up. He told me that he was of the nation of Yankton Sioux who lived on the Des Moines River. That he was not out for war but for the hunt and that the women and children would soon arrive and that I might come to them in safety.

I replied that I had very little to make me believe it and that they might deceive me. He threw up his hands toward the sun and bowed them to the ground, doing as witness that he spoke the truth. He then recited all the chiefs of his nation by their names. He recalled many deeds of which I had gained knowledge myself during the time when I had visited this people. He named for me all the French both old and new who had moved among them.

Without knowing that he spoke to me, he named me by the name which I had previously borne among them. All these correct citations, justified me in judging that he spoke the truth. As for his village, being known by this nation of the Sioux called Yanktons, savages sufficiently civilized, I had reason to hope, that I could withdraw more easily from them than from any other village of the Sioux.

But for yet better assurance of the truth, I demanded that two of his men only should cross a great sandbar which separated us. Three crossed by swimming. I made an advance toward them with three armed men. I recognized them for such as they had told me they were and they recognized me also. I caused them to smoke which they did with a good grace. At last they gave me every expression and assurance that no harm would befall me.

We took them to our pirogue where I gave them something to eat. We saw then arriving at the other bank of the river the women and all their baggage, which confirmed the statement that they were a hunting and not a war party.

I set out then with these three rascals in my conveyance. They wished to descend below where they had planned to put up their lodges. Having no shelter for my canoe in case of wind, I did not wish to do this. I set a course by marking out to gain a point of woods which appeared higher up. All these rascals following along the river, just like a pack of wolves following a buck as he is about to land, in order to devour him. Before arriving at the fatal point, I found a little channel of which the entrance was not sufficiently deep to accommodate our pirogue. All these tigers took hold of it and dragged it toward their encampment. All their flattering statements which they made to me, were not able to convince me of their sincerity and honesty. I knew too well the trickery and knavery of savages to place any confidence in them. This predicament in which I found myself forced me to appear joyful at having met them, although in my heart I detested the moment.

The orders which the directors of the Company had given me were to make alliances, give promises, open commerce with all the nations which I should discover above the Poncas. I ought then to seek them rather than to flee from them. But I protest that all *voyageurs* who undertake to gain access to the nations of the Upper Missouri ought to avoid meeting this tribe, as much for the safety of their goods as for their lives even. One will be able to understand that from what is happening to me here. Here I am then in their hands, in a channel nearly dry, without being able to advance or to return, my pretended friends from the Des Moines, having told me some truths. But they had hidden from me that they were only three lodges of their nation and that this band was largely composed of Teton Sioux, a ferocious people, little civilized, who wandered around constantly for food, filled with barbarous customs and manners. The vast prairies, which they cross north of the Missouri, were presently stripped of wild animals and they were obliged to come to hunt the buffalo and wild cows on the banks of the Missouri, and even to cross over to the west bank for hunting. These were lean and skinny. They had lived on roots and some wild

269

rice, which they had gathered on the banks of certain swamps which they had passed.

This is the sort of men among whom I had fallen. And thus I could not hope for any relief in the way of food. They were arriving in great numbers, and were putting up their lodges at the edge of a wood. They lit a great fire near to our conveyance and there all assembled. I started off by presenting them little pieces of tobacco, with great care to make them smoke it, some accepted it, others refused it, even to shake hands with me. I suspicioned evil from this refusal for among all these peoples the calumet is a symbol of peace and friendship.

They asked me where I was going. I told them I was going to the Arikaras. I was not able to hide it, for they saw that I was loaded with merchandise for trading. They raised a murmur among themselves at this news. I spared nothing in trying to soften the disposition of these wild beasts through my words.

I asked them if they had some notable chiefs in their band. They told me that they had none. I told them that their father, the great chief of the Spaniards, had sent me to the home of the Arikaras, that having been informed of their misery, and that of the Tetons, he had pity on them and wished to procure for them a charge of powder and a knife, that as soon as I had been to the Arikaras I would return to the Tetons in order for them to listen to the words of their Spanish father and to smoke the peace pipe. That they should be assured that they would be able to find all their wants in the village of the Arikaras in exchange for the hides which they would carry there.

They replied to me that the Tetons did not have one great chief greater than all the others. That each man was chief of his cabin; that we French did very wrong to carry powder and balls to the Arikaras. That this powder would be used to kill the Sioux. That the French who had already been to the home of the Arikaras were bad French, always talking evil against them, and exciting the Arikaras to kill them when they had gone there under promise and we were going to do the same. The rest of the day passed in some feast of bad wild rice which only the Yanktons gave us. They demanded some powder and balls in order to go on the hunt the next day, promising to give us the meat. I gave it to them. They wished to borrow all the guns of my men who let them take three. I was opposed to giving them any more. My friends of the Des Moines River made the demand. I foresaw that I would have absolute need of them in order to snatch myself from the scrape into which I had fallen.

It was necessary not to rebuke them harshly. The night had come, they all assembled around our fire. My men lay down in the pirogue and kept a good guard. I put up a little tent near the fire so that I could watch their actions and more easily hear their discourse whether good or bad. The

Yanktons approved all their words that I had spoken to them, saying that their chiefs had been at different times in the country of the French, that they had been well received by the great chief of the Spaniards, the father of all the Red skin nations. That since that time they had always had abundance of merchandise so useful to life. That the French were traveling over all the earth. That they rendered all nations which received them very happy and on the contrary the people whom the French did not frequent were miserable, exposed to die of hunger, and to be conquered by their enemies, from want of defensive arms which the white men alone were able to procure for them.

All this discourse hardly affected the dispositions of the ferocious beasts. They saw a great pirogue loaded with merchandise which it would be easy to seize through violence, therefore they persisted in their evil thoughts.

The Yanktons seeing them obstinate in wishing to maltreat us, said to them that they wished they would not do evil to me in particular; that I had visited their nation for a long time; that I was their ally and parent; that their chiefs and old men would reproach them if we were killed in their presence; that they had promised me through an oath to the sun and to the earth to get me to come to them that no evil would befall me; that I had smoked and eaten with them. The night passed with just such contests on one part and the other. The next morning they retired. The Yanktons alone remained with us. Some of them made believe they were going on the hunt and returned without having killed anything. I saw that my pledges were giving way. The one who had spoken for me took me into his lodge where he caused me to eat. He told me that the Tetons were bad men; that he feared much for me and my Frenchmen; that there were so few of their nation that they feared them themselves. I encouraged him to help me in this occasion. He promised that he would do his very best, but he told me that the French would open up the bad road by giving presents, that this was the only means to pacify the Tetons, all of whom had a bad heart, that they thought that I would think well of it, which is to say that I would spare nothing for our freedom. I told him that when some of the principal rascals who were on the hunt should return I would talk to them definitely. He led me to the conveyance and for a time awaited the return of the hunters, he called together all the young and old men, the women and children of all ages and each sex and obliged me to give to each individual, little and big knives, awls, combs, vermillion and other gifts of all kinds. One can easily judge that the expense was no little matter. I was in despair from such profusion. This however was not the worst point; what to do in a meeting so dangerous? What to offer them in defense in such simple words when they so little valued my words after this distribution. They brought some beaver and deer hides to me and

271

demanded to trade them for cloth, powder and balls. They crowded around the conveyance in a throng. My men had every possible difficulty in keeping off the robbers. They took from me powder, balls, cloth, white blanket, hatchet, pickax, vermillion, knives, etc., without giving me time to count their hides, yet less to settle on a price, in spite of any effort I made to resist them. This was a real pillage. My safe guards from the Des Moines river, were not in the least left out of it. The eagerness for booty in all these savages is a dominant passion. These forgot in a moment their oath and their care of me.

After this assault they retired, only some young rascals remaining who tried to make us mad.

One of them, called me into his cabin. While I was absent they stole two cooking kettles, and took two guns from my men.

I returned immediately to them, I swore, I prayed, I supplicated, but all in vain.

They told me that an old wicked man, supported by many boys his children and other relatives, had asked that these things be done—and he had used all his efforts in order to pillage me.

My embarrassment and my pain was unequalled.

I judged that the sooner I could get away from them the better. Some old women had warned me that they had sent couriers to warn other bands which were in the neighborhood, that they should come promptly to this place.

If they arrived before my departure it would be all up with my merchandise. In order to depart it was not only necessary to secure their consent but also their aid, in order to take our pirogue out of that confounded channel, nearly dry, into which they had dragged us.

I prepared them promptly and arranged on the shore the present that I was obliged to make them, which consisted of seven or eight ells of cloth, a barrel of powder, balls in proportion, four carrots of tobacco, two packets of knives containing two dozen each, four white blankets, four pickaxes, four hatchets, two sacks of vermillion, flints, wormscrews, hammers, etc. I asked the leaders to come. A part of them came, some refused, in the number of which was the infernal old man of whom I have spoken.

I placed on the sand the blue cloth, symbolic of the clear road which I demanded of them. I told them that I desired to leave that day. I took back the word which the great chief of the Spaniards, their father, had charged me to carry to the Arikaras, to the Teton chiefs, his children, which is done that I might render myself absolutely to following his wishes.

I asked them to send some young men to warn the great chief of their nation of my arrival among the Arikaras, that I would await them there the following spring, at the latest, that they should set about hunting beaver, otter and other peltries; that I would give to them in exchange [for] their needs; that they should have no fear that they would not be well received by me and by the Arikaras. That my heart was not like the other Frenchmen of whom they complained. I would take the Yanktons who knew me to witness. These last approved me but the demons of Tetons responded to me as insultingly as the day before and in addition telling me that they had no Spanish father. That they had sent couriers to all the bands of Sioux who were on the upper or lower river to warn them that they had found a great pirogue loaded with merchandise for the Arikaras. That I was foolish to desire to go among this nation which had run away in the middle of the summer, having been attacked by the savages of the North, having abandoned their lodges without giving themselves time to gather their crop. Do you think, they said to me, you can escape the hands of the Sioux, who border the Missouri on both sides, even to the village of the Arikaras and even above that. They are warned, they will hunt for you, they will rob and perhaps kill you, and your men, for, they said to me, the Tetons do not have a good disposition. Remain with us, build a house here for the winter. All the Sioux would come to trade with you many hides because of the desertion of the Arikaras. I did not wish to believe them. The *voyageurs* newly returned from the Arikaras having assured me that they were established in their habitations, going alternately by bands to hunt the buffalo, and knowing the savage fertile in ruses and lies, I judged that these had invented this news in order to deter me from the resolutions which I had to take myself there.

The Yanktons, not daring to express their thoughts openly, fearing to displease them, made signs to me to not accept their demands.

I took care not to accept them, after the bad treatment I had received from them, and because they were yet ready to commit the same offense again. I had much to fear over the arrival of some other brigands of this bad nation, who would have entirely robbed me, rather than consent to take up my residence among them. By what means would I be able to withstand an entire winter with these people which had a peculiar ferocity, who have no ties, who wander ceaselessly in a group, not being able to gather together in a village without stealing, fighting, killing, it may be for women, perhaps for the possession of horses of which one may have more than another. People filled with evil prejudices, attributing ordinary misfortunes, sickness, deaths, to the merchandise or food which they have received from us; men greedy for goods which they see without ever wishing to pay the value for it; violent tempers always ready to strike at the least contradiction which they may receive, who do not know such a thing as subordination and do not fear any stranger, who violate without scruple the words or assurance of peace and alliance which they give to or receive from their neighbors. What tyranny would they not exercise against the French whom chance has placed in their hands, and who they know very well are destined not for them but for their enemies? To what excess will the jealousy not carry them. The Sioux, insulted by Garaut and Lauson, have they not themselves the greatest reason for revenge? They would have robbed us not only of our merchandise, but also of our guns, and they would have left us to die of hunger if they had not taken our lives themselves.

I refused haughtily to accept that which they proposed. I told them that I wished to depart immediately, that they should come to learn what I would give them for the support of their wives and children. I asked them to give me back the two guns and two kettles that their men had taken, representing to them that we had nothing in which to cook our food. They replied to me that it was impossible that I could set out inasmuch as I and my men were seeking our own death. They all got up and carried away the present with bad grace, finding it not large enough.

We were then for some minutes alone. I was not able to go from this place without aid. To unload my pirogue in order to lighten it would be to expose it anew to theft and pillage. Time was pressing me. I could not see any more my men; the Yanktons, they had abandoned me. There unexpectedly appeared some old women who had known me on the Des Moines river, who told me again all the wicked designs that the Tetons had had concerning me and still had against us; that their men were opposed to these wicked designs because of me; that they assured me that there were five bands of this nation which would march before us on each side of the Missouri; that twenty two lodges of the same people would shortly set out from the neighborhood of the White River. They counseled me to march only during the night and to hide during the day, saying that if they would see us we would be lost. I promised them to do this. But I was not able to depart from this place, for immediately other women called loudly those here and caused the children who were near us to retire, I judged and not mistakenly that there was some evil gathering against us.

I promptly went up the bank, marched straight to the lodge of the one who had first given me the hand on the sandbar, and demanded of him what was going on.

He did not reply. I reproached him for having abandoned me against his promise. He told me that he did not have a contented heart, that the Tetons had divided the present among themselves. That neither he nor his men had received any part of it; that the old man, of which I have already spoken or his children had not been willing to be present at the sharing of it. Finally that he wished to strike against us.

I pressed him, getting him to promise to come with his men and aid me in leaving the place.

The old women of his lodge aided as they could, he set out and came with us, accompanied by six other of his men. Scarcely had we arrived at the conveyance when we heard a great noise in the savage camp; lamenting; cries of the women who were weeping; they were going to shoot the French. They all appeared to interest themselves in our conversation. It was perhaps as a recognition of the knives, awls, etc. that I had been forced to distribute among them the day before.

Many men appeared to us who were rushing here and there with arms in hand. Some were following them to oppose them in this evil plan. Those who accompanied me to the number of six, urged me to depart. I prayed them yet to aid us in getting our pirogue into deep water. I promised to give each of them a *brasse* of cloth, therefore they aided us in placing our conveyance in the deep channel with more celerity than in the coming in, although we were then many more people, because the approach of peril gives strength and courage to shun it. I then kept my word and gave them that which I had promised them.

I crossed immediately to the other bank. The sun was just setting. I then started up stream, always in sight of the rascals, thinking over in what manner I would be able to escape the hands of these tigers or their like.

In this place the river makes a bend—From the White river to the great bend 20 leagues, from the great bend to the Little Missouri 25 leagues, from the Little Missouri to the village of the Arikaras 15 leagues—from four to five leagues long, so that the savages which we had just left would be able to join us again by going over land in three or four hours. Taking a day for the route by water, I had every reason to believe that they would pursue me the next day with the same disposition in which I had left them. I felt assured that there were others above and below us whom I would not be able to avoid, it being impossible for us to navigate by night a river which is so shallow at this season, that we were often obliged to lighten our boat of the lead and other heavy loads, making little portages at certain places. Besides, according to the indications which Jacques d'Eglise and Quenneville had given me, and which I had traced on a piece of paper, concerning the size of the rivers which discharge into the Missouri from the mouth of the River Platte up to the village of the Arikaras, and other notable places, I would judge that we must be about forty league from the Arikaras.

It would be most unfortunate, after having come thus far in order to succeed, to turn back. To hide ourselves and our effects would not be possible. The savages whom I feared would be able to hunt all autumn in these places; besides we were without food. Hunger was tormenting us. There remained to me for all provisions about thirty pounds of flour and a quarter of a *minot* of maize. It was little for nine hungry men. In this extremity I could find no other way to do than to place what remained of our merchandise and our pirogue in hiding and all go overland to the Arikaras, who I was assured resided at all seasons in their village, proposing to return with a good escort to seek the pirogue and the merchandise. I executed this resolution, which was not at all times without some risk, for the Sioux might be able to find our hiding place and rob it. But I doubted that they would cross the river at this place; believing that we would continue our journey all that night and the next day, they would pursue us along the other bank of the Missouri which without doubt was the shortest and best way. For on the western bank at this place where I was going to hide our goods, the banks and rocks raised themselves so precipitously that the way there was impossible. We then traveled along these *cotes* for the distance of two leagues. Then we stopped and set about hunting the proper place for our plan. The moon which was just then full made it easy for us. At this moment it seemed that nature wished our safety for having penetrated by a little crooked foot path into a deep ravine, we found a cave, the most proper place in the world to do our hiding.

We promptly transported all our effects there. Having placed them in good order we returned to our pirogue. It was necessary to hide it, which would be not a little difficult for it was so heavy and so large that we were not able to drag it onto the ground in any place. We rowed it up as high as we could and sank it in the water by means of many holes which my men bored with an auger in the bottom of the boat and by a quantity of stones which they threw within it. This work finished the day approached. It was necessary to flee, fearing to be seen. We climbed many deep ravines filled with thickets, which tired us very much during the remainder of the night. At sun up we found ourselves on a vast prairie, where one could see only sky and earth.

We remained the entire day hidden in a hole without eating or drinking. In the evening pressed by thirst, we gained a little streamlet where we cooked pancakes from the flour which we carried with us.

It was the third day of the month of October. During the night we covered more than two leagues from the river out on the prairie and we marched the 4th the entire day without finding water. The 5th, pressed by hunger and thirst we approached the river running the chance of being discovered. We had the good fortune to kill a roe. We spent the remainder of the day and night in drying the flesh after having our hunger well satisfied. We saw the fires of the Sioux who were all above and below us and even around the part where we were.

None of us knew this country. We were not able to follow close to the river, fearing to be discovered. It was necessary to march two or three leagues at a distance, taking good care not to show ourselves on the heights. We did not find in the course of the day any stream where there was water to quench our thirst.

In the evening it was necessary to go out of our way more than two leagues to find water. Yet several times we found only some bad salty water. At length, in the day having the sun for a guide and in the night the stars, we marched five days with fear, thirst, and hunger, our feet always covered with stickers which the *voyageurs* call *pomme de requete* with which the surface of the prairie is covered.

The sixth day in the morning, the 9th of the month, we discovered the village of the Arikaras.

All contented, we believed our troubles ended, and our lives in safety, but our joy was not long in duration.

For having carefully examined, from a hill, the place where the lodges appeared, I could see no one around, not even any appearance of smoke coming from the top of their houses. I supposed at once that they were all empty, and that the Sioux who had captured us had spoken the truth. We continued our march and entered into the abandoned lodges. For more than two months the lodges had been in a ruined state and half burned by the enemy. We found a quantity of shoes, of tanned buffalo skins, and all sorts of utensils for their use, which they did not take time to hide or carry away in their flight. We passed the night very chagrined and worried over the future. Our hopes had fallen and our only resource vanished through the desertion of the Arikaras. Some of my men thought that it would be well to follow their road even to the place where they had stopped for the winter, others said it would be better to continue our route even to the village of the Mandans situated a little over a hundred leagues from here. I did not accept any of this advice. It was extravagant to undertake so long a journey in an unknown country without food, still more imprudent to give up to chance the merchandise placed in hiding, without knowing at what time we would be able to return. It might be found by the savages or damaged by injuries from the weather. I resolved to return there promptly; to descend the Missouri with caution even to the ordinary crossings of the Sioux, being determined to fight even to the death before allowing ourselves to be taken, either by water or by land by these demons.

The next day the 10th of the month, after taking a good supply of shoes and shoe leather, we retraced our footsteps.

We stopped in the neighborhood of three leagues from there where there appeared to be deer. One of my men found a deer which the wolves had killed, which made us a good repast. The 11th and 12th we frequented the same route which we had taken in going. We passed the night in a level country without water, fire, or food. The third day in the morning we arrived at a little river named the Little Missouri to the left of the Missouri. This river is very small. The water does not flow at this season of the year and we found it there only in holes. Seeing there the footprints of deer, my men asked me to remain there for a day or two in order to hunt and in order to rest themselves. I willingly consented, not having had anything to eat for two days and being fatigued with the journey which we had already made traveling both day and night. We remained at this place both this day and the next, the 14th of the month. My men killed two deer. The

15th, 16th, and 17th, we continued our journey with the same trouble about water, and always in the fear of being discovered by the Sioux whose fires we had seen very near us. The 17th we killed a very thin cow. My men took some parts of it. Finding ourselves near a water hole they cleaned the belly of the cow and made a sort of portable urn and filled it with water to drink on the march.

That afternoon we crossed a road where the Sioux had passed the day before. I followed it even to their encampment. There were twenty eight lodges of them. They appeared to be going toward the Little Missouri whence we had come.

God preserved us from meeting them, but I very much feared that they had passed near the place of our hiding. We knew upon our arrival at the Missouri that they had come from another part, and had crossed higher up. The 18th we marched along the banks of the Missouri until we came to the boat which we found just as we had left it.

Having bailed out the water, we descended to the hiding place of our merchandise which we found in the same condition. The next day, the 19th of the month I resolved to hide twelve or thirteen hundred pounds of lead, one hundred fifty pickaxes and hatchets, and one case containing four gross of knives. Two good reasons led me to take this position; the first, the waters being low at this season, I could not descend without a great deal of trouble, having a load so heavy as to drag on the sand; and if unhappily I met the Sioux, who were hunting on the lower river, it would be impossible for me to escape from their hands under cover of night, being so loaded.

The second, before returning in the spring my boat would be lighter and consequently I would be able to make better time. This hiding being accomplished, I set out and went into camp three leagues below.

The 20th we traveled down the entire day. Two hours before the setting of the sun two of my men going hunting saw the footprints of a man who had passed that same day. The next day, the 21st, our hunter, Noel Charron, having been on a hunt, returned soon to report to me that he had found the place where a deer had been killed, the blood of which still appeared on the leaves. I thought it was the Sioux who had come to hunt wild cattle and that their lodges were quite distant, even on the other bank of the Missouri. I was mistaken. I was nearer to them than I thought. I remained that day in the same place in order to see if I could discover where they were, without being seen. I myself tried to make the discovery in the evening. I neither saw nor heard anything. It was the third day that we had eaten nothing but rose-buttons, which we found here and there. My men weak from hunger, tried to boil two fresh deer hides, which we ate (bad feast). The 22nd in the morning a deer appeared on a sandbar near our encampment. We embarked in order to go to shoot it, with great intention, in our necessity, to kill it. Providence preserved us there from a new misfortune. The deer fled, and even so swiftly that we were not able to shoot it. We pushed on, thoughtful, chagrined with so many accidents and trouble. We were permitting ourselves to drift easily on the course of the waters, when we heard cries, howling of dogs being beaten. These cries came from the center of a thicket of trees which we were following. I promptly approached the bank. Reaching a high bank by the aid of some stumps I got off the boat and crept along even to a little hill where I could make discovery without being seen. I saw a number of women and children with their following of dogs and horses, who were coming from the edge of the woods at twenty arpents from us. I easily distinguished their language. I knew that this was a party of Sioux who were on the march, and who were marching on the prairie while going up the Missouri.

Having heard the voice of a man who appeared to be coming toward us, I hurried to embark and placed ourselves at a distance by force of our oars. The waters were so low that we could touch bottom at each stroke, but the point of the woods which was long and deep saved us from being seen by them. We forced our way ahead this day very late and the next day all day long. One of my men killed a little year old deer, which we ate at one repast. Arriving at some leagues below the White River, we felt a little more assured, being outside of the places most frequented by the Sioux. We found ourselves in the midst of wild beasts, sufficient for food. We made part of a day's trip. Deer, roe, and wild cattle hurried along the banks of the river in herds. Now we were in a great abundance of food after having been fasting.

I and my men are very much chagrined at not having been able to go to the nations where we had set out to go in the autumn, by the meeting with the Sioux and the flight of the Arikaras which had most contributed to our giving up.

Our hopes commenced to grow again, especially as we no longer lacked food, for I have had many discussions with my men, who had often believed themselves lost on the prairies or absolutely dead perhaps from hunger or from thirst, or by the hands of the Sioux, cursing the very moment when they had embarked on such a trip. I had always reanimated their courage through my word and example. But anyway the most infallible way to regain joyfulness and procure quietude in the minds of certain men, is to let them fill up their bellies. The only question now was to select a place convenient to pass the winter and live from the hunt, and to settle in a place not frequented by the Sioux or any other nation while awaiting the return of spring in order to ascend the Missouri again. I stopped in the neighborhood of ten leagues above the village of the Poncas, knowing that this nation at this season was away hunting wild cows and the Sioux never came to hunt on their territory, being their enemies. It was the 4th of November, when we chose a place for a winter home wishing ourselves to be well fortified against the attacks of the savages.

Always in the fear of some unforeseen event, I had them dig a very deep hole in the ground in order to place there the merchandise most advantageous to the nations of the Upper Missouri where I ought to be going, wishing to make a second hiding of the rest of the effects in the center of our cabin when it should be built, reserving only that which was absolutely necessary for us to live on.

The loss that I had received from the Sioux was great enough for the hides that I received from them did not come to two hundred pounds. This verification made, I set about burying the greater part of the stuff in the hole, after taking an inventory of it and putting it in good condition. My men, the better to hide the place, made a little hunting canoe above the opening so that the quantity of wood chips which was heaped up over it was effacing the least traces.

The 10th of the month the work was finished.

The 11th my men cut down trees for our winter cabin. The 12th our hunter, Noel Charron, being on a hunt as usual, returned bringing with him a savage. I was surprised at the sight of this man, for I had not expected to see any of them here.

I asked to what nation he belonged. He told me he was an Omaha; and that twenty-two lodges of his nation were encamped at some leagues below us, who would arrive the next day. The chief of this band is named by the French, Big Rabbit, and is also recognized as a great rascal.

I experienced a sharp grief over their arrival. I had not yet hidden all the merchandise which remained with us.

I foresaw all the bother they were going to carry on in order to procure ammunition for the hunt on credit, for they had already informed me that part of their village was out of powder, balls and other necessities. That no one had come to them from the French this autumn; that Jean Muniers had arrived there in the middle of the summer in order to obtain food to carry him to the Poncas; they had stopped him, but he was carrying so little merchandise that the greater part of their men were not able to have any of it; that the lack of food having no maize this year, had obliged them to set out and to disperse by bands on all sides in order to seek a living for the women and children who were half dead from hunger. In fact there came to us this day many men who threw themselves on our food like famished wolves. We had at that time scaffolds well filled with deer and turkeys and wild animals.

Towards the evening the chief Big Rabbit arrived who told me the same things that the first arrivals had told me. He told me that he and his people were very glad to have met with us; that the French alone are the support of all the red skin nations; that they felt today more than ever the necessity of having things better, failing absolutely to nourish themselves, through lack of guns, powder, balls, etc.; that the French only could procure them for them, (flattering and deceitful talk which they had continued to hold with the French since the first sight) seeking ceaselessly to deceive us, and to extort our merchandise by all sorts of means.

All the savages of this river, as elsewhere, I speak of those who have been visited by us, are shrewd and deceitful. They have more knowledge than many people believe. The chief Big Rabbit told me that the great chief named Toangarest, (in French, the Village Maker) was still with the man named Jean Muniers, hoping that the French would come in the last of the autumn, that this chief had been displeased when he had learned that I had passed his village without stopping, with a great boat loaded with merchandise for the nations of the Upper Missouri. I gave him an amplified story of what had happened to me at the home of the Sioux. I exaggerated the amount of merchandise which the Sioux had pillaged from me, for he did not fail on seeing our boat to say to me that it was not believable that so great a boat had carried only such merchandise as was apparent. I gave him to understand that the Sioux had robbed me of the greatest part and even of my cooking kettles. The hides of the Sioux which he recognized caused him to believe that I spoke the truth and then he bothered me no more on that score.

The 3rd of the month the old men, women and children arrived. It was true that they were out of food, eating only herbs, so they crowded around us when we ate our meals, fighting among themselves as to who should have our soup, gathering up the bones which we threw for them to gnaw on. It was a strange sight.

I conducted myself on this occasion so as not to irritate these hungry men, and not to expose ourselves to a certain shortage of things to eat. We gave them some of our food, distributing small portions principally to the children. They represented their misery to me, for the most of them had no guns and asked for ours to hunt deer which we did not like to do, but willing or not it was necessary to consent, for they took possession of them without waiting our approval and we found ourselves dependent upon them for food.

The next day they assembled to demand powder, balls, and knives on credit. I resisted their demands for a long time, representing to them that I had very few. They persisted which obliged me to give them some.

In order to avoid the tumult which arose when they took things by force, I consented to give them some, provided they would take only for twelve or fifteen hides for each hunter, which was carried out in an instant. The chief Big Rabbit and some of the *considérés* forced me to give them credit for thirty or forty hides. He made great promises for himself and his men, but I have some fear that he will deceive me.

They set out first for a hunt of wild cattle and returned at the end of fifteen days hunt loaded with dried meat. In recognition of the assistance which they had received from us, they sold me food at exorbitant prices. All the savages, and more than one among them, did not know or at least did not wish to recognize the benefits which they had received from us, believing that we were obliged to accommodate them.

The expense which I have been obliged to bear here for the nourishment of nine men is exorbitant. Not having any maize for food I am reduced to buy dried meat, bit by bit, from this mob, our hunter Noel Charron, not being able to kill anything among them, the wild animals having run away. They returned to the hunt for beaver and deer, they said in order to pay me well.

The 18th of December there arrived the great chief of the Omahas, [Blackbird] of whom I have spoken above. A repetition of surprise and displeasure for me. The arrival of the first inconvenienced me very much for our departure in the spring and occasioned me much expense, which I would not have had if he had not come, as much for food as for merchandise which I was forced from time to time to give him. The arrival of this last named chief put a climax to my difficulties.

This great chief of the Omahas [Blackbird] was the most shrewd, the most deceitful and the greatest rascal of all the nations who inhabit the Missouri. He is feared and respected and is in great renown among all strange nations, none of whom dare to contradict him openly or to move against his wishes. They do not set out either for war or for the hunt unless he has given his consent to it. His name is recited in all assemblages and speeches are made in his absence in the most distant places to which they go. All the neighboring tribes hear his word and crown him with presents when he goes to visit them. If any of his men acquire beautiful merchandise or beautiful horses and he appears to desire them they instantly give them to him. He never goes about on foot, but always mounted on the most beautiful horse in the village. He has slaves for his work, and better to say, they are all his slaves, for should he wish to sleep he has one or two hired attendants who gently rub his legs and feet while he sleeps. If these ordinary valets are absent, he presses into that service even the greatest and bravest of the tribe.

When it is time to awaken him it is necessary to do it with caution, being careful not to cry in his ears nor to stroke him with the hand, but they use a feather which they pass lightly over the face or tickle gently certain parts of his body. Finally he is a man who by his wit and cunning has raised himself to the highest place of authority in his nation and who has no parallel among all the savage nations of this continent. He is able to do or cause to be done good or evil as it pleases him. It is not his warlike actions that have brought him so much power, for he has been inclined towards peace, but because of the fear that his men and his neighbors have of certain poisons which he uses, they say to kill off those who displease him. He takes from the French who come to trade with him their most beautiful merchandise and gives them in exchange very few hides, that those who have lost only one hundred to one hundred and fifty percent from the cost price are fortunate. He promises much and never keeps his word. He takes every year from the Poncas and from his own men a quantity of beaver and otter hides. But he saves them for the nation situated on the Mississippi which brings him every spring in exchange, scarlet cloth, china ware and unwrought silver, and some little brandy for which he has a great passion, and the greater part of his men follow his example only paying hides of deer good or bad for guns, kettles, powder, balls, etc., which they take on credit. If they trade with beaver or otter it is at the price they set, and always to the loss of those with whom they trade. The chief pretended for some time to take an interest in the French, but at the bottom all the beautiful talk which he held, the grand promises which he made, having nothing for an end but the pillage for himself, under a false cover of friendship which he seems to display for them; and after being satisfied he leaves the trader to debate with his men to snatch his goods at the best bargains possible. In this extremity it is always necessary to have recourse to the chief of the second rank, to the braves and to the soldiers, who are so many bloodsuckers who extort from you the other third of the goods for their good services.

This man knows how to make the Frenchmen realize how much they are in need of him, perhaps in commerce with his nation, perhaps in the distribution of the credits which without his presence would be made long and noisily, perhaps also in getting payment. Having the policy of leaving the trader on such occasions in the embarrassment of disputes, threats, and robbery from his men, who are naturally brutal and ferocious and coming immediately to his aid, restores calm and order. The poor traders finding themselves fortunate for his support, are forced to load him with glory, with caresses and with good treatment, and no one dared to refuse what he desired.

As for his men, he caused them to know that they depended on him for their welfare. He determined the measures of powder and the price of the merchandise: Sometimes of an immense size and the price of the merchandise moderate, wishing he says to have pity on them; at other times they are very small and the prices high, which happens very rarely. By this changeable attitude of good and bad he holds all of them in fear and hope. But as for his private life there has not been for many years a change. On the contrary he takes freely a third at least of the merchandise which comes to his village. Upon the arrival of the French at his villages he causes an exhibition of the goods to be made and then carries off and appropriates whatever is pleasing to him. The *engagés* are even forced to open their cases or haversacks which he examines. He takes from them a part of their tobacco and other little effects which they may have. The second chief[s] carry on their robbery also, and one is not able to object to them, and always with promises of good pay which ease their own mind and are a loss to the trader. As to the common people the trade is carried on with much profit, but the loss which this chief and his followers bring to the traders which takes from them the better or greater part of their effects at a low price, places them in a condition to make no gain. This Omaha post is about the most disadvantageous on the whole river at the present time as much through the great knowledge they have of trading through the English on the Mississippi, as through the evil disposition of this nation and of their chiefs in our regard. It is said that some *coureurs de bois* formerly made great profits. They had not at that time this pernicious communication with the nations dependent upon the English. There was only one chief among them who lately recognized as chief by the commanders of Illinois, devoted himself entirely to the interest of the traders. His individual conduct was honest. He always paid well for the merchandise which he took. For some years past he has been entirely changed toward us. He talks to us in one way and thinks and acts in another. His mind is occupied only with deceptions and lies in order to deceive us and to steal our merchandise. Every day he reproaches us that the French are great liars and deceivers. He told me that many years before he had asked for a certain medal, greater than all ordinary medals, which M. Montardy had brought to him, but not finding it equal to the others, because of four portraits which were inlaid thereon and because the exergue was missing and the edge was plain, he had returned it to his Spanish father, for it to be remade with only one figure, not having four hearts, he said for four fathers, that this medal belonged to him in as much as it had been sent to him by his Spanish father, that he had not refused it nor had returned it to lose it entirely. He said that every year the traders who had come to his place had told him that this medal had been sent to a great village of the Spanish in order to be remade (which was false, for M. Montardy had kept it) and made him believe that it would come the following year. He plainly sees that he has been deceived and he loses no opportunity in causing a loss to the French who come to trade with him, or who wish to pass through his country in order to go to the upper country.

He said that every day he was on the brink of giving full liberty to his men and permit them to rob and kill all the French wherever they could find them, that his nation only had never killed any Frenchmen because of the opposition which he had always made, that presently very little would hold him back. He especially accused M. Montardy of having made great promises to him which had never been carried out.

All these reasons are for him a legitimate pretext for robbing, blocking the road and forcing burdensome tribute.

So, Gentlemen, if I have dwelt a little long on this subject of this chief and his nation whose character I have studied this winter, his way of thinking and acting, it was to instruct you with the truth of what takes place among this nation, for I forsee that you have need of direct communication with it in order to procure a free passage and safety for your boat in going up as well as in descending the Missouri. Do not hope to continue secret voyages with safety. Sooner or later all your goods will be taken or stolen and perhaps your people killed.

For it is certain that knowing now the plans of the French to trade on the Upper Missouri, and the time when they are accustomed to go up, they will watch and search in war parties, both the upper and lower country in order to surprise them. They are already very roused up against us on this subject and particularly against Jacques d'Eglise, who hastens stealthily along the road every summer they say. I have persuaded the chief that I had stopped at his village on passing in order to see him and talk with him, but having found no one I had continued the route.

The village of the Omahas would be a most propitious place to establish a post for merchandise and provisions to supply the trade on the Upper Missouri, it being situated about half way to the Mandan villages. From there the transportation of merchandise to the Mandans would be much quicker and less risky, being able to profit by the seasons when the Sioux were ordinarily away from the Missouri. In order to pass above, this is absolutely necessary, in order to place the great chief of the Omahas in our interest, as well for the commerce with his nation as with those of the Upper Missouri, which will not be easy to do without his consent, except to content him by giving him this medal, which he has demanded for so long a time, and a great flag and every year the Company in concert with the government should send him a present. By this means you will be able to procure through this nation's territory a free passage, and to obtain there some help in food for so long a journey in going as well as in returning. Every day this chief talks to me of the enterprises of the French on the Upper Missouri, of the risks and dangers to which they expose themselves through meeting with the Sioux. He does not always disapprove of the fact of visitation being made with the Arikaras and the Mandans. He admits that they are good savages by whom the French will be well received. But he is unable, he says, to forgive us for passing and hiding from his village. I replied to him that the French always find so much trouble in passing villages situated on the Missouri, that they often decide to pass secretly, that the French went through all the country, that the road was free to them everywhere; without any savage nation placing obstacles to them. That along this river alone did the nations close their ears to the words of their Spanish father, hindering the French from going to seek pelts anywhere they wished; that if on the contrary they left the road free and open they would see all the time boats loaded with merchandise pass and repass their village, where they would stop in safety as in their own places, just as the nations on the Mississippi do where the French come and go freely. What jealousy, I said to him, gets the better of you when you see us carry needs to the nations situated farther on from you? Why do you impede us so obstinately in our course? Are you not content and happy that the French have reached you and bring to you every year your needs? Why do you hinder us in carrying them to others and seeking hides? These nations of the Arikaras, and Mandans, whom you say yourself to be good savages, they will not thank you. Why not leave an open road for the French who bring them a charge of powder and a knife? Then your name will be made public and spread abroad to all nations even to the source of this river. Your father, the great chief of the Spaniards, when he learns that you hear his word, that you join your heart to his, in order to procure the needs of all his people situated on the Missouri, will it not content him? I do not discover any reasons, just and true, which would give you occasion to close the road to the French on these trips, on the contrary I see only good for you and this nation; you will be assured of seeing them in every season. The nations whom you can reach would be able through our help to visit you and to bring quantities of horses at a better price than among the Panis whom you always have to pay very dear.

He replied to me that that was good; that he was not ignorant that the white nations were anxious to seek hides among all the savage peoples, whom they could discover, and that without doubt the first French who would penetrate from nation to nation would open the road between them and each village through which they passed, announcing the words of their great chief, making presents on his behalf when it was necessary; placing the savages in union everywhere, sparing nothing to calm their ferocious and changeable spirits, and that he knew very well that in spite of the good heart of the French and their presents that they had often been robbed and killed by the nations whom they visited (except the Omahas). That the road which they had opened had been red with their blood and covered with merchandise as much given away as stolen; that today our chief and ourselves do not follow the same footsteps as our ancestors; since instead of marking out the road with good understanding with all the nations who are situated on our way, in announcing the words and plan of our chief, in place of employing the ordinary and convenient means in order to bring accord among them, and in order to calm the spirit and heart of the merchant, we have sought only to irritate them by hurrying along the road secretly, that without doubt the plan of our chief and of ourselves was to open the road with blood and pillage. You have yourself, he said to me, just felt the hand of the Sioux, who have nearly closed your life, others will lose their lives, it may be by the Poncas as well as the Sioux. As for me, you cannot say that I have harmed you since you have always been so well hidden from me.

You reproach me, he said to me, with having stopped the man named Jean Munier who had been destined for the Poncas. It is true if I did it, it was to preserve him from the insults which this nation would have given him, if he had gone to their place. I had been informed of their bad disposition toward the French, and for him in particular, saying that after his departure from there a certain number of their braves and headmen had died, attributing this mortality to a certain calumet which Jean Munier had caused them to smoke.

Besides I am more and more discontented with the French. They carry great boats loaded with merchandise to the Poncas, the Arikaras and the Mandans and to all the nations who inhabit the Missouri, people for the most part who kill them every day, and my people who have never killed a white man, are deprived this year as I am myself of my medal.

Then, after having waited even to the last season of the autumn in the neighborhood of my village, I have seen arrive a second conveyance by a man named Salomon Petit, loaded with merchandise for the Poncas and none for me. I have been greatly provoked against the French. I have abandoned them, and I went to hunt wild cattle with all my family in the number of seventeen lodges for something to eat.

Sieur Jean Munier, not having been able to make any provision for food, has sent six men to winter with the savages. They have arrived here with the last band. They have assured me that upon the arrival of the last boat, this chief had treated them very badly; that he had even pushed two of the *engagés* so rudely that they fell head over heels over the bluff, threatening to take the powder from the said Jean Munier; that having appeased him, he forced them to winter very near his village and to give credit to his men for powder and balls, using as a measure a horn, whose contents three times full were given for one hide (more than a pound of powder), and that he himself had taken more than four *pièces* of cloth and twenty white blankets with things to match, without giving him a single beaver.

On his arrival here he asked me to relate what had happened and having caused me to enter into my magazine, he obliged me to show him what remained of the merchandise. He pitied me for the misfortune which had happened among the Sioux adding that he did not wish his men to cause me to weep. But for a precaution, seeing that I had little stock and before I trade it, he took away much of the merchandise, telling me that he would pay me well for it. Every day he fleeces me. I had as yet received only small bits of food. I fear that he will treat me as he has treated all the others.

I have had great difficulty with the chief Big Rabbit, chief of the second rank, who, not content with having taken from me three hundred ninety one *livres* of merchandise, according to the invoice value, and having given me in exchange only sixteen beaver, four otter, fifty deer and four hides of roe, wished to force me to give him ten *brasses* of cloth and ten white blankets, on credit payable in the springtime at his village. I firmly refused. But I believe that without the presence of the great chief, who had taken my side on this occasion, he would have treated me very badly.

For, Gentlemen, with what can I oppose them, only simple words which have no more effect than if they were spoken to the trees and rocks, and the angry threats of their father, our chief, and of the deprivation of their needs? Their ears are tired with this sort of threats which never happen, for which they laugh and mock us, treating us as robbers, saying that we bring to them only bad merchandise; even our guns are valueless, for the most part breaking in their hands, or the spring failing them when the hunt is half over; that our hatchets are not made of durable iron, breaking at the first blow against the softest tree; that finally it is too much to pay two beaver or otter hides and two or three deer hides for a *brasse* of cloth, a white blanket, since the English merchandise, which is more beautiful and better, is sold cheaper on the Mississippi. As to the rest of the smaller articles which they have taken always in quantity they apportion that among themselves freely, as due to their number of chiefs and soldiers. I have been paid almost entirely by the remainder of this band to whom I have given for two hundred thirty one hides, a credit for powder, balls, knives, flints, etc.

I have lost sixty two hides by the soldiers and *considérés*. They have used twenty five days on the hunt for deer and beaver, and have killed only a very few, the fault they say, of not having good guns for the deer and of the thick ice for the beaver.

Aside from the chief and the soldiers one sells to the common people of the village with profit. But the first take at a low price the greater part of the merchandise, and never leave enough for us to take up the hides of the latter which are always the best.

Very timely after my arrival here last autumn, I hid the merchandise which would be best for the nations on the Upper Missouri, for if all these rascals of chiefs and *considérés* had seen it they would have taken away the best of it.

The second day of February three young savages who had gone to hunt wild cattle reported that they had heard many shots of a gun, and had seen three men. They sent out ten young men the next day to find out who had fired the shots.

The fourth they reported that they had found six lodges of Poncas at some leagues above us.

In announcing this news to me, they brought also very distressing news affecting Jacques d'Eglise and myself, and consequently which caused a notable prejudice against the Company. They told me that the Poncas has surprised Jacques d'Eglise that summer a half day's march above their village; that having spent some moments in deliberating whether to kill him or not, they had contented themselves with taking from him twenty-five guns, two barrels of powder, balls in proportion, tobacco, knives and other merchandise of which I do not know the exact number or quantity.

I was greatly grieved over this loss. I believed these guns safe within the hands of Jacques d'Eglise, to whom I had confided a commission, for the reason which I have cited on other pages. Besides if I had kept them in my boat they would have been stolen by the Sioux. This news has not been announced to me peaceably. The Omaha chiefs have burdened me with reproaches and insults, and they threaten especially to maltreat Jacques d'Eglise if they catch him traveling stealthily, and also, all others who undertake it in the same way.

I defended myself by telling them that I did not know that Jacques d'Eglise had come up the Missouri after me, and that no doubt he had passed me at the time when I was marching overland in trying to reach the Arikaras.

I told them again the intentions of their Spanish father, who wished to satisfy the needs of all the nations situated on the Missouri. That the French who wished to visit all the savage peoples of the Missouri sought only to do good and not bad, and that on the contrary they were the ones who had caused the robbery, loss, maltreating them everywhere they met them and even in their own villages.

I told him that these secret voyages of which he made so much reproach had not caused him any damage, and that if the French acted so, it was because of their knowledge of their evil intentions toward the French and once through difficulties which they always offered before permitting them to pass, and if on the contrary they would leave the road free we would stop there with pleasure.

If all the savage people, I told him, who are situated along the road of the French from the country where the merchandise is made even to you had closed the passage, you would never have received from us the needs which you want so much, but on the contrary all these nations contented with having the French among them who give life to their women and children, hear the word of their Father, are always in accord with their brothers, the white man, who go and come at any time in all seasons from one village to another, as they please, without finding any opposition. You alone, Omahas, Otos and Poncas, who have a greater need of us than any other nation, close the ears to the words of their father, our chief. Your spirits and your hearts are full of evil sentiments toward us, seeking only to rob us, to deceive us, injuring us in our enterprises by all sorts of means. Finally after as many disputes, for I would not end even if I were to cite all the impertinent discourse, which he held with me every day, this cunning chief always wants to persuade me that it is for the safety of our effects and even for the life of the French, if [that] he finds fault with the trips to the Upper Missouri.

The loss of the effects of Jacques d'Eglise by the hand of the Poncas and of mine by the Sioux gave a great weight to these reasons, although the true motive of his discontent was over not having been able to snatch the most beautiful and best part if we had stopped there.

The 16th of February two of the employees of Jean Munier have set out to return to him.

I have sent two of my men with them to seek a letter written to me by my wife and carried by Salomon. I had thought to prove to the Omahas and to the Poncas through this letter that the guns taken by the latter, while in the hands of Jacques d'Eglise, had belonged to me, saying that as there had been no guns in the French village on my departure, I had commanded Jacques d'Eglise to bring me twenty-six if they happened to arrive there before he set out. I did not know if this ruse would succeed.

The 8th of the month of March the great chief of the Omahas and all his family have set out from here to return to their own village without giving me a single hide, saying that the hides were buried in his village, but I hope for nothing from this rascal for two hundred twenty three *livres,* according to my invoice price.

The 9th two men arrived whom I had sent for the letter accompanied by Salomon and two other employees, with some effects with which to buy food, having fasted the greater part of the winter, eating only wild beans.

The 10th two great chiefs of the Poncas arrived here, (the one named Kichetabaco, the other Morrest Naugÿ). I received them well. I have told them that their Spanish father, protector of all the nations which inhabit the Missouri, wished to procure their needs for them, sending them every year a conveyance loaded with merchandise for them, but that the Omahas, cunning and deceitful had closed the road, saying that the Poncas were bad men, accusing them of desiring to rob and kill the French who came among them, attributing their sickness and deaths to their merchandise, that the Omahas alone were the cause of their misfortunes. I exhorted them to treat the French well wherever they might find them, that the intentions of their Spanish father was to have a good road among his children. I asked them to pay for the effects which they had taken from Jacques d'Eglise.

I assured them, by showing them the letter which Salomon had brought me, that the guns belonged to me, besides the powder and the other merchandise which they had taken, coming from the same village and from the same house as mine; also that they would do well to give me the hides which they had meant to pay to him and not to trade them to any other Frenchman nor to the Omahas which would surely happen if they did not give them to me for Jacques d'Eglise, not being able to at once return to their village; that if they caused us to weep the Omahas would be content and would confirm their wicked words against them.

And on the contrary if they would render to us a contented heart that would prove that all the bad talk of the Omahas was false. That their Spanish father would be satisfied with them and that they should be assured that the French, learning of their good conduct, would make every effort to come again to their village, carrying them their wants.

I advised them to lend a deaf ear to the flattering and deceitful talk of the Omahas, which tended only to stir up trouble with us and would render them unhappy.

They told me that all the bad discourse of the Omahas was false; that there was nothing on earth better than the white man and his merchandise. That the chief of the Omahas was an evil one who deceived them and always placed them in a pitiful condition. That I would find out for myself when I entered into their village that they were as they were accused. That it was true that they had taken twenty-four guns, powder and balls from Jacques d'Eglise. That necessity, seeing that the Omahas had stopped every boat, had caused them to do it. That moreover it was for revenge on the Arikaras who had received them badly and wished to kill them when they had talked with them last summer in their village. That the *considérés* of their nation had determined to make the young men pay well for that which had been taken. That they would not detach any hides until the payment was complete. That when they had all arrived at their village, he would hold a council on the matter, and that he would recommend to me that as soon as navigation was open I should render myself there immediately, that they thought I would be contented.

They represented that they were out of powder and that that alone might cause some of their men to keep their hides and get powder with them from the Omahas. In order to encourage them in saving their hides I promised them that if they would pay me well, I would sell them some, as well as some cloth and a white blanket which I had reserved for them. For the time they appeared very content and promised me earnestly to save them. The Omahas did everything possible to take away the pay for that which they had taken from Jacques d'Eglise. This man had shown to the Poncas the five medals and five flags which he was carrying to the chief of the Mandans. This sight has brought about a great jealousy between these two nations and occasioned bad words against us.

In speaking to these Ponca chiefs of the Arikara nation, among whom they had been last summer, they told me that five French were staying at the home of this nation, and that they had seen only two of them, that the

Arikara had told them that three other Frenchmen had set out, some considerable time before, with seven *considérés* of their nation, to go to speak to savage people far away, that not having returned they believed that they had been killed and that they were planning to go to war to avenge their death.

The 11th the chief Big Rabbit left here with his family. The 12th twenty lodges of Poncas arrived on the banks of the Missouri opposite to us. The 13th I paid them a visit. They gave me a great feast. Salomon bought much dried meat cheaply.

I proposed to the chief of this band that he make the men who had my guns pay me for them. He did not wish to, saying that it was necessary to assemble all in a village to do that.

The 14th they broke camp and set out. I have sent Pierre Berger who understands their language passably with them, having given him some pieces of tobacco in order to have a smoke with the *considérés* of each band and to encourage them to save their hides for me.

I am very impatient at not being able to set out from here promptly; the ice yet covers the surface of the waters. We have had a very mild winter. There having fallen only four inches of snow which lasted only ten days.

But the waters of the Missouri are so low that the ice will not be able to move without its rising.

The 21st, the ice in the Missouri has broken up and passed down. The 22nd and 23rd I had two men set out to descend with the furs which I had received from the Omahas and the Poncas. Jean Munier has promised me through Salomon to crate all the furs together.

I am going up to the nations of the upper country with six men, the few furs that I sent down are not worth sending more men.

Upon my arrival at the Arikaras and at the Mandans, if I am able to pass the first freely, I will trade for the pelts which are to be found among these peoples and I will send them to you by three of the employees as soon as possible. If I see Jacques d'Eglise as I hope, by furnishing him with two or three men and if necessary my big boat and one other that he has without doubt made this winter, sufficient to descend with his furs and mine, and for the time I will propose to keep his old boat in order to navigate if it be necessary.

I am sending from here two little boats which my men have made this winter. It has not been possible to make them bigger and better. There was no wood in this place suitable to make boats of.

If Jean Munier descends with only one of my boats I have recommended to my men to place the other in hiding in some marked place which the second party which descends will be able to pick up in passing.

292

It did not work out that way. I have decided to send the large boat and one of the smaller ones, using myself one of the middlesized ones which my men have made this winter for the up trip. The threats and the bad words given by Salomon to my men on his departure, having recommended to two of my men employed by Jean Munier to trade with the Poncas, to make a canoe of hides in order to take their hides below and to leave my two men on the sand with their boat and merchandise, has caused me to fear that he will persuade Jean Munier to deceive me some evil day and that the two men would find themselves inconvenienced at having to travel alone.

That is why I am determined to send three men to take to you the pelts which I had received from the Omahas and the Poncas. I was not able to set out from my winter camp until the 25th of March, and I arrived the same day near the village of the Poncas. The next day I entered their village. Their lodges are built about half a league from the Missouri.

Time does not permit me to give a full narration of the character of this nation.

I will tell you for one thing that they are great rascals. They copy the Omahas exactly in all their ways of dealing with the French buying the merchandise as they please, or taking by force what is refused them. The chiefs are the principal robbers of merchandise. I have made a bad deal with them. These two chiefs have taken half of the cloth and white blankets which I carried for three hides of deer, the blanket, little and big hides equally, for a sack containing twenty-five pounds of powder and another of sixty pounds of balls they have given me only thirty hides. These are the men who look over all the merchandise generally and take what suits their fancy and at the price they set. All representations and complaints can have no effect on their evil hearts. They tell us continually that the Omahas have done worse to us than they have. The latter do not cease their evil councils instructing them at the bottom of all their deceits and trickeries to rob the French. These follow their advice too much.

This great rascal of the Omahas especially is heard by the Poncas as an oracle. He is their protecting god. He and the other chiefs of this nation have used all the efforts to prevent the Poncas from paying me for the guns taken from the hands of Jacques d'Eglise. Every day coming to camp near us, they send messengers to spread lies and hold evil discourse against us. I denied as much as possible all these lies and tales, causing the Poncas to understand that the Omahas were seeking only to make them miserable, depriving them of meeting the French; so as to force them to give up their pelts.

They agreed to the truth of my words, but acted always only on the words of their protecting god, the great chief of the Omahas. This bad man, learning that the Poncas had not treated me so badly as he had desired, has had the maliciousness to send a last messenger to report an evil slander, which has almost occasioned me great injury with this nation.

He had warned them, as being their father and seeking only their safety, that the man named Salomon Petit passing through his camp had assured him that I sought to kill the Poncas and Sioux by some evil medicine which I threw in the fire, the first for having robbed Jacques d'Eglise, and the latter for having taken my merchandise and that Salomon had solicited him and his people to withdraw immediately from near the Poncas, fearing to be enveloped in this evil contagion which I wished to throw over the first, saying that from the books which he had seen of mine and the letters which he had seen me write this winter, he knew me to be a man of medicine.

Judge, gentlemen, to what extent this chief forces his lies and trickery against us.

This new report in the evening caused a great trouble among this people, full of false prejudice and superstitions. There can be heard in the camps the speeches and songs of death. Chiefs, old men, and *considérés* come to demand the reason for this news. I have persuaded them to the contrary with a thousand reasons and proofs, that it will take too long to report here. Finally their terror has vanished from their spirits at least from the principle men.

For I believe always that the majority of this credulous, superstitious, and wicked people yet believe the word of the chief of the Omahas, that I am capable of having them all killed. Also since the moment when the news was received, I did not dare to touch book, papers or pen before men so ignorant.

———

[*The First part of the journal ends abruptly as above. On June 1st following he resumes as abruptly*]

———

PART SECOND[3]

The Sr. Jacques d'Eglise departed from the village of the Ricaras on the 24th day of May, 1795. I sent with him two men, *engagés* of the Company, to deliver the few skins which I had obtained from the Cheyennes [*Chaguiennes*] only; the Sr. Jacques d'Eglise, before my arrival here, during the winter and also in the spring, having traded for all of the peltry of the Ricaras. Then I sent four men, two of whom, named Quebec and Savoie, are men capable of making pirogues to search for a tree sufficiently large for the construction of a boat [*voiture*] in which I might transport, as

[3]*Missouri Historical Society Collections,* IV, 21-48.

soon as possible, my remaining goods to the Mandans. I hoped that the Ricaras would consent to this upon my leaving a man here with powder and other necessities, while awaiting the arrival of the pirogue which the Company is to send up during the summer.

Na. Lecuyer and the Srs. Quebec and Savoie, wishing also to reach the Upper Missouri for beaver hunting this autumn, would have helped me with my pirogue as far as the Mandans. They returned after fifteen days of fruitless search, having traveled through all the woods along the Missouri River a distance of about seventy-five miles above the Ricara village. It is true, indeed, that for the distance of about one hundred and twenty-five miles below the village of the Ricaras and for the same distance above, the country is composed of hills and prairies, with an occasional patch of woods, the trees being willows and short and slender cottonwoods. For fuel and the building of their cabins these nations use only the drift wood which is piled up by the rising waters of the Missouri. Because of this lack of timber it would be most difficult for us to construct either houses or forts in this locality; we would need many people and much time to succeed.

I remained here without a pirogue, as it is absolutely necessary that I stay until the arrival of the boat which is due here this summer. Besides, my presence here is needed in case of emergency as much to preserve peace and union between these nations and those situated on the Upper Missouri, as to prevent their going to war with those who wander through the country west of the river, who are very numerous.

A war party of the Ricaras arrived on the fifth of June with the scalp of a man of the Crow nation, a people who live near the Rocky Mountains.

The eighth of the same month another party which had gone to avenge the death of three of their people whom the Sioux had killed last winter, returned after having killed a man of the Sioux village called Ysanty, the people of which are sworn enemies of the Ricaras.

A few days later two men from another Sioux village called Ta Coropa brought the news that three villages belonging to that nation had assembled and formed an army of five hundred warriors, intending to attack the village of the Ricaras.

The Ricaras have fortified their village by placing palisades five feet high which they have reinforced with earth. The fort is constructed in the following manner: All around their village they drive into the ground heavy forked stakes, standing from four to five feet high and from fifteen to twenty feet apart. Upon these are placed cross-pieces as thick as one's thigh; next they place poles of willow or cottonwood, as thick as one's leg, resting on the cross-pieces and very close together. Against these poles which are five feet high they pile fascines of brush which they cover with an embankment of earth two feet thick; in this way, the height of the poles would prevent the scaling of the fort by the enemy, while the well-packed earth protects those within from their balls and arrows.

The Sioux nations are feared and dreaded by all of these others on account of the fire arms with which they are always well provided; their very name causes terror, they having so often ravaged and carried off the wives and children of the Ricaras. Our being here gives them great assurance, consequently they every day await the coming of the Sioux with courage, and with the resolve to make a strong fight.

It is apropos, for the lucidity of this Journal is to make known to you the character of the Ricara nation, their number, the way in which they are divided, the position of their villages, as well as those of the neighboring nations; for they hold, so to speak, the key to the passages which we must traverse to reach all of the nations higher up the Missouri, where lie their villages which are in great number.

CHARACTER

The Panis Ricaras are of a rather gentle nature; they respect and defer to the White Men. (I will hereafter make use of these words in the continuation of these *mémoires* to designate civilized people; as the Indians of this country do not know any distinction between the French, Spanish, English, etc., calling them all indifferently White Men or Spirits.)

It is said that formerly the Ricara nation held us in such great veneration that they gave us a sort of worship, having certain festivals at which they offered us the choicest morsels, and even threw into the river robes which had been dyed and dressed skins decorated with feathers as a sacrifice to the White Man.[4]

I have been assured that the Cheyennes and other more distant nations still practice this custom; while the Ricaras, through having for so many years associated with the Sioux and the Panis Mahas have changed the ideas which they have inherited from their ancestors in regard to the White Man whom they regarded as divinities. Now they consider us only in so far as we supply them with the merchandise which we bring, and which is so necessary to them, particularly ammunition which they obtain from us and which protects them from the onslaught of so many formidable enemies who so often carry off their children.

I have never discovered in them any malice towards us. Up to the present time we have been able to freely enjoy our possessions without fear that there are any who will harm, molest or tyrannize over us. He who is not satisfied with what is offered him in exchange for his peltries carries them away without a murmur or a threat. Indeed, I will say that having frequented all of the Indian nations living East and West of the Mississippi

---

[4]Marginal notation: "Several old people of this tribe have told me this as a fact".

as well as those living on the Lower Missouri, I have found none who approach these in gentleness and kindness towards us. There is as much difference between these and the others as there is between day and night. But, according to some French hunters who are here and who have seen much of the Cheyennes, Mandans and Gros Ventres, they far surpass these, in goodness, kindness, and in reverence for the White man.

The French who came to trade with the Ricaras nation two years before me described them very unfavorably; they accused them of being thieves, slanderers, liars, cheats, and capable of all sorts of wickedness; giving nothing for nothing, refusing to render any service to the French without pay, and even willing to let them die of hunger if found empty handed.

I believe them, but—

From stealing, slander, lying and cheating, I say that one can easily protect himself and avoid being duped, by being careful of his acts, moderate in his conversation, especially with young people (in which the French are too commonly at fault). As to any actual malice I have, up to the present time, experienced none. It is true that they are dour towards the French in the matter of food, giving nothing for nothing, and never doing us a service without reward, but they have these faults in common with all savage nations who have intercourse with civilized ones and become infected with their peculiar faults and vices. Those Indians who have had little or no intercourse with us are more civil, kinder, and more humane than those whom we habitually visit, for they observe in their manner of life the laws dictated only by reason, nature and humanity. Certain it is that if these people whom we call barbarians and savages knew the disposition of the White Men whom they class as divinities, if they knew their manners and customs, their ways of living and their lack of charity for one another: if they could witness all the vile and contemptible deeds done by them for the sake of money, the worries and torments of body and mind imposed upon them by the sword, the gown and the counting house; if they knew these tricks, the frauds, the crimes even which they practice against the rights of nature, of blood and of humanity in order to satisfy their ambition and to accumulate riches, they might justly apply to us the designation of savages and barbarians which we have given to them.

Those same Frenchmen (Garraut and his companions) who, as I say, had come among the Ricaras two years before me, have contributed largely by their bad conduct to diminish the favorable opinion and good will which they formerly had towards us.

Instead of finding these white men, as they had believed, incapable of folly or unreason, they found them dissolute, prodigal and wicked. They quarrelled among themselves to such an extent that some counselled, begged and even paid the Indians to maltreat, to rob and to kill the others. The Indians, more reasonable than the Whites, without performing the

297

evil deeds to which they were urged, profited by the liberality and the discord of the Whites, and took their merchandise whether it was spent for women, or for other follies and excesses which they gloried in committing. Instead of bringing peace among the Indian nations which should be the first aim of the White Man, when he goes among them, these people were the cause of quarrels and dissensions among the chiefs and families with whom they lived, and even embroiled them with their allies. Far from upholding these people in their former simplicity and in their estimation of the value of our merchandise, they made them believe that we considered it no more than grass growing on the prairie, and that we preferred to use it for bad purposes rather than to trade it for peltries. They also paid the Indians three prices for food, a habit and rule which took such deep root in the minds of these people that had I not taken the precaution to provide myself with dried meats from the Cheyennes and the Sioux, who sell them more cheaply, I should have run great risk of fasting; having abandoned, on my arrival here, the pernicious custom of paying at each meal for each dish, be it soup, corn or cooked meats, as it was served, which had been followed by my predecessors.

The Sr. Jacques d'Eglise failed to reform this way of living, which must involve any one who finds himself obliged to remain for any length of time with this nation in very heavy expense.

I will say, however, to the credit of Sr. Jacques d'Eglise, that he regulated thoroughly the fur trade with the Indians; having established a very high price for merchandise, and having held to it with firmness. But, since I am impartial, I will say of him that he did not search out ways of attracting strange nations to him nor of maintaining this nation in union and accord with its allies by speaking or sending proper words [quelques paroles] to that end. I will say, further, that he neglected to encourage the hunting of beaver and other good furs, being too much bent upon trading for robes, leggings [mittasses], moccasins, women's garments, dry cow hides, etc., which sufficed to meet the needs of the Indians. They find it extraordinary that I refuse to trade for this sort of articles, as well as to submit to their method of selling us food.

It will be easily seen from what I have reported that we often contribute to the wickedness and depravity of the heart of the Indian nations. It would only require a second Garaut and like companions to make these nations like all the others living on the Lower Missouri, which is to say crafty and bad. There is no gainsaying that there are some Indians of a gentler and kinder nature than others. The Ricaras nation, which I consider as having a good character, is said by some to be less docile and more wicked than any of the nations living beyond them; that the young people do not heed the old ones; that the remonstrances of the elders, urging peace and harmony with their neighbors, are listened to without contradiction, but the young men continue to act as their [own] whims and caprices prompt them.

NUMBERS AND DIVISIONS

The many families or tribes of which these villages are composed, each having its own Chief, proves a great obstacle in keeping harmony amongst them.

In ancient times the Ricara nation was very large; it counted thirty-two populous villages, now depopulated and almost entirely destroyed by the smallpox which broke out among them at three different times. A few families only, from each of the villages, escaped; these united and formed the two villages now here, which are situated about half a mile apart upon the same land occupied by their ancestors. The differences of opinion and the wrangles for authority which arise among the Chiefs, although the Indians live independently and without subordination, cause discord and misunderstandings among them and give to the young men occasion to make trouble and attack nations, which otherwise would wish for peace and union. This nation formerly so numerous, and which, according to their reports, could turn out four thousand warriors, is now reduced to about five hundred fighting men, as I have said, and what is more the lack of harmony which exists among the Chiefs has caused the nations to be divided into four parts. Two of the Chiefs, jealous no doubt of the kind of superiority and consideration acquired by the two Chiefs who now dominate in these villages, as well with us as with the other nations, seceded last spring with their bands; one is gone to make his residence with the Pani-Mahas, the other with the Mandans.

Jealousy among the heads of this nation is the sole cause of their discord and their divisions, for they know no interest and are without ambition to accumulate riches; they live in a sort of equality conformable to the dictates of nature, in such a manner that it might be said that what belongs to one belongs to another, each priding himself on helping his neighbor, whether it be with food or other necessaries. They are far removed from the sentiments prevailing amongst civilized nations, where a man is esteemed and respected only according to his wealth; with them, to be a man and honored it is necessary to be dignified, courageous, generous, charitable, and wise in counsel; therefore, they have no quarrels or feuds caused by theft, slander or cheating. If any one among them is discovered to have been guilty of such conduct, they content themselves with telling him that he has no sense, or that he has a wicked heart, and usually in a case of theft, they say that the chief must have been in sore need, and do not carry the matter further.

It is perhaps surprising[5] that these people who have no knowledge of the written law, whether human or divine, and are therefore fearless of the punishment which God has destined for the wicked in the next world and of the corporal punishment in this, should not be more addicted to stealing and other crimes so common to the civilized nations. But one rarely hears of robbery among them, and never of assassination or murder; although their cabins are open all night as well as by day, and every one goes in and out freely. And, besides, several families live together in one house; a thing which we Europeans could never do without a multitude of laws, a throng of judges, lawyers, notaries, and a train of police, who, while they should be the foundation and support of our societies, are often leeches and tyrants because of the wrong use they make of their power. We must ask of the free thinkers [*esprits forts*] of the century, who are more familiar with the systems of morals than I am, the reason for so great a diversity of manners and sentiments between animals of the same species [men] who have equally at birth the germs of justice and equity at the bottom of their souls.

The women never cause battles among them for not having that kind of blind frenzy which we call love, they are not susceptible to jealousy, and do not know that passion.[6] When a man dies, they say, he has not even his wives with him in the land of the dead, so that those who fight and kill each other for women are fools and mad men.

The girls and young women who seem to be common property among them, living in full liberty, are so dissolute and debauched that according to the reports of those who have studied them, there is not one whose modesty is proof against a bit of vermillion or a few strands of blue glass beads; what is more, the fathers, brothers, and even the husbands offer and take the youngest and most beautiful daughters, sisters and wives to the White Men for their diversion, in exchange for a few trifles which they receive.

Our young Canadians and Creoles who come here are seen everywhere running at full speed, like escaped horses, into Venus' country, from which they rarely emerge without being afflicted with the ills which are almost inseparably connected with it, for the foul distemper is more common here than the smallpox is in the northern countries of Canada. The Indians cure themselves of it very easily. They showed me some who six months ago were rotting away who are now perfectly cured.

The two villages belonging to the Panis-Ricaras are situated near the Missouri; the first one at a distance of eight hundred paces from the river, and the other about one hundred paces further on; both are at a distance of

---

[5]A marginal note says that this paragraph is misplaced and should come in later on.
[6]Marginal note: "I except the Sioux and the Cheyennes, who are jealous to the last degree."

nearly four hundred and thirty leagues from the Illinois. South of them on a fork of the Platte River live the Pados [Comanches], a great nation living at a distance which the Ricara warriors would cover in a seven days' march, which would mean about eighty of our leagues.

On the Southwest and to the West, on the branches of a large river (which I name the river of the Cheyennes) which empties into the Missouri about three miles above the second Ricara village, are situated several nations called the Cayoguas, the Caminanbiches, the Pitapahotos, etc., all of different speech. The Cheyennes wander over the country along the river; a little below those first named [plus bas que les premiers]. The vast country, not far from here, over which these different nations roam, abounds in beaver and otter, since they have never hunted these animals, not having had any intercourse with the white men. It would be easy, by means of the Cheyennes who are their friends, to extend our commerce with those nations and obtain from them fine furs. To this end, however, some expenditure would be necessary to get horses and people to transport the kind of merchandise that would attract them most; for this river, of which I have just spoken, though sufficiently wide, is so very shallow that one cannot venture on it in a pirogue; it could be traveled only in the spring, when the snow melts, or after abundant rainfalls, and then only with boats made of buffalo skin, such as are used on the Platte river. To attempt to have them come by way of the Missouri to the place where the merchandise depots are established would be an impossibility; not that the Ricaras or Mandans would offer any opposition, but owing to the fear which they have of the Sioux, their sworn enemies, and whose very name causes all of the people of this continent to tremble.

The northern part of the Missouri is inhabited by the great Sioux nation, almost all of whom are enemies of the Mandans, the Gros Ventres and the Ricaras, and other nations also. The Sioux nation are of those who hunt beaver; and almost every spring they obtain great quantities from here, which they trade with those Sioux who frequent the St. Peter's River and that neighborhood.

The high price held here on merchandise [is the cause of this]; and above all the amount of powder which we give for beaver; which until now, has been only ten *livres* for each pack,[7] and some trifle for *lagniappe;* now they demand a double handful for each beaver and each otter, and unless we yield they will never consent to trade their furs with us.

As for me, my orders being to maintain very high prices on merchandise, though I see with much regret so many fine skins being taken out of our territory to strangers, I cannot, without a new order from the Company, better the price.

---

[7] *"dix louis les chaque"*—this translation is a guess.

One thing is certain; if the English merchants, who are unquestionably much more enterprising than those of Illinois and Louisiana, were in possession of this river [the Missouri] on which from its mouth to its source navigation is so easy for the largest pirogues, having no cataracts or portages, they would establish a large trade with all the nations, those which are known to us as well as those which are still unknown, and obtain from them a great quantity of fine peltry; a thing which these gentlemen, the merchants of the Illinois, have never dared and may, perhaps, never undertake, because of the reluctance they have always had and still have of making expenditures, and because of their fear of failure, they being too easily disheartened by the first obstacles and losses which are encountered; things which have never stopped the English in their commercial ventures.

It will doubtless be said that the Company formed in St. Louis for the purpose of doing business on the Upper Missouri has for its aims and object, in establishing a store house at the Mandans, the discovery of distant nations with whom it might open a fur trade. Such is, indeed, the intention of the Company; and I have been instructed to send out the *engagés* of the Company on voyages of discovery North, South, East and West. But will these *engagés,* who, for the most part, come from Canada, and who have been chosen because of the small wages they are willing to accept, and who are unfamiliar with the Indians and with the routes, will they, I say, make discoveries without leaders and without guides? Will the guides and leaders cost nothing? Will they be able to pass from nation to nation, unsophisticated as they are, without some cost for little presents to the Chiefs? It is required, however, that I execute all of these projects without expense, according to my instructions.

The Director has enjoined upon me to retain only [word blotted] men with me, and to send the other *engagés,* after the winter season is done, back to the Illinois. These two men, will they be ubiquitous? Will they be able to render the needed service at the post, and explore the country from sunrise to sunset and from South to North? Such a thing does not stand to reason.

The greatest obstacle to the voyager on the Upper Missouri is the pass at the Mahas and at the Poncas. Will the Company make the necessary effort to free these passes? There is little risk of meeting the Sioux. They are easily evaded by precaution in passing the places where they frequent. Above all it is necessary to know how to choose the time to make the passage when they are away, which is in the early spring.

I conclude by saying that if the ways were once opened, and if *Messieurs,* the merchants of the Illinois would employ the necessary forces to reach the many different nations who live on the Upper Missouri and in the neighboring country, and the means to prevent the people North of the river from carrying their furs to the English merchants, it would double and treble the value of their own trade. The capable men among the Indians, and the young men who are accustomed to remain inactive, would have a better chance to earn a livelihood and pay their debts, and in consequence this country which can barely support itself by its fur trade and its hunting, would be much better off than at present. [In the copy at Washington there is a page following this which has been so carefully erased as to be illegible.]

CONTINUATION OF MY JOURNAL

On the twelfth of June, several horses were stolen during the night from the second village of the Ricaras. This horse robbery caused a great tumult in the village, as it was realized that it had been committed by the Nations of the Upper Missouri. They accused the Mandans and the Gros Ventres, and were much inclined to go to war against these nations. I begged the Chiefs to calm their young men and made them understand that it were far better to hold them back than to allow them recklessly to make war. I urged them to send some of their own people among the Ricaras who are harboured by the Mandans to find out exactly who was the author of this theft; that I myself would write on this subject to the Frenchmen living among the Mandans, and that I would send some tobacco to the Chiefs of those Nations, entreating them to have the horses returned if they had been stolen by any of their young men. They consented to do this, and on the seventeenth of the month, three Indians started out on this errand. They returned the following day and reported having seen a great number of men on horseback, who seemed to be coming on, ready for war, either with them or the Sioux who are their allies, which statement proved to be false.

On the twenty-fourth of the same month, two Frenchmen named Quebec and Chorette started out on the same trip; they returned on the third day, saying that they had seen a warlike party, whom they thought might be Sioux, by whom they were not discovered, as they left under the cover of night.

On the second day of July, six other Indians started out on the same errand carrying the words of the village from which the horses had been stolen, and three pieces of tobacco which I was sending to the chiefs of the Mandans and Gros Ventres and the band of Ricaras who had taken refuge with the first.

These words were to this effect: that being friends and allies and having given no cause for having had their horses stolen they were sending their own people to ask for them and they believed that the Chiefs, be they Mandans or Gros Ventres would have them returned, owing to the regard in which they held the White Men and in consideration of the words of their Spanish Father who advised them to live in peace and harmony, he

303

who made them restrain their young men who lacked neither courage nor legs to avenge this robbery.

I sent a letter by them to Menard and Jussaume who were living among the Mandans, in which I impressed them with the fact that the intention of the Lieutenant-governor of the Illinois was to provide all the necessities of life, to all the Nations situated along the Upper Missouri, and for this reason had formed a Company, composed of several merchants of St. Louis, for whom I was agent, to establish a trading post among the Mandans for several years; that unfortunate and unforeseen events had prevented my reaching there last Fall, that I would certainly reach there during the coming Summer after the arrival of a pirogue laden with merchandise which I was expecting during the coming months of July or August. I assured them that the Company of the Missouri was ready to favor and help them, that it was hoped that on their parts they would contribute with enthusiasm to the success of the proposed undertaking; and that they must stop trading with the English on the Red river. I begged them to spare no pains in maintaining peace and harmony among all nations particularly those of the Mandans, Gros Ventres and Ricaras; to make the Mandans understand that the route which the French must take to reach them depended entirely on the Ricaras. I implored them to have returned to these last, the horses recently stolen from them and to assure the Chiefs of the Mandans and Gros Ventres, to whom the Great Chief of the Spanish, and the universal Father of the Red Skins, was sending by me medals, flags and swords with which to bind their friendship and to insure benefits to all their villages; that, I say, should they insist upon keeping the horses, they will infallibly light the torch between them and the Ricaras and ultimately prevent our reaching them despite our desires to do so. Above all, I pleaded with Sr. Menard who has the reputation among the Indians of being a man to be depended upon, frank and honest, to distribute in person the tobacco which I was sending to the Chiefs of the Mandans and Gros Ventres, until I myself could deliver to them the words of their Spanish Father. These new ambassadors promised me to be back by the thirteenth day, taking five days walking to reach there, three days to remain and five in which to return.

On the sixth of the month three men of the Cheyenne Nation, from a village called Ouify [Ouisay], which has not yet come here, arrived, having heard the news that among the Ricaras, had come some strange White Men bringing with them much powder and merchandise; their Chief had sent these here to find out if the truth had been told to them; they reported that the Cayoguas, the Caminanbiches, the Pitapahotos of whom I spoke above, had drawn near, and were camped just beyond them, that on the reports they had received concerning the arrival and residence of the White Men among the Ricaras, they wished to form an alliance with these last, in order to obtain from them ammunition and knives, of which they were so much in need, but that the dread they felt, either of the Sioux or the Ricaras, who often killed them without provocation, prevented their approaching.

In the meantime some young men, belonging to the Ricaras, formed a war party, in order to attack the Nations on the Upper Missouri, among whom were possibly those just mentioned. I reproached the Chiefs and the old men, that they should allow their young men to become so unmanageable and show such hostile feelings, wishing to do harm and to make war on the neighboring nations who were seeking only peace and harmony.

I proved to them their poor policy in antagonizing every one, retaining no allies or friends; that if on the contrary they would but form closer ties with the nations west of them and who are well supplied with horses, they would derive great benefit from them and acquire many things which were lacking to them; that we White men would trade with them in beaver and other furs, which were so plentiful in the country.

The Chiefs and the old men approved all that I said but seeing their young men obstinate and determined to go to war, the Chief of the first village of the Ricaras, named Crazy Bear, in whose cabin I lived, became angry and remonstrated with them sharply, telling them to go on and make war and so drive back the White men to their own villages with all their powder and other merchandise, while he and his family would withdraw with the Cheyennes. In order to reduce these turbulent young men to tranquillity I proposed to this Chief that we should ourselves go with the Calumet to the nations who were making instant demands for peace. He applauded my plan, but he said he must first call a meeting of the principal men of the Nation, to impart to them our plan and obtain their approval.

The following day on the 7th of the month he bade all of the Chiefs and *considérés* to his cabin, he placed a flag before the door and placed his medal around his neck. At the furtherest end of the hut, exposed on a mat, the letter patent which his Spanish Father had sent him by me, having placed before it some live coals on which was burned a certain kind of dried grass the smoke of which produces a very strong odor, and which they use as we use incense. They hold such things as medals, flags, and letters in such deep veneration that whenever these are taken from their wrappings, they are smoked and hold the most important place at their feasts.

To this assembly, he recalled the desires and advice of the great Chief of the White Men (of which they saw the evidence), which was to make peace and not war on the neighboring nations. I repeated to them what I have already said on page—about acquiring horses from the Western people; for in order to win over all sorts of Nations to our views, it is well to mix in their own interests and clearly show them their own advantage to be gained.

305

The whole assembly applauded our speeches and approved the plan which the Crazy Bear and I had formed, of going to the nations which I have named, bearing the Calumet. They summoned the war chief of the party, who was preparing to go; they induced him to smoke and he consented to remain quiet. They called the three men of the Cheyenne Nation who had just arrived and, having found out through them, just where these strange Nations had stopped, decided that they were still too far away to go to them at once, and that it would be more suitable to send them tobacco, to make them smoke to the White men and to the Ricaras Pawnees, urging them to approach without fear and assuring them that the white men desired to see them and that the Ricaras unanimously wished to make an alliance with them, that here they would find guns, powder, knives, etc., in exchange for their horses to the Ricaras and their furs with the White men, who advised them to hunt beaver during the Fall, Winter and Spring.

That as soon as it should be learned that they were near here, the Chief "Crazy Bear" with a few *considérés* among the Ricaras, and myself would go to them with the calumet to form a sincere alliance with them, and if instead of approaching, they withdrew, it would prove that they cared little for the White men or for peace with the Ricaras.

All of these words were repeated to the Cheyennes by an interpreter, for their language is entirely different from that of the Pawnees. I gave them three pieces of tobacco, to be delivered to the three Nations which I mentioned above, and after having given to each one a knife, a bit of Vermillion and a piece of tobacco, which they might show in their village, to prove the good faith of the White men, they left on the morning of the eighth.

On the tenth of July, I unfortunately lost one of my Frenchmen, named Joseph Chorette, who was drowned, while bathing alone at dusk, in the Missouri.

Two little Indians aged about ten and twelve years old, came running to us to say, that they had seen a white man, who was washing his body on the bank of the Missouri, and while playing had wandered a little farther away from him; a few moments later, they looked towards the spot where he had been and had seen him no more; then going to the spot where he had gone into the water, they found his clothes, which were still there.

Accompanied by the other Frenchmen and several Indians, I ran to the edge of the river; we found his clothes, just as these children had told us.

The Indians jumped into the river just at this spot, also some distance below, to make a search, but without avail. For the last few days this man had taken the habit of going to bathe in the Missouri, in spite of all we could say, telling him that the bed of the river being uneven, full of holes and precipices and he being unable to swim, he would undoubtedly be drowned; but incredulous to the last, he obstinately continued his bathing and unfortunately was drowned. I was most unhappy over this misfortune. During the twenty-six years and over, in which I have been making my trips, neither I, nor any one of my companions, has met with a serious accident. I had him searched for, during several days, but without success.

On the fourteenth of the month, the six Indians whom we had sent to the Mandans, returned; they brought me two letters from Messrs. Jussome and Menard, assuring me that the Mandan and Gros Ventres Nations had received and smoked the tobacco which I had sent to them with inexpressible joy, incessantly raising their hands toward their Father, the Chief of the White men, in thanksgiving for his benevolence, and that they had promised to do nothing against the will of the White men. They tell me that all of the Indians and the French who make their residence there are impatiently awaiting my arrival, being disposed to do all in their power to serve the Company; that so far as the stolen horses are concerned, which I and the Ricaras claim, there would be no difficulty whatever in returning them had they been stolen by the Mandans or Gros Ventres, but that the robbery had been committed by some young men of the Ricaras Nation who had taken refuge among the Mandans and they would not consent to return them, saying that the stealing of these horses had been done in revenge for some other horses, which had been withheld by those from below, at the time of their separation, and that besides, these discussions and controversies between those belonging to the same Nation was no business of the French or the Mandans, and that they scorned the threats of their own kind.

So our so-called ambassadors returned without horses. The discontent of the second Ricaras Village may be easily imagined.

On the sixteenth of July, one of the great chiefs of the village from which were taken the larger number of the stolen horses, and who since my arrival here, had always shown us much consideration, came to visit me; he said that he was leaving with many young men, to war on the nations above; that since my arrival, they had consented to all for which I asked, for the sake of peace, but since the Indians above us had not heeded my words, nor theirs, they intended to avenge the stealing of their horses; that he being Chief and not being in sympathy with the movement of these young men of no sense and no ears, had not wanted to leave, without warning me, and to find out from me my views on the subject.

I easily understood the object of his discourse, which was, to be retained by me or to get my consent to make war on the nations farther up.

I was undecided as to how I should answer this man. Stop him? That would be expensive, for you will notice that among all savage people the most wise words and discourses, whether for peace, whether for war,

307

or in regard to the reception of strangers, are not fruitful, if unaccompanied by feasts and by presents of horses, of guns or other merchandise given at the end.

After so many losses and expenses due to unfortunate events, since my departure from the Illinois, by which the Company finds itself much aggrieved, and those which I have made and am obliged to make since my arrival here, whether it be to maintain peace with the Cheyennes and the village of the Sioux settled here, who were at variance with one another and whom it is necessary to keep on friendly terms, they being the ones who can best furnish us with good furs.

What with food and small gifts which I cannot refuse, now and then, to the two Chiefs decorated with the Ricaras medal, when they ask me. It being wise to propitiate and not offend them too much, by unnecessary refusals while not seeming to grant them too readily. So I take good care to not only avoid heavy expenses, but also not to give these newly bemedaled Chiefs, the bad habit of exacting from traders, a quantity of merchandise as due to their positions of Chiefs, a custom which the French have unfortunately introduced among all the Nations situated along the Lower Missouri. I try to yield to their demands only on necessary occasions, where it is a question of giving a few trifles to strangers, who come to visit them, or when it is to appease some mutinous or discontented ones of their own nation, who would insult or maltreat their allies. To refuse them under such circumstances, would be to cause them great displeasure and change their kindly sentiments, with which we wish to inspire them, such as peace amongst themselves and kindly feelings toward strangers and, above all, not to alienate us in their minds.

All of these losses and expenses made me hesitate as to how I should act this time towards this Chief. To recall to him all the advice of his Father, the Chief of the White Men, and to repeat my usual arguments for maintaining peace and free passage among the Nations of the Upper Missouri, without at the same time giving him anything, was to throw my words to the winds, especially to a man who had just lost all of his horses, by which he counted his wealth, and who would not have failed to reply as he had already done, that these same Nations from above had been the first to disturb the peace and harmony which I was anxious to maintain.

To tell him that he should do as he pleased, was to countenance all of the evil which he intended doing, beside trying to check all the youths of this Nation without being able, when the time came, to hold them back. I therefore thought fit to make a few more sacrifices, although burdensome, by giving out some more merchandise to stop this war party, rather than allow it to proceed, for one thing is certain, that should war break out

308

between these Nations and those farther up, all passages leading to the latter would be closed to us, which would only bring great harm to the Company, by putting obstacles in the way of Commerce which it had planned and which was to extend to all the Nations on the Upper Missouri. I summoned the Chief "Crazy Bear" and some *considérés* of the Ricaras, who made him smoke with me in order to divert him from his purpose. I gave him a present and bade him to make known to the others of his village who had lost horses by robbery.

In order to displease no one, he accepted the Calumet and the gift, saying that it was not on account of the booty which I gave and which was but small in comparison to the loss of his horses, if he agreed to remain quiet, but in consideration of the White Men, whom he did not wish to displease, that he would forget them and would make every effort to appease those who like himself, had lost their horses.

This Chief did at once all that he had promised me, and there was no more talk of war with the Nations higher up.

On the eighteenth of the same month ten men of the Cheyenne Nation arrived; they reported that their entire village was approaching, traveling by slow stages, being too heavily laden to move faster. That the young men of their Nation had started off, carrying tobacco to the three Nations which I had named, the Cayoguas, the Caminanbiches, and the Pitapahotos, and that they had not yet returned.

They also told me of a most wretched accident which had happened to them recently; I would not repeat it to you, if the cause of it were not attributed to us, on account of the high opinion they have of us and all that belongs to us.

When I had summoned the most important ones from both Cheyenne villages on my arrival here last Spring, to announce to them the words of their Spanish Father and to deliver to them the medal, the flag, the letter patent and the present which he sent them, I asked them to choose from among their number, the one whom they deemed most worthy to wear the medal and to be made the great Chief of their Nation. They had me to [sic] give it to a young man whom they called "The Lance," who accepted it and promised to do all the good which had been recommended to him, in the letter which his Father, the Chief of the White Men, had sent him.

These newly arrived Cheyennes youths reported to me, that this young Chief, far from having followed my advice after taking possession of the medal, flag and letter which came from the great Chief of the White men, had continued with a wicked heart for strangers, and even for his own people, getting angry and treating them badly on every occasion; that he was the author of a recent murder committed in their village, that of a Sioux, his wife and three children, who were living among them, in spite of the fact that he had promised me to live in peace with those of the Sioux village who lived there, and to which belonged this man and his family. They had even eaten and smoked together.

Instead of maintaining peace with the Mandans and Gros Ventres, he had had their horses stolen. That without doubt the medal, the flag and the letter, who were great spirits, had become angry, for three of his children had died, and what is more, lightning had struck the hut of his own brother who, with his wives, children, dogs and horses tied before the door, had been reduced to ashes.

This accident happening to befall this man, above all others, known to have broken his promise to the White Men, and not having behaved in the manner imposed upon him, in the presence of all the esteemed ones of his Nation, had a terrible effect on the minds of all these Nations and confirmed anew their belief that the White Men were great spirits and all powerful.

Most of the old men of the Cheyennes, according to reports, openly denounced the conduct of this young Chief, reproached him for his wicked heart, his lack of attention and submission to the words of the White Men by whom they were now visibly punished by the Master of Life, just as I had predicted.

The Ricaras Nation, as I have said, is a little more enlightened than those farther away and yet this occurrence gave them much to think about.

On the 20th of the month, a Sioux village which they call "Ta Coropa" numbering eighty huts, came to join the Sioux village, which has settled here, and who are really the only friends of the Ricaras, having the same sentiments and character; these newly arrived Sioux, as well as another band called Chahony, who are soon to come here, usually wander over the country North East of the Missouri, but not finding any wild oxen or cows thereabouts, are forced to the West of this river, where these animals are found in great numbers.

The Ricaras and this Sioux Nation live together peacefully. The former receive them in order to obtain guns, clothes, hats, kettles, clothes, etc., which are given them in exchange for their horses. They humor them through fear and to avoid making too many enemies among the Sioux, who would inevitably overpower them.

The last frequent the Ricaras and make them great promises to live with them in peace and harmony, in order that they may smoke their

310

tobacco, eat their Indian wheat and hunt freely wild oxen and beaver, on their lands during the Fall and Winter. In the Spring they withdraw to the other shore, from whence they usually return to steal their horses and sometimes to kill them.

It is their custom every spring to meet the other Sioux villages, situated on the St. Pierre and Des Moines rivers, with whom they trade their furs for merchandise.[8]

Journal kept by J. B. Truteaux, Agent for the Company of the Upper Missouri, addressed to Messrs. Clamorgan and Reihle, Directors of the Company.

Commenced the first of June, 1795

---

[8]Following this are three lines carefully erased and illegible.

CHAPTER III

1795

I

MERCHANTS OF ST. LOUIS TO THE EDITOR [*1795?*]

Supplement to the previous *mémoire*[1]
Copy of the observations addressed by the majority of the commerce to the editor

Mr. le Fidel Spectateur

The commerce begs you to insert in your supplement some observations concerning the safety and tranquillity of each individual merchant and his operations in his trade with the savages of the Missouri, as well as, with those savages who come to St. Louis.

First. That one be absolutely forbidden to take any intoxicating liquors into the Missouri, trade it with the savages or with the whites or even sell it to the *engagés* in payment for their wages, during the course of their trips.

Second. That one can advance to the *engagés* only one-half of the wages for the trip during the course of the trip.

Third. That when there are several traders in a single post of a savage nation, there should be an established price among them to sell their merchandise to that same nation. This price cannot be decreased without the consent of all the traders of this same post and in case of viola-

---

[1] Written in French., A.G.I., P. de C., leg. 211. This document is undated but probably 1795.

tion by some of them, the offender will pay one hundred *piastres* fine to the profit of the public works.

Fourth. That from the month of July, the traders, or their representatives, and their *engagés*, will leave the nations where they will have traded, or leaving sooner if the traders for the following year appear before that time.

Fifth. That the traders will not be able to sell in the Missouri any merchandise to whites, mixed bloods, or savages, for the purpose of trading for their account or for the account of these same traders under penalty of one hundred *piastres* fine for each person who will have been employed.

Sixth. The said traders, if necessary will be able to have as agents [*comis*] only whites whom they will have brought with them. They are expressly forbidden to make use of other persons under penalty of one hundred *piastres* fine, applicable to the public works for each person [so] employed. This is done in order to prevent vagabonds, who are on the river or who live with the savages, even the said *chasseurs,* eluding or evading the precautions of the government for the prosperity of each individual merchant. The reason for this is that these same vagabonds and *coureurs de bois* are pernicious to the whites, on account of their continual sojourn with the savages to whom they give knowledge prejudicial to the interests of the traders.

Seventh. That it is forbidden to give to the *chasseurs,* at the time of their departure from St. Louis or during the course of their trip, anything but the objects necessary to their hunt, in order to avoid the fraudulent trade that one might make with the nations, etc. In case of violation there is a penalty of confiscation of the value of the merchandise traded, exchanged, or given in presents to the savages, in order to receive said value. In order to prevent abuse, the merchant equipping the *chasseur* will make him a memorandum [*bordereau*] in duplicate, signed by him and examined by the syndic, who will keep one and remit the other to the *chasseur.*

Eighth. The traders will not be able to take with them as *engagés,* either negroes, mixed bloods or savages. That will be done in order to favor the work of the whites established in the dependency.

Ninth. No traders, *engagés, chasseurs* or others will be able to trade, receive in presents or exchange, any horses branded with iron marks, considering that that would induce the savages to new thefts among the whites, in order to re-sell them or trade them for merchandise, under penalty of confiscation of those horses which will not be reclaimed by any owners to whom they will be sold without repetition of the purchase price.

313

Continuation of the observations made by the merchants to the editor.

Mr. le Spectateur: The trade with the Indians in the village of St. Louis has no less need of correction than that of the Missouri. That is why it is suitable to give to your supplement the following observations.

First. That the corps of merchants will establish at St. Louis a general warehouse where each one of them will place in equal portions, the merchandise necessary for the trade with the savages, who come there or who trade in the environs.

Second. That this fund be regulated by a syndic and managed by the one, who will have been chosen by the majority of the interested parties in the manner and under the terms which will suit their interests, in order to avoid the same abuse existing in the Missouri.

Third. That there also be a general warehouse to sell to the nations who come to St. Louis the liquor that they wish to trade there; that this same liquor not be delivered to them until the time of their departure, and that not a single bottle be given, exchanged, or traded to them, during their sojourn at the village.

Fourth. That all other persons regardless of any quality and condition be forbidden to trade any intoxicating liquor to the savages, or to give or exchange [any], under penalty of corporal punishment or fine. This is to avoid the disorders of the nations in the village of St. Louis.

Fifth: That in case of some questionable points, foreseen or anticipated, relative to the commerce of the Missouri or with the village of St. Louis for the trade with the savage nations, the interested and recognized members at the time will vote, assisted by the syndic who will have two votes, as to whether there is need to diminish [?] the difficulty which will be written down by the syndic. The conclusions taken by the majority [will be] deposited in the hands of *Monsieur* the commandant, in order to give thereto the necessary authenticity.

Sixth. That in case there would be need of forming some rule, convention, enterprise, company, for the present trade of the Missouri and for that which might be extended in the future, the members of the corps of commerce will resort to their vote, assisted by the syndic for a final decision.

Seventh. In case of petition, demand, or remonstrance to be made to the general or individual government, the syndic alone will be authorized thereto when the majority will have judged it best, and that in order to avoid the *cassement de têt inutile* [useless worry] that is given to the government.

314

It is with respectful sentiments that I take the liberty of calling myself.

Monseigneur

Your very devoted, very submissive and very grateful citizen

Le Fidel Spectateur
[rubric]

II

CARONDELET TO TRUDEAU, NEW ORLEANS, JANUARY 27, 1795[1]

I have received the three memorials from some merchants that you included in your letter no. 202,[2] merchants, who solicit exclusive trades in the Indian Nations of the Missouri. To pay any attention to these particular graces would be ruinous at once, since it would annul the commerce of the Missouri Company, would impede the good effects that are hoped for from their disclosure, and introduce confusion and disorder among the same nations. It is my decision:

That you recommend Santiago la Yglesia,[3] discoverer of the Mandanas, to the Company in order that, in view of his having been the real discoverer, you will be able to permit him to introduce himself [into the Mandan country] as you did last year with the merchandise furnished by the same company which would want improvements. Since this company, as you inform me, has an offer from La Yglesia to take interest in all its operations, this is really advantageous, and [it] should be carried out as much to please this man, as to promote his discoveries in which he can be useful.[4]

To the appointed Roland,[5] with respect to the expenditures that he made the four years over which he counted, the present year can be conceded as you propose, although the Company may take his merchandise for the valuation that there would be made, recompensing him for the expenditures that he may have made, and employing him in one of the trades of the Company.

But what he does to the trades of the Cances, which Don Ventura de Collell[6] solicits, does not lend sufficient merit for it to be needed, and that is the way the lot of the others should run.

Nevertheless, you shall instruct the directors of the Company, very carefully, to try to distribute their trades with impartiality, pleasing those

---

[1] Written in Spanish. A.G.I., P. de C., leg. 22. In connection with this document see Nasatir, "Jacques D'Eglise on the Upper Missouri" in *Mississippi Valley Historical Review*, XIV, 47-56; 62-63.
[2] Chapter II, document XX.
[3] Chapter II, document XIII.
[4] See document XV.
[5] Chapter II, document XVI.
[6] Chapter II, document XVII.

neighbors, in order to disperse the rumors and suspicion that is caused by the new establishment which, handled with activity and prudence, should some day enrich those establishments and make those inhabitants happy.

May God keep Your Honor many years. New Orleans, January 27, 1795.

El Baron de Carondelet
[rubric]

Señor Don Zenon Trudeau.

III

TRUDEAU TO VALLÉ, MARCH 4, 1795[1]
[EXTRACT]

Yesterday I had certain news that Benito and Quenache de Rouin, two traders coming from the Kansas, were pillaged and rudely beaten by a party of one hundred and sixty Iowas, who have carried off two of their *engagés* to their nation where the English traders ransomed them, clothed them and sent them back here where they arrived after the greatest misery in the world. They left Benito, as well as the other on the seventh of the month of January at the entrance of the Kansas river, without arms, food, or clothing. It is greatly to be feared that they may yet have very disastrous accidents.

---

[1]Written in French. Missouri Historical Society, Vallé Collection no. 7. See document V.

IV

TURNER TO EVANS, KASKASKIA, MARCH 10TH, 1795[1]

Sir,

Agreeably to your desire, I enclose here a few ideas, hastily thrown together, as hints, upon which you will, doubtless, improve in the course of your travels up the Missouri. Such as they are, however, I shall be happy if, in any degree, they may prove Serviceable to you.

Mr. Chouteau[2] assures me, that the Pacific Ocean can lie at no great distance from the Missouri's source. This information, derived from such respectable authority (for Mr. Chouteau has himself travelled 500 leagues up the Missouri) must afford you consolation amidst all your fatigues.

The same Gentleman tells me that at a great distance up that River, you will meet with some new animals—animals unknown in our Natural

---

[1]A.G.I., P. de C., leg. 213. Written in English. Printed in Nasatir, "John Evans: Explorer and Surveyor" in *Missouri Historical Review*, XXV, 434-435. For an account of John Evans see *Ibid.*, XXV (1931) 226-239.
[2]Auguste Chouteau. See A. P. Nasatir, "The Chouteaus and the Fur Trade of the West 1764-1865," Ms. thesis in University of California Library.

History: particularly one, of the size and nearly the colour of the elk, but with much longer hair. Under this hair, he is clothed with a fine and very long fur. He has two large horns which, issuing from behind the ears and turning backwards in a circle, terminate in two points projecting before the head, in a horizontal direction. Do not fail, good Sir, to procure me a couple of the Skins (male and female), so that they can be stuffed to exhibit the entire form and natural attitude of each—I shod be glad to receive half a dozen of the horns also.

You will likewise, it seems, find another new animal, and which appears to be of the Goat-kind. The hair on the back and belly is white; on the flanks it is reddish. Two *complete* skins *of both* sexes of this quadruped, to be aftds. stuffed like those of the former, would be very desirable.

Wishing you all imaginable Success, and hoping to hear *frequently* from you, I remain

Sir,

Your very Obedient Sert. and
Well-Wisher
G. [?] Turner[3]

P. S.   Since writing this,

Your favour of the same date was put into my hands. In a letter to Mr. Trudeau, I had before mentioned you particularly to him, and also to your desire to take a companion. This, I doubt not, will receive the commandant's approbation. Present my best compliments to Mr. Trudeau & family.

Mr. John T. Evans

[3]There is a Benjamin Turner listed among the American residents in the Illinois in 1787; C. W. Alvord [ed.] *Kaskaskia Records 1778-1790 (Illinois Historical Collections,* volume V., Springfield, 1909), 422, 444.

V

TRUDEAU TO [CARONDELET], ST. LOUIS, MARCH 12, 1795[1]

Answered.

Mon Général:

I have just received all the letters with which you have honored me, from the eighteenth of August up to the thirty-first of October. It has pleased *Monsieur* Peyroux to keep for forty-five days at New Madrid, the letters with which he was entrusted, in spite of the very excellent occasions which he had to send them to me. It would have been the same, even if you had ordered me [in those letters] [to do] something important for the service or public utility.

[1]A.G.I., P. de C., leg. 217.   Written in French.

Don Luis de Vilemont has just arrived here and he appears to be charged with a mission of the court. He has occupied my time by visiting the environs of the country. As I am leaving tomorrow, it is only with great haste that I am able to tell you that everything is perfectly quiet in our establishments and that we have hopes of preserving this tranquillity, at least on the part of our neighbors. This is the feeling of *Monsieur* Don Luis Vilemont who has passed through the center of the country which is to be feared.[2]

Two *voitures* [boats] of our traders, coming from the Kansas nation, were stopped by one hundred and sixty-four Iowa Indians, who were going in war against the same nation. The said traders were pillaged by them and soundly thrashed with blows of sticks. They brought two *engagés to* their villages where they were ransomed by the English traders who sent them back to me.[3] This nation is not at all at war with us, but such is the custom of these cursed barbarians, that when they are at war they make victims of all those whom they meet on their way. The chiefs have sent me a *collar* to show their regret, for that which they were unable to forsee or [for] such disorders; and in the impossibility in which they found themselves to give me satisfaction, I can not forsee effectively how to force them to do so. Notwithstanding that, I propose to succeed in it.

For more than three months I have not had the slightest news from the Osages, except that the commandant of the Arkansas informed me that they [Osages] had pillaged some hunters of that river. Now is the time for the communication that I should have from *Monsieur* Cadet Chouteau, and, if he has obtained satisfaction for this last insult, they [in any case] have not appeared in the environs of our establishments as they used to do every year. Nor have they done any harm to our hunters whom they have encountered. On the contrary they have been treated by them better than by any other nation.

The Sacs, who are very numerous, hunting on the Missouri, killed ten or twelve Osages, after having shaken hands with them and promised peace. I believe that it is very interesting that these two nations are continually in discord, in order to stop the communication of the Osages upon

---

[2]The original of the project of Louis de Vilemont is to be found enclosed with a letter of Carondelet to Alcudia, New Orleans, July 30, 1795. A.H.N., Est., leg. 3890 *expediente* 34. In this *expediente* there are letters to Carondelet and to Vilemont giving the decision of the court. Previous to this time Vilemont had been traveling in the United States as a naturalist. Langlois to Carondelet, New Madrid, April 14, 1795, A.G.I., P. de C., leg. 210. Vilemont visited St. Louis, New Madrid, Ste. Geneviève, Cape Girardeau, Arkansas, etc. See *Ibid.*, and also Rousseau to DeLuzières on *La Venganza* Arkansas, April 11, 1795, A.G.I., P. de C., leg. 211, etc. I have many documents from the archives of Spain that deal with Vilemont. The Supreme Council of State discussed Vilemont's project in its session of November 13, 1795 (A.H.N.), A. P. Nasatir and Ernest R. Liljegren, "Materials Relating to the History of the Mississippi Valley" in *Louisiana Historical Quarterly*, XXI (1938), reprint pp. 55-61.
[3]Document III.

[with] the Upper Mississippi. They are doing little damage to each other and never go away to wage war—the one against the other. It is only accidentally that the most feeble remain victims. If the Osages should penetrate into the Upper Mississippi they would be badly advised by the English, who, in addition, would provision them, and would draw them away from being somewhat subordinated to us, because of receiving their needs from us. I will fulfill exactly all that you order me concerning them, as well as favoring the establishment projected among them by Chouteau, who has already caused some poor families to go there.

Our priest has been a charming person for a long time but, in spite of this, he keeps me on my guard. I have told him something flattering from you, about the fact that for a long time he had not written to you.

Monsieur De Lassus, always interesting to me, told me that you wrote to him that you have solicited your recall to Spain. Don Luis de Vilemont also assured me that he knew about the steps that had been taken on your behalf at Court to obtain your request. I can only make vows for your satisfaction, but allow me to lament, *Mon Général,* that I find myself on the eve of losing the fruit of your good deeds. I certainly cannot flatter myself of ever being treated by your successor, with as much goodness and benevolence, as you have for me, which makes me have recourse once more to it, by supplicating you to glance favorably upon a request, which I am addressing to my colonel, for a fixed appointment which will make me independent from caprice and fantasy. My well-known infirmities, my numerous family, and my poverty, force me to attempt to be liberated from the service of my regiment. Some post or other in the colony, my rank as captain, [and] the same salary, are what I desire, and if I ask for the Illinois, it is only because a displacement [transfer] would be too expensive for me. If my request is indiscreet, I pray you to be indulgent and to annul it; but if, on the contrary, you find it reasonable, heap upon me a last good deed, for the support of six little unfortunate children who will not cease, as I, to remember the happy fate which you will have procured for them.

The one named Coiteux has been arrested at Ste. Geneviève and I have sent an order to M. Vallé to have him embarked for New Madrid under a good escort.

Pardon a thousand times, *Mon Général,* my verbiage. I can only hope for your indulgence because of the profound respect and lively gratitude with which I have the honor of being

    Mon Général

      Your very humble, obedient Servant

              Zenon Trudeau [rubric]

St. Louis, March 12, 1795.

Trudeau to Carondelet, St. Louis, April 18, 1795[1]

Answered.

Mon Général:

Monsieur Pierre Chouteau has just arrived from the Osages to profit by the high waters of the season, in order to transport his family and the artillery of the fort,[2] all the wood for which is made and delivered to the place chosen and the most advantageous for its defense. In three months at most, it will be entirely finished. *Monsieur* Auguste Chouteau is also going there to hasten the work. This is going to bring people there, which will contribute a great deal toward familiarizing the young men with the whites and to restrain them from doing evil.

This year has passed with much tranquillity except for a single pillage made on the Arkansas river, according to what the commandant of that place wrote to me, but he not having pointed out to me its nature, I could not inform M. Pierre Chouteau of it. Only a few days ago, some young men who arrived here told me they had stolen some rifles. Immediately these men ordered a small *voiture* sent out to inform the chiefs of it and they assured me that there would be no difficulty in the restitution, and that I could inform *Monsieur* de Vilemont that the carbines would be sent to him immediately and that all the hunters could be confident that they would not be disturbed at all.

The savages have never been seen as tranquil as they have been this year. They are all proud of having a fort, whites, and domestic animals with [among] them. They regard it all as their own property. Indians have come from very distant nations to compliment them, which has flattered their *amour propre* [pride], they believing themselves distinguished and with preponderance over [being considered more than] the other nations. Their expressions at the time were quite original: "You see our friends the whites among us. When they keep themselves distant, we have no nerves in our arms and we can scarcely move our bows. Now that they will not abandon us any more, we have them so large and so strong that we can break trees."

I continually hope, *Mon Général,* that this nation will be restrained [kept in obedience] better than any other. The evil that it has done, I grant, is great—but it has been spoken of because it is the only one by its power, that can frequent the districts which have had [reason to make] complaints. All other savages would do worse, as we have proof daily in the Illinois.

---

[1]A.G.I., P. de C., leg. 211. Written in French.
[2]This is Fort Carondelet of the Osages. The complete documentation concerning this fort is in Nasatir, *Imperial Osage.*

As soon as *Monsieur* Chouteau returns, peace will be made with the Arkansas. It has been made with the *Panis* and the *Kance* and begun with the Laytane who asked it of them [Osages]. I shall not enter into any other detail concerning this nation in the fear of fatiguing you. It suffices to tell you that it [Osage Nation] seems entirely well disposed [to do good] and that *Monsieur* Chouteau just as his brother, has an authority there that no other white could have. The former is greatly feared and the other greatly loved, a contrast which did no harm in restraining them.

I have the honor of remitting to you a petition of the administrator of the *Compagnie du Commerce* of the Upper Missouri, which requests the exclusion of a certain trade, in order to favor the Company in its enterprises.[3] I grant that all the inconveniences that are exposed are true and the Director [*géreur*] of the Company who left last year makes it very evident as you can see by the copy of the enclosed letter. But all the commerce of the Missouri has been divided into twenty-nine portions:[4] sixteen belonging, at present, to M. Chouteau by the exclusive trade that he has of the Big and Little Osages; and one of the remaining thirteen belongs to the commandant. Thus if the six requests were accorded, there would remain only six for the rest of the commerce of the Illinois which, evaluated at twelve hundred *piastres,* would make only a capital of seventy-two hundred *piastres* to divide among at least thirty persons. This I am laying before you, despite the fact that I am interested in the Company which does not yet know whether by these discoveries, it will find a market for the merchandise sent the first year, and even less for the second which is going to leave immediately, which expedition is more considerable.

The man named Baptiste Lami, *patron* of a *berge* of *Monsieur* Chouteau and bearer of the present, although a very honest boy and from one of the esteemed families of the country, has caused trouble in a numerous family by a little prank of youth. Warned by the priest, I fear the despair of this one who is offended who can still give himself to some regrettable excess in the future. This young madcap is about to depart. I would rather consult you, than expatriate him for some time from the country. If you believe he merits it, inform me of it or give him an order, permitting him, however, to reascend the *berge* which he is conducting to Ste. Geneviève, in order not to leave the owner in the embarrassment of finding another *patron* whom, he is certain, cannot be found at New Orleans.

Several letters from *la Belle Rivière* give credit to the news of the peace; [but] mention is not made of the conditions.

---

[3]The Company had petitioned for a ten year exclusive trade (Chapter II, document IX).

[4]See Chapter II, Document IV.

I have the honor to recommend myself to your bounties, begging you to believe me to be, with the most respectful attachment,
Mon Général,
Your very humble and very grateful servant,

Zenon Trudeau
[rubric]

St. Louis, April 18, 1795.

VII

Trudeau to [Carondelet], St. Louis, April 30, 1795[1]

Answered.
Mon Général:

Since my last letter to you by a barge of Mr. Chouteau, there arrived here one esteemed by the Poux nation [Potawatomi], sent by the chief to assure me that those Indians had decided among themselves that the first one of their nation to do evil on our district would be brought to me in order to dispose of him at my will. I should like to believe that those who sent me the embassy are all well intentioned, but the number of rascals is great and I doubt greatly that the others can stop them, when they will be disposed to do evil to us. However, I am informed that different villages have taken arms against the one from which came a man who committed a murder [among] us. This disposition in our favor and the necessity to dissimulate our resentment against a nation which inhabits a foreign district and which is very close to us, has caused me to receive well the embassy and adhere to its propositions, until the effects will be seen.

I am enclosing for you a request which was presented to me by the man named Duchêne Pero, the only trader of our district in the *Rivière des Moins,*[2] where the English are introducing themselves more than ever, penetrating even into the Upper Missouri. They have already indoctrinated the savages so well that one cannot any longer, without risk, go to the Mahas, Hotos, and Poncas, from where they have been removing all the beaver and otter, as well as, the other fine furs.[3] These same three nations every year mistreat our traders, from whom they extract great contribu-

---

[1]Written in French. A.G.I., P. de C., leg. 211. Parts of this letter are quoted in Nasatir, "Anglo-Spanish Frontier on the Upper Mississippi 1786-1796" in *Iowa Journal of History and Politics,* XXIX (1931), 204-206.

[2]Duchêne Perrot is mentioned in A. P. Nasatir, "Anglo-Spanish Rivalry in the Iowa Country 1797-1798" in *Iowa Journal of History and Politics,* XXVIII (July, 1930). Duchêne Perrot's petition and letter to Trudeau dated April 22, 1795, gives the information here detailed in much greater clarity. He complained bitterly of the wrongs committed against him by the British. A.G.I., P. de C., leg. 29.

[3]See the journal of Truteau, Chapter II, document XXII, and the experiences of D'Eglise recounted in documents in Chapter II.

tions, for the privilege of remaining in the nation to such a degree that those who returned this year had two thousand *piastres* loss in that of the Hotos alone. The others still absent will surely not have been treated better. The only way that I see of opposing the wrongs inflicted upon us by the English is by having an establishment between the *Rivière des Moines* and that [blank in ms][4] which is ten leagues distant one from the other, an establishment which will meet with great obstacles on the part of the savages, [who have become] too accustomed to receiving at a cheap price all their needs from the English and who will be pushed by them to vex us, as far as St. Louis. If it were possible for our government to come to an agreement with the Court of London to reserve for us at least these two rivers, placing obstacles to their trader[s] approaching [the savages or district], then the savages will have recourse to us. We would be tranquil; and we would have a thousand packets [of furs] more a year; and we would be able to compel all the savages of the Missouri to remain peaceful and allow us a free passage to the upper part of the last named river, which already carried competition to Canada by the new Company formed to make commerce and which might attract to it a large part of that which the English do in the whole western Canada.

By only a small *galiotte* armed as that which M. Langlois commands [*La Flecha*] could respect be imposed, which would hinder the entrance of these two rivers and make the English fear to introduce themselves there.[5] This *galiotte* would only be present there, during the first three months of autumn, in order to withdraw at the ice; but there would still be fear that it might be destroyed by the savages, which would only embolden them as well as their traders; despite that, I advised the commandant of McKina that I was going to employ all means to seize all those who introduced themselves in these two rivers and who have been responsible that the traders of the Missouri, of the Kansas nation, have been pillaged by the Iowas, to whom they had offered to pay double for all the furs that they might be able to bring back. I am sending you a copy of my letter.[6]

Mr. Peyroux is at St. Louis where he asked me for a passport to New Orleans which I gave him. He has a thousand plans and has determined nothing. He sought at first to buy a house at St. Louis. He wanted to form a habitation at Ste. Geneviève. Today he leaves and tomorrow he will change his mind, which makes me believe him to be as cracked as his brothers.

---

[4] Possibly Iowa river. There is a blank space in the document.

[5] Although this had been advocated for quite some time it was not done until 1797; see Nasatir, "Anglo-Spanish Rivalry in the Iowa Country 1797-1798," *op cit.* Clamorgan offered to build a fort in the environs of the mouth of the Des Moines river in return for exclusive trading privileges. Clamorgan to Carondelet, St. Louis, December 15, 1795, A.G.I., P. de C., leg. 2371; see *infra.*

[6] In A.G.I., P. de C., leg. 29—attached to copy of Perrot's letter to Trudeau cited in note 2.

I also gave a passport to M. the Abbé Flagier, priest of Vincennes Post, whom I know particularly and who has been coming frequently here where there was no difficulty in inducing him to remain, either for the parish of St. Charles or that of Ste. Geneviève, which is going to be made vacant by the recalling of M. de St. Pierre. You will be able to judge that he is of very good education and a very good preacher. The aim of his trip is to go to Baltimore where the bishop asks for him. The regret that we have at seeing him leave is a guarantee which will assure you that he is a perfect ecclesiastic whose acquisition would be precious for us. He has two *confrères* here: one at Kaskaskias and the other at Kaokias. Both are equally praiseworthy. Their cures are of so little importance, that if the colony needed people [priests] one would have no difficulty in persuading them to go there, and, in that case, I beg you to remember [*ressouvenir*] the parish of St. Charles of Missouri, as likewise that of Ste. Geneviève which is to become vacant as soon as M. de St. Pierre departs.

A newspaper which was sent to me from the American district does not speak of peace as has been announced. This same newspaper announces the taking of Barcelona in the month of November, last year, which appeared to me to be a lie, besides the thing is not affirmed as certain.

The *berge* of Mr. Bolduc arrived at Ste. Geneviève and I have not yet received a letter. Doubtlessly MM. Soulard and Derbigny are bearers of them [letters]. I do not expect them until May 25 at the soonest, unless they come by land from New Madrid. It is only indirectly that I learned of the burning of the Capital and that I found myself included in the number of unfortunates burned. I had in my house all my furniture, beds, even linens; and they saved me only a mirror. I will find myself reduced to nothing if it is necessary to leave this post which, although scarcely advantageous, is already [such] a resource for me that I have asked you to have the goodness to conserve it for me. I would not dare to annoy you in my behalf, if it were not that my large family forces me to this indiscretion. It is not that I have more at this post than at any other. All those of the colony would be equally good for me, since in one, as in another, I would find the life that is no longer possible for me to procure at the capital, that I no longer see except shuddering. Glance favorably on my situation, *Mon Général,* and believe that you will never have favored another person more sincere and respectfully attached than the one who is, with gratitude,

Mon Général,
Your very humble, obedient
Servant,
Zenon Trudeau [rubric]

St. Louis, April 30, 1795.

VIII

CARONDELET TO TRUDEAU, NEW ORLEANS, MAY 22, 1795[1]

Although the zeal and extended views of the instructions[2] given by the Company of Commerce of the Missouri merit my approbation, articles eighteen and nineteen cannot be put into practise, because the trade with the Pele [sic] and Laytane nations would fire up the *Provincias Internas,* which suffer greatly from the incursions of these nations. Neither is it best that the traders of the Company mix, in any direct or indirect way, with the nations who trade with the *Provincias Internas,* and it is of the greatest importance that the nations who make war upon the Spaniards of those said provinces be induced by all possible means to make peace. If they see themselves forced in their trips to give them some presents, it is necessary *not* to give fire arms to those nations which trade with the Spaniards and who do not have them, and even to give very sparingly of them to the Indians who might have knowledge of them.

Most especially is it of greatest necessity to have care and vigilance, since upon the very strict observance of these points depend the security of New Mexico and the *Provincias Internas,* as well as that of the establishments of Natchitoches, Arkansas and the Illinois. Therefore you will order altered articles eighteen and nineteen, which must be reduced to what I have said and you shall remit them for my approval.

May Our Lord keep you many years.

New Orleans, May 22, 1795.[3]

El Baron de Carondelet
[rubric]

Señor Don Zenon Trudeau.

[1]Written in Spanish. A.G.I., P. de C., leg. 22.
[2]Chapter II, document XVIII.
[3]Trudeau sent Carondelet a copy of the *reglamento* of the Company and the original instructions given to Truteau with articles 18 and 19 annulled "as I am forewarned, in order to merit Your Excellency's approbation." Letter to Carondelet dated St. Louis, September 24, 1795, A.G.I., P. de C., leg. 32.

IX

TRUDEAU TO CARONDELET, ST. LOUIS, MAY 30, 1795[1]

Number 227

[Marginal note :[2] Order medals
made if there
are none in
the storehouse]

I have received the eighteen new model commissions which Your Excellency has sent me in your official letter of October twenty-eighth,

[1]A.G.I., P. de C., leg. 31. Written in Spanish.
[2]By Carondelet.

last, for the Big and Little Osage Nations and the new ones in blank for the Ricaras and Mandan nations, and I am informed that the medals, gorgets, and flags which were also solicited will be sent to me.[3]

Without doubt I probably made a mistake in the *relación*[4] which I sent to Your Excellency when I solicited these commissions. Since two big medals have come for the Osages which should have been small ones, I am returning them to Your Excellency and, in order, not to retard the replacement of them, I will use two of those blank commissions for the Mandan nation, for whom I beg Your Excellency to remit two others.

The commandant at Fort Carondelet of the Osages, Don Pedro Chouteau, solicits two large medals, one for *Gredomanse* [Cheveux Blancs], small [medal] chief of the first nation, and another for the small [medal] chief of the second, Cayechingá [*le petit chef*] ; a small one of captain of the same, for Renombas [*Les Deux Cornes*]. I am proposing these to Your Excellency because these are Indians from whom good service is expected, because of the authority which they have with their people.

The Kansas nation does not have chiefs nor captains named by the government. Because of this I propose to Your Excellency two for large medals, two for small ones, and six captains, whose names, as well as the others, are found in the same *relación*[5] which includes the six Osage captains, for whom Don Pedro Chouteau had previously asked. They form the *relación* which I am enclosing.

As in the Oto, Mahas, and Poncas nations, some good *considerados* are found whom it is best to reward and, at the same time, they can divest of authority the chiefs who comport themselves badly with us, I beg Your Excellency to remit some medals, gorgets, and blank commissions to take care of the most useful of them.

May God keep Your Excellency many years.
St. Louis, May 30, 1795.

Zenon Trudeau [rubric]

Señor Baron de Carondelet

———

List of the Indians of the Big and Little Osage Nations for whom new model commissions for Chiefs, gorgets and commissions of the same model for captain are being solicited from the *Señor* governor general.

———

[3]Chapter II, document XX, note 6.
[4]This *relación* is in A.G.I., P. de C., leg. 127. I believe this *relación* was sent with Trudeau's letter no. 204, dated St. Louis, November 26, 1794, A.G.I., P. de C., leg. 30. See Chapter II, document XX, note 6. The names listed in the next paragraph were listed in the *relación*.
[5]The names of the Kansas chiefs are not included in the *relación* cited in the previous note. That *relación* contained the names of five Big Osage and fifteen little Osages and is dated St. Louis, November 17, 1794. None of the Osage names here given were in the other *relación*.

Indian names	French names
Patente [commission] of big medal	
Tawhangage	Clermont
Patentes of first medal	
Nonbonbechie	Le Mangeur de Canards
Opuchigie	La Bombarde
Pawrangy	Les Beaux Cheveux
Kuchechire	La Grande Piste
Whacetonchiga	Le Petit verd de gris
Escamany	Le Poux Blanc
Gorgets and *patentes* of captains	
Kane Angá	Le Kance Sage

Kansas

Large medals	
Kayguechinga	Le Petit Chef
Jhahoangage	Les grands Chevaux
Small medals	
Kueéhagachin	Le Batard
Whachanguia	Le Geur qui brule
Gorgets	
Manchiamany	Le petit Maigre
Chiabey	Le Couteau
Sesemany	Le Gauché
Chido Whaguegran	Le gendre du Coupiqué
Osibedocá	Le foulier Monillé
Whahon gaché	Le gendre de la Butte

Otoes

Small medals: Two blank *patentes* and two medals.
Gorgets: Four *blank patentes* and four gorgets.

Mahas

A large medal two blank *patentes* for the same.
A small medal.

Poncas

A large medal two blank *patentes*
A small medal

Two blank *patentes* for the Mandan nation to replace those which were given to the Osages.

St. Louis, Illinois, May 30, 1795.

Zenon Trudeau [rubric]

327

X

Trudeau to Carondelet, St. Louis, June 4, 1795[1]

Mon Général:

I have the honor of sending you the relation[2] of the one named Truteau, agent of the Company of the Upper Missouri on the voyage undertaken last year to penetrate the sources of this river. The innumerable obstacles which he encountered held him hidden ten leagues above the Ponca village, from where he seemed to leave again to go to his destination. The enclosed relation, although poorly copied, will sufficiently instruct you of all the troubles and risks of such a voyage. Therefore I will not tell you anything about it. It was about forty days ago that the Company sent its second expedition.[3] I do not augur for it a more fortunate success. In order to give a little encouragement, I joined the *Société* from which I would have retired this year, except for this same reason. I cannot continue it any longer and I do not believe that there are many others who are in any better condition that I to do it—which makes me forsee that it will be impossible to make the slightest disbursement next year, while it [the expedition?] has already cost the Company twenty thousand *piastres,* for which I am responsible for two thousand that *Monsieur* Chouteau did me the pleasure of advancing to me, the greater part of which I still owe him.

There just arrived on the American bank two French priests paid by Congress to preach to the savages with whom peace should be made this month. There has been granted by the Illinois district alone twenty thousand *piastres* in presents for the various nations. There is a *commissaire* appointed to oversee them. I do not know to what to attribute this change of *politique.* It has been a long time since one has heard from Europe. Peace was promised in the month of January and here we are in June and nothing has yet been terminated.

Monsieur Portell has just officially written me [torn] that a number of armed militiamen from Cumberland, having solicited the navigation of the Mississippi to go to *Écors à Margot,* and he having refused it, some threats towards an establishment were made, and then these same militiamen crossed by land to the said place where they should have met *Monsieur* Rousseau. I am waiting to know the result which can only be hostile— likewise our establishments of the Illinois are exposed by some *gens sans frain* [men without restraint] who somewhat like our savages of the Missouri follow only their caprice.

---

[1]A.G.I., P. de C., leg. 207B. Written in French.
[2]This was the first part of Truteau's journal—Chapter II, document XXII.
[3]Under Lecuyer. See Nasatir, "Anglo-Spanish Rivalry on the Upper Missouri in *Mississippi Valley Historical Review,* XVI (1929), reprint p. 19. See Introduction.

I am awaiting with impatience the barge of *Monsieur* Chouteau, which should have left New Orleans the twentieth of last month and which should be here about the first of August, in order to know finally if peace will have been made between us and France, which they say here has conquered the whole of *Catalogne* [Catalonia]. This is quite difficult to believe and does not give me either anxiety or inquietude, in view of the fact that rarely is the American news confirmed. The harvest of our settlements is threatened with ruin by caterpillars, and there remains no other hope at the villages near St. Louis to escape this plague but a large quantity of storks which have suddenly just appeared and are devouring these insects. I hope that they will save us. The Americans have been less fortunate—everything of theirs has been destroyed.

I have the honor of being with sentiments of the most lively gratitude and the most profound respect, *Mon Général,*

Your very humble and obedient servant
Zenon Trudeau [rubric]

St. Louis, June 4, 1795.

XI

Trudeau to Carondelet, St. Louis, July 4, 1795[1]

Number 229.

The one named Pedro Vial, who two years ago[2] was commissioned by the governor of Santa Fé to come to these establishments of Illinois, arrived this year (with four *mozos* who accompanied him) as far as the Panis nation (commonly called republic) which has its village on the bank of the Kansas River. There he met our traders with whom he remained fifteen days. He said that he came in order that the said Panis nation might make peace with the Comanches [Laytanes]. He delivered a medal, a complete suit of clothes and other things to the Chief. He

---

[1] Written in Spanish. A.G.I., P. de C., leg. 22. This letter was answered by Carondelet on December 10, 1795, A.G.I., P. de C, leg. 22. See in this connection document VIII.

[2] This refers to Vial's journey to open a road from Santa Fé to St. Louis. His diary of the journey to St. Louis is in A.G.I., P. de C., legs. 1442 and 2362 and translated and printed in Houck, *Spanish Régime in Missouri*, I, 350-358; and in A. B. Hulbert, *Southwest on the Turquoise Trail* (Denver, 1933), pp. 45-54. Copies of Vial's complete diary are extant in A.G.I., P. de C., legs. 1442 and 2362; *Archivo General y Público, Mexico, sección Historia*, volume 43; *sección Provincias Internas*, Vol. 102. His return trip from St. Louis to Santa Fé has been published in translation by A. B. Thomas in *Chronicles of Oklahoma*, July, 1931, pp. 195-208. I have collected a mass of materials from various archival and other repositories concerning Pedro Vial, without doubt the best scout, Indian guide and explorer in the service of Spain in the southwestern portion of the United States. I hope to publish in he near future a volume of documents on Vial and his contemporaries under the title of the "Genesis of the Santa Fé Trail" which in reality is the successor to this volume.

caused peace to be made as he desired, conducting our traders as far as the Comanche nation. In proof of the intentions of the government of both provinces that the said Indians live in friendship, he desires to take our traders to Santa Fé, very near to which vicinity they had arrived, but the latter refused, in order not to abandon their interests.

The mentioned Vial said he traveled from Santa Fé to the Panis in eight days; from this nation to St. Louis the traders regularly arrive by water in ten days, which infers that we are very near.[3]

May God Keep Your Excellency many years.

St. Louis, July 4, 1795.

Zenon Trudeau [rubric]

Señor Baron de Carondelet.

---

[3]See Nasatir and Liljegren, "Materials Relating to the History of the Mississippi Valley," *Louisiana Historical Quarterly* XXI (1938), reprint pp. 36-37.

XII

DECLARATIONS OF FOTMAN AND JONCQUARD, ST. LOUIS, JULY 4, 1795[1]

In the government house of St. Louis, Illinois, the fourth day of July in the year seventeen hundred ninety-five. I, Zenon Trudeau, Captain of the Louisiana regiment and Commandant of this western district of the Illinois, [was] informed by the above-mentioned Santiago Léglise, who has tonight arrived from the Missouri River, that he had brought with him two men whom he had found among the Pawnee nation and who had declared to him that they had been in the pay of some English merchants from the North who had sent them to the Mandan nation to trade and to form a trading-post in that nation; [on] learning this, I had one of the men appear before me in order to discover and make clear whence he came, how he had got in, [and] for what purpose he had come on the aforesaid Missouri River. Having made him take oath to tell the truth in proper form before the captain of militia, Antonio Soulard, and the first sergeant, Manuel Gonzalez Moro, witnesses in my behalf, I asked him for his name, country, and his religion. He replied that he was called Juan Fotman,[2] that he was a native of the province of Normandy in the kingdom of France, and a Catholic of the Apostolic Roman faith.

---

[1]Written in Spanish. A.G.I., P. de C., leg. 172bb; certified copy is annex no. 5 to Carondelet's dispatch no. 65 *reservada* to the Prince of Peace, dated New Orleans, January 8, 1796, A.H.N., Est., leg. 3900; edited and annotated in English translation by A. P. Nasatir in his "Spanish Exploration of the Upper Missouri" in *Mississippi Valley Historical Review*, XIV (1927), 63-69. The translation here given is from the original in A.G.I., P. de C., leg. 172bb. This is enclosed in document XV.

[2]Or Tremont.

Questioned as to whence he came, how he had entered into the Missouri river region, what his purpose was in coming, and told to give an account of his entire trip, he replied that he had left the city of Montreal in Canada on the fifteenth day of June 1794, employed as an oarsmen in a canoe, belonging to the trading company commonly called the Company of the North,[3] and had gone to the fort which that company has at the confluence of the Assiniboine and La Souris rivers. [On] the seventeenth day of the following October the agents of the same company had him leave with five others, led by the merchant Jussome with five horses laden with merchandise, powder and guns, with orders to travel with the greatest speed in order to reach the Mandan nation before the other traders who were established at that fort did. They traveled eleven days, during which they went astray several times and arrived at the above-mentioned Mandan nation the twenty-seventh day of the same month of October. They crossed the Missouri River and were well received and welcomed by that nation. Then the afore-mentioned Jussome divided his merchandise into two parts, giving one to the Canadian named Menard, who had been sixteen years with the nation for the purpose of trading with it, while the other half was taken by Jussome himself to the Gros Ventre nation, a league and a half away from the first. There Jussome ran up the English flag and began his trading, while the witness with the other five assistants were occupied in building a small fort and a hut between the Mandan and the Gros Ventre villages. [On] the nineteenth of April of this year, Jussome took his skins and went back to the fort from which he had come, leaving the witness with three others to continue the work on the fort and the house, on which they were to run up and did run up the English flag every Sunday. Tired, as he said, of the toils of his life in a region, which made desertion by way of the Missouri River easy, and fearful that on Jussome's return (which ought to take place a month after his departure) he would be employed in a remote region, he resolved to escape without saying anything to his companions. This he did at night. After traveling two days he killed a cow, from whose hide he made a canoe in the manner of the country and embarked in it. He traveled until the twentieth of May, when he met among the Pawnee Hocá nation Juan Bautista Truteau, agent of the Upper Missouri Company, and Santiago Léglise, trader for the same company, with whom he embarked four days later, arriving at St. Louis last night.[4]

[3] Northwest company.
[4] See Truteau's journal, Chapter II, document XXII. See also L. R. Masson, *Les Bourgeois de la Compagnie du Nord-Ouest* (Quebec, 1889); G. C. Davidson, *The Northwest Company* (Berkeley, 1918); C. M. Gates [ed.] *Five Fur Traders of the Northwest* (Minneapolis, 1933); *Wisconsin Historical Society Proceedings, 1915;* H. A. Innis, *Fur Trade in Canada* (New Haven, 1930); D. A. Stewart, *Early Assiniboine Trading Posts of the Souris-Mouth Group 1785-1832* (*Historical and Scientific Society of Manitoba Transactions* number 5, n.s., July, 1930).

Questioned what the several trading companies were which he had said had established posts or forts on the Assiniboine River and also were about to send traders to the Mandan nation and others on the Missouri, he replied that one was called the Great Company of Montreal under the name of its director, Grante; another was the small company of the same city under the name Piter Grante; [and] the Hudson Bay Company which had established its fort about two years ago and was trying to destroy or ruin the other two.

Questioned if the Mandan, Gros Ventre, and other nations that he had seen on the Missouri were armed with guns, and [whether or not, they] had given up their arrows to use them, he replied that all the nations that he had seen on the above-mentioned river, and particularly the Mandan and Gros Ventre, were all very well provided with guns, pistols, and swords, and did not lack ammunition, since they traded directly or indirectly with the English at Montreal and [at] Hudson Bay. [Because of this] they had not given up their arrows, still using them for hunting, while keeping the guns for war, for which they were very ready.

Questioned if, besides the three nations, Mandan, Gros Ventre, and Pawnee Hocá, about which he spoke, he had seen or heard mentioned others on the Missouri or in its vicinity, and ordered to tell what he knew about them, he said that below the Mandan nation there was a village of Pawnee Hocá which had two chiefs, and he did not know the number of its population; a hundred leagues farther down were other villages of these same Pawnee Hocá, more numerous than the first, who had four chiefs. A short distance from these he had seen about a hundred and fifty tents of the Cheyenne nation. All these Indians always stayed in the district south of the Missouri; in the district to the north were the Sioux, who had withdrawn at the time he went down the river, to take their skins to the different English posts, as they were accustomed to do every year. (Menard had told him) that a hundred and fifty leagues above the Mandan there was a beautiful river that had its source on the slope of a high cliff, which they commonly called among themselves the Rocky Mountain, in some lakes which are there. This same Menard likewise had told him that it was that Mountain of Cliffs [*Montaña de Peñas*], from which the Missouri River flowed by a cliff more than three hundred feet high. The Indians of these regions had told him that the Missouri was as navigable on the upper part of the mountain as on the slope, and these same Indians said that this river had its source within some other high mountains which were always covered with snow. He was also informed by the aforesaid Menard that going from the Mandan by the Missouri to the mountain of Cliffs, one always found the following nations: *Les Gens des filles, Nasseniboines, Les Sarcis, Les Gros Ventres*

332

des Prairies, Les pieds noirs, Les Gens des feuillets, [and] *Les Gros Ventres de la Montagne des Roches,* which are the same nations that go to trade with the English posts on the Nasseniboine River.

Questioned if he had knowledge, as to whether the nations which he had seen or heard mentioned communicated directly or indirectly with some Spanish posts that are to be found south of the Missouri, or beyond the *Montañas de Peñas* of which he had spoken, he said it could not fail to be true that the Mandan and Gros Ventre and the other nations nearby communicated with them, since all these Indians were well provided with bridles, which proved it, and almost all their horses, as well as many of their mules, are marked with well-known letters, and that these animals are ridden from the Rocky Mountains, whether they came for the purpose of war, or to trade when they are at peace, according to the information Menard had given him.

And, having read to him this declaration of his, he said that it was the same that he had made under oath, and that, because he did not know how to write, he had made the sign of the cross in the presence of the above-mentioned witnesses in my behalf who signed with me, the aforesaid Commandant.

Manl Gonz Moro [rubric] [There is a cross] Zenon Trudeau [rubric] Ane Soulard [rubric]

On the same day, month, and year, I, the above-mentioned Commandant, accompanied by the same witnesses, had appear before me a man who said that he had arrived this last night from the Missouri River. When he had taken oath to tell the truth, I asked him his name, his country and his religion. He said that he was called Chrisosthomo Jonca,[5] was a native of Canada, and a Catholic of the Apostolic Roman faith.

Questioned as to whence he came, how he had entered into the Missouri, what his purpose in coming was, and told to give an accurate account of his journey until he arrived at this city, he replied that he had left Montreal the seventeenth of April, 1788, with a man named Frebucher, employed by the Great Trading Company of the same city to navigate Lake Superior where he had passed a year; following that, he had spent another year at Grand Portage, another on the river *Qui Appelle* or *Catepoé,* another at *Fort L' epinette,* another at *Fort Recoude* [or *Reconde*] *de l'homme,* and another, for the second time, on the river *Qui Appelle,* or *Catepoé.* On the second of December, 1793, the witness with eight others begged leave of Roberto Legrante, the Company's agent, to go to the Mandan with some trinkets to trade with those Indians for buffalo skins. Having obtained it, they left the same day and after seventeen days of traveling through the

---

[5]Chrysostome Joncquard. For this expedition see the diary of John MacDonell as printed in Gates, *Five Fur Traders of the Northwest,* e.g. pp. 112ff; and also Masson, *op. cit.*

snow, they got lost, and after resting, they reached the Gros Ventre nation the nineteenth of the same month. The twenty-ninth of the following March, seven of his companions returned to the River *Qui Appelle* and the witness remained there with another named Laggrave. A certain Loison, the bondservant of the trader of this city [St. Louis] called Garreau, having arrived a few days later, he embarked with him and in five days' journey they came to the Pawnee Hocá nation in which they expected to find Santiago Léglise, with whom he wished to go to these posts. Being dissappointed in this hope, he remained with the above-mentioned Pawnee Hocá some time; then he went to the Cheyenne nation where he remained until the last winter, when he learned the the aforesaid Santiago de Léglise had arrived among the Pawnee. Immediately he went to join him, in order to take advantage of the opportunity. In this he succeeded. Having arrived this last night at this city, he had learned that his father was living at St. Geneviève. It was on his account that he had desired so much to come to this district.

Questioned if he knew of other trading companies established on the river of the Assiniboin, in addition to those by which he had been employed, he said that there are three trading companies established on the designated river, the Great Montreal Company, the Small Company of the same city, and, for two years in this place, the Hudson's Bay Company.

Questioned if he has seen on the Upper Missouri any Indian nations provided with fire arms, and if he knew, whether any of them had abandoned their arrows since they had been able to secure these arms, he answered that all the nations that he saw on the Missouri, and especially the Gros Ventre and Mandan, were sufficiently provided with guns, javelins and pistols, and did not lack the necessary ammunition since they trade with the English of Montreal and Hudson Bay and [also] they have not given up their arrows since they use them when circumstances demand in case of urgent necessity.

Questioned if, besides the nations he had frequented, he had seen others or heard them mentioned on the Missouri or its vicinity, and told to give the details he knew about them, he replied that there is a village of Pawnee Ocá below the Mandan nation; at a great distance farther below are found other small villages [*pueblozuelos*] of the same people, whose population is much greater, and a very short distance from there is the Cheyenne nation; that these nations always remain to the south of the Missouri, and on the north side are the Sioux. He is likewise informed that there is a very beautiful river about a hundred and fifty-leagues above the Mandan nation, that its headwaters rise in some lakes that are on the slope of the Rocky Mountain, and it then empties into the Missouri on the south side. He said likewise that he heard it said that the Missouri flows out of this Rocky Mountain by a precipice more than three hundred feet high, and that from the Mandan to the Rocky Mountain are found the following Indian nations: *Les Gens des filles, Nasseniboines, Les Sarcys, Les Gros Ventres des Prairies, Les Gens des feuillets,* [and] *Les Gros Ventres de la Montagne de Roches.* All of these nations do their trading with the English [who are] established on the Nasseniboine River.

Questioned if he knew whether these nations, which he said he had known, had any communication, direct or indirect, with any Spanish dominions that may be to the south of the Missouri or beyond the Rocky Mountains, he said that without doubt the two nations of Gros Ventre and the Mandan [at least] must have some dealings; if not with the Spaniards, at least with some Indian nations that are nearby those dominions, since there are evident signs which prove it; such as their horses and mules marked with very distinct letters and not lacking bridles and other trappings which go to prove it.

Having read this declaration to him, he said that it was the same that he had given under oath and that he is twenty-eight years old, and, because he does not know how to write, he made the sign of the cross in the presence of the afore-mentioned witnesses in my behalf, who have signed with me, the aforesaid Commandant.

Manl Gonz Moro [rubric] [there is a cross]

Zenon Trudeau [rubric]
Ane Soulard [rubric]

XIII

REPORT OF SANTIAGO CLAMORGAN AND ANTOINE REIHLE, ST. LOUIS, JULY 8, 1795[1]

In reply to your favor of the 6th inst., by which you request that the Company of the Missouri present to you the present condition of its matters and business in order that you may give a report to the Governor-General, we shall briefly review the steps of our operations to show the extent of our disbursements by the several expeditions made for the purpose of exploring the territory of distant nations; and to make more clear the weakness of the essential parts of our operations, from which, nevertheless, ought to result the reward for our labors.

---

[1]Written in Spanish. A.G.I., P. de C., leg. 2364; copy in Library of Congress. This report, forwarded by Carondelet to the Prince of Peace after the former had signed it, forms annex no. 7 to dispatch no. 65 *reservada,* dated New Orleans January 8, 1796. A.H.N., Est., leg. 3900, copy in Library of Congress. Printed in Houck, *Spanish Régime in Missouri, II,* 173-178. See also *American State Papers, Public Lands,* VI, 720. I have carefully collated, retranslated, and corrected Houck's translation. This report was forwarded to Carondelet on July 20. Document XVI.

At the time of the creation of this Company in the month of May, 1794, nothing seemed to be more urgent to it than to follow the trend of the explorations by which it found itself animated; its expectations were to advance rapidly towards the west and [it was] already marching with long strides upon unknown soil; but the experience which now shows us the difficulties which were incessantly to impede and combat our efforts, retards and defers the moment of our success; nevertheless the perserverance, which we have resolved upon as a rule and guide on this thorny way, must most assuredly lead us either to the glory of a felicitous result, or bury us under the ruins of our fortunes, and in whatever way fate may decree, we shall be satisfied if at the expiration of the required period, we open a useful way to our posterity.

In order to remove the chief obstacles which incessantly oppose us, it is necessary, do not doubt this, to buy the good-will of every nation and tribe which may oppose our communications; these expenses grow to a large sum on account of the frequent repetitions, and sap our fortunes; hope alone consoles and sustains us, but *Señor,* if in the midst of our career our means can no longer nourish our hope, to what shall we have recourse? We ought to anticipate that fatal moment, and seize with alacrity the opportunity of disclosing to you, how important it would be to the private interest of the Governor-General to come to our aid and support, aiding us in one of the expeditions which we undertake annually; the purpose and designs of our operations are in so many ways connected with the prosperity and preservation of the interior of the territory within the established limits and which we propose to extend to the shores of the Pacific Ocean, consequently His Majesty, desirous of maintaining his possessions, ought to encourage and support our Company in sharing its sacrifices.

On the other hand, the commerce of the English daily encroaching on our possessions requires a check in this far and distant region. You know that the habits and customs adopted by the English towards the possessions of others in time become in their eyes rights and property which they will always claim under the title of an acquired possession, without formal possession [i.e., legal right].

These claims which the learned prudence of our Governor should have anticipated by establishing several agencies, scattered and located at different points over this vast territory, would thus from the very beginning have stifled such an invasion [by the English].

If our observations are just and well connected [founded], will you have the kindness to explain to the Governor-General this incontestable truth, which we will make manifest [show] when the circumstances present an occasion.

You know well the effort and the repeated enterprises of various British companies that are drawing near to us: that of the Hudson Bay, which seemed a dream to us on account of the distance and which is today at our doors; the building of many of these forts situated on the Osseinbunes [Assinniboine], which statement is confirmed by two of their deserters who arrived here in one of the Company's piroques,[2] surprises and frightens us; those forts, which have not yet been constructed to the west and of which we have only heard, are to be built instantly. It seems that an invasion menaces all that extent of land [territory] which separates us from the Pacific Ocean: the English banner hoisted over the forts built in the territory of the Mandana nation on the Upper Missouri to take possession of land which seems to them unoccupied on account of our distance from it ought to fall instantly and retire to its own territory, otherwise it will be a tacit confession and consent on our part that our Government approves of this.

Although it is our right to destroy the commerce of the English under the protection of their banner in the heart of the dominions of His Catholic Majesty, are the forces of a Company recently subjected to untold costs, losses, expenses and presents to be feared by these strangers and is it simply a question of opposing them? We may consider ourselves fortunate if their ambition does not seek the means of precipitating us into an abyss in order to remove us from their vicinity.

If you believe it of importance to preserve the possessions of His Majesty from invasion which is rapidly moving forward to the frontiers of the Californias, crossing a territory which belongs to us, we ought not to permit this occasion to pass by without beseeching you to arouse your intelligence, your patriotism, and your talent to make known your observations to the Governor-General, pointing out to him the necessity of maintaining a militia to protect and defend the line which our Company is extending from the Maha nation to beyond the Rocky [Mountain] Chain about 50° north latitude to approach the Sound of Nootka.

This distance, which is not less than seven or eight hundred leagues, demands a chain of forts located at intervals which our Company has already begun to build, and which ought to continue in the same direction, at the places most exposed to the attempt [to invade our territory] of the foreigners both to destroy their projects and to place the Indian tribes that we may meet under the protection of our nation. This assistance from the militia sent by the Governor, united with the small force which our commerce will oblige us to maintain, will form, from now on, a barrier which the foreigners will not dare to cross, and still less when it is supported by the affection of the Indian nations which we must continuously bind to our

[2]Document XII.

interests by presents given for that purpose in the name of the Great Chief, their Father, the Spaniard, in order to give him more importance.

If, unfortunately, our weakened forces ever oblige us to interrupt our course of operations, we shall soon behold the English raising a clamor on the horizon, laying claim to taking possession [to which their banner, planted without opposition in] of different parts of the Dominions of His Majesty, [will bear witness³].

In these circumstances the Company offers to maintain for the whole period of its exclusive privilege, a garrison of one hundred soldiers in the different forts which it is obliged to erect on the line described above for the security of its commerce, if His Majesty will have the kindness of paying annually one hundred *pesos* for each one of the soldiers under the orders and commands of the general agent of this Company in this territory, and if His Majesty will grant such a subsidy as he may judge proper, in order to prevent the invasion of a commerce by foreigners advancing under the protection of their banner.

You know that the first expedition in the month of May, 1794, was made only to open a way for our discoveries, and that the agent of our Company who was in charge of it received orders to act with utmost prudence in order to assure and win the friendship of the nations through whose territory he would pass.

The capital outlay for this expedition, a statement of which we shall give below, was sent under the escort of valorous and picked men, and nevertheless in the course of a year it was not able to proceed farther than to the territory of the Ricara nation on account of the delays caused by the ice.

The second expedition, dispatched in the month of April of this year, strong and of greater consequence, under the command of a leader who was to shun nothing to remove all the obstacles from a thorny and difficult route, will be very fortunate if it reaches the Mandana nation at the end of fall, and before the severe cold, so as to be able to go overland to the Rocky chain [Mountains] whither he has orders to go without delay in order to reach, if possible, by next spring, 1796, the shores of the Sea of the West.

A third expedition, of which we have had the honor to announce to you the preparation, is to set out by the end of this month under the escort of more than thirty men and under the direction of a new agent, whose ability we have had the honor to make known to you. Presents shall be taken along in the name of His Majesty for the Ottos, Mahas, Poncas, and other nations whose territory the expedition may traverse, even to the most distant places which have already been explored and for those which may yet be explored with which we are partly acquainted, advancing far to-

---

³The words in brackets are omitted in the Library of Congress copy.

wards the northwest as well as to the southwest, in which places, the said agent shall give orders to construct forts along the first of these lines at all the places where it will be proper to place them to prevent the commerce of our neighbors and to prevent the hoisting of the English banner among the nations who are in our dominions.

In view of this we feel it our duty to beg you to obtain for us from the Governor twelve swivel-guns or little cannons of one pound caliber for the forts which we are beginning to construct, and we ask that they be sent to us as soon as possible. We shall now proceed to report the expenses and costs which this vast enterprise has caused us up to the present time, and of which we do not expect great returns until many years shall have passed.

May Our Lord keep you well many years.

St. Louis, July 8, 1795.

J. CLAMORGAN
A. REYHLE.

Among the merchandise which we expect from Michelmakinak to complete the stock of our present expedition, there was to be some powder, but we have just been informed that the capture of several boats destined for Canada makes it impossible that the powder be sent to us which we have asked for; that necessary article, which is indispensable, obliges us to have recourse to you, asking you to provide us with about five hundred pounds; whatever more we need we expect to secure in this town, in order to send out the third expedition.

Subscribed by the above.

Report of the first expedition of the Company of the Missouri for the remote nations of the west.

May, 1794

Value of the merchandise sent in a piroque of which one half is intended for presents to the Indians of different nations	20,000
Cost of the armaments, equipment, useful things, and provisions	4,000
Salaries of employees	8,800
For the furnishing of things that were necessary on leaving	900
For different expenses [made] indispensable by the promises of the Lieutenant-Governor, together with banners he sent for nine nations	2,000
By the expenses of a second piroque of merchandise which escorted the first	6,647
By expenses of armaments and salaries of men	4,000
For the furnishing of things given to them at their setting out	400
	46,747

Value of the merchandise and for a large [*bercha*] boat from which were to be taken the presents suitable for the different Indian nations 25,251

For expenses of the armament, utilities, and provisions...... 8,581

For salaries of the men 14,000

For their equipment on setting out 1,200

For the salaries of those who remained among the Ricaras with the agent of the Company 5,000

96,779 [*sic*]

Third Expedition, July, 1795

The merchandise of four piroques or *berchas,* one intended for the Ricaras, another for the Sioux, whom it is necessary to flatter in order not to risk being beheaded [headed off], another for the five villages of the Mandana nation, and the last one to reach the Rocky Chains [Mountains] with orders to go overland to the Far West.

Total merchandise............. 50,000

For the expense of the armament of the four vessels which are to set out 15,000

For the salaries of thirty men 30,000

For the things necessary to furnish them on setting out 3,000

For the salaries of many employees who are not able to return by the end of the year 6,000

104,000

46,747
96,779
104,000

200,779 [*sic*]

Enormous capital, the repayment of which ought to be favored by the Governor-General .... [247,526]

[This is the total when added and is also given with the totals of the three expeditions in annex no. 7 of Carondelet to Alcudia, no. 65, *reservada* A.H.N., Est., leg. 3900]

---

⁴Houck incorrectly prints the total at 200,779. The correct total when added is 247,526 which is the figure given with the totals of the three expeditions in annex no. 7 to Carondelet to Prince of Peace no. 65 *reservada,* cited in note 1.

XIV

Carondelet to Trudeau, New Orleans, July 8, 1795[1]

I have received the list of the distribution of the trades of the Missouri which you had divided into eighteen shares in order to place the same number of merchants who did not have entry during the first year, which I approve, as also that you manage prudently the trade of the Poncas nation in order to keep the passage open for the Commercial Company of the Upper Missouri.

May God keep you many years. New Orleans, July 8, 1795.

El Baron de Carondelet
[rubric]

Señor Don Zenon Trudeau

---

[1]Written in Spanish. Original in A.G.I., P. de C., leg. 2364; copy in Library of Congress; copy and transcript in Bancroft Library; draft in A.G.I., P. de C., leg. 127. Printed in Houck, *Spanish Régime in Missouri*, II, 163. I have retranslated this document.

XV

Zenon Trudeau to Carondelet, St. Louis, July 15, 1795[1]

I[2] have approved the appointment of Mr. Mackay as agent for the Company, and as regards the fort that they think has been built in the Mandan nation nothing can be decided, until it is definitely known whether one

Santiago Eglise, discoverer of the Mandan nation, without having been able to reach the same nation a second time because of having been detained on his way by the Ricaras, has returned to this town of St. Louis with two deserters from the English merchants of Montreal who joined him and whom he has presented to me. I am enclosing for you the statements[3] I took from them, which will easily inform you as to how those English merchants got on the Missouri where it appears they have run up the flag of their nation, and built a small fort at the place where our Company had the intention of building[4] a storage place and the larger of their buildings.

---

[1]Written in Spanish. Bancroft Library. This document has been edited and published in Nasatir, "Spanish Exploration of the Upper Missouri," in *Mississippi Valley Historical Review*, XIV (1927), 69-71.
[2]This is written in Carondelet's handwriting and has his rubric at the end of the note. This notation is a part of Carondelet's reply, dated New Orleans, December 10, 1795, A.G.I., P. de C., leg. 2364, Spanish original and copy in French. There is also a copy in the Bancroft Library. It is printed in Nasatir, "Spanish Exploration of the Upper Missouri," *op. cit.*, XIV, 71. Document XXIII.
[3]Document XII.
[4]See Truteau's "Instructions," Chapter II, document XVIII and Truteau's "Journal," Chapter II, document XXII, etc.

As you will see by the continuation of Juan Bautista Truteau's diary,[5] which I enclose, he also has not been able to go beyond the same Ricara nation where he had to remain awaiting the second expedition of the Company which left in the month of May just past.[6] Since the above-mentioned Truteau only pledged himself to serve that Company for two years[7] and this makes it necessary to send another agent right away so that he may arrive in time for him to retire from its interests before the return of the first [named], and since no native of the country has been found with sufficient intelligence to be entrusted with the important management of the discoveries that are proposed and the control of their interests, they have suggested to me Mr. Mackay,[8] a Scotchman, but a naturalized Spaniard, whom I have approved because of his honesty and intelligence. The Company will give him a part of its profits and four hundred dollars a year [besides], while the special privilege which you granted to the Company continues. It [the Company] is going to form a third expedition,[9] larger than the first two, which, leaving the fifteenth of the coming August, will go as far as it can before the winter, in order to continue its journey the following spring.

exists or not, but for the advantage of the Company permission should be secured from the king to send a well armed ship as far up the Missouri as it can go without danger.

The documents are with the correspondence of his excellency the Minister of State.[10]

Santiago Yglesia has not been willing to take a share in the Company and work through it. He has preferred to take out a hunting license which the Company has forced him to renew, equal to theirs for three years, and the agency for the trading post that he will establish in the Mandan nation; besides, they are to give him two men free of charge this present year for his trip, which he will begin in a few days. He will pass the winter among the Ricaras, and in the spring of the coming year he intends to pass the mountain of Rock [la Montaña de Roca], and reach the

---

[5]This is the missing part of Truteau's "Journal," as yet not found.

[6]Lecuyer's expedition—See Nasatir, "Anglo-Spanish Rivalry on the Upper Missouri," *Mississippi Valley Historical Review,* XVI (1929), reprint, pp. 19-20.

[7]Douglas says he was employed for three years. See *Missouri Historical Society Collections,* IV, 16.

[8]On Mackay see documents *infra:* Nasatir, "Anglo-Spanish Rivalry on the Upper Missouri," *op. cit.* and Nasatir, "John Evans: Explorer and Surveyor," *Missouri Historical Review,* XXV (1931), 219-239; 432-460; 585-608.

[9]Mackay's expedition.

[10]This is in the margin below the other marginal note, and seems to have been written by Carondelet's scribe, or secretary.

sea. He seems determined to make this discovery and, since he is full of courage and ambition, he is capable of so dangerous an undertaking; it is a pity that he should not have instructions that would make [it] easy for him to secure all the benefit of a trip which might [also] be of interest to the government.[11]

May God keep Your Excellency many years. St. Louis, July 15, 1795.

Zenon Trudeau [rubric]

The Baron de Carondelet

---

[11]See document II and Nasatir, "Jacques D'Eglise on the Upper Missouri," *Mississippi Valley Historical Review*, XIV (1927), 47-56.

XVI

TRUDEAU TO [CARONDELET], ST. LOUIS, JULY 20, 1795[1]

Mon Général:

With the present letter I am sending you via New Madrid, two official letters which have as their subject particulars which only pertain to this post, which is perfectly tranquil. Its inhabitants are occupied with their harvesting which will be more abundant than one could have hoped for, and there will even be some persons who will harvest more than thirty to one of wheat.

The arrival of Mr. Gayoso at Écors has surprised me. I believe he is the peaceful master of that place. Our neighbors are complaining a great deal about the establishment that he has formed.[2] Governor Sainte Claire should have been here a month ago. It is said that his trip was delayed by reason of the peace treaty which should have been made with the savages the fifteenth of last June, and which has been postponed until the same day of next August. It still seems that the English of Detroit are defending [sustaining] and diverting the nations from this peace which will never take place unless they are annihilated.

Some American newspapers have announced the taking of Frigniera [*sic*] and Rosa, as well as the surrender of all Holland. That is all that I have heard concerning Europe. The general peace which was announced has doubtlessly been delayed [due] to the continual misfortune of humanity.

I have just received a letter from Mr. Chouteau who informs me that [on] the 10th of next month the palisade of Fort Carondelet will be finished and all the buildings well advanced. He has with him 90 of the best men

---

[1]A.G.I., P. de C., leg. 215A. Written in French.
[2]At Écores à Margot. Gayoso's trip up the Mississippi River to the Illinois in 1795, during which he established the fort at Barrancas de Margot, had conferences with men from Kentucky, etc., is described in his letters and diaries. The present editor has collected, edited and translated them and hopes to publish them soon.

[20 of the King's best men] of the country. All the Osages are on their summer hunt. One chief with 40 men has been to the Arkansas without anyone knowing why. It is [will] only [be] upon their return to their village that one may find out if they have done any evil which we shall endeavor to repress.

Besides the men that Mr. Chouteau has with him, the Company of the Upper Missouri has also employed a large number who descended to New Orleans this spring with two *berges,* while a number of canoes have left for Mackinac. I was obliged to force the sedentary and cultivating people to embark in a vessel to transport food to *Écors* for the account of the king, which caused a scarcity of laborers and now is disturbing the harvest of wheat which is in progress, a part of which will be lost, if the weather becomes the least bit contrary. Those inhabitants who were able to obtain men are paying them four *piastres* a day.

Having requested Mr. Clamorgan, director of the Company of Upper Missouri, for an account of disbursements made by the said company to date in order to inform you that this same company has made efforts which some day will be able to drive out the English who have established themselves among the Mandans, the aforementioned Mr. Clamorgan has given me an enumeration of things to propose (which I shall not have the indiscretion to do), although in it [in fact] he exposes many realities of which it is your perogative alone to know their tenor. So without any aim, I am enclosing to you the letter of *Monsieur* Clamorgan, who, I believe, has at heart his own interests rather than those of the others, which he is trying to have considered, concerning all of which you will be able to judge very easily.[8]

The Company is going to organize next month a strong expedition which has frightened several members [of the Company] who, like myself, have resigned. This effort [of the Company] is going to exhaust everything, since it is not possible to expect returns [from it] before [it will be] necessary to form a fifth expedition, which it is [will be] indispensable to send out next spring; those having merchandise will only advance it when they have the assurance of seeing certain returns which, I believe, will exist some day, but a little too late for those who do not have sufficient means.

The one named Jacques de Léglise, discoverer of the Mandans, has not wished to take any interest in the company or to work for it. He is tormented with the ambition to discover the sea beyond the Rocky Mountains, which he will undertake next year, by starting out within a week to go to the place where the ice will stop him this winter.

_____

[8]Document XIII.

With the confidence that I have in your goodness, I would not dare, *Mon Général,* to write to you such boring letters which inform you of nothing interesting. On the other hand, I would believe it lacking in me, if I were to allow a single occasion to slip by to testify to you my respectful sentiments of attachments with which I shall be all my life,

> *Mon Général,*

> Your very humble and obedient servant,

> Zenon Trudeau
> [rubric]

St. Louis, July 20, 1795.

XVII

Trudeau to [Carondelet], St. Louis, August 30, 1795[1]

Answered

Mon Général:

The barge of *Monsieur* Chouteau arrived here with the news of the prospect of the insurrection of the negroes of Pte. Coupée, where the crew saw some culprits punished, during the passage of the barge. There is no doubt here that your prudence will have stamped out all of the germ of this conspiracy,[2] and that the lower part of the colony is to enjoy, as we, the most perfect tranquility.

Several days ago, I sent an express to give warning to the commandants of New Madrid, and Écores à Margot, (today St. Ferdinand), that one of our neighbors received a letter which assures him that North Carolina, the territory of the South, and the Georgia people were rising to join the people of Cumberland and the savages in order to come to drive us out of the new establishment which has been made at the said *Écors.* Since then, another letter reports the same thing, and also that they were determined to drive us out to the thirty-first parallel, and that there had already arrived at Cumberland thirteen companies of seventy-five men each, four cannons, and three mortars. If this enterprise is real, I believe that you are better informed than anyone, through ways easier than those that I can have.[3]

Monsieur Chouteau, the elder ,has just arrived from the Osages, who only returned from their summer hunt the seventh of this month. They

---

[1]Written in French. A.G.I., P. de C., leg. 211.

[2]See Gayarré, *History of Louisiana, Spanish Domination;* and Liljegren, "Jacobinism in Spanish Louisiana 1792-1797," *Louisiana Historical Quarterly,* XXII (1939), reprint p. 19.

[3]Discussed in Whitaker, *Spanish-American Frontier;* Bemis, *Pinckney's Treaty;* and other works.

robbed and pillaged a hunter of the Arkansas river. Chouteau made them return the horses and arms, placing a price upon the head of the first partisan whose band would do evil; furthermore, they will cover the dead, in order to stop the resentment of the families. It is in this manner that Mr. Cadet Chouteau wishes to get rid of some evil subjects, upon whom devolve all the disorders that they attribute to the corps of the nation, which for eighteen months has comported itself perfectly with all our establishments of the Illinois. The fort is finished, the *maison forte* well advanced, but the small artillery that you sent arrived too late to be transported this year since the waters are lower than ever.

One of the nations of Natchitoches has destroyed a Big Osage dwelling, in which was found the father-in-law of the principal chief, Clermont. A party of a hundred men left in pursuit of the murderers. At the departure of Mr. Chouteau they had not yet returned. They had employed every means to stop the vengeance, but it was impossible to attain that goal, since the *loge,* considered as being destroyed, was a matter involving the courage of all the warriors of the village.

There arrived here by way of Canada a young officer, *émigré* from *the régiment de Flandre,* supplied with papers from the British Minister which ordered his admittance to all the countries of this domination, and invited the foreigners who were not at war with it [England] to be favorable to him, etc. The good upbringing of this young man, his indigence, joined to the fact that he was attached to an officer whom I knew very well, the brother-in-law of M. Daunois, my compatriot, engaged me to welcome him and to be of some aid to him, until he would be able to find some means of placing himself in a position to be able to gain a livelihood.

The Company of Commerce of the Mandan nation, or Upper Missouri, has just dispatched its third expedition,[4] composed of thirty-three men, well provisioned. These expenses are considerable, in relation to the means of those who compose it, who are playing double or nothing. They have to overcome the ferocity of the savages [which is necessary to overcome because that is necessary in order to make them free],[5] which they can only succeed in doing by their keeping up their credit, which will fall or strengthen, according to the success of these first operations. If they are successful, they will deliver a large quantity of fine skins in the lower part of the colony. By banishing the English from our possessions, they will be aiding us, by going through and knowing these districts.

---

[4]Mackay's expedition—see Nasatir, "Anglo-Spanish Rivalry on the Upper Missouri," *Mississippi Valley Historical Review,* XVI (1930); Nasatir, "John Evans: Explorer and Surveyor," *Missouri Historical Review,* XXV (1931), and documents *infra.*

[5]This is the literal meaning; it is difficult to translate.

We know positively that the merchants of Montreal have given orders to their agents in the trades of the Northwest to thwart the operations of our Company. This additional obstacle will have to be overcome in these trips which they [the Company] can intercept by having them attacked by the nations who in general do their hunting on the banks of the Missouri, and who would neglect nothing to make them act and conserve them [their hunting ground] for themselves. This can only be changed by time and means. I am enclosing a letter from Montreal which makes known what I am saying.[6]

Up to now persons coming from Canada have not been able to give me any news from Europe. It has also been a long time since there has been anything said of America, in such a way that we are absolutely ignorant as to, whether or not, the peace you had the kindness to tell me of has taken place or is terminated, which is as necessary in this country, as in all other parts of the world. We lack the most essential things; skins are without value; the savages, discontented with the price of the merchandise, are hunting less; and, as long as the war will last, we shall always fear the Americans, who have just concluded peace with all the nations who forcibly await them in the posts which have been ceded them by the English,[7] which, once given up, will without a doubt make a change in the trade, and cause us to experience vexations, which can no longer be borne from an old enemy. This in turn will cause the Americans to make laws and perhaps [even] excite them to do evil against us.

I have just as this moment learned that *Monsieur* Gayoso is on his way here, and that he will arrive in five or six days.[8] I am most flattered with his coming which will enable him to tell you in detail how interesting this country is, and how much it merits encouragement, both for its physical beauty and for the neighboring Americans, who are increasing every day and who will increase much more when an office for the sale of lands is opened. Many honest families have asked my permission to cross to this bank, which I have accorded them, as you permitted me by one of your letters. A certain number of these men, the good cultivators, can do nothing but great good for our inhabitants, who need an example to put aside their old methods of cultivation, and to substitute a better one.

The savages have just killed one more inhabitant on the other bank. That same day three savages fired on one of our men, who received two bullets which fortunately only grazed him, and, by grace of having a good

---

[6]See *e.g.*, document XII and Nasatir, "Anglo-Spanish Rivalry on the Upper Missouri," *Mississippi Valley Historical Review*, XVI (1929), reprint pp. 22 ff.
[7]By Jay's Treaty. Wayne's victory and Treaty of Greenville are probably referred to.
[8]An account of Gayoso's visit is contained in Gayoso de Lemos to Carondelet, New Madrid, November 24, 1795, A.G.I., P. de C., leg. 2364.

horse, he was able to withdraw from the affair and go to the village of St. Ferdinand where he advised them [villagers] to give chase to them [Indians]. This they did but they did not succeed in reaching the Indians. Moreover there are always so many of them in our environs, that, often falling upon the evil doers, one does not dare arrest them for fear of mistaking and angering those who might be innocent.

I am always annoying you when I have the honor of writing to you. I beg you to pardon me for it, in favor of the desire that I have of informing you of my respectful attachment and the sincere gratitude with which I shall be all my life,

Mon Général

Your very humble and obedient servant,

Zenon Trudeau [rubric]
St. Louis, August 30, 1795

XVIII

TRUDEAU TO CARONDELET, ST. LOUIS, SEPTEMBER 26, 1795[1]

Mon Général:

I have received the letter with which you honored me dated June 28, last, which informed me that the Court had continued your former salary. I feel the liveliest satisfaction about it, because that makes you [feel happy], and assures us hope that you will not leave our colony. As long as the calamities of the globe menace it—you will continue for us the good fortune, which despite turbulent elements, your prudence has conserved for us. Your pains and your cares, Mon Général, will immortalize for ever your name in Louisiana, which can only make prayers for you to acquire elsewhere the recompense which it cannot offer you.[2]

General St. Clair arrived ill at Kaos. His great age, his rank, as well as the high virtues which characterize him, have made me think that I have not in any way compromised the honor, the decency and the dignity of the command confided to me in anticipating him by a visit which I paid him yesterday. Despite a great fever he did all that he could to receive me with distinction, as well as all those who accompanied me. I do not doubt that he will come to see me as soon as his illness will permit him. I shall do my best to receive him and he will excuse, I hope, the inadequate facilities of a poor infantry captain who has greater desires than means of honoring his command. It appears that the object of his trip is to examine the conduct of the lesser tribunals, appoint judges there, inspect the

---

[1]Written in French. A.G.I., P. de C., leg. 211.
[2]Carondelet had asked for (1) return to Spain; (2) Captaincy-General of Cuba.

militia, and make a promotion there. Within eight or ten days he is to return and go to Philadelphia. This general assures us that peace has been made between France and us, and he believes that peace with all the powers will not be delayed very long. From Canada we are also assured that the posts of McKina [Michilimackinac] and Detroit will not be delivered, as the English had previously agreed. They say that orders have been given to repair the fortifications, which have been neglected since the peace of '83. *Monsieur* St. Clair has scarcely any difficulty in believing this news.[3]

Monsieur Gayoso is coming here and has *relaché*. It has been a time since I have seen anyone from New Madrid, and I do not know whether or not I shall have the good fortune to see this amiable governor. We already feel the severe cold which, joined to the ordinary maladies of the season, I fear may place before him obstacles to the project of a second voyage.

I am sending to you the *Reglement* of the Company of Commerce of the Upper Missouri and the instructions given to its agent.[4] I have poorly understood what you prescribed to me in your official letter in this regard; the copies that I have had the honor of sending to you have not been returned to me, and I believed them sufficient for your secretariat. This Company is perfectly well arranged this year for the Ponca, Maha, and Oto nations which they wish to have. The man named Jean Meunier who had the exclusive privilege of the Poncas,[5] not finding anyone to make advances to him, has resigned his privilege with some profit. The four traders, chosen by lot for the Mahas, have not dared to engage themselves [in trade] there; while those of the Otoes have sold their profits, which thus overcomes all obstacles in the Company's favor. The Company has undertaken much more than one might have hoped, and has today sixty men in its service, the least of whom is paid two hundred *piastres* per year. These great discoveries could only be done during the course of the next year in order to have news for the following [year].

---

[3] Arthur St. Clair, governor of the Northwest Territory. See C. W. Alvord, *Illinois Country* (Springfield, 1920); Smith, *St. Clair Papers;* etc. Gayoso de Lemos visited St. Clair when he was in St. Louis.

[4] Chapter II, documents IX and XVIII. In acknowledging receipt of this letter of Trudeau, Carondelet said that he had received the "original *reglamento* and instruction of the Company of Commerce of the Upper Missouri which you enclose to me in your official letter of September 24—" Carondelet to Trudeau, New Orleans, December 10, 1795, A.G.I., P. de C., leg. 22. Trudeau enclosed the originals in his letter of September 24, 1795—A.G.I., P. de C., leg 32—Carondelet acknowledged receipt of the copy of the original *reglamento* of the Company and instructions to Truteau in his letter to Trudeau, dated New Orleans, December 10, 1795, A.G.I., P. de C., leg. 22. On January 14, 1796, Carondelet wrote to Trudeau (draft in A.G.I., P. de C., leg. 138) that he had in his possession the *reglamento* of the Missouri Company which "you enclosed to me under date of September 24th [*sic*] of last year."

[5] Chapter I, document XXXIV, and Chapter II, documents I, III, VI, VIII, and XVI.

349

I should have desired that the Abbé Flagier would wish to accept the curacy at St. Charles.[6] It is true that he had already told me that he would not be free until after a trip to Baltimore. We have here *Monsieur* Abbé Janin, *le curé refractaire* of the ville D'Angers, a respectable and very learned man, who, although placed at Kaskaskia by the Bishop of Baltimore, is very unhappy. This position of parish priest cannot even support him. Through the charity of the judge of the place, he has informed me of his situation, begging me to claim for him from your goodness, *Mon Général,* what humanity and religion urged me to do. I am persuaded that you will pardon me this new importunity and that you will graciously give me a consoling reply for this *curé,* who has already been assisted in Spain by the Bishop of Zamora, who has supported him for two years, during which he had sufficient time to learn the Spanish language well enough to exercise his ministry. St. Charles is too distant from St. Louis for Don Didier to offer to go there; the customs are so depraved there due to its being in a most out of the way location and its residence of the savages, mongrels and the worst scoundrels in Illinois. A *curé* would be for them a God who would restrain them in their vices, and would insensibly fix them to the work of the land [agriculture], thus rendering them all the more happy. St. Ferdinand is practically in the same condition but the population is small, while on the contrary St. Charles is increasing every year. The last news that I have received from Mr. Pierre Chouteau concerning the Osages, indicates that they have been perfectly tranquil, without any one leaving for war beyond [their village]. The one [group of Osages] which had been pursuing the men of Natchitoches to revenge some deaths returned at the end of eight days without having done anything.

Mon Général, how can I express my gratitude for all your past goodness and for the new grace that you have yet deigned to favorably support my *petit mémoire*? I have nothing more to desire for my good fortune and that of my family, valetudenarian for ten years, [although] my hopes were ruined twice by fires. I had no other hope than to establish myself permanently with my position and salary in this small nook of the province, and for that I would have sacrificed all the accumulation of the savings that I owe to you, if I had been able to have appointed for me at [to] Madrid an *apoderado* [an authority] who might continue your support, upon which I base the felicity of the rest of my old days, which will be employed to impress [*engravé*] for ever in the memory of my children that they have, as I, a benefactor who is responsible for their happiness, and for whom we all together

[6] See Document VII.

should send prayers for his prosperity. It is in these sentiments that I shall be all my life with the most profound respect,

Mon Général

Your very humble, obedient servant

Zenon Trudeau [rubric]
St. Louis, September 26, 1795

XIX

MACKAY TO CLAMORGAN, OCTOBER 24-27, 1795[1]

Copy extracted from a letter written by Sr. MaKay, agent-general of the Company, dated October 24th, last, from the village of Octoctata at the entrance of the Platte River.

To Messrs. Clamorgan and Reyhle, directors at St. Louis,

I arrived here the fourteenth of this month after a forty-four days' march.[2] The bad weather and one of the pirogues of my convoy, which has continually filled with water, delayed me, and will delay me in reaching the Mahas.

I must recommend to you never to load your barges or *voitures* too much and always to have at the head some leaders of ability. I ought not to [have to] tell you, nor to forewarn you, of the indispensable necessity of having a person possessed of a great talent with the Indians remain at the post of the Mahas at the head of your operations. You know that this is a place of importance for the new commerce and for communication with the Mandans.

I am informed at this time by the Othos that the pirogue which left in the month of April last, in order to go to the Mandans, consigned to Truteau and conducted by Léquiyé [Lecuyer] is at the Poncas where the merchandise has been pillaged. The one named Breda whom you dis-

---

[1]Written in French. This is an original or contemporary copy, unsigned, in the Bancroft Library. It is annotated and published in Nasatir, "John Evans: Explorer and Surveyor" in *Missouri Historical Review*, XXV (1931), 436-441. I have made several changes in this translation. This document was sent to Carondelet on December 19, document XXV.

[2]This would place the date of his departure from St. Louis at about the first of September. There have been some divergent opinions concerning the date of Mackay's departure from St. Louis. Mackay states in his "Journal" (document XX), that he left about the end of August, 1795. This date is corroborated by Trudeau (document XVII). André Michaux states, "I was informed at Illinois that Mackay, a Scotchman, and Even [Evans], a Welshman, started out at the end of July, 1795 from St. Louis to ascend the Missouri." *Travels in Kentucky*, entry for December 11, 1795, in R. G. Thwaites [ed.], *Early Western Travels* (Cleveland, 1904), III, 79-80. Carlos Howard said the expedition left in July. Howard to Carondelet, St. Louis, May 13, 1797, Bancroft Library. Trudeau in a letter to Carondelet, St. Louis, July 15, 1795, said the expedition would leave the fifteenth of August. Document XV. Clamorgan stated the expedition would leave in July. Document XIII.

patched after him must have arrived too late to give aid and take possession of it.[3]

If the Company is to continue its commerce in this distant country, it is absolutely indispensable to have the village of the Othos in your power. Otherwise, your pirogues will be more or less pillaged each year. I have promised them that you will have a fort built among them next year, in order to protect them against their enemies;[4] and that they would have many guns for their hunt; for they complained of not having a fourth of that which they have need. In these two types of promises, I hope that you will not make me out a liar, seeing that the first, under the guise of favoring them, will serve to hold them in check, and that the second is absolutely inseparable from our interests. I have contracted this obligation with them, on condition that they behave well towards the agents that you will send them and toward the boats which might ascend to the Mandans. They have decided on the spot where they wish the fort to be built—at the entrance of the Platte River, where they intend to place their village. This situation will be advantageous. The agent that I have placed there for the trade with them will apprise you of their conduct, and of means of subjecting them to our interests. If it should occur that the Othos do not keep their word and behave themselves badly, deprive them of all help the next year. We will gain much from this by showing them that their need depends absolutely on the good will of the Company, and that, in default of us, they must no longer count on the aid of other traders, each accustomed to lie to them in pursuance of his own interests. But if their conduct is honest remember well to carry out my promise. You can not conceive the difficulties one has in passing through this nation, in spite of the presents we must give them. The chiefs have no command, and this nation is so rough that one has trouble to move them, even in their own interest. They complain that Motardi, Quenell and the other traders who have come among them for several years, have spoken so much deceit, have cheated so much, and have made them so many promises of which not one has ever been fulfilled, that they wish to believe nothing now without seeing. To tell you the truth, they are in a kind of anarchy which will lead them to become dangerous enemies of all the commerce of the Upper Missouri. [This danger will increase] if this post continues to be open as usual each year to all types of traders who are only interested in the present, and do not worry about the future.

I am satisfied enough with the equipment of my whole convoy, but I wish that you had given me better interpreters for the Maha. Many of

---

[3]See Nasatir, "Anglo-Spanish Rivalry on the Upper Missouri," *Mississippi Valley Historical Review*, XVI (1929), reprint, pp. 19-20.

[4]Fort Charles was located about six miles below the present site of Omadi, Nebraska.

those people at St. Louis who think they understand the Indians and who on that basis, wish to be sent out to the [Indians], when they arrive here, are only children. We need some good, shrewd interpreters.

If the government, as well as the merchants, do not take combined measures for the continuation of the commerce in the Missouri, by prohibiting the entrance of those who are capable of breaking away or eluding them, this country is lost for all time, both to His Majesty and to his subjects. The commerce of foreigners on the one hand and the bad behavior of our traders on the other are enough to throw all the nations into insurrection and anarchy at once. Only one year is necessary for that; but how many would be necessary to restore them to order and submission?

The Othos desire that the same agent whom I left them for the trade be continued. He appears to be well-liked there; consequently will be more than any other capable of leading them to our purpose, for [which is] the passage to the Upper Missouri of the boats, which could not escape them, due to the continual stationing of various strong parties, hunting all along the banks of the river, where they will establish themselves more than ever, in order to intercept our communications—whenever they are tempted to do so by their usual inclination to do evil—now that they know of our new enterprise. If the government does not grant the Othos to you as the key to our distant interests, it is absolutely necessary to purchase [that trade] from those men who might be [its] proprietors, if, however, you think that we might be able to sustain the increase of expense. Otherwise, we must retire [withdraw] as well as we can from the career of discoveries, and renounce now, rather than later, our ruinous [enterprise].[5]

In case the favors of the government are distributed far enough in advance to us, so that we may have them, and arrange at our pleasure the absolute needs of all these nations, through whom we must pass, do not fail to give at least two swivel guns to the agent of the Othos, in order to have the fort that you will have built there respected.

This will especially please that nation, since it will consider them a protection against an attack by their enemies.

27th of October, eight leagues above the Platte River.

This morning six men belonging to the Company and coming from the Poncas arrived at my camp. They belonged to Lecuyer's expedition or that which Antoine Breda was leading which you had sent after him, but which arrived too late to help him. This autumn the Poncas killed a Ris who was coming as a messenger [en parole]. I am much afraid that I will experience great difficulties in passing through this nation next spring to reach my destination. The thing which has just happened to our merchandise has entirely destroyed our stock, and I do not know how to replace it.

---

[5] See document XVIII.

Tabeau,[6] one of the *engagés* of Lecuyer's expedition, not only should be deprived of his wages, but also severely punished, in order to serve as an example to the future. He is an infamous rascal. Lecuyer, the leader, who has not had less than two wives since his arrival among the Poncas, has wasted a great deal of the Company's goods, even as you will see by the account which I have received, and am sending to you.

I have a difficult task to fill, but I do not lose courage. Next spring I will inform you of all that I will have done.

I am,

---

[6]See A. H. Abel, *Tabeau's Narrative of Loisel's Expedition to the Upper Missouri* (Norman, 1939).

XX

MACKAY'S JOURNAL, OCTOBER 14, 1795-JANUARY 18, 1796[1]

No. 78 *reservada*

Your Excellency:

I am sending to Your Excellency the enclosed relation, no. 1, of the voyage of the Scotchman, Mackay, general agent of the Trading and Exploring Company of the Missouri River toward the South Sea, which I established in the year 1794, and confirmation of which I have solicited by communication *reservada*, no 65,[2] under date of January 8, of the current year.

The relation of Mackay confirms the previous information of the introduction of the English from Canada into the domains of the King, both among the Mandan tribe who are located on the south shore of the Missouri River, and of which I informed Your Excellency by the above-mentioned communication *reservada*, no. 65, and on the Chato River which flows into New Mexico, to the point where they have erected a blockhouse [*casa fuerte*], in order to assure their clandestine trade with our [many] Indian tribes, and, perhaps even, with the natives of Santa Fé. The letter written to me by the Commandant of the Post of Natchitoches, Captain Don Luis Deblanc, a copy of which is enclosed no. 2, agrees with the relation of Mackay. In respect to the fact that, notwithstanding that the said

---

[1]Written in Spanish. The original of this letter of Carondelet to the Prince of Peace, no. 78, *reservada*, is in A.H.N., Est., leg. 3900; draft in A.G.I., P. de C., leg. 2364 From the latter draft it has been printed in Houck, *Spanish Régime in Missouri*, II, 181-182 I have collated, checked and corrected the printed translation with the original. Perhaps this Journal was forwarded by Trudeau in his letter of April 3, 1796 (A.G.I., P. de C., leg. 212A). See Chapter IV, document V, note 4. It was sent in Trudeau's letter to Carondelet of May 1, 1796. A.G.I., P. de C., leg. 193.

[2]A.H.N., Est., leg. 3900, Chapter IV, document III.

letter attributes to the Americans the construction of the blockhouse above mentioned, it is a fact that the latter have not allowed themselves to be seen as yet on the Missouri and its neighborhood. The fatal consequences of such an attempt on the part of a nation as enterprising as the English are related in the above-mentioned *reservada* communication, no. 65.

There are two means, in my judgment, which may be employed, in order to prevent the English from the beginning from forming claims, in regard to these domains of His Majesty. One of them, the more efficacious, more permanent, and less costly, and more honorable, is detailed at length in the above-mentioned communication *reservada* no. 65. The other, which will be no more than a relief for the moment and an uncertain palliative, consists in forming an expedition in Santa Fé[3] to explore the most northernly part of New Mexico, and driving the English from it, by destroying the fortified post which they have on the Chato River. I am ignorant of the forces which that province can employ in such an expedition, as well as whether the Indian tribes of those districts will view it with tranquillity, or whether they will take the part of the English. But I am sure that if His Majesty will empower me to undertake it from St. Louis, Illinois, with two hundred men, picked for the greater part from our settlements of the Upper Mississippi, and some Indians, we shall succeed in destroying that settlement with sufficient secrecy, although the distance is very great. Since the expedition can be directed by water and made under the name of the Company without its true object being understood, its outcome will be so much more secure, for the Company will be able to carry some light pieces of artillery to bombard the blockhouse, and scatter the savages who may wish to side with the English, who cannot carry artillery to such vast distances.[4]

I can do no less than represent to Your Excellency with this motive how advantageous it would be to assure and fix in the service of Spain the agent Mackay, a person of great intelligence and merit, whom the English employed with such great success in the explorations of the countries,

---

[3] See among many letters that can be cited, the letter of Pedro de Nava to Alcudia, no. 2, *res.*, Chihuahua, August 6, 1795, and its enclosures. A.G.I., Sección, Papeles de Estado, legajo 37.

[4] This was done by Evans. See documents, *infra;* and Nasatir, "John Evans: Explorer and Surveyor," *Missouri Historical Review*, XXV (1931). These plans were part of the secret instructions given to Carlos Howard by Carondelet, dated November 26, 1796, A.G.I., P. de C., leg. 2364, and translated in *Missouri Historical Society Collections*, III, 71-91; and excerpts in *Wisconsin Historical Collections*, XVIII, 449-452. See also three letters nearly identical, all dated New Orleans, December 1, 1795, Carondelet to Prince of Peace, no. 85 *res.*, A.H.N., Est., leg. 3900; Carondelet to Azanza, no. 1, *res.*, index in *Ibid.*, draft in A.G.I., Sto. Dom., 86-7-2 (old numbering), translated in Houck, *Spanish Régime in Missouri*, II, 133-138; and draft [Carondelet] to Las Casas with two additional paragraphs in A.G.I., P. de C., leg. 178B. See also Nasatir, "Anglo-Spanish Rivalry in the Iowa Country 1797-1798," *Iowa Journal of History and Politics* XXVIII, (1930), and Liljegren, "Jacobinism in Spanish Louisiana 1792-1797," *Louisiana Historical Quarterly*, XXII (1938).

located north of the Missouri, with the intent of opening communication with the South Sea. A commission as captain in the army with the full pay of his rank would flatter his ambition, causing him to sacrifice himself for the service of Spain, and the success of the Company of the Missouri in which he is interested.

May God, Our Lord, keep your Excellency many years.

New Orleans, June 3, 1796

Baron de Carondelet [rubric]

Most Excellent *Señor*, the Prince of Peace.

[Mackay's Journal][5]

Voyage of *Monsieur* Mackay, General Agent of the Company of the Missouri, dispatched by Don Santiago Clamorgan, its director, to ascertain the discovery of the Pacific Sea, escorted and convoyed by a certain number of picked men who left the city of St. Louis, Illinois, at the end of August, 1795.

October 14, 1795

On this day I reached a place one league below the mouth of the Chato River [Platte].[6] I camped in that place in order to visit the Othochita [Otoes] and take fresh provisions there. On the following day I reached a place one-half league above the said river, in order to construct a house for the wintering of the traders whom I left there on the 20th day [of the same month] following. The principal men of said tribe arrived to the number of sixty. On the following day I assembled the chiefs in council, in order to chide them, and point out to them with vigor, their evil conduct with the whites whom their Spanish Father had sent to them for the purpose of furnishing them the goods that they needed. Convinced of the truth, they gave me weak excuses. I made them perceive the consequences that might result, if they did not change their conduct immediately. Their reply reduced itself to saying in effect that they would change their conduct toward the whites, if I kept the word which I gave them; in respect to the fact that they had never, until the present, had any but traders who deceived them by telling them all sorts of lies, in order

---

[5]A.G.I., P. de C., leg. 2364, transcript in Library of Congress, and printed in Houck, *Spanish Régime in Missouri*, II, 183-192. I have carefully checked and corrected the printed translation with the Library of Congress transcript. This journal was dispatched to Carondelet accompanied by several other letters from Mackay and by Trudeau's letter of May 1, 1796, A.G.I., P. de C., leg. 193. Carondelet in his letter to Clamorgan dated New Orleans, July 9, 1796, acknowledged receipt of the journal; original in Bancroft Library and copy in the Missouri Historical Society. See also Chapter V, document II.

[6]See Document XIX.

to get hold of their furs, only giving them [in return] great promises which never were fulfilled. I told them that their Father, in his desire to render them happy, had formed a Company to supply them with all the things that they needed; that this Company, of which I am here as its agent, would never deceive them in its promises, if they behaved well toward us. In that case the Company will have a fort built for them next autumn, in order to protect them from their enemies; in which there will always be merchandise, without them having to go to the English, who desire to deceive them more than do the traders. After this speech which I made to them through my interpreter, I perceived that it had not failed to produce an effect, because, although they were accustomed to pillaging the boats destined for the most distant posts, they absolutely did not touch a thing, except what I wished to present to them of my own accord, and they did not even dare to enter into any of the pirogues laden with goods for the Mandans and other tribes of the Upper Missouri.

I remained eleven days with the Othoctatas [sic] in order to make them some suggestions and attract them by means of mildness to our side. I imagine that my harangues will not fail of success. If such be the case, will Your Excellency remember to fulfill the promises which I have made to them. In case of the contrary, I beg Your Excellency, for the future prosperity of the Company, to deprive them entirely of everything they need. In that regard Your Excellency may interest yourself with the Government, in order that no one may be permitted, for the general welfare of the country, to penetrate to this tribe, whether for trade or hunting. Without doubt Your Excellency will find the necessary aids for preventing those who go to the Panis and the Lobos [i.e., Wolves] and Abenaquies from giving them any aid secretly, by passing through any other road than the abovementioned Chato River, on whose banks are located the Othocatatas who would doubtless pillage them. In case that their conduct with the Company permits the sending of goods next year, I must inform Your Excellency that at least one hundred guns are needed for this tribe, without which, as has happened, the returns will be very doubtful, since threefourths of the tribe are idle all winter, so that the trader suffers a considerable loss in furs.

On November 3, the son of Pájaro Negro [Blackbird] who was in St. Louis the past summer, came to meet me with a band of young men, as soon as he heard of my speedy arrival among his tribe. His father sent him to protect me from the obstacles that I might meet on my way. They accompanied me overland for the two day's march to their village. The cold and the snow have been so great that my voyage has been retarded considerably.

On November 11, I reached a place below the village of the Mahas with the great chief Pájaro Negro who came to meet me a day's journey distant. He showed great affection and friendship to me, as did the other smaller chiefs who accompanied him. As soon as we reached the village, he placed a guard in my boats to watch all night, and to see that his people did not take anything.

On the 12th and 13th, the weather was so bad that I was unable to unload my boats. Consequently, during these two days, I held long conferences with the Great Chief on various important matters, both for the Government and the Company. I found him in those conferences, to be a man full of experience, intelligence, and capacity.

The rigor of the weather having moderated on the fourteenth, I unloaded my *berchas* and pirogues and placed them in securtiy.

On the 15th I assembled the Great Chief and the principal men of the tribe in Council, and represented forcibly to them the bad conduct that they had observed toward the traders who went to their tribe. I told them that their Spanish Father sent me, in order to ascertain whether they had any intention of changing their conduct; that, if they acted well, a Company, formed for the Missouri, would never allow them to want for anything, and they would not need to have recourse to the goods which the English bring annually; that then they would have whites with them all the year whom the Company would leave for their needs; and that, if they did the contrary, they would be deprived of everything.

They answered me that the traders who had been sent to them hitherto were very bad, and the last of all the men whom they had seen among the nation [were the worst?]; but that now they were satisfied at seeing in their village a white chief whom they could call their Father, on whose word they could count; and that they would behave better if they had many guns with which to hunt, in order to support their families. Now Your Excellency may see how important it is for the Company to supply them with arms and ammunition, although it may be necessary to make a present of it to them; for when a savage has many furs, trade is easy with him; but when he has few, quite the contrary happens.

This village contains seven hundred warriors, and I have promised them two hundred muskets for next year, even though this number is too few for the number of men there. If this is not possible, Your Excellency must expect a general discontent on their part, and the sure loss of the trade that might be carried on with them. They care for only the English guns and not the French ones which burst in their hands, and good powder, for bad powder is regularly sent to them, which is of the greatest consequence for the hunt. Today I began to trade with them, which I stopped at the setting of the sun. That has surprised them greatly, since they are accustomed to trade at all times, and when they please, without considering the convenience of the trader. I announced to them that the first one who dared to violate my intentions would repent it, and that threat has had all the effect that I desired.

The Mahá Chief, their sovereign, is the soul of the village and many others. He appears to be my sincere friend since my arrival. He is more despotic than any European prince, and, in addition, is most courteous and of great talent. His present conduct toward us must not be forgotten, since he is the one to decide whether our communication remains open and free.

November 21, the Indians, contented and satisfied, went to hunt and it was necessary for me to send part of my men with them, as there were no provisions in the village, for maize was totally lacking, and there was not one-half minot of this grain which has not cost me a blanket [demande (?) sic]. This scarcity of food retards a trifle the construction of the fort which I am building, but will not prevent me from finishing it soon. I saw a Ponca chief who left on the next day for his village. Through him I have sent severe reprimands to his tribe. I showed him my bercha, and, in order to mortify him, I told him that it was charged with goods for the purpose of going to his tribe; but that since his whole village was incapable of anything else than doing evil, I would punish it by never sending any more, and depriving their women and children of whatever they needed; that now they would get no guns or powder with which to get their living; that they would die of hunger; and that the Great Maha Chief would unite with me, in order to avenge me. After hearing my long and severe speech, he could do naught but shed tears over the conduct of all his tribe.

After that, I declared a plan to the Maha prince in regard to my voyage to the head of the Missouri, presenting to him the famous medal and patentes which pleased him greatly, especially as they were accompanied by the present given him by the Company. However he was surprised at not finding in it a large flag, telling me that the English always gave one with the medal, and that though they had frequently invited him to accept both, he had never made use of either of them, abandoning them to his children, in order to make it clearly understood by the English that he had no intention of abandoning the friendship of his Spanish Father. However he believed that the latter did not appreciate the affection which he professed for him, and besides, it would be shameful for him not to receive a large banner and a present proportional to his importance, since the English, his neighbors, constrained him to receive their friendship and their presents which they send him annually, in order to attract him with this tribe to the San Pedro River, in order to trade his furs with them.

Thus they insinuated to him and his tribe the scant heed that their Spanish Father gives them, who did not love them, while, on the contrary, their English Father was so affectionate to them, and showed such great generosity to the red men that they would not lack anything, if the latter would give him their hand. In proof of this they annually receive presents in his name, both for the support of their families and to clothe them; and, notwithstanding, without heeding so many promises on the part of the English, and without trusting to the deceits of the traders of the Missouri, he only desired to conserve the friendship of his Spanish Father, for his heart was happy because the latter had sent a chief to visit him, and truly make him recognize his word, which so many other traders had hitherto falsified, deceiving him. On that account he would endeavor to assist me in all my plans, especially in opening a road of communication with the Upper Missouri, and reuniting the various tribes, who could oppose the conservation of the peace and tranquillity. He himself in person with his tribe would go to convoy my boats to the Ricaras, if there were the least sign of danger or opposition. He would reduce the Poncas to their duty, avenging the wrong and injury which they had committed against our boat, conducted by Lecuyer. He ended his speech with testimonies of regret over the past, protesting that his heart had never been happy until this day, and that he saw in me his true friend whom his Father had sent him, and that he was speaking the truth.

Seeing that I was constructing a fort in which large guns, that is to say canons, were to be placed, in order to protect their tribe from all those who refused to enter into relations of peace with them, I told him that, reckoning on his good actions in favor of the Government and of the Company, he could be absolutely sure of their friendship and protection against all those who attempted anything against his tribe or who disturbed the good harmony and concord in which his Father, the Spaniard, desired to have them live. Consequently, he would send them two great guns next summer, in order that they might be placed in the fort, and they would remain there continuously, both to protect them from their enemies, and to open the road from [to] the Upper Missouri; in regard to which, I hoped that he would keep his promise. He answered me that the Master of Life was witness of his promise and of mine, and that the universe would see which of us two failed. On that score we, respectively, reiterated our promises, and took as witness of our oaths the sun which lighted us. Afterward he asked me for my patents or despatches from his Great Father, the Spaniard, who lived on the other shore of the Great Lake, that is, in Europe, in order that he might see whether, as I told him, I was the bearer of his word among the tribes of this continent, in order to direct, assist, or compel to peace the evil tribes, whether by mildness or by force, clothing me with his authority in order that I might clear the road of the Upper Missouri, and remove all the obstacles placed there by the tribes through whom one must cross, in order to reach the proposed end; that, without it, he would not dare to undertake a task which could grieve his Father, the Spaniard, who would be angry with him and with me, if he did it without his permission. I replied to him that in such a question he demanded from me prudence to convince him that the word which I gave him had already been announced to him three months before by our Spanish Father, Don Zenon Trudeau, by means of his [i.e., the chief's] son when the latter presented himself in St. Louis in the month of July last; that the desire of our Great Father was to make all the red men happy; and that our Father, Don Zenon Trudeau, was entrusted with this commission, in consequence of which he had sent a member of the Company to announce to him his word. I told him that our Great Father, being informed that for many years the tribes of the Missouri were showing evil inclinations against the whites and his trader, had made him take the precaution of sending a chief to him, who, showing him his friendship and good intentions, should be supported by his power through the likeness which he has with him in authority, judgment, and sentiments, to bring the tribes of the Upper Missouri to reason, who might oppose themselves to the good-fortune and tranquillity of those who desire to live in good fellowship with the whites, who can at any moment deprive them or procure for them whatever they need when they judge it suitable. He answered me that his Father, the Spaniard, as well as myself, has always charged him to be good; that such have always been his intentions; but that he did not have sufficient ascendency among the other tribes to cause himself to be perfectly respected, without making presents to their chiefs, in order to show them his superiority by means of his power and generous conduct, which he had with the common chiefs of each tribe, whenever they assembled to form a pact of friendship and alliance among these same tribes and the whites, who came sent by his Father, the Spaniard; that, in such case, the presents would make them adopt my advice and my counsels, receiving the calumet of peace and the Spanish flag, notwithstanding how ordinary it might be; for the Sioux, as well as other tribes of the northern district, who, receiving only silk flags from the English, would cause them to despise ours. Notwithstanding, he is about to send to seek out all the tribes, but he tells me that this cannot be done without great presents of cloth, blankets, kettles, tobacco, guns, and ammunition; [and] that he was not asking for these articles for himself, but rather for me, and to make it known that his Father, the Spaniard, loved and showed his affection to the Indians who behaved well. He told me that he would send [correos] posts this winter with a calumet to all the tribes, especially to the Sioux, who frequenting the Missouri between

361

the Poncas and Ricaras, might be induced to come to see me next spring, with the object of adopting measures and means of peace with them, and opening forever a free communication with the Upper Missouri; [Thus] allowing my boats to pass without committing any outrage; but that, when they came, presents would be necessary, and he had nothing to give; consequently, it would be necessary for me to stand the expense; [also] that a large flag was absolutely necessary for him, in order to distinguish him from the other chiefs, and to lend importance to his mission.

A few days after my arrival here, I received information that a Ponca had killed a Ricara, who had come to his village with a message last summer. This occurrence, together with the previous outrages committed upon the Sioux, placed great obstacles in my passage. I hope, nevertheless, with the aid of the Maha prince and with a number of presents suitably placed, to find a means of opening the road, although these two casualties will occasion reiterated expenses, and will retard our march.

November 24. Not having had any information of the Ricaras, and not being able to send by water, I had a well-accompanied detachment set out overland with the order to go to said tribe, and inform me of what is happening there. But, unfortunately, they had to return, because they discovered a considerable band of Sioux who were hunting buffalo, at sight of whom, believing that their lives were not safe, they came here on the sixth of January, on which occasion the great Maha Chief renewed his promise to me that he would assist me to succeed in my enterprise.

On the 29th, the Prince came to visit the fort which was being built in a plain located between the very village of the Mahas and the Missouri River, on the shore of a small river which flows into the latter, and is fairly navigable. This plain is very extensive, the land excellent, and never inundated by the waters. The location of the fort seems to have been prepared by nature. It is in a commanding district, which rises for a circumference of about one thousand feet. It looks on the shore of this river, as if to command the rest of the area. I have established my settlement and my fort there, although at a distance from the woods; however, the horses of the Prince are at my service.

On December 18, the Missouri had ice, and on the 19th of December, was completely frozen.

January 18, 1796

Two Mahas arrived from the hunt.
[the clerk or official who copied or translated the original journal here merely synopsizes]. Note: *Monsieur* Mackay goes into great details here on the pillage of the Poncas, which it is useless[for me] to mention, since I had already given information of what happened among this tribe, because of the bad conduct of the conductor [of the boats], Lecuyer.

He continues after to say: The autumn having passed, I ordered Antonio Breda, our commissioner, to hide the rest of the goods, which the Poncas took, and which remained in their village, announcing to them that I was sending for them in order to give them to the Mahas. Antonio Breda executed my orders faithfully. That mortified the Poncas greatly who counted on taking possession of the rest, which is very little, at whatever price they wished. I hope that in the future, it will not be so, if my friend, the Great Chief, the Maha Prince keeps his word with me. He expressed himself as greatly irritated against the Poncas. Some time ago he sent them a message, and he himself, accompanied by the chiefs of their village, is going thither to make them deliver the few furs that they have obtained in their hunt, on account of what they have stolen. I believe that his journey will not be without success, and, although he will not bring back more than a little from a hunt to which no necessity incited them, the consequence will always be advantageous for the interests of the Company, since it will serve as an example to the other tribes in the future. And then, Your Excellency, do not doubt that my friend the Maha Prince has a right to a generous recompense [and this will] increase our losses and expenses. But it is important to sustain the authority of this intrepid man by the ostentation and particular distinction of elevating him above every other chief, especially for his personal interest. This man deserves consideration, and must not be abandoned, for I consider him one of the chief instruments of our projects. A present worthy of him and one of consideration ought to be given him annually. It is necessary to give this on account of his character, and does not Your Excellency believe that that is a small thing; it is better to fatten one who rules as a despot over various tribes, than to feed many at less expense. However, the Government must come to our aid, for he is one of the chief supports for our navigation. The intrigue of the English, in order to attract the tribes of the Missouri, has planted such deep roots among these peoples, that it is necessary to apply a prompt remedy, unless we desire to see ourselves exposed to abandon this magnificent country which must some day be a great resource to the prosperity and glory of the state.

The presents which the English send annually to the various tribes, where they can penetrate, give much weight to their intrigues. The English of the river of San Pedro had concluded among this tribe last autumn the construction of a fort for them on the shore of the Missouri, which they were resolved to maintain against all resistance. My arrival here changed all their projects, while the presents which I have given to the tribe and to my friend, the Prince, have turned them in such manner to his favor, that they have made disappear and have destroyed the measures agreed upon with the English.

The latter have at present thirty pirogues of goods on the San Pedro River within four days' journey from these places. They sell the blanket for two furs, and the rest in proportion. It is probable that they will come this spring to visit the Missouri. The jealousy that has always existed among the merchants of Canada, has not only ruined trade with the Indians in their territory, but also with the vassals of His Catholic Majesty on the western part of the Mississippi to which they daily penetrate.[7]

The traders of the River of Monigona [Des Moines][8] have sent twelve horses, laden with goods, to trade with the Panis and the Loups [Lobos or Wolves] on the Chato River. The caravan crossed the Missouri in the month of last December. I would be glad to be able to deal them a blow on their return.

Since my arrival here, I have sent many messages to various tribes, which has occasioned me great expense, although that is inseparable from our interests, if we wish to open up communication for our explorations and to reach the Pacific Sea, we must expect to see them increase daily, until our project sees complete fulfillment. We need the aid of the Government to resist and destroy the ambition of foreigners. Otherwise, the ruin of the Company in its infancy is inevitable.

Through my fear of arriving late next summer at the Mandans, I am going to send out a detachment within a few days under the charge of *Monsieur* Even [Evans], until he meets Trudeau [Jean Baptiste Truteau who was in command of the first expedition of the Company], who must have already constructed his fort among the above-mentioned Mandans, if he has experienced no opposition on the part of the English, who have had the audacity to unfurl their banner there. *Monsieur* Even is to leave there with picked men, who occasion us great expense, in order to visit the head-water of the Missouri and *La Cadena de Rocas*, [chain of Rocks or Rocky Mountains], and follow to the Pacific Sea, according to the enclosed instructions of which he carries a copy.[9]

---

[7]See Nasatir, "Anglo-Spanish Rivalry on the Upper Missouri," *Mississippi Valley Historical Review,* XVI (1929-1930) ; and "Extracts from Mackay's and Evans' Journal" in *Wisconsin State Historical Society Proceedings,* LXIII, 190-195, Chapter V, document II.

[8]On December 15, 1795, Jacques Clamorgan who knew of the activities of the British traders in the Iowa country proposed to build a fort near the mouth of the Des Moines river in order to stop the incursions of the British traders and to protect the open passageway on the Missouri for the traders and boats of his Missouri Company. He also suggested the fort in order to protect the Spanish dominions and to establish a settlement there. In return for establishing this fort Clamorgan asked for the exclusive trading privileges with all the Indian nations which frequented or inhabited the banks of the Des Moines, Skunk and Iowa rivers for six years. Project of Clamorgan, St. Louis, December 15, 1795, A.G.I., P. de C., leg. 2371. See document XXV. See also Nasatir, "Anglo-Spanish Frontier on the Upper Mississippi 1786-1796," in *Iowa Journal of History and Politics,* XXIX (1931), 207-208.

[9]Evans' instructions is dated Fort Charles, January 28, 1796, Bancroft Library and printed in Nasatir, "John Evans: Explorer and Surveyor," in *Missouri Historical*

[Letter to Trudeau:][10]

I am sending to You the dispatch as Commandant of the forts established by the Company, in favor of Mr. Mackay,[11] so that after having examined [recognized] it, you may deliver it to the director, Don Santiago Clamorgan. May God keep you many years.

New Orleans, May 12, 1796

Baron de Carondelet [rubric]

Addressed: *"Señor* Don Zenon Trudeau."

[Letter from Deblanc:][12]

My General: On the return journey made by Don Francisco Lamate [sic] through the tribes, he assured me that he has been well informed that in the vicinity of the savages and Ambaricas [sic—Ricaras], (who although nomad as a general thing, are very frequently found encamped between this Colorado River of the Natchitoches and that of the Arkansas which unite above, having their rise near the mountains of Santa Fé in New Mexico), there was found a band of Americans fortified in a blockhouse. If this is so, it must be inferred that they have crossed from this side of the river into the district of Illinois, and that they have crossed the Missouri between the villages of the Osages and others to the place above mentioned. This is very possible, since the road from Santa Fé to Illinois was discovered last year by one Pedro Vial, called Maniton [or Manitou].[13] I charge the above-mentioned Lamate [*sic*] to deliver this to Your Excellency. I informed him as soon as I arrived at the city what I had discovered regarding the matter. Also, he has promised me that he would offer his services to the Government to go in person to drive the American thence. Accustomed, as he is, to the fatigue of the longest voyages, and knowing perfectly the methods, manners, and customs of the Indians, I believe that he would really be very proper for this expedition. I have the honor to remain, with the most profound respect, My General, your most obedient and humble servant.

Luis Deblanc

Natchitoches, February 22, 1796.

Addressed: "Baron de Carondelet."

Review, XXV, (1931), 441-447; Chapter IV, document IV. See also "Extracts of Evans' Journal" in *Wisconsin State Historical Society Proceedings,* 1915, LXIII, 190-195, Chapter V, document II; and Nasatir, "Anglo-Spanish Rivalry on the Upper Missouri," *op. cit.,* reprint pp. 30ff.

[10]A.G.I., P. de C., leg. 2364, transcript in Library of Congress. I have checked the printed translation in Houck, *Spanish Régime in Missouri,* II, 192.

[11]See Chapter IV, document XII.

[12]A.G.I., P. de C., leg. 2364, transcript in Library of Congress. I have checked the translation printed in Houck, *Spanish Régime in Missouri,* II, 192-193. See Chapter IV, document XVIII.

[13]See document XI, note 2.

XXI

Trudeau to Carondelet, St. Louis, October 26, 1795[1]

Mon Général:

I have had the honor of having a visit from General St. Claire[2] who dined at my house. I have had a conversation with him concerning the propositions which were made to me by Judge Tourner[3] to reciprocally return the deserters, and the necessity of making arrangements for the slaves who cross as fugitives to their bank. There, he informed me, their constitution[4] freed them, and obliges, and force debtors to present themselves at the tribunal of the district where they had contracted their obligations, in order to be heard there, and judged according to the laws of the country. This general told me that the judge had no commission or authority to make such propositions, since that belongs only to Congress to treat what concerns deserters. [He told me that] Fugitive negroes at all times and in all cases will be pursued, and returned to the owners without need of convention; that the constitution of the United States could not compel a debtor citizen to go to a foreign district to plead a lawsuit which they could pursue there; and that for desertion it seemed agreeable to him for the two banks to make arrangements, but that he, as you, could not decide it, nor, moreover pursue the savages who, having committed murders, take refuge in the opposite district. Seeing his sentiment, I did not push this conversation any further, and I only profited by the moment to speak to him and make known to him the sarcastic [caustic] character of the lawyer Jones[5] whom you have seen, aside from his wranglings, has a talent destined to trouble us. He assured me that he knew him, and that for this reason he did not wish [even though he was educated] to employ him at any *place* in the administration for which he preferred honest men with good sense, with whom I shall always have the most perfect harmony. At the same time he informed me that there had just arrived at their place a man named Micheaux,[6] already known for having been in the intrigue of Genêt in his former project against our colony; also, that this man might have some friends; but if that happened, he could assure me that he would not be successful in his district. That

---

[1]Written in French. A.G.I., P. de C., leg. 211.
[2]Arthur St. Clair, Governor of the Northwest Territory. See document XVIII.
[3]Judge Turner.
[4]Ordinance of 1787.
[5]John Rice Jones.
[6]André Michaux, *Travels in Kentucky,* in Thwaites, *Early Western Travels,* III. See also some of his correspondence in connection with the Genêt intrigues in American Historical Association, *Annual Reports, 1896,* vol. I, and *Ibid., Annual Report, 1903;* See also James, *George Rogers Clark,* etc. The literature of the French intrigues in the West is quite voluminous.

was an enigma for me, in that I cannot conceive the projects that he is planning, which makes me (after this advice) keep on my guard. I learned that he mistrusted our district where, in effect he would be arrested, if he appeared there.

I had the honor of receiving your letter of July 14, and in reply I have nothing that I can tell you about M. Portell, eighty-five leagues distant from here. Communication between his post and mine is as rare as that with New Orleans. Perhaps the circumstances in which we find ourselves will have contributed towards ridiculing him, which at another time he would have avoided, at another time, [being] obliged to survey all the *esprits* and to contain them within limits. This just motive would have brought discontent and bickering about the most innocent things, and would take this occasion to complain of them. It is true that New Madrid below the *Belle Rivière* would give him a true advantage for his population, but the circumstance of the expedition of Clark, which for two years, we have been circumspect in the choice of persons who we must admit, would have made timid many people, who not being known, would have presented themselves to establish there. It is necessary to hope that peace will give us a fortunate change which will increase the population; as this is susceptible to destroy all calumny against me, I haven't much to praise in M. Portell, I having avowed my confidence in him as a comrade. He daily testifies of being as jealous of my reputation as of his own. However, one attributes to him proposals which only tend to make me lose your confidence and honor, and I can only believe in coming to a verbal understanding with him.

Mr. Bte. Vallé was wrong in telling you that merchants of Ste. Geneviève have not been included in the repartition of the trades of the Missouri. I appeal to the statements that I sent you in which MM. Bolduc and Pratte were placed, together with the man named Hubardeau, last year,[7] and they are the only three who are living at that place; moreover, one of whom for more than four years has not traded. It is certain that if *Messieurs* Vallé had had some rights to these trades, despite their easy circumstances, I would have preferred them more than all others; but having never passed for anything but a cultivator, I would have deviated from the *reglement* by including them in it. Besides, *Mon Général,* in following the first distribution, I have only four shares of one thousand *piastres* each with the *Kansas,* three with the *Panis,* and one with the Republic, which make only eight. The other nations have been granted to Mr. Chouteau and the Company of the Upper Missouri. For these eight shares there are forty merchants who have a right to make claims thereto. It is only then after five years that all might have passed there, alter-

---

[7] See *e.g.,* Chapter II, document IV.

nately observing the drawing of lots. If you do not foresee any inconvenience, I believe it would be more advantageous to place these eight shares every year at auction for the profit of improving and beautifying St. Louis. A general advantage would result from it by the production of about 2,000 *piastres* a year, which would give relief to the poor inhabitants in certain toils, etc. What I propose is against my interests, for it would be necessary to sacrifice the 25 *piastres* which are given me by each of the eight passports as I deliver them, conforming to what you granted me. I shall do it gratis (despite the fact that this is my only emolument), in favor of the public good, although I am experiencing importunities from the ambitious ones who would like to have everything and leave nothing to the others. Do not believe that those who obtain these trades do it themselves; they do it with stock-jobbing which passes from hand to hand, and ends by ruining the unfortunate trader who, whether by ambition or necessity, acquires the permit which costs him very dearly, and the merchandise which is overcharged, as well as hindering him from joining the two ends of these outlays or advances which he receives.

The twenty-seventh of the last month, Mr. de Volsey died after an illness of ten months duration. He made a will by which he leaves to a natural daughter the little that he had, which does not amount to 400 *piastres;* and he recommended to me to recall his cross of St. Louis to have it sent to you in thanks for the kindnesses that you have shown him (which I am doing herewith enclosed). He gave his sword to my son, and gave me marks of the greatest confidence, while avowing to me that he had sought to pester and harm me, because he believed that he was dependent on me to give him one of the trades of the Missouri. He was confused and ashamed, and begged me not to abandon him in his last moment, which I did not [instead, I cared for him], as if he had been my father. I have never been able to succeed in having him receive from our curate the last sacraments. He asked me for the one from Kao, neighbor to us. I had him come, and he partly fulfilled the laws. In his last moment Dn. Didier tried to give him Extreme Unction. He still refused it, and I believe that he had no other reasons than his own caprice.

There is absolutely nothing new in this post which merits your attention. I am occupied with the annual census. I shall take unceasing care to immediately send it to you, with the amount of the tax to be imposed on each slave head, contributable to the payment for those who have been executed.[8]

[8]Trudeau sent Carondelet a *resumé* of the general census of the Illinois establishments with his letter no. 239 dated St. Louis, November 28, 1795, A.G.I., P. de C., leg. 2364. The original of the census, dated October 31, 1795, is in the same legajo and a copy is in the Bancroft Library.

I have the honor of being with the most respectful attachment and the greatest thankfulness for your bounties.

Mon Général,

Your very humble, obedient servant,

Zenon Trudeau
[rubric]

St. Louis, October 26, 1795.

XXII

TRUDEAU TO CARONDELET, ST. LOUIS, NOVEMBER 14, 1795[1]

Mon Général:

Monsieur de Gayoso has at last, as I desired, made his trip to St. Louis,[2] where he spent eleven days, during which he glanced over our establishments and the country, of which, I hope, he will give you favorable information which will only increase the projects that you have formed for a long time for their prosperity. Already I see by your letter of July fourth which the lawyer Jones has just given me, that you proposed *à la Paix* to obtain an increase of garrisons for this vast country. This lone expenditure by the King is sufficient to double the population within a few years, attach the inhabitants to work, and render us capable of furnishing the colony with all the flour that it can consume. I await this moment with great impatience, although persuaded that my rank, as mediocre as my capacity, will not permit me to remain for long commandant in a profitable place, whose rapid prosperity will soon form a government of as great consequence as that of the present [government] of this [entire] province. *Monsieur* Gayoso, who has seen everything from the point of view of an enlightened man, and who desires the augmenting of the province, will instruct you in a non-suspicious manner, concerning this district so very interesting on account of its soil, and a good basis for the inhabitants whom we already have, and who, religiously attached to our Sovereign, are beginning to occupy themselves seriously with agriculture, which should make for their perfect happiness.

Your views on the Company of Commerce of the Upper Missouri will be seconded by me, as much as I can. This same Company has made this year efforts beyond facilities, and it is necessary to await the result, in

---

[1]Written in French. A.G.I., P. de C., leg. 211.
[2]Gayoso arrived in St. Louis on October 30 (Gayoso to Carondelet, St. Louis, October 30, 1795, A.G.I., P. de C., leg. 43) and left November 10, 1795. Gayoso's report is dated New Madrid, November 24, 1795, (A.G.I., P. de C., leg. 2364.) His diary is in A.G.I., P. de C., leg. 2354. I am preparing this and other relative diaries for early publication.

order to know what should be added by the government—to favor it advantageously. The exclusive trade of the Otoes, Mahas and Poncas nations gives to it a passage and point of departure for the spring, in order to go further up. I do not believe that there is anything more to be desired for the time being, in that a *galliot* would not be able to give a great aid in this navigation, and the Company itself ignores the success or difficulties that will be experienced by these expeditions from which they do not expect news of the principal [expedition], until July, 1797.

The mill of Mr. Chouteau is in the most perfect condition and gives us flour as superb as the finest in Philadelphia, but with a much better taste. It awaits the iron-fitting necessary to make a saw [mill], which would give us *chalons,* and facilitate the transport of these same flours as far as the capital, which at first could only be in small quantities but would increase progressively to [meet the needs of] the population of New Orleans, which would some day be entirely provisioned by us; we will also be able to do the same in lead and in iron. The latter object [iron] is very interesting and lucrative, and, at any moment, persons well off [wealthy] may be found to establish a forge—the speculation of which will aid the inhabitant and can only enrich him.

As you have permitted me, I am proposing the name of Soulard to fill the employ left vacant by *Monsieur* de Volsey.[3] I do not see anyone else who can claim it. This rank will put him in a position to occupy himself in the position of surveyor, in favor of the new poor inhabitants, who can come here, and to whom it is proper to give land gratis and without expense; at the same time I am the only military and public official here, and very often there are found opportunities when one has need of an intelligent and confidential aid, which facilitates the operations and always renders them more certain and profitable. *Monsieur* Peyroux appeared to me to desire this same post, but, undecided in all these desires, he spoke to me of ten claims [demands], that is the third passport that I have given him within six months for New Orleans, where he will remain,

---

[3]Soulard was appointed. He was captain of militia, adjutant to the lieutenant-governor of Upper Louisiana, and surveyor for St. Louis and Ste. Geneviève. See Soulard's petition to the King, dated New Orleans, May 22, 1802 wherein he relates his experience and accompanies it with documents. He was adjutant to Carlos Howard during his stay in St. Louis and assisted Vandenbemden in the fortification works in St. Louis. A.G.I., P. de C., leg. 155A. See also Portell to Carondelet, New Madrid, May 15, 1795, *Ibid.,* leg. 33; Trudeau to Gayoso de Lemos, No. 313, St. Louis, January 10, 1798, *Ibid.,* leg. 49; draft [Carondelet] to Morales, New Orleans, April 19, 1796, *Ibid.,* leg. 89; Las Casas to Governor of Louisiana, Havana, April 1, 1796. *Ibid.,* leg. 153A; Carondelet to Trudeau, New Orleans, January 27, 1795, A.G.I., P. de C., leg. 22; Somuerlos to Governor of Louisiana, Havana, May 24, 1799, *Ibid.,* leg. 154B; Gayoso to Santa Clara, New Orleans, April 26, 1798; and other documents in *Archivo General de Simancas, sección guerra,* leg. 6920; Soulard to Gayoso, St. Louis, March 10, 1799, A.G.I., P. de C., leg. 212B; *Id.* to *Id.,* May 31, 1798 (*Ibid.,* leg. 215A) and December 15, 1797, (*Ibid.,* leg. 13).

doubtlessly, as undetermined as he is here, where he has constancy only in the *Procès*.

Monsieur Loisel, bearer of the present, will give you two barrels of apples and, despite your recommendation, a small pacquet of twenty-four martins, six lynx and six *pécans* [*sic*], which I owe to the compliments of my attainments, and which I beg you to permit me to offer you in gratitude.

We have not had the slightest news here for a long time. Everything is peaceful and in harmony. *Monsieur* Gayoso, whom we have seen, left us with regrets [although] at the same time we were persuaded that he will give information, which will merit for us the continuation of your protection, which gives satisfaction to the one who is with the most respectful attachment.

Mon Général

Your very humble, obedient servant

Zenon Trudeau [rubric]

St. Louis, November 14, 1795.

XXIII

Carondelet to Trudeau, New Orleans, December 10, 1795[1]

In your official letter, no. 230,[2] you inform me of the return of Santiago l'Eglise, discoverer of the Mandan nation, and of his third departure with the intention of going as far as the sea, in which I hope he succeeds.

I have in my possession the statements of the deserters from the Montreal company,[3] and the continuation of the diary of Juan Bautista Truteau, agent for the St. Louis company; with these documents I shall do what is fitting for me to do.

I[4] approve also the nomination of Mr. Mackay, as agent of that company, in place of Truteau who is about to complete his term. As for the English fort that is thought to have been built in the Mandan nation, nothing can be decided, until it is definitely known whether it exists; but in order to favor that company, I shall solicit permission from the king to send a well armored *galiotte* to go up the Missouri,[5] as far as it can without danger.

May God keep you many years. New Orleans, December 10, 1795.

El Baron de Carondelet [rubric]

Señor Don Zenon Trudeau.

---

[1] Written in Spanish. A.G.I., P. de C., leg. 2364, a copy in French is also found in this same *legajo*. There is a copy in the Bancroft Library.
[2] Document XV.
[3] Document XII.
[4] This paragraph is to be found in the margin of document XV.
[5] See document XXV.

XXIV

TRUDEAU TO GAYOSO DE LEMOS, ST. LOUIS, DECEMBER 18, 1795[1]

My dear sir and most beloved Governor:

I received Your Excellency's letter dated the second of the current month,[2] in which you favored me with the news of the peace which has filled us all with satisfaction, and no less, since Your Excellency has taken into consideration our unfortunate country which has no other splendour than the favor of Your Excellency's protection, for which we are greatly thankful and grateful, particularly the one who is writing, having no other merit that his respectful affection for Your Excellency, which he will conserve all his life.

Morgan told me he [was] finished some days ago with the manufacturing of salt from our saline. The latter never told me anything of any saline.

The Poncas Indians robbed us of a *pirogue* with 700 *peso's* merchandise. Because of [despite] this the Company of the Missouri is not discouraged, and will continue its expeditions, as soon as the navigation of this river permits.[3]

Two days ago, Chouteau saw a letter from the Commandant of Post Vincennes to the Commandant of the Militia of Kaokia, in which he tells him that General Wainn sent two *parlamentarios* to Your Excellency via Los *Écoies*; that a third *parlamentario* had set out; and that, while awaiting results, they were preparing themselves in a hostile manner. As Your Excellency tells me nothing, and as I see the peace concluded, I believe that there will be nothing to fear. However, a word from Your Excellency, before abandoning our inclosures, will greatly fortify my opinion cencerning the future.

This country is always the happiest on earth and lacks nothing, but the fomentation that peace will bring us. Your Excellency will see its population by the census which I am enclosing,[4] in which there are many persons missing, since they do not have fixed [permanent] homes, and, were not included as permanent, due to being employed outside. But I believe that I can estimate without difficulty the latter at 150 men. I have mislaid the *relación* of the population of the Indian nations, which I had offered to Your Excellency, and had in my hand a minute ago. I do not know whether I will be able to enclose it without delaying this occa-

[1]Written in Spanish. A.G.I., P. de C., leg. 48.
[2]Written from New Madrid.
[3]See document XXV.
[4]A general census was sent to Carondelet by Trudeau enclosed in his letter no. 239, dated St. Louis, November 28, 1795, A.G.I., P. de C., leg. 2364. A copy of the census dated October 31, 1795 is in the Bancroft Library, the original of which is in A.G.I., P. de C., leg 2364, of which I have a photostat copy.

sion which is going to Sainte Geneviève, and which I am charging to take advantage of the first occasion, so that this letter may reach Your Excellency whom I beg to receive and forward the one enclosed, although of little importance.

Mr. Brion, my wife, and my entire family offer Your Excellency the most attentive and courteous expression, and I remain begging God to preserve Your Excellency's life many years.

St. Louis, December 18, 1795.

Your most attentive and loyal servant kisses Your Excellency's hand.

Zenon Trudeau [rubric]

Señor Don Manuel Gayoso de Lemos.

XXV

TRUDEAU TO CARONDELET, ST. LOUIS, DECEMBER 19, 1795[1]

Answered

Mon Général:

Don Didier has just informed me that the priest of Kaokias (*abbé* de Vadon) has communicated to him different papers, which accuse the *curé* of Ste. Geneviève of not being a priest, which I am hastening to inform you opportunely, in order to give you time to have copies of the said papers that Don Didier proposes to send to *Monseigneur* the Bishop. Despite the fact that the said papers should be extremely suspicioned, having come from a very bad subject, who escaped from Canada (*abbé* de Lavalinière), I believe it is prudent to examine them, and to have Father Bernard of Pte. Coupée inform you of what it is about. He was at the place and has been mediator in the affair, having been apparently more in favor of Father St. Pierre, than the other whose reputation is a horror in this country.

The second of this month, *Monsieur* de Gayoso had the goodness to announce the peace to me.[2] I do not know any of the circumstances of it, but it does not flatter me any the less at a time when M. Chouteau had told me of seeing a letter from the commandant of the Post Vincennes to the commandant of the militia of Kaokia, in which he says that General Wainn has already sent two *parliamentarios* to M. de Gayoso in order to summon him to withdraw from *Écors;* [also] that a third *parliamentario* was on its way, and while awaiting the result, their army was preparing in a hostile manner. The peace made, we are without obstacles, and within

---

[1]Written in French. A.G.I., P. de C., leg. 211.
[2]See document XXIV.

reach of making ourselves feared. Moreover, I hope that we will remain, more than ever, tranquil.[3]

The second expedition of the Company of the Upper Missouri has been pillaged by the Poncas nation. The loss amounted to 7,000 *pesos,* and causes a delay of a year for the discoveries further up. Much of the fault is attributed to the conductor of the *voiture.* His bad conduct on the way warned those who had engaged him to send another man to supplant him, but he arrived eight days too late.[4] I am enclosing for you a copy of the letters from the agent of the third expedition, which should winter among the Mahas.[5] He is asking for swivel-guns and some blunderbusses. The Company recommends itself to you, because they can not procure them. He will need eight of them, as well as six flags of a certain size for the forts that he has to construct. The English whom these savages have under their eyes, make a show of ostentation which we must imitate; besides, the King's flag[6] is imposing to them, and glorifies them infinitely, when coupled to the fact that it will be hoisted in a territory where it has never been seen and where it is high time it appears. Further, *Mon Général,* I repeat to you the request for medals. I have only received two of them so far for the Mandans, although some time ago I asked you for some for the Hotos, Mahas, Poncas, and Ricaras.

I again chatted with the directors of the Company, concerning the use of a galiot to aid them in their trip. They are, as I, of the opinion that it would be of little use against such a large number of savages, [who are] entirely lost to our own traders and to the English whom they see every year. It is only with patience and choice men who are rare, that we will succeed in the end, especially when we are in a position to deprive them of all aid, as we shall soon be able to do. The proposition that M. Clamorgan makes you[7] by the enclosed memoir might contribute thereto, if I believed I could count on his plan; but stripped of means, I believe that ambition makes him promise more than he will be able to execute. However, I

---

[3]See Whitaker, *Spanish American Frontier;* Bemis, *Pinckney's Treaty;* etc.
[4]See documents XIX and XX.
[5]Document XIX.
[6]In an undated letter written by Clamorgan [?] which is in A.G.I., P. de C., leg. 211 is written: "In consequence of the power of His Majesty granted to the Missouri Company to hoist the royal flag over the forts and on its vessels, Your Excellency is begged to have some of these delivered to the Director of the Company in order to put his intentions into execution and by that to render the places that it oversees more respectable to their neighbors."
[7]Clamorgan's project for a fort and settlement at the mouth of the Des Moines river in return for a six year exclusive trading privilege on the Des Moines, Skunk, and Iowa rivers is dated December 15, 1795, A.G.I., P. de C., leg. 2371. See document XX, note 8. Todd was granted the exclusive trade of the Mississippi north of the Missouri—decrees of Carondelet December 21, 1796, A.G.I., P. de C., leg. 129, and draft [Carondelet?] to Clamorgan, New Orleans, December 21, 1795, *Ibid.* See Nasatir, "Anglo-Spanish Frontier on the Upper Mississippi 1786-1796," *Iowa Journal of History and Politics,* XXIX (1931), 215-216.

have been told that he had ties of interest with M. Todd, a Montreal merchant, who they say has gone to New Orleans to establish a house there.[8] If that is true, the thing will be very practicable; however, it remains to be found out if it is agreeable to you that it be [accomplished] by this means. I believe it can, for if the house of Todd has been established at New Orleans, then the skins will be able to be sent down there. Despite that I believe that it is suitable to bridle Morgan in such a manner as not to have an affair elsewhere, because the foreigners will still be those who will draw the profit from it.

Monsieur Chouteau will descend at the beginning of next March. I do not forsee being able to write you directly before that time. The ice restrains us, and the cold is already too rigorous for a valetudinarian like myself. Thus, I am profiting by this opportunity to present to you my respectful attachment, and make prayers for the conservation of your days in the new year which is going to commence.

I include my thinks for your bounties to me, for which I shall be all my life, with the most perfect gratitude.

Mon Général,

Your very humble, obedient servant,

Zenon Trudeau [rubric]

St. Louis, December 19, 1795

---

[8]See A. P. Nasatir, "Jacques Clamorgan: Colonial Promoter of the Northern Border of New Spain" in *New Mexico Historical Review,* XXVII (April, 1942).